# A HISTORY OF RUSSIA

## BY GEORGE VERNADSKY

*VOLUME II*

## KIEVAN RUSSIA

# KIEVAN RUSSIA

BY

GEORGE VERNADSKY

PROFESSOR OF RUSSIAN HISTORY
YALE UNIVERSITY

NEW HAVEN AND LONDON
YALE UNIVERSITY PRESS

Library of Congress catalog card number: A43–1903
ISBN: 0–300–01007–9 (cloth), 0–300–01647–6 (paper)

Printed in the United States of America by
The Murray Printing Company, Forge Village, Mass.
Seventh printing, 1973

Published in Great Britain, Europe, and Africa by
Yale University Press, Ltd., London.
Distributed in Canada by McGill-Queen's University
Press, Montreal; in Latin America by Kaiman & Polon,
Inc., New York City; in Australasia and Southeast
Asia by John Wiley & Sons Australasia Pty. Ltd.,
Sydney; in India by UBS Publishers' Distributors Pvt.,
Ltd., Delhi; in Japan by John Weatherhill, Inc., Tokyo.

# FOREWORD

MY BOOK *Kievan Russia* was published twenty-five years ago. I am satisfied that it has passed the test of time and still is basically sound. In preparing a paperback edition, I have had to make only a few minor corrections and to add to the Sources and the Bibliography the titles of scholarly works that have appeared since 1948.

In the section headed "Concluding Queries: on 'Political Feudalism' in Kievan Russia" (pages 209–13) I attempted to show that there was no developed feudalism in Kievan Russia in the western sense of the term. There could not be any, for Russia in that age belonged to a different socio-political formation: that of commercial capitalism, partly based upon slavery. I still believe this in spite of the new publications of Soviet historians. For a good discussion of these sources I recommend A. G. Mazour's *The Writing of History in the Soviet Union* (Stanford, California: Hoover Institution Press, Stanford University, 1971). Pages 46 to 57 are especially pertinent.

*New Haven, Connecticut,*
  July, 1972.

# FOREWORD TO FIRST EDITION

KIEVAN RUSSIA—that is, Russia in the period from the coming of the Varangians to the Mongol invasion—is much better known to us than ancient, pre-Kievan, Russia. The student of the Kievan period has more written sources at his disposal than the ancient era provides and, in contrast to the preceding period, Slavic documents occupy an important place among those sources. Moreover, the Russians of the Kievan period were themselves already interested in their history; the first history of the Kievan period was written by a contemporary, in the early twelfth century. Since then the Kievan period has been covered in all major histories óf Russia and in the course of the nineteenth and twentieth centuries several generations of historians have studied in more detail various aspects of life and civilization in that period. A revival of interest in Kievan Russia is particularly noticeable in Soviet historiography and many valuable monographs have been added recently to those published before the Revolution.

Thus, at first glance, the task which the student of Kievan Russia faces seems not as difficult as that of exploring ancient Russia, and yet the study presents enough riddles and moot problems of its own. While there are contemporary written documents which constitute important evidence, they are few compared with those which are available for the study of western Europe for the same period, and the gaps left are often too wide to be fully bridged.

Also, while there exists ample literature on many important topics in Kievan history, there are gaps in it too, and in many cases there is no consensus of scholarly opinion even on major problems. I have therefore had to offer my own interpretation of many aspects of Russian history of the period. Though not every reader may accept my solution on all points, I hope that the attempt at reappraisal of disputed historiographical issues and criticism of sources may help toward a better understanding of Russian history.

The conscientious reader may wish to turn to the sources himself in order to obtain a more immediate acquaintance with the society described and to use his, or her, own judgment in understanding its life. It is fortunate that at least three of the major sources for the study of Kievan Russia are now available in English. The so-called

Russian "Primary Chronicle" (*Book of Annals*) has been translated by the late Samuel H. Cross and published by the Harvard University Press (1927). Cross has also prepared a new translation of the *Lay of Igor's Campaign* which is to appear in the "Igor Volume" of the *Annuaire de l'Institut de Philologie et d'Histoire Orientales et Slaves* (1948). The most important juridical document of the period—the oldest Russian Code of Laws (*Pravda Russkaia*) has been translated by the author of the present volume. This is published in the collection entitled *Medieval Russian Laws* (Records of Civilization, No. 41 [Columbia University Press, 1947]) and the reader of *Kievan Russia* may well use it as a companion volume to the present one.

A few words should be said concerning the organization of this volume. Chronological narrative alternates in it with a systematic treatment of various aspects of Kievan civilization. The last chapter is an attempt to give a general picture of the interrelations, in the Kievan period, of the Russians and other nations in order to help to understand Russia's specific gravity in the medieval world. The disadvantage of this organization is that it makes some repetitions unavoidable. The author believes, however, that the advantages of the method outweigh its inconveniences, since no adequate idea of the development of a nation—the Russian nation in this case—can be obtained from a mere chronological survey of facts.

As in the preparation of *Ancient Russia,* I have profited much from the help and advice of friends and colleagues. Roman Jakobson was kind enough to read the entire manuscript. His comments and suggestions, in philology as in other matters, have been invaluable. Among the problems discussed with him was Slavic paganism, on which I also had the advantage of consulting Walter Bruno Henning and Vsevolod Basanoff. It goes without saying that none of these scholars is responsible for any of the unorthodox conclusions contained in this book. George P. Fedotov let me read his *Russian Religious Mind: Kievan Christianity* in manuscript and, while I am unable to accept all of his conclusions, I have profited greatly from the reading. I wish also to express my gratitude to Jacob Bromberg, Nicholas N. Martinovitch, and Vladimir F. Minorsky for valuable suggestions, and to Pierre E. Kovalevsky and Sergius Yakobson for bibliographical references. Last but not least, I am indebted to my wife, Nina Vernadsky, for assistance in preparing the section on Russian music. The map has been drawn by Nicholas N. Krijanovsky of the American Geographical Society.

The author's thanks are also due to the staff of the Yale University Library for their kind coöperation; to the Editorial Department of the Yale University Press and to Miss Annabel Learned and Mrs. Frank McMullan for their assistance in preparing the manuscript for the printers.

Acknowledgment of their courtesy in granting permission to quote from books published by them is hereby expressed to the Columbia University Press (quotations from J. W. Burgess, *The Foundations of Political Science*); Methuen & Co. (quotation from J. A. R. Marriott, *Anglo-Russian Relations, 1689–1943*); and Pantheon Books, Inc. (quotation from *Russian Fairy Tales*).

The publication of this volume would not have been possible without the financial support of the Humanities Fund of New York City, and the author wants to express his gratitude to that organization.

*New Haven, Connecticut,*
   May, 1947.

# CONTENTS

# KIEVAN RUSSIA

# Chapter I

## KIEVAN RUSSIA'S PLACE IN HISTORY

### *1. Is Russia Europe?*

GEOGRAPHICALLY, Europe is but a western extension of Asia—an
Asiatic promontory, as it were. In conventional school geographies,
however, the area is considered a separate continent extending eastward to the Ural Mountains. According to this view Russia is assigned
a sort of intermediate position, being divided into two parts: "Asiatic
Russia," east of the Ural range, and "European Russia," west of it.
Thus from the point of view of elementary geography the question, "Is
Russia Europe?" may be answered without much hesitation. Only
part of Russia is Europe.

And yet such an answer, although definite, is hardly satisfactory,
since the traditional division of the country into two parts is artificial;
the Ural range is low and does not break the continuity of the latitudinal landscape zones so characteristic of the Russian geographical
background. Moreover, it is not in the geographical sense that the
question has been persistently asked. By "Europe" is meant not a
geographical but a historical and cultural unit.

The inquiry, then, should be made more specific: Is Russia Europe
in the historical and cultural sense? Does Russia belong, historically
and culturally, to the European comity of nations?

This form of the question has been answered more often than not
in the negative, in any case by non-Russians. Sir J. A. R. Marriott
may be chosen as a typical exponent of the negative view.

Russia is not [he writes], and has never been, a member of the European
family. Ever since the fall of the Roman Empire, and the migrations conse-
quent upon Norse and Teutonic conquests, there has been a measure of
kinship, despite wide diversities of development, between Scandinavians,
Englishmen, Germans, Frenchmen, Iberians, and Italians. Even Poland,
thanks to its adherence to the western form of Christianity, had some affini-
ties with Europe. Russia during long centuries had none.[1]

1. Sir J. A. R. Marriott, *Anglo-Russian Relations, 1689–1943* (2d ed. London, Methuen
& Co., 1944), p. 1.

Among Russians themselves there have always been two schools of opinion, of which the "Slavophiles" and the "Westernizers" of the nineteenth century may be considered the classical representatives. The Westernizers looked upon Russia as the eastern part of Europe and explained the divergencies between Russia and western Europe by a "retardation" of the historical process in Russia, due to the unfavorable geographic background, the Mongol invasion of the thirteenth century, and various other causes.

The "Slavophiles," on the contrary, were ready to recognize the basic difference between Russia and Europe and, instead of speaking of a retardation of Russian civilization, dwelt on its originality and self-sufficiency. The chief spokesman of this school, as to the question which interests us here, was Nikolai Danilevsky. In his book, *Russia and Europe,* this author expounded a theory of differing "cultural types" as represented by the various nations and groups of nations in their history. He admitted the greatness of the "Romano-Germanic" civilization but refused to recognize it as *the* civilization—the only path to progress. By this theory he attempted to assert the rights of the "Slavic cultural type" to an independent development.

In his opinion, the civilization which is usually called "European" should be called "Romano-Germanic." To identify "European" with "Romano-Germanic" would be a logical error from his point of view. But, since the identification has generally prevailed, he asks himself: "Does Russia belong to Europe in that sense (i.e., to Romano-Germanic Europe)?" His answer is an emphatic "No." [2]

What position shall we take in regard to this old controversy? It may be suggested, first of all, that the very premises of the argument are now out of date, since from the point of view of the historian there is no longer a Europe in the traditional sense. In the course of the last three centuries Europe has expanded politically, each of the leading European states subjecting to itself vast territories on other continents; nay, absorbing whole non-European nations. The area has also expanded demographically by emigration, as a result of which new "European" nations have asserted themselves in the Americas, in Australia, in Africa. More recently still, Europe has expanded

---

2. N. Ia. Danilevsky, *Rossiia i Europa* (St. Petersburg, 1871), p. 60. More recently the contrast between Russia and "Romano-Germanic Europe" has been brilliantly discussed by the late Prince N. S. Trubetskoy, founder of the "Eurasian" school of thought. See his *Europa i Chelovechestvo* (Sofia, 1920).

technologically and industrially, putting in motion forces which, once released, she has hardly been able to control.

As the European powers one by one—Spain, Portugal, Holland, Great Britain, France, and more recently Germany—each built for itself a colonial empire, and as they thus stepped out of Europe proper, they finally shattered the unity of the region. While Russia acquired no colonies overseas, she expanded steadily eastward through a continuous territory until she found herself controlling a vast subcontinent. As a result of all this, several "world powers" have come to being, while the core of Europe, crushed by the effects of two world wars, is now politically divided and culturally confused.

What about these world powers in their relation to Europe? Is the United States "Europe"? Yes, in the sense of her cultural background and traditions; no, in the sense that she has created a civilization of her own which is now affecting Europe in its turn.

Is Britain Europe? Again yes, in the sense of historical derivation; and again no, as, being the leading body of the British Commonwealth, she lives a life of her own.

Is, then, Russia Europe? Yes, in the sense that her civilization has had many contacts with the European culture—even by the Romano-Germanic interpretation—since the Middle Ages. No, in the sense that she is a world apart, a subcontinent within herself, not only geographically but also politically and culturally.

Even world powers are transitory. The levelling effect of technology and industrialization is rapidly erasing old cultural differences between single nations. The harnessing of atomic energy makes "one world" imperative, although world unity cannot be achieved overnight. To this unity each nation is destined to contribute and each has already contributed a share. Projecting this argument back into the earlier periods of history we begin to realize that one cannot gauge the whole historical process by European standards, the less so since there have always been centrifugal trends in Europe itself.

To answer the question posed at the beginning of these pages, therefore, we have first to come to common agreement on another point: What is Europe? The argument thus leads to a dead end. But the very fact that the question has been asked about Russia indicates the feeling that, if Russia is Europe, she is only partly so and that more often than not her historical ways have been different from those of other European powers.

It is significant that both those who would exclude her from Europe and those who would not, agree that in the course of history some basic divergencies between Europe and Russia have been revealed. When all is said, Marriott's point of view on the complete cultural isolation of Russia is certainly untenable. Throughout the long passage of time there have existed not only divergencies but parallels between Russian and European history, and both should be taken into account. Contacts between Russia and Europe have been manifold at every stage of medieval and modern development and, putting aside for the moment the modern age, one may say that they were especially close in the Kievan period.

## 2. Russia's Place in the Medieval World

A nation's history is conditioned not only by its own material and spiritual resources but by its international environment as well. No nation has ever been, and none is, completely isolated. This is plain enough in our day but even in earlier periods, long before the revolution in means of communication, some kind of intercourse between nations was unavoidable.

Owing to her geographic position, China seems to have come closer to isolation than any other country. Yet, even in ancient times, a trickle of maritime commerce connected China with India and Arabia and through the latter with the Mediterranean area; in addition, the overland commercial road through Turkestan, controlled by the nomads, assumed great importance in the Roman and the early medieval periods.

In the Roman period, which corresponds to the Sarmatian period of Russian history, Russia was certainly not isolated; on the contrary, the proto-Russian tribes were engulfed at this time in an alien sea.[3] Similar conditions prevailed in the Hunnic and Khazar periods. In a still later age, the prosperity of the Kievan state was based on foreign commerce.

The question now before us is to examine the international environment of Kievan Russia and the changes it underwent within the Kievan period (878–1237). It must be emphasized at the outset that in early medieval times the dynamics of international relations were quite different from those of the modern age. The main European nations were already in the process of formation but the center of grav-

3. See *Ancient Russia*, chap. III.

ity, both politically and culturally, was located neither in western nor in central Europe but in Byzantium.

The Byzantine Empire outstripped by far the Carolingian Empire in the field of economics as well as in diplomacy. As a matter of fact, it was one of the two world powers of the period, the other being the Moslem Caliphate.

By no means could western Europe claim at this time any leading role in the advancement of science and technology. Such a role belonged to the Caliphate, where the traditions of Hellenistic scholarship were being revived. Arabic became the language of leading scientists and physicians. To a certain extent, until the Crusades, Byzantium served as an intermediary between the Arabic world and western Europe. Spain, conquered by the Arabs in the eighth century, was another channel through which the west absorbed Arabic science.

While Russia was in close contact with the nations of central and northern Europe, it was the Byzantine influence which prevailed with her, as might be expected in view of the predominant role of the Empire in that age. As to the Caliphate, she was deprived of any direct contact with it. It was unfortunate that Khazar control of the Pontic steppes was, from the late tenth century, replaced by that of wild nomadic tribes such as the Patzinaks and the Cumans; the fact that the Russians themselves had destroyed the Khazar Empire hardly made the situation easier for them.

However, the barrier of the steppe nomads was not impenetrable and there was always some intercourse between Russia and the Christian states in Transcaucasia and, through them, with Syria. Behind the steppe area dominated by the nomads also lay such important commercial and cultural centers as Khoresm and Bukhara. In the tenth century Bukhara was ruled by the enlightened Persian dynasty of Samanids. Later, in the eleventh century, the wild Seljuqs replaced them, undermining the level of civilization in Turkestan.

In the north, the Moslem state of the Volga Bulgars, with whom the Russians were in close commercial relations, seems to have achieved not only material prosperity but also a comparatively high level of culture. Potentially, it might have served as an intermediary between Russia and the Arabic culture but it does not appear that Russia profited much by this opportunity.

Economically, Russia kept lively relations with the East, both through the Volga Bulgars and through Tmutorokan, until the end of Russian control of that city in the late eleventh century. Later on, the Cumans—in periods of peace, at least—allowed the Khoresmian and other Eastern merchants to trade with the Russians. The influx of Oriental silver to Russia ceased, however, about A.D. 1000, probably in connection with the overthrow óf the Samanids by the Seljuqs.

The era of the Crusades (1096–1270) brought about radical changes in the international situation. Byzantium's power was now declining and that of the west ascending. In 1204 the western knights conquered and mercilessly sacked Constantinople, after which a "Latin" empire was established in Greece, to last until 1261. Russian commerce, which in the earlier period had gravitated toward Constantinople, now shifted to the western markets.

Politically, through Hungary, Poland, and Bohemia, Russia in the period of the Crusades became involved in European affairs much more closely than she had been in earlier times. Now belligerent, now peaceful, the Russians in their relations with the west succeeded during the twelfth century in establishing a kind of equilibrium in eastern and central Europe. This balance was upset in the early thirteenth century by the formation of German crusader states in Prussia and Latvia. Simultaneously the Mongols gave their first warning by a raid into the Cuman steppes in 1223.

To sum up, the international constellation in the Kievan period, so far as it affected Russia, was favorable to her in the south, less so in the west, and decidedly unfavorable in the southeast, where constant nomadic raids sapped her strength and drained her resources.

### 3. Divergent and Parallel Trends in Russian and European History

The division of "universal history" into the ancient, medieval, and modern ages is one of the traditional generalizations which become almost meaningless with closer approach, especially from any truly universal point of view—that is, taking into account the historical development not only of Europe but of other continents as well. As a matter of fact, the conventional division was formulated with only the history of Europe in mind, and only in regard to European history has it any meaning.

In Europe the Middle Ages were the era of feudalism par excellence. Feudal institutions developed as a result of the degeneration of the Roman Empire, its disintegration under the pressure of the "barbarians"—chiefly Teutons—and an adaptation of Teutonic institutions to the Roman and vice versa.

Not all of the Roman Empire was destroyed, however, in the catastrophes of the fifth century—only its western half. In the east the Empire survived to last for another thousand years under the name of Byzantium. The development of the Byzantine Empire was in turn affected by new social and political trends and gradually some institutions similar to the feudal appeared in the east but never assumed such momentum as in the west until the conquest of Constantinople by the Crusaders. In the period of the so-called "Latin Empire" (1204–61), feudal institutions of the western type were transplanted wholesale to Greek soil. But the restoration of the Byzantine Empire once more checked this process of feudalization.

As we turn farther east, certain feudalizing tendencies are noticeable in the social organization of the Moslem states but these were of a different pattern from the western. As to the nomadic tribes of the Eurasian steppes, they lived in an entirely different environment, not only geographically but economically and socially as well.

While Russia was never part of the Roman Empire (so much we may concede to Marriott), the Antes and other proto-Russian tribes were in some contact with the northeastern fringe of the Empire, as in the Crimea, for example. In the later period Russia was drawn into the Byzantine orbit both economically and culturally.

On the other hand, the Russians lived from time immemorial in close contact with the steppe nomads; they were at times almost submerged in the Iranian and Turkish sea. The steppe empire thrived on commerce, and the protection of the transcontinental overland roads, especially the "silk road" from China to the Mediterranean, was always one of the primary tasks of the steppe emperors.

One might well expect that, built on a different foundation, Russia's economic and social structure in the early Middle Ages would be different from the European. And so it was in many respects.

As is convincingly shown by Henri Pirenne, the Arab conquest of North Africa, Sicily, and Spain severed for a time commercial relations between Western Europe and the Levant,[4] and it was the urge to open new roads to the Orient which guided the Norsemen in their audacious drive from the Baltic Sea to the Azov region. In Carolingian

4. Henri Pirenne, *Economic and Social History of Medieval Europe* (New York, Harcourt, Brace and Co., 1937); also *Medieval Cities* (Princeton, Princeton University Press, 1925) and *Mohammed and Charlemagne* (New York, W. W. Norton & Co., 1939), by the same author.

Europe (from the eighth to the tenth century) trade was at its lowest level in long ages. Carolingian feudalism had as its economic foundation an impoverished agricultural civilization and, with all due reservations, the growth of early feudal institutions corresponded to the establishment of a "natural," or "closed," economy.

Against this agrarian and feudal Europe, Byzantium with her extensive commerce and profitable industries stood out in bold relief. "Money economy" and not "natural economy" prevailed in the Byzantine Empire. Note that Italy, from the Age of Justinian, was partly controlled by Byzantium until at least the tenth century. Economically, in the Carolingian period Italy belonged to the Byzantine world rather than to the European.

Russia was likewise a part of the Byzantine world, besides being directly connected with Oriental commerce. Although, contrary to the opinion of Kliuchevsky and his school, agriculture was as important an element of Russian economics as commerce, the sociological implications of its development in that period were not the same for Russia as for the West because of the closer connection in Russia between the two spheres of activity, especially in the form of a lively grain trade. In any case, in Kievan Russia as in Byzantium, a money economy prevailed over natural economy. And, in contrast to the West, not the feudal manor but the city was the dominant factor in the country's economic and social development.

But if there were important divergencies in the Middle Ages between the sociopolitical development of Russia and of western Europe, there were also many similarities. In Kievan Russia the regime of "commercial capitalism" was superimposed over a primitive tribal and clan society. The early social organization of the Slavic and Teutonic tribes was similar in many respects, as a result of which there are striking parallels in the old customary laws of the Slavic and Teutonic peoples. The early version of the Kievan code of laws—the *Russian Law* (*Pravda Russkaia*, or *Lex Russica*)—may be considered, together with the *Lex Salica* and other western *Leges*, as belonging to the same general type of "Barbaric Laws."

There were also many similarities in the organization of princely administration. In Russia as in the west, the public administration of the rulers developed out of their household administration. The rise of the *maire du palais* (Major Domus) in the Frankish monarchy in the seventh and eighth centuries is but one of the characteristic expressions of this process. In Russia as in the west, the prince tried to assert his authority by granting special protection to his assistants in the management of his estates. The *Pravda* of Iaroslav's sons has many a common feature with the *Capitularia* of the Carolingian kings.

Politically there was, however, a great difference between a ruler's authority in the west and in Russia. Both the prince in Russia and the king in the west had to share their rule with a powerful aristocracy but, in addition, in Russia there was a third important political element lacking in the west at the time: the city.

## 4. The Notion of East European History

So far I have spoken of the Europe of this period as if it were a single socio-political body. Actually, various nations lived together there, whose integrated or similar functioning was only relative. The universal church and universal empire are commonly considered the two pillars of unity in medieval Europe, feudalism being recognized as its third fundamental institution. However, we must not forget that the area in which these three factors were at work did not cover the whole region geographically.

More often than not, when we speak of "medieval Europe" we mean western and central Europe only. The alleged "universal empire"— the Holy Roman Empire of the German nation—was actually not universal but local, since it was counterbalanced by the Byzantine Empire in the southeast. Nor was the Roman Catholic Church universally recognized; many an east European nation preferred Greek Orthodoxy. And, as we have just seen, the economic and social foundations of the Byzantine east were markedly different from those of the feudal west.

It appears that we must recognize the existence of two medieval Europes rather than one—a western and an eastern Europe. Of these, the historical role of eastern Europe has long been underestimated. Even now, in general outlines of medieval history, by "Europe" western Europe is usually meant, while eastern Europe is treated as a superfluous appendix, if at all.

Ethnically, western Europe is populated for the most part by Latin and Teutonic peoples, eastern Europe by Slavs, Greeks, and a number of other groups. In the neglect of east European history, racial prejudice, especially the Teuton's traditional contempt of the Slav, must have played a not inconsiderable role. It is significant that even such a powerful thinker as Hegel could find no room for the Slavs in his *Philosophy of History*. As he explains,

These peoples did, indeed, found kingdoms and sustain spirited conflicts with the various nations that came across their path. Sometimes, as an advanced guard—an intermediate nationality—they took part in the struggle between Christian Europe and unchristian Asia. The Poles even liberated beleaguered Vienna from the Turks; and the Slavs have to some extent been drawn within the sphere of Occidental Reason. Yet this entire body of peoples remains excluded from our consideration, because hitherto it has not appeared as an independent element in the series of phases that Reason has assumed in the World.[5]

To what extent German nationalist theories have influenced even modern American scholarship may be seen from John W. Burgess' *Foundations of Political Science,* first published in 1917 and reprinted in 1933. In that author's opinion both the Greeks and the Slavs have manifested "a low order of political genius," because of which it is "absolutely necessary that the political organization, in highest instance, of the Greek and Slav nations should be undertaken by a foreign political power." [6] He then suggests that the Teutonic nations "as the political nations *par excellence*" should "assume the leadership in the establishment and administration of states." [7] One reason for the possibility of such advice from an American scholar is precisely the lack of understanding of the historical role of the Greek and Slav peoples.

In regard to the Greeks, old ignorance and prejudices have long since been overcome by the splendid development of Byzantine studies. Since the labors of the great Du Cange and others in the seventeenth century, the Byzantinological tradition has been kept alive by a number of French and Belgian scholars, as well as by Russian, Ger-

5. G. W. F. Hegel, *Lectures on the Philosophy of History,* translated from the third German edition by J. Sibree (London, Bell & Daldy, 1872), p. 363; for German original, see G. W. F. Hegel, *Sämtliche Werke,* H. Glockner, ed. (Stuttgart, 1928), XI, 447. It must be noted that Hegel foresaw the possibility of a great future for the Slavs and especially for Russia. In his letter of November 28, 1821, to Boris von Yxkuell, a Baltic German and a Russian subject, he writes as follows: "You are fortunate to belong to a country which occupies so great a place in the field of universal history and which undoubtedly has an even higher destiny. It seems that other contemporary states have more or less reached the goal of their development; it is possible that they have already passed their peak and their position has become static. Russia, on the contrary, potentially already the mightiest state of all, carries in her womb immense possibilities of further development of her intensive nature." See Kuno Fischer, *Geschichte der neuern Philosophie* VIII, Part 1 (Heidelberg, 1911), pp. 118–119; also D. I. Chizhevsky, *Gegel v Rossii* (Paris, 1939), p. 13.

6. John W. Burgess, *The Foundations of Political Science,* with an introduction by Nicholas M. Butler (New York, Columbia University Press, 1933), p. 32.

7. *Idem,* p. 40.

man, British, American, Italian, Hungarian, Romanian, Polish, Czech, Bulgarian, and Yugoslav Byzantinologists, and of course by the Greeks themselves. Tremendous progress has been made in this field in the last fifty years and the great historical role of Byzantium has now been clearly revealed.

Byzantium, however, was but one of the political and cultural centers of eastern Europe in the Middle Ages. The church schism prevented Roman Catholic peoples such as the Poles from accepting the cultural leadership of the Byzantines. On the other hand, while pledging allegiance to Rome, the Poles—as well as the Hungarians—belonged geographically and economically to eastern Europe, not to the west. They may be said to have constituted an east European group of their own, with which a number of other peoples, such as the Lithuanians, the Belorussians, the Ukrainians, and the Romanians, were in close contact. Moreover, the peoples of this area maintained a lively intercourse with central Europe, in particular with the Czechs and the Slovaks.

It is the Polish sphere of cultural influence, then, which may be called the nucleus of eastern Europe in the late Middle Ages and early modern period. And it is to the Polish, Ukrainian, and Czech historians that the credit must go for setting the problem of east European history as an independent branch of research.

The first chair of east European history in a European university was founded in 1894 in Lvov, western Ukraine (then Lemberg in Austrian Galicia). Its first holder was the prominent Ukrainian scholar Michael Hrushevsky (Grushevsky). In 1904 he published a valuable study on the interrelation between Russian history and the history of the eastern Slavs, in which he treated the Ukraine as a part not of Russia but of eastern Europe.[8] In the interval between the two world wars the problem of east European history was the subject of a lively discussion in which several Polish and Czech historians took a prominent part.[9] The main point in the debates was how to establish

8. M. Hrushevsky, "Zvychaina skhema russkoi istorii i sprava ratsionalnogo ukladu istorii skhidnogo slovianstva," *Stat'i po Slavianovedeniiu*, V. I. Lamansky, ed., I (St. Petersburg, 1904), 298–304.

9. See O. Halecki, "L'Histoire de l'Europe orientale," *La Pologne au V-e congrès international des sciences historiques* (Warsaw, 1924) ; M. Weingart, "Le Passé et le présent de la solidarité slave," *Monde Slave,* February, 1926, pp. 187–210; W. Lednicki, "Existe-t-il un patrimoine commun d'études slaves?" *Monde Slave,* December, 1926, pp. 411–431; J. Bidlo, "Ce que c'est l'histoire de l'Orient européen," *Bulletin d'information des sciences historiques en Europe orientale, 6* (Warsaw, 1934), and, by the same author, "L'Europe orientale et le domaine de son histoire," *Monde Slave,* October,

a proper relation between the notions of "Slavic Europe" and "eastern Europe."

The main difficulty in this connection is the question of how to place Russia. She is indeed a predominantly Slav nation but is she an organic part of eastern Europe? Are we to include Russia in the group of eastern European nations or not? When it comes to modern times it is obvious that Russia is a unit by herself, and by Russia I mean here the Soviet Union, including both Ukraine and Belorussia.

What was the situation in the Middle Ages? In the late Middle Ages—that is, in the fourteenth and fifteenth centuries—both the Ukraine and Belorussia were part of the Polish-Lithuanian federation; both, therefore, may be conveniently placed in eastern Europe from the political point of view.

In the Kievan period, the Ukrainian and Belorussian lands belonged to the Russian federation and their place in history must be considered together with that of all Russia. As the territory of Kievan Russia did not extend beyond the limits of "Europe" from the conventional point of view, there is no formal objection to including it in "eastern Europe."

This would be rather misleading, however, and little would be gained by it for our understanding of either Russian or east European history. In spite of her ties with the Balkans on one hand and with Hungary and Poland on the other, Russia even then formed a distinct sociopolitical body of her own. Moreover, historically Kievan Russia was the nucleus of the later continental, "Eurasian" Russia. From the geopolitical point of view the area of the Kievan state may be defined not only as "eastern Europe" but likewise as "western Eurasia." Culturally, Russia may be thought of in this period as the northern frontier of Byzantium.

## 5. The Challenge of Geopolitics

The expansion of Russia resulted in her occupying a vast and continuous territory stretching from the Baltic Sea to the Pacific and from Pamir to the Arctic Ocean. This subcontinent is best called "Eurasia," not only because it comprises parts of both Europe and

1935, pp. 1–20; November, pp. 204–233; O. Halecki, "The Historical Role of Central-Eastern Europe," *Annals of the American Academy of Political and Social Sciences,* March, 1944, pp. 9–18; R. Jakobson, "The Beginnings of National Self-Determination in Europe," *The Review of Politics,* 7, No. 1 (January, 1945), pp. 29–42. For a German approach to the problem, see J. Pfitzner, "Die Geschichte Osteuropas und die Geschichte des Slawentums als Forschungsprobleme," *Historische Zeitschrift, 150* (1934), pp. 21–85.

Asia but also because it represents a geographic unit which is as distinct from Europe as it is from the non-Russian parts of Asia.[10]

In regard to soil and vegetation, Eurasia consists of latitudinal landscape zones, such as the tundra, the forest zone, the intermediate forest-steppe zone (*lesostepie*), the steppe zone, and finally that of deserts. These zones have played and, to a certain extent, still play an important role in Russian economics. No less significant have been the political implications of the interrelation between the forest zone and the steppe zone. The latter, together with the adjacent deserts, served in old times as the abode of various nomadic hordes of Manchu, Mongol, and Turkish extraction. Powerful steppe empires were built in this zone from time immemorial, following upon each other with brief intermissions.[11]

The steppe zone stretches from Mongolia westward to the Carpathians and has an extension into the middle Danubian area. In old times it offered an excellent road for the Mongolian nomads, with no natural obstacles to bar their way until the Carpathian Mountains. Once a nomadic military empire had established itself in the Eurasian steppes, it tended to subject to its control the whole steppe zone as well as at least portions of the adjacent forest-steppe area.

At times, instead of one huge empire, a belt of lesser khanates dominated the steppes, some of them allied among themselves, others opposing each other. Thus after the fall of the Hunnic Empire the Avars established themselves in Hungary, the Khazars and Magyars in the north Pontic area, and two Turkish khanates in Kazakhstan and Mongolia.

In the late ninth century the Magyars migrated westward to the middle Danubian area (present-day Hungary) and a century later the Khazar Empire was destroyed by the Russians. But the Russians were not able by themselves to control the Pontic steppes, since new Turkish hordes were constantly pushing from Kazakhstan; after contesting the steppes against the Patzinaks they were pushed northward by the Cumans. Then, in the thirteenth century, the Mongolian invasion flooded the whole of European Russia.

The Mongol Empire was vaster than even the Hunnic and the Mongols united the whole of Eurasia under their authority. After the emancipation of Russia from the Mongol yoke the process was gradually repeated in reverse, with the result that in the course of

10. See P. N. Savickij, *Šestina světa* (Prague, 1933).
11. See *Ancient Russia*, pp. 64, 65, 78–84, 122, 123, 178, 179, 206, 213.

time the Russians succeeded in uniting under their own authority most of the area of the former Mongol domination.

It is interesting to note that in their drive the Mongols had advanced westward through the steppe zone and while advancing had gradually extended their authority to the forest zone. The Russians, on the contrary, expanded eastward through the forest zone and only after controlling it penetrated into the steppe and desert zones.

Bearing all this in mind, let us now consider the position of Kievan Russia from the geopolitical point of view. In the Kievan period the Russians occupied the European part of Russia only, and not all of that. In the south they at first extended their control to the Crimea and the Azov and lower Volga regions but lost those areas by the late eleventh century, when they were compelled by the Cumans to evacuate the steppe zone and retreat northward to the forest-steppe and forest zones. In the east the middle Volga region was held by the Volga Bulgars, with whom the Russians were in close commercial relations from the ninth century and with whom from time to time they also clashed. In the beginning of the thirteenth century the east Russian princes showed their obvious intention of subjecting the Bulgars to their control as a preliminary step to controlling the whole course of the Volga River. But their drive was barred by the Mongols, who conquered both Bulgars and Russians.

Even if the Russians failed to control all of European Russia in the Kievan period, the space they occupied seems large enough, especially as compared with the areas of their European neighbors. Geographically, the Dnieper riverway was the pivot of Kievan Russia and the Russians had access to both Baltic and Black seas, although the Cuman raids made the use of the Black Sea precarious.

Speaking in terms of geopolitics as represented by Mackinder and his followers, the Russians in the Kievan period controlled a considerable portion of the European "heartland," [12] yet, in spite of this, proved unable to parry the Mongol invasion. One reason for the vulnerability of their position was their failure to round out a full control of the heartland; had they succeeded in controlling the whole course of the Volga River as well as the southern steppes they would have been in a much better position to meet the Mongol onslaught.

12. H. J. Mackinder, *Democratic Ideals and Reality* (New York, H. Holt, 1919; 2d ed., 1942); K. Haushofer *et al., Bausteine zur Geopolitik* (Berlin-Grunewald, 1928); see also G. B. Cressey, *The Basis of Soviet Strength* (New York, Whittlesey House, 1945), pp. 231–237.

Another cause of the Russian disaster in the thirteenth century was the fact that Russia was subjected to simultaneous pressure from both east and west. The German drive from the west assumed momentum exactly in the period of the Mongol invasion from the east.

But perhaps the main cause of the Russian failure was the lack of protection of the heartland on the eastern side. The Eurasian steppes represented the real heartland in the conflicts of that period. Owing to the westward extension of the steppe zone, European Russia was geopolitically a part of Eurasia and prior to the era of field artillery there was little hope, if any, for the Russians to stop the nomads once the later were united.

The Kievan period was one of disunity among the nomads; though suffering from Cuman raids, the Russian people were at this time in no real danger of being crushed by them. But the Mongol invasion overthrew the balance of power between forest and steppe zones in favor of the latter.

The lesson which the Russians drew from the Mongol yoke was that security from the nomadic east could be obtained only by controlling Eurasia altogether. To that goal they approached gradually and by stages. The eastward expansion started in the middle of the sixteenth century; Russia's first move was to secure control of the whole course of the Volga River. Within the next century all Siberia was occupied. The colonization of Siberia was a spontaneous movement of Cossacks and trappers rather than a formal military conquest but the Muscovite statesmen knew how to take full advantage of the popular movement. In the case of the expansion into Kazakhstan and Turkestan in the eighteenth and nineteenth centuries the initiative belonged to the government rather than to the people.

In the course of the same period the southern steppes, as well as the Crimea and the Caucasus, were conquered—or, if we may refer here to the events of the tenth century—reconquered. Thus the task which the Russians failed to achieve in the Kievan period was completed.

## 6. The Significance of the Kievan Period in Russian History

Old Russia is usually associated, in the mind of the American reader, with autocracy and serfdom. It has even been suggested that totalitarianism emanated directly from the "Russian soul." And, indeed, in 1833 a Russian, Count S. S. Uvarov, proclaimed that Russia rested upon "Orthodoxy, Autocracy, and Nationality." Looking back to Uvarov's time with the benefit of our knowledge of subsequent events, we know that, when he made his statement, undiluted autocracy had less than four score years to live. Serfdom was abolished less than thirty years after Uvarov's declaration.

In fact, during the whole imperial era (1721–1917), periods of reaction alternated with those of liberalism. The last twelve years of the imperial regime were those of constitutional experiment, however limited in scope. But even prior to that, since 1864 autocracy had been somewhat checked by the local institutions of self-government (zemstvo) and a well-balanced judiciary.

In the tsardom of Muscovy of the sixteenth and seventeenth centuries, the authority of the tsar was limited, actually if not legally, by a people's assembly (zemsky sobor), a system of local self-government, and the church. Simultaneously, democratic institutions flourished in the Cossack communes, especially in the Zaporozhie and the Don Host.

The fourteenth and fifteenth centuries were the period of the formation of the Muscovite state. The nascent Muscovite autocracy was itself subordinated to a much more rigid and implacable absolutism —that of the Mongols—and the power of the Moscow grand dukes was partly shaped on that forceful pattern. However, in the Mongol period Muscovy controlled only a corner of present Russian territory, the central Russian "Mesopotamia"; that is, the basin of the upper Volga and Oka rivers. Other Russian lands at this time had a different political and social milieu.

Paradoxical as it may seem, the Mongol age was the period of blossoming of democratic institutions in the north Russian city-states of Novgorod and Pskov, in spite of the fact that north Russia was under the nominal authority of the Mongol khans and that the grand duke of Moscow was more often than not elected prince of Novgorod.

In Ukraine the Mongol domination came to an end in the middle of the fourteenth century—that is, about a century earlier than in Muscovy; in Belorussia the period was even shorter. These two nations eventually exchanged Mongol rule for that of the grand duke of Lithuania, while the western Ukraine (Galicia) was occupied by Poland in 1349. In 1385 a union was formed by Poland and Lithuania, at first dynastic only, to become a real union later on.

In the fourteenth and fifteenth centuries the grand duchy of Lithuania was a loose federation which the Ukrainian and Belorussian lands joined as so many autonomous units. An aristocratic constitution was eventually established and thus, in contrast to both autocratic Muscovy and democratic Novgorod, an aristocratic Ukraine and Belorussia asserted themselves.

These three elements of power—monarchic, aristocratic, and democratic—which in the Mongol period developed separately in three distinct geographic regions of old Russia, coexisted in each of the Russian lands during the Kievan period in various proportions and combinations in each case. It is this variety of political experience which makes the Kievan period a fascinating study for the student of government.

Thus a glance at the political history of Russia is sufficient to dispose of the myth of totalitarianism's being inherent in the Russian mentality. It was not because of any alleged innate sympathy of the "Russian soul" to autocracy that the tsardom of Moscow came into being but out of the stern necessity of organizing a military force sufficient to overthrow the Mongol yoke and then of securing control of a territory vast enough for strategic defense. In the fifteenth and sixteenth centuries Muscovy became a military camp. The energy of both rulers and people was concentrated on defence. Political freedom was sacrificed for national survival.

It is probable that the Russians would have emancipated themselves from Mongol domination much earlier than they actually did, had they not been threatened simultaneously from the west. Faced by the dilemma of war on two fronts, two Russian princes of the thirteenth century each tried an opposite course of policies. In western Ukraine Prince Daniel of Galicia made a bid for the support of the west, and lost. In eastern Russia, Prince Alexander Nevsky accepted Mongol suzerainty in order to have his hands free in the west, and won. By defeating the Swedes at the mouth of the Neva River in 1240 he secured to Novgorod an outlet to the Baltic. Two years later he saved Russia from a German invasion by crushing the German knights in the famous "battle on the ice."

Serfdom was another price paid by the Russians for the sake of survival. Although slavery existed in both Kievan and Muscovite Russia, slaves did not represent a large proportion of the population. In Kievan Russia it coexisted with a "capitalistic" economy just as in the United States prior to the Civil War.

On the other hand, serfdom as a feudal institution was hardly known in Kievan Russia. In the Mongol period the process of attaching free peasants to the large estates made rapid progress in both

Muscovy and Lithuanian Russia. Serfdom was officially introduced in Ukraine and Belorussia by the charter (*privilei*) of the Grand Duke Kazimierz of 1447. In Muscovy, from 1581 certain years were proclaimed "prohibited"—that is, no migration of peasants from one estate to another was allowed in these years. Serfdom was finally confirmed by the Code of Laws (*Ulozhenie*) in 1649.

As a contrast to both Muscovite and Lithuanian states, Kievan Russia was a country of free political institutions and free interplay of social and economic forces. The Kievan period was also that of the Christianization of Russia; it witnessed the rise of a brilliant civilization, revealed especially in architecture, literature, and applied arts, such as filigree and enamel.

While the Mongol invasion administered a heavy blow to Kievan institutions and culture and resulted in the formation of an absolutist state in Muscovy, the development of the elements of Kievan civilization was not altogether stopped. Some traditions of the Kievan period evolved in Novgorod and Pskov, others in Ukraine and Belorussia; still others in Muscovy itself. From the point of view of legal history, the foundations of the charter of the City of Pskov (1397–1467), the first Lithuanian statute (1529), and to a certain extent even the first Muscovite Code of Laws (*Sudebnik*) of 1497 are to be sought in the *Russian Law* of the Kievan period.

Besides the positive achievements of the Russian people in the Kievan period, life in Kievan Russia had many negative aspects as well. Constant raids of the Turkish nomads from the southeast as well as the internecine wars between Russian princes harassed the population and made life insecure more often than not. The ever-widening gulf between the upper and the lower classes resulted in periodic economic and social crises. In spite of all its deficiencies, however, Kievan Russia was warmly cherished in popular memory, as manifested by the Russian epic songs—the *byliny*. No other era of the country's history is referred to in Russian folklore with so much sympathy and gratification as the Kievan.

There must have been something in Kievan Russia which made people forget its negative side and remember only its achievements. That "something" was the spirit of freedom—individual, political, and economic—which prevailed in the Russia of that day and to which the Muscovite principle of the individual's complete obedience to the state was to present such a contrast.

# CHAPTER II

# THE IMPERIAL PLAN AND ITS FAILURE, 878–972

### 1. The Imperial Plan: Dreams and Realities

THE political history of Kievan Russian opens with a century of bold adventure: with an attempt on the part of the Norse rulers of Kiev to build up a vast empire stretching from the Baltic to the Black Sea and from the Carpathian Mountains to the Caspian Sea. A series of daring campaigns was undertaken, both by sea and by land, with Constantinople and Transcaucasia as the two main objectives; at one time the mouths of both Volga and Danube were controlled by the Russians.

This ambitious effort may be considered from two angles—as an episode of viking expansion and as a stage of Russian history. Toward the close of the ninth century the vikings controlled both the North and the Baltic seas and not only raided adjacent parts of the European continent and the British Isles but were able to establish themselves firmly in northwestern Europe. Even earlier, as we know, they had entered Russia and penetrated as far to the southeast as the Azov region. Cruising along the western shores of France and the Iberian peninsula, they also explored the Mediterranean and eventually built a state of their own in Sicily.

Constantinople—Miklagard, the Imperial City—was the focal point where the Black Sea and Mediterranean drives eventually met. It is against this background of the adventurous spirit of the vikings that the imperial dreams of the Russian princes of Kiev should be studied. Amazing as is the wide range of their political plans, it fits well into the general picture of Europe in this period. However, we must not forget that by the end of the ninth century the Norse newcomers in Russia had already merged with the native population to a considerable extent, becoming part of the Russian background. This is particularly true of the Swedes in the Azov area, who borrowed their very name—Rus'—from the natives.[1] That name was now assumed by the Kievan Norsemen as well. Sviatoslav, the most dar-

1. See *Ancient Russia*, pp. 274–275.

ing of the first Kievan princes, not only bore a Slavic name but both in physical appearance and in attire was a typical Slav of the south, a prototype of the Zaparozhie Cossacks. His grandson Iaroslav the Wise had few Nordic features, if any, anthropologically speaking. And, while the bulk of the *druzhina* or retinue of the first Kievan princes consisted of Norsemen, Slavs were not excluded from it and both Norsemen and Slavs were interested not only in war but in commerce as well.

The Russian Slavs had old traditions both of long-range military campaigns and of international trade behind them, beginning at least as far back as the sixth century when the Antes penetrated into the Danubian area. In the seventh century some of the Antian tribes firmly established themselves in the eastern part of the Balkan peninsula, later to be known as Bulgaria. In the seventh and eighth centuries the Antes and the Rus' helped the Khazars to ward off Arab raids on the Caucasus.[2] Under the auspices of the Khazars the Antian Slavs took active part in international commerce, and from Mas'udi and other Oriental authors we know that Antian-Slavic merchants had permanent quarters in the Khazarian capital Itil and presumably in other Khazar cities as well. Antian-Slavic troops constituted an important element in the Khazar army.[3]

It thus appears that the Norse princes of Kiev must have found considerable support to their imperial plans among the upper classes of the Slavs. In their imperialist undertakings plunder was a preliminary to trade—the driving motive of the imperial plan of the first Kievan princes was essentially commercial; their strategy aimed at the control of a vast network of commercial highways in the Pontic and the Caspian areas. Geographically the cornerstone of this system was the Azov region, more specifically Kerch Strait, already held by the Russian kagans since the late eighth century. To round out the structure they needed control of the lower Volga and lower Danube areas. In case of the complete success of their undertakings, the seizure of Constantinople—that is, of the Bosporus and the Dardanelles—loomed as the crowning prize. However, their attacks on Constantinople were motivated not so much by the hope of capturing it as by a desire to compel the Byzantines to open their markets to the Russian trade. We find here an exact parallel to the aspirations of the Huns in the past. The last Byzantino-Hunnic war, in the late fifth

2. *Idem*, pp. 220, 259, 260, 273.
3. *Idem*, p. 214.

century, was the result of the refusal of the Byzantines to throw the Danubian market towns open to the Hunnic commerce.[4] Commanding the Black Sea and entrenching themselves in Bulgaria, the Russians would be in position to dictate their conditions even without actually controlling Constantinople. Thus even a partial realization of the imperial plan promised rich rewards.

But, if the driving motives behind the great plan and the advantages expected from it were obvious, so were the tremendous difficulties to be overcome. First of all, there were two centers of Russian action in the period—Kiev and Tmutorokan—and, while a certain degree of coördination between the policies of the princes of Kiev and the Russian kagans must have been reached, it was not so easy, if possible at all, to achieve complete unity. Furthermore, the Kievan realm consisted both politically and socially of heterogeneous elements, not to mention ethnographic variations. The authority of the Kievan prince was recognized at first by only a few Russian tribes. Later, other tribes were brought within the Kievan political sphere but some only reluctantly; thus in some cases the link between Kiev and local centers was weak and unstable.

There was a great divergency between single tribes in regard to their respective economic and cultural levels and even greater divergency within each tribe. While the upper classes in most cases could be interested commercially in the projects of Kievan princes, the bulk of the population was rather indifferent. We have here the traditional contrast between cities and rural communes. Some of the tribal aristocracy, moreover, must have been suspicious of Kievan imperialism.

Thus Prince Oleg and his immediate successors had a twofold task before them: to organize their own state and to lead their campaigns of conquest. Each of the tasks was in itself tremendous; in addition, in their foreign policies the attention of the first Kievan princes was perforce divided between the Byzantine Empire and the Khazar kaganate; either problem, again, was one to require the full attention of the Kievan rulers and, for the successful solution of either, vast resources were necessary.

As it proved in subsequent events, the princes did not have strength enough for a war on two fronts: against Byzantium and against the east. Sviatoslav came closer to success than any of his predecessors but overreached himself and ended in failure. Yet his victory over

4. *Idem*, p. 151.

the Khazars had fateful consequences for Russia, since the breaking
of the Khazar kaganate opened the gates for the Patzinaks, to be
followed by other Turkish tribes from beyond the Caspian Sea, and
neither Sviatoslav himself nor his successors had sufficient power to
prevent the Turkish flood from spreading over the Pontic steppes.

## 2. First Successes: Oleg

Around the year 878 Oleg, originally ruler of Novgorod in north
Russia, seized Kiev and eventually established his authority in south
Russia.[5] It is he rather than his predecessor in Novgorod, Riurik,
who may be considered the first Norse prince to become the sovereign
of all Russia. For this reason if for no other, the personality of Oleg
made a deeper impression on the historical memory of the Russian
people than that of Riurik. In the Russian chronicles as well as in
oral tradition Oleg is known as Veshchi, the Far-Sighted, the Wise,
the Holy. This epithet seems to have originated from a play upon
the meaning of the name in the Norse: Helgi (the original Norse form
of Oleg's name) means "the Holy"; the Russian adjective *Veshchi*
is thus but a translation of Helgi. In Norwegian, Oleg Veshchi is called
Helgi Helgi.

In Russian tradition Oleg is glorified as a wise ruler and a successful
warrior; he is particularly praised for his shrewdness in dealing with
his enemies. The story has it that after his victorious campaign against
the Greeks, which brought him to the gates of Constantinople, the
Greeks opened negotiations by sending him choice food and wines.
With quick penetration Oleg refused to partake, feeling that both
food and wine were probably poisoned. Whereupon the Greeks abandoned treachery and accepted his peace terms.

With this wisdom of Oleg the last legend concerning him—that of
his death—is in obvious contradiction. According to the legend, popu-
larized by the poet Pushkin in his magnificent "Song of Oleg the
Wise," the ruler had been warned by a sorcerer that his death would
come through his steed. Impressed by the prophecy, he took care not
to ride it. Later, being shown the horse's carcass, he stepped upon it,
abusing the sorcerer; at that moment a snake crept out of the carcass
and bit him, causing his death.[6]

The legend is obviously didactic, its object to prove that even the
wisest man is helpless before Fate. The same idea was poetically

5. *Idem,* pp. 363–368.
6. Cross, pp. 150, 155.

expressed in the famous *Lay of Igor's Campaign* of the twelfth century: "And said Boian the sagacious poet: 'Neither a shrewd and successful man, nor a fledgeling can escape the God's judgment.' " [7]

It is characteristic that the Russian legends of Oleg, including that of his death, have close parallels in the Norse saga of Odd. The saga has it that Odd died—of snake bite—in Norway, whither he allegedly returned after his Russian exploits. [8]

It is patent that Kiev could not be the final objective of Oleg's drive from the north. It was to serve him as a base for further campaigns southward aimed at opening paths to the Black Sea and the Sea of Azov, with Transcaucasia and Constantinople as his ultimate goals. However, his immediate task was to make the base itself sufficiently strong and his control over the riverways between Novgorod and Kiev absolutely secure. According to the *Book of Annals* it was Riurik who began to build a network of forts in the lands of the Slovene, the Krivichians, and the Merians [9]—that is, in the regions of Novgorod, Smolensk, and Rostov. Bands of Varangians were stationed in the newly built forts and the three tribes had to pay tribute for their maintenance. Thus, Oleg had only to follow Riurik's policy to consolidate his authority in the north.

The Kievan base itself was enlarged by his conquest of the Drevlianians, a warlike tribe whose abodes were at this time in the Pripet basin, northwest of the land of the Polianians, that is, of the Kiev region proper. Oleg imposed on them a tribute in furs (around 880 A.D.). Further expansion to the south and southwest, down the Dnieper and the Bug rivers, was barred by the Magyars. The lands east of the middle and lower Dnieper were controlled by the Khazars.

The Khazar problem was the first to be approached by Oleg. Like his predecessors in Kiev, Askold and Dir, he must have been anxious to establish a connection with the Russian kaganate in the Azov and Tmutorokan region. Presumably in the first or second year of his reign in Kiev, Oleg partly succeeded in this undertaking. His envoys and possibly some of his troops sent along to reënforce the army of the Russian kagan may have used the riverways extending across the steppes from the Dnieper bend to the Sea of Azov.

Encouraged by the help received from Oleg, the Russian kagan

7. *Slovo*, p. 37.

8. A. I. Liashchenko, "Letopisnye skazaniia o smerti Olega Veshchego," *ANORI, 29* (1924), 254–288.

9. Hyp., col. 15.

sent a plundering expedition to the Caspian Sea, which landed at its southeastern corner in the Mazendaran region around the year 880. The expedition ended in disaster, however.[10] Obviously the situation called for a closer union of forces between Kiev and Tmutorokan. In order to achieve this, Khazar control over the Slavic tribes east of the middle Dnieper had to be done away with. And, indeed, Oleg's next move was to extend his authority over these tribes. Around 882 he defeated the Severians, after which they discontinued their tribute to the Khazars and instead agreed to pay a "light tribute" to Oleg.

Impressed by his victory over the Severians, the latter's neighbors to the northwest, the Radimichians, voluntarily agreed (885) to pay to Oleg the tribute they had hitherto paid to the Khazars. In this case the tribute was in silver coins (*shcheliag*). At that juncture Oleg's attention shifted to the southwest. The chronicler mentions vaguely that he waged war against the Ulichians and the Tivertsi, two south Russian tribes who inhabited the lower Dniester and Bug basins.[11] Both tribes were at the time to a certain extent controlled by the Magyars and we may assume that in their opposition to Oleg they acted as vassals of the Magyar *voevoda* Arpad. Thus, while the chronicler presents that conflict as a war between Oleg and the two south Russian tribes, it must actually have been a war between Oleg and the Magyars.

The Magyars controlled at this time the whole southwestern corner of the Ukraine—the basins of the lower Dnieper, Bug, and Dniester rivers. Previously, one may suppose, the Magyar voevoda had also been suzerain of Kiev, where Askold and Dir acted as his lieutenants or vassals.[12] Oleg's seizure of Kiev meant the end of Magyar authority over it and, after his murder of Askold and Dir, the relations between Oleg and the Magyar voevoda must have been strained. Each side had its claims against the other. Presumably the Magyars meant to recover their hold on the Kiev region; the new ruler of Kiev, on the other hand, needing access to the Black Sea, had either to come to terms with the Magyars or to push them out of his way.

The conflict between Oleg and the Magyars, the Ulichians, and the Tivertsi must have taken place around 890, in any case not later than 893, for in the next year the Magyars were already engaged in

10. Dorn, p. 5.

11. Cross, p. 147. See K. Menges, "Etymological Notes on Some Päčänäg Names," *Byzantion, 17* (1945), 261–263. According to Dr. Menges, the Tivertsi were of Turkish origin.

12. *Ancient Russia*, pp. 341, 342.

a war against the Danubian Bulgars.[13] Judging from the tone of the passage alluding to it in the *Book of Annals,* the war between Oleg and the Magyars was indecisive.

It is to Byzantine diplomacy that the initiative in arranging for a Magyar invasion of Bulgaria around 894 may be ascribed. To quote the *Book of Annals,* Emperor Leo the Wise "hired" the Magyars against the Bulgars, who at this time threatened the safety of Byzantine possessions in the Balkans.[14] The Bulgars were defeated and their country plundered. In despair they appealed for help to the Patzinaks (Pechenegi), a Turkish people whose abodes were in Kazakhstan and of whom a band was then roving in the Pontic steppes. Whether the Patzinaks managed to pierce the Khazar defences along the lower Volga and the lower Don or the Khazars for some reason of their own allowed them to cross the Don westward, is not known.

Simultaneously attacked by the Bulgars from the south and the Patzinaks from the east, the Magyars were completely defeated (around 897) and had no alternative but to evacuate south Russia. A group of them went westward up the Danube and eventually reached Pannonia. Another group went north toward Kiev and pitched their tents on its outskirts.[15] Failing to take the city, they turned westward to Transylvania. This group is called the "Black Ugrians" in the *Book of Annals.* Eventually the two groups were reunited, establishing their control over the region of the middle Danube and the Tisa River—that is, over present-day Hungary (around 899).[16]

The occupation of Hungary by the Magyars proved a fateful event in the history of the Slavs, of which the three groups—the western, eastern, and southern—were now partly separated from each other by the Magyar wedge. The immediate result of the Magyar invasion was the downfall of the kingdom of Great Moravia. Most of it was occupied by the Magyars. White Khorvatia—that is, Galicia—pledged

13. On the Magyar-Bulgar relations of this period, see K. Ia. Grot, *Moraviaa i Madiary* (St. Petersburg, 1881), pp. 282–304; V. Zlatarski, *Istoriia na Bulgarskata Drzhava prez Srednite Vekove,* I Pt. 2 (Sofia, 1927), pp. 290–294. On the date of the Magyar-Bulgar war, see n. 14.

14. Hyp., col. 22; Cross, p. 149. The event is dated, in both Hypatian and Laurentian versions, in 902, obviously a mistake. According to Zlatarski the war between the Bulgars and Magyars started around 894; according to Grot, around 889. I accept Zlatarski's dating. See G. Moravcsik, *Byzantinoturcica,* I (Budapest, 1942), 58–59.

15. The appearance of a Magyar horde before Kiev is dated in the *Book of Annals* in the year 898 (Hyp., col. 19).

16. See Grot, *op. cit.,* pp. 305–327.

allegiance to Oleg. In the chronicler's narrative of Oleg's campaign of 907 against Constantinople, both the Khorvatians and their neighbors the Dulebians (in the Volyn region) are mentioned among the Russian tribes participating in the campaign. For Oleg the most important result of the Magyar migration was that the whole Dnieper riverway from Kiev down to the Black Sea was now at his disposal. In later sources the island of St. Gregory (Khortitsa) on the Dnieper, below the cataracts, and that of St. Ætherius (Berezan) in the Dnieper estuary are mentioned as the two main stations of Russian merchants on their way to Constantinople. Presumably naval bases on both islands were established by Oleg immediately after the withdrawal of the Magyars.

In the list of Russian tribes which took part in Oleg's campaign of 907 we also find the name of the Tivertsi, whose abodes were at the mouth of the Dniester. They may have been conquered by Oleg in a naval expedition started from Berezan. However, Oleg's troops may also have reached the Tivertsi from the north by descending along the Dniester from Galicia.

Let us now turn to Oleg's campaign of 907. According to the *Book of Annals* it was a combination of a cavalry raid across Bulgaria and naval operations.[17] In the latter, two thousand boats are said to have participated. The Russians reached Constantinople simultaneously from land and sea and the outskirts of the Imperial City were mercilessly plundered. The Greeks barred access to the inner port of Constantinople—the Golden Horn—by chains, but according to the chronicler's story Oleg ordered boats to be put on wheels and in this way part of the Russian squadron at least sailed overland to the upper reaches of the Golden Horn. The Greeks sued for peace, agreeing to pay tribute and to conclude a commercial treaty favorable to the Russians. Before withdrawing from Constantinople Oleg is said to have posted his shield at the gates of the city.

There is no direct mention of this campaign in Byzantine sources and many a historian has expressed his doubt of the authenticity of the Russian story. Among those who refuse to accept it are the German scholar Gerhard Lähr and the Belgian Byzantinologist Henry Grégoire.[18] However, the majority of students of both Russian and

17. Cross, pp. 149, 150.

18. G. Lähr, *Die Anfänge des russischen Reiches* (Berlin, 1930), pp. 95–99; H. Grégoire, "La Légende d'Oleg et l'expédition d'Igor," *Bulletin de l'Académie Royale de Belgique, 23* (1937), 80–94.

Byzantine history still consider the story of the *Book of Annals* reliable on the whole. The Byzantinologist George Ostrogorsky has subjected Grégoire's views to a detailed criticism,[19] the validity of which, to be sure, Grégoire is so far not willing to accept. I do, however.

In my opinion, the best proof of the authenticity of the story of the *Book of Annals* is the contents of the Russo-Byzantine treaties of 907 and 911. Of the first we have only a brief exposé in the *Book;* of the second, the full text. The authenticity of the latter is self-evident, since the wording of the Russian text makes it absolutely certain that it was a translation from the Greek, showing all the features of the formal style of Byzantine documents of this kind. Now, the contents of both these treaties are so favorable to the Russians that no Byzantine emperor of this period would have agreed to sign such documents without being compelled to it by a military defeat.

Furthermore, as Ostrogorsky points out, while there is no direct mention of Oleg's campaign in Byzantine sources, some indirect evidence may be procured. In his book, *De Cerimoniis Aulae Byzantinae*, Constantine Porphyrogenitus mentions the participation of auxiliary Russian ships in the Cretan expedition of 910. These must have been sent by Oleg as a token of his friendship to the emperor.[20] It may also be pointed out that in the Arabic work *Taba'i al-Hayawan* by Marvazi (written around 1120) the Russians are said to have reached Constantinople "in spite of the chains in the gulf." As V. F. Minorsky suggests, this is possibly a reference to Oleg's campaign of 907.[21]

According to the provisions of the treaty of 907 the Greeks had to pay a huge indemnity—computed on the basis of twelve *grivna* for each rowlock of the two thousand Russian boats—and, in addition, to assign special funds for each of the important Russian cities (Kiev, Chernigov, Pereiaslav, Polotsk, Rostov, Liubech, "and others"). Out of these funds the Byzantine Government undertook to provide ample food for the merchants of those cities throughout the stay of each in Constantinople; also to provide them with food and all necessary equipment for their boats for the return trip from Constantinople to Russia. During their visits at Constantinople the Russians were to be quartered in a suburb of the city, near the Church of St. Mamas.

19. G. Ostrogorsky, "L'Expédition du prince Oleg contre Constantinople en 907," *AIK, 11* (1939), 47–61.

20. Constantine Porphyrogenitus, *De Cerimoniis Aulae Byzantinae*, II, chap. xlvi; cf. Ostrogorsky, *op. cit.*, pp. 53, 54.

21. Marvazi, pp. 36, 119, 120.

They were allowed to enter the city, carrying no weapons, in groups of not over fifty men accompanied in each case by a Byzantine commissar. Characteristically enough, the Russian merchants in their commercial transactions were exempt from paying any customs duties.[22]

The treaty of 907 laid the foundation for further commercial intercourse between the Russians and the Greeks. In the treaty of 911 a number of juridical technicalities were added.[23] The settlement of mutual offenses, murders, thefts, and other crimes perpetrated by the nationals of one state against those of the other was regulated, with special attention to the case of fugitive slaves. All provisions were made in the spirit of complete equality of the two nations. Perhaps the most remarkable feature of the treaty is the promise on each side to help the shipwrecked merchants of the other. This was contrary to the so-called "strand law" practiced in most European countries at the time, by which in a case of shipwreck the local rulers were entitled to confiscate all stranded goods of the shipwrecked merchant and to enslave him and his crew. The law was abolished in Italy in the twelfth century, in England and Flanders in the thirteenth century, at first only with respect to the Hanseatic merchants. General abandonment of the practices of strand law in Europe took place even later.

## 3. First Setbacks: Igor

Oleg's success in opening the Black Sea to Russian trade cleared the path for a lively commercial intercourse between the Russians and the Greeks, and on the profits from this trade the prosperity of the Kievan realm was founded.

A good idea of how Russian trade with Constantinople was managed in the tenth century may be obtained from Constantine Porphyrogenitus' *De Administrando Imperio*.[24] According to this authority there was a regular timetable for collecting goods and shipping them. In November the prince of Kiev and the members of his druzhina would start their tour of the Slavic tribes subject to tribute (*poliudie*) in order to collect it. From other sources we know that the main items of the Russian export trade at the time were furs, wax, honey, and slaves. All these were to be furnished to the prince of Kiev,

22. For a résumé of the treaty of 907, see the *Book of Annals,* Laur., cols. 31, 32; Hyp., cols. 23, 24.

23. For the text of the treaty of 911, see Laur., cols. 33–37; Hyp., cols. 25–29; also *Khristomatiia,* I, 1–7.

24. *DAI,* chap. ix.

as he visited them, by the tribes subject to tribute in kind. Some tribes, as we know, paid in money. The prince and his druzhina would spend the whole winter in this way, to return to Kiev by April. Simultaneously, the Slavs living in the upper reaches of the Dnieper would be engaged in making boats by hollowing out the trunks of trees, and as early in the spring as the lakes and rivers were free from ice these were floated down to Kiev and there sold to "the Russians"—that is, to the prince, his acolytes, and the Kievan merchants.

Then the boats would be equipped with rowlocks and loaded. We may easily imagine the feverish activities of assembling the flotilla, in which presumably thousands of people were engaged. Each year in April and May Kiev must have looked like a great shipyard bursting with human effort. As soon as everything was ready, the flotilla moved downstream until it reached the Dnieper cataracts. There the boats were unloaded and hauled overland, together with the goods, along the bank of the river to a point below the rapids where they were reloaded. Later on, when the Patzinaks came to the Pontic steppes in strength, to pass the cataracts became a dangerous operation for the Russians; busy hauling loads, they were severely handicapped in case of a Patzinak attack.

Below the cataracts the newly assembled flotilla stopped at the island of St. Gregory, where the pagan Russians sacrificed cocks to their gods under a huge oak. The next stop was in the Dnieper estuary, at the island of St. Ætherius, where the boats were equipped with sails. They then sailed westward along the northern shore of the Black Sea into the Dniester estuary, whence, after another stop, they cruised to the mouth of the Danube. From the Danubian delta they proceeded to Konstantsa, Varna, and Mesembria, which at the time of Constantine's writing (around 953) was the terminal point of the Russian journey.

On their return trip (not described by Constantine) the Russians carried goods of a more delicate kind—silk fabrics, spices, wines, and fruits. Since the return load required much less shipping space, part of the boats were probably sold to the Greeks and the Bulgars or simply abandoned after being stripped of rowlocks, sails, and other equipment.

It is hardly possible to determine with any degree of accuracy the volume of goods shipped every summer from Kiev to Mesembria; however, it will not be amiss to speculate on it. From Constantine's picture we gain the impression that the flotilla was a huge affair. Presumably it consisted of several hundred boats, possibly over a thousand. To be sure, they were *monoxyla,* as Constantine calls them: that is, each made of a single tree trunk. But such trunks, cut in the primeval forests of northern Russia, must have been enormous.

Similar boats were used by the Zaporozhie Cossacks in the sixteenth and seventeenth centuries.[25] As a matter of fact. the Cossacks had boats of two kinds: river boats and seagoing boats. The Cossack word for "boat," *chaika,* derives from the Turkish *chay,* "river," and was applied originally to small boats only but later came to designate the other type as well. The river boat was a monoxylon pure and simple—a canoe. It was used for fishing and for carrying small loads; its capacity was ten men. Such canoes were undoubtedly used by Kievan Russians for similar purposes but a Kievan monoxylon intended for the Byzantine trade must have been much larger, of the type of the sea-going Cossack chaika. For this the tree trunk served as a foundation only, on which the boat proper was built of heavy oak boards. The chaika had a length of from fifty to seventy feet; its width was from eighteen to twenty feet, and height about twelve feet. It carried from fifty to seventy armed Cossacks, from four to six falconets, and ample supply of munitions and food. It was equipped with a mast and twenty to forty oars. Assuming that the boats of the Russian flotilla of the tenth century were similar to the Cossack sea-going boats and that the annual flotilla consisted of no less than five hundred of them, the total load of goods shipped must have been not short of ten thousand tons. Assuming again that half the amount was used for the transportation of "live goods"—slaves—as well as for other purposes, this leaves around five thousand tons for the goods proper, as a conservative estimate.

This is a small load for a commercial fleet by our standards. However, it is much more impressive when compared with common medieval practice. Even in the fourteenth and fifteenth centuries the total goods transported annually from Italy to Germany over the St. Gotthard Pass—one of the main gateways of European continental commerce in the Middle Ages—averaged 1,250 tons.[26] The aggregate tonnage of the Italian and Hanseatic commercial flotillas at that period was much larger but in the tenth century western maritime commerce

---

25. See D. I. Evarnitsky, *Istoriia Zaporozhskikh Kozakov,* (St. Petersburg 1892), I, 454–456.

26. I. M. Kulisher, *Lektsii po istorii ekonomicheskogo byta Zapadnoi Evropy* (5th ed. Petrograd, 1918), p. 173.

could show nothing comparable to the Russo-Byzantine trade.

Thus, if we think of the annual Russian flotilla in the terms of Carolingian trade, we must come to the conclusion that the volume and scope of Russian foreign commerce was far above the west European standards of the period.

Constantine's description of the Russian trade flotilla is a valuable source not only for the study of Russian commerce but also for that of the Russian state and government of the first half of the tenth century. According to this writer the core of the Russian state was in Kiev and the Kiev region alone was called Russia proper. Everything else was the "periphery of Russia" (exo Rossia), consisting of Slavic tribes paying tribute to the prince of Kiev.[27] However, it would be wrong to conclude that all these lands were merely Kievan colonies. The picture given by Constantine is not complete and must be supplemented with evidence available from other sources. First of all, it should be mentioned that the various tribes submitted to Kiev on different conditions. Some paid tribute in kind, others in money; some paid a heavier amount, others but a "light," i.e., nominal, tribute. Then we must consider the evidence of the Russo-Byzantine treaty of 907, according to which the Greeks were obliged to assign separate funds for each of the leading Russian cities—Kiev, Chernigov, Pereiaslav, and so on. As the chronicler remarks at this point, in each of these cities sits a prince of its own. And indeed, from the preamble to the Russo-Byzantine treaty of 911 as well as that of the treaty of 945, we know that neither Oleg nor Igor was the sole ruler of Russia. Both in succession had the title of "grand prince" (velikii kniaz') of Russia but other princes are mentioned as under the authority of the grand prince. Thus we have a feudal ladder with the suzerain at the top and his vassals beneath. Furthermore, while we know very little about the relations between Kiev and Tmutorokan at that time, from the scant evidence we have we may surmise that the latter city was still ruled by a prince of its own—the kagan.

In any case, the political structure of Russia in the first half of the tenth century, although primitive, was much more complex than one might think solely from the evidence of Constantine Porphyrogenitus' narrative. One may suppose that the degree of subordination of tribal princes to the prince of Kiev differed in the various cases. Some must have been allies rather than vassals.

The position of a tribal prince in provinces where tribute was col-

27. See A. Soloviev 'Η˙ΕΞΩ 'ΡΩΣΙΑ, Byzantion, 13 (1938), 227-232.

lected in kind by the grand prince himself was probably the hardest. However, even in such cases there must have been a definite agreement as to the share of the grand prince in local collections and if the agreement was violated on his part the local prince was entitled to resist, as we may see from the story of the death of Prince Igor in the *Book of Annals*.

Let us now turn our attention to Igor and his policies. According to the tradition Igor was a descendant of Riurik and there is no reason to doubt the accuracy of the tradition. However, one may guess that he was Riurik's grandson rather than his son as stated in the *Book of Annals*. Under Oleg, Igor must have played a totally subordinate role. He is mentioned only once, on the occasion of his marriage, and even here it is stated that the alliance was arranged by Oleg (903).

Igor's wife was Olga, a native of Pskov. Her name is Scandinavian but she must have been a Slav girl as will be explained presently. While Igor is portrayed in the chronicle with little sympathy, his wife is glorified as "the wisest of women." As Olga eventually became a Christian, her popularity with the chroniclers may be easily explained. However, neither Oleg's nor Sviatoslav's paganism deprived those princes of the chronicler's praise. There must have been something in Igor's nature which caused the chronicler's coolness toward him. In the story of his death he is portrayed as a greedy and treacherous man. He probably was.

According to the *Book of Annals,* Igor and Olga had but one son, Sviatoslav. At the time of Igor's death (945) he was an infant, born in 942 according to the Laurentian chronicle. If the date of Igor's marriage in the *Book of Annals* (903) is to be credited, Olga must have been in her late forties, or even in her fifties, at the time of Sviatoslav's birth, even if we suppose that she had been a mere girl at the time of her marriage. We are led thus to think that Sviatoslav may not have been her first child. If we admit that he might have had elder brothers, we may tentatively identify one of them as "Halgu, King of the Rus" mentioned in a Hebrew document, the so-called "Letter of a Khazar Jew of the Tenth Century" first published by Schechter in 1912. Of him more will be said at the close of this section. Suffice it to note here that Halgu is obviously the same name as Helgi, in Russian pronunciation Oleg.

According to the *Book of Annals* Prince Oleg died in 913 (perhaps in 912). It seems probable that after bringing his negotiations with Byzantium to a successful conclusion and securing the Black Sea for

Russian commerce, he must have shifted his attention to the Caspian Sea and Transcaucasia. For this, close coöperation between the Kievan Russians and the Tmutorokan Russians was essential. In 909-10 sixteen Russian boats, presumably sent by the Tmutorokan kagan, appeared along the southern shores of the Caspian Sea. The Russians attempted a landing at Enzeli but were repulsed.[28] This was clearly a reconnoitering expedition to be followed by a real campaign, for which preparations must have started immediately afterward.

The campaign took place after Oleg's death (913). His successor Igor must have personally led his druzhina to Tmutorokan, the natural base for the drive. However, he did not go farther, the news of the revolt of the Drevlianians compelling him to return to Kiev with part of his entourage. The other part remained in Tmutorokan, whence the Russians went up the Don River to the Volga portage and down the Volga to the Caspian Sea. They received the permit of the Khazar kagan for the expedition in return for a promise of a share in the booty.

The Russians plundered the southwestern shores of the Caspian, using the Apsheron peninsula (the Baku region) as their base of supplies and for storage of booty. They maintained the base for several months, after which, their ships heavily loaded with plundered goods, they set forth homeward. In spite of the fact that they sent the kagan his agreed share, as soon as they entered the Volga estuary they were treacherously attacked by his guards and completely defeated. According to Mas'udi around thirty thousand Russians perished and only few escaped (914).[29]

Meanwhile Igor crushed the revolt of the Drevlianians, imposing on them a heavier tribute as punishment. His troubles were not over, however, for in 915 the Patzinaks invaded Russia (that is, the Kievan land) for the first time. Somehow an agreement was reached and they retired to raid Bulgaria. Five years later (920) they appeared again and Igor had to fight them. From these brief statements in the *Book of Annals* it may be seen that at this time the Patzinaks did not yet represent any real danger for Russia. Their main horde was still east of the Volga. Subsequently, in Igor's Balkan campaign of 944, the Patzinaks acted as his allies.

There is no information in the *Book of Annals* about Igor's policies from 920 to 941. Presumably this was a period of peace during which

28. Dorn, pp. 4–6.
29. *Idem,* pp. vi–viii, 15, 16, 28; Markwart, pp. 333–335.

the Russians accumulated strength for further expeditions against
both Anatolia and Transcaucasia. The *Book* describes only the Anatolian campaign (941); Arabic sources speak of the Russian campaign in Transcaucasia (943-44), while Hebrew documents throw
some light on the connection between the two.

Let us start with Igor's Anatolian campaign.[30] Asia Minor was at
this time a part of the Byzantine Empire. The reasons for Igor's break
with the Greeks are not known; his naval expedition to Anatolia in
941 was apparently a joint undertaking of the Kievan and Tmutorokan Russians. The "Letter of the Khazar Jew" mentions the name
"Halgu, King of the Russians," in connection with the Russian war
against the Greeks and the subsequent "withdrawal" of the Russians
to "Persia" (Transcaucasia).[31] According to my conjecture, Halgu,
or Oleg, was Igor's son. He could not have been king of the Kievan
Russians, since the Kievan throne was occupied by Igor himself.
Therefore we may suppose that he was king, or kagan, of the Tmutorokan Russians.

The Russians landed on the Anatolian shore of the Black Sea and
plundered the Byzantine provinces of Bithynia and Paphlagonia,
penetrating as far west as Nicomedia before the Byzantine generals
had time to muster sufficient troops to repel the invaders. When the
latter took to their ships, their flotilla was attacked by the Byzantine
naval squadron and easily defeated by the use of the famous "Greek
fire." [32] It appears that, while Igor himself returned to Kiev, the
bulk of what remained of the Russian army went to Tmutorokan,
whence two years later they undertook a campaign against Transcaucasia.

This time the rich city of Bardaa in Azerbaijan proved to be the
main objective of the Russian drive. Thus the Russians in this case
followed the path of the Savarti, who attacked Bardaa between 750
and 760. By my conjecture, the Savarti may have been Swedes.[33]
The Russian campaign in Azerbaijan is described in detail in the

30. Cross, pp. 157-158. See also K. Bártova, "Igorova výprava na Cařihrad r. 941,"
*BS, 8* (1946), 87-108.

31. P. K. Kokovtsov, *Evreisko-Khazarskaia perepiska v X veke,* p. 120. See also I.
Brutskus (J. Brutzkus), *Pismo Khazarskogo evreia X veka* (Berlin, 1924); V. Moshin,
"Khelgu khazarskogo dokumenta," *Slavia, 15* (1938), 191-200.

32. Cross, pp. 157-158. "Greek fire," also called "liquid" or "marine" fire, was an ex-
plosive compound, projected by special tubes or siphons, which burst into flame when
it struck a vessel (A. A. Vasiliev, *History of the Byzantine Empire* [Madison, University
of Wisconsin, 1928], I, 261). See *Ancient Russia,* pp. 165, 198, 247, 299.

33. *Idem,* pp. 270-273.

Arabic chronicle of Ibn-Miskawaih who lived in the late tenth and early eleventh centuries (died *ca.* 1030). He writes: "In this year A.H. 332 [A.D. 943-44] the army of the nation called the Russians invaded Adharbaijan, where they attacked and seized Bardha'ah, taking its inhabitants captive. They are a mighty nation with vast frames and great courage. They know not defeat, nor does any of them turn his back till he slay or be slain." [34]

As they approached the city the Russians issued the following proclamation: "There is no dispute between us on the matter of religion; we only desire the sovereignty; it is our duty to treat you well and yours to be loyal to us." Since the city refused to capitulate, however, the Russians stormed it and ordered all the population to evacuate it within three days. Those who remained after that term were either slain or obliged to pay huge ransom.

Using Bardaa as their base the Russians plundered the country around it and amassed immense booty. They spent several months there but were eventually surrounded and defeated by superior Moslem forces. Their commander was killed in battle. Finally the remnants of the Russian army "made for the river Kur where the ships in which they had issued from their home were in readiness with their crews. They embarked and departed, and God saved the Moslems from them."

Now, in the Hebrew document quoted before it is said that King Halgu perished "in Persia" with most of his troops. We may assume, then, that the "commander" of the Russians mentioned in Ibn-Miskawaih's story was Halgu.

The disastrous result of the Transcaucasian campaign and the loss of his son Oleg (if Halgu was his son) did not deter Igor from another attempt to strike at Byzantium. According to the *Book of Annals* he hired a band of Varangians "across the sea" (i.e., in Scandinavia) as well as a horde of Patzinaks to reinforce his Kievan troops. Of Slavic tribes, the Slovene, the Krivichians, and the Tivertsi agreed to participate in the campaign.[35]

In the summer of 944 Igor's army reached the banks of the Danube River, where they were met by the envoys of the Byzantine emperor

---

34. Ibn-Miskawaih, *The Eclipse of the Abbasid Caliphate*, V, 67-74. See also A. V. Florovsky, "Izvestiia o drevnei Rusi arabskogo pisatelia Miskaveikhi," *SK*, I (1927), 175-186; A. I. Iakubovsky, "Ibn-Miskaveikh o pokhode Rusov v Berdaa," *VV, 24* (1926), 63-92; V. Minorsky, *Hudud al-Alam* (Oxford, Luzac & Co., 1937), pp. 144, 398-400.

35. Cross, pp. 158, 159.

who brought rich presents both to the Russian and the Patzinak chieftains and offered peace. Igor convoked his retinue for a war council. Memories of the devastating effect of the "Greek fire" still haunted the Russian boyars and the council voted to accept the Byzantine offer. A formal treaty of peace was signed in 945.

The Byzantino-Russian treaty of 945 may be characterized as a confirmation and expansion of the treaties of 907 and 911. It is more detailed and more precise than the earlier treaties. In one point only were the privileges of the Russian merchants curtailed: the provision concerning freedom from customs duties was not included in Igor's treaty. In addition to the commercial and juridical clauses there are two noteworthy political clauses dealing with the Crimea ("the Korsun land," *Korsunskaia strana*) and the Black Bulgars (arts. 8 and 11, Vladimirsky-Budanov, ed.).[36]

The text of these clauses is rather obscure and their content has been interpreted by scholars in various ways. As I understand them, they constitute a special agreement between the "Russian prince" (*kniaz' Russkii*) and the Byzantine emperor, according to which the prince undertook to defend the Crimea against the Black Bulgars and the emperor promised his help to the prince in the latter's conflicts with those cities in the Crimea (apparently under Khazar domination) which would not recognize his authority; thus the agreement amounted to an alliance between the Russians and the Byzantines against the Khazars and the Black Bulgars.[37]

The question now is, who was the "Russian prince" mentioned in Articles 8 and 11 of the treaty?[38] It could not be Igor, since the latter's title was "grand prince" (*velikii kniaz'*). The title is mentioned in several articles of the treaty (1, 2, 16). However, according to Article 1 the treaty was concluded not in the name of the "grand prince" alone but in the name of "Igor, the grand prince of the Russians, and all of the princes, and all of the men of the Russian land." Each member of the princely family, including Igor's wife Olga, was represented by an envoy of his or her own. There are two other Rus-

---

36. *Kristomatiia*, I, 13. J. Bromberg in his "Toponymical and Historical Miscellanies," *Byzantion*, 13 (1938), 33–50, has attempted to prove that under the name "Land of Korsun" not the Crimea but the Dobrudja is meant. His hypothesis is not convincing.

37. See my article, "The *Rus'* in the Crimea and the Russo-Byzantine Treaty of 945," *Byzantina-Metabyzantina*, 1 (1946), 249–259.

38. See N. D. Znoiko, "O pokhodakh Sviatoslava na vostok," *ZMNP, 18* (1908), 280–282.

sian women represented, each by a special envoy: Sfandra, wife of
Uleb (Gleb), and Peredslava. Could not Peredslava be the widow of
Halgu (Oleg) of Tmutorokan?

In any case, the Tmutorokan Russians must have been represented
in the negotiations which led to the conclusion of the treaty and it is
probably the ruler of Tmutorokan who is meant under the title of
the "Russian prince" in Articles 8 and 11 of the treaty.

From the text of the agreement—if I rightly understand it—it is
then obvious that in the middle of the tenth century the prince of
the Tmutorokan Russians controlled some sections of eastern Crimea
in addition to Tmutorokan. He also appears to have controlled both
the eastern shore of the Sea of Azov and the mouth of the Don River.
This region had been one of the centers of the Alani-As since the
second century.[39] Since, according to my surmise, by "Black Bulgars"
the Volga Bulgars are meant,[40] it was because of his control of the
lower Don basin that the "prince of the Russians" was in a position
to prevent the Black Bulgars from raiding the Crimea.

The treaty of 945 must be considered an important achievement of
Igor's policy. Yet personally he derived little satisfaction from it,
since the presents he received from the emperor were not sufficient
to cover the expenses of his abortive campaign of 944. For that campaign, as we know, he had hired both the Patzinaks and the Varangians to assist him in his drive toward Constantinople. Apparently he
intended to pay them with shares of the booty. But there was no
booty and the auxiliary troops demanded payment just the same.
Igor satisfied the Patzinaks by letting them loot Bulgaria. But there
still remained the Varangians with their claims. It is in the light of
the settlement of these claims that we may best understand the relations between Igor and his general (*voevoda*) Sveneld. Sveneld played
an important role in the events which led to Igor's death and later
became one of the chief assistants of Igor's son Sviatoslav. Yet his
name is not included in the list of the Russian notables of the treaty of
945. The obvious conclusion is that at the time of the signing of the
treaty he was not considered Russian (i.e., either Kievan Russian
or Tmutorokan Russian). Presumably he was one of the hired
Varangians; more exactly, the commander of the Varangian band
hired by Igor.

39. *Ancient Russia*, pp. 257–260, 317.
40. *Idem*, pp. 203, 223.

According to the Nikon chronicle, Igor granted to Sveneld the right to collect tribute from both the Ulichians and the Drevlianians.[41] This was apparently done to settle the Varangian claims. Incidentally, the Ulichians had at this time not yet recognized the authority of the grand prince and Sveneld had first to conquer them.

While the Varangians were thus satisfied, Igor's Russian druzhina now started to grumble. "The servants of Sveneld are adorned with weapons and fine raiment, but we are naked. Go forth with us, oh Prince, after tribute, that both you and we may profit thereby." [42] Thereupon Igor led his druzhina to the land of the Drevlianians and in spite of the latter's protests collected tribute from them in addition to the amount obtained by Sveneld. Apparently most of it went to the members of his entourage and Igor returned once more to the Drevlianian land, accompanied by but a few retainers, to round out his personal share in the tribute. This time the Drevlianians were not prepared to stand the extortion. According to the colorful story of the *Book of Annals* their prince Mal said to the people: "If a wolf comes among the sheep, he will take away the whole flock one by one, unless he be killed." [43] The Drevlianians then attacked Igor and his small retinue and slew them all.

### 4. A Breathing Spell: Olga

At the time of Igor's death his son Sviatoslav was a mere boy and it was therefore his widow Princess Olga who assumed power. Because of her eventual conversion to Christianity and her following canonization, Olga was given a prominent place in Russian chronicles as well as in historical tradition. Even the cruel punishment she inflicted on the Drevlianians to avenge Igor's death is described by the chronicler with obvious admiration of her cleverness and resourcefulness.[44]

In a sense, Olga's decision to embrace Christianity is in itself an evidence of her sound judgment and keenness of intellect. But in addition there is other evidence of her abilities as a ruler. All along she must have been a remarkable woman.

41. *PSRL*, IX, 26–27. This information about Sveneld is inserted in the Nikon chronicle following the statement on Igor's suppression of the Drevlianian revolt. The date, 914, refers to the latter only.

42. Cross, p. 164.

43. *Idem*, p. 164.

44. *Idem*, pp. 164–168.

Olga was born around 890 in Pskov, probably in a Slavic family. In attempting to determine her nationality we have to start with anthropological data on her great-grandson Iaroslav the Wise, son of Vladimir the Saint. According to the recent examination of Iaroslav's skeleton his cranium is not of the Nordic type; it is similar to the craniums of the Novgorod Slovene. From whom could Iaroslav acquire those Slavic features? His mother was Rogneda, Princess of Polotsk, of Scandinavian ancestry. His father Vladimir was the son of Sviatoslav and of Olga's housekeeper Malusha. Vladimir's grandfather Igor was, as we know, of Scandinavian origin. In order to explain the Slavic anthropological type of Vladimir's descendants we have to suppose that either his mother or grandmother or both were of Slavic origin. According to Shakhmatov his mother Malusha was of Norse origin, and the name Malusha is a Russian adaptation of the Scandinavian name Malfrid. If so, Olga is the only one of Iaroslav's ancestors who could be responsible for his Slavic type. There remains, however, the possibility that both Olga and Malusha were of Slavic origin. The name Olga is of course Scandinavian (Helga); she might have received it at the time of her marriage.

Olga was a rich woman. Even before Igor's death she held landed estates in various parts of the realm. It is mentioned in the chronicles that the town of Vyshgorod near Kiev belonged to her; besides, she owned a village, Olzhichi, in the Desna region and a number of villages in the Pskov and Novgorod regions. After Igor's death Olga must have become the largest landowner in Russia. This is an important point because her administrative reforms were started and tested in her own domains.

Her main objective was to prevent incidents such as the one which led to her husband's death from being repeated. Therefore she abolished the custom of *poliudie*—the prince's winter expeditions for collecting tribute. Instead, the country was divided into a number of districts, each under the authority of a princely agent or a local board in charge of collecting taxes. Such a local unit became known as a *pogost*. In other words, tribute exacted from autonomous tribes was replaced by uniform taxes paid by the whole population. In the course of the realization of this reform most of the local princes must have been deprived of their authority and the autonomy of tribes drastically curtailed. It amounted to centralization of the financial administration, in any case with respect to western Russia (the land of the Drevlianians) and northern Russia (the Novgorodian land). The Kievan land had been under regular princely administration even prior to Olga's reign.

Let us now turn to her conversion. At the time of Igor's death a considerable number of the Russian boyars must already have been baptized. Both "Christian Rus' " and "Pagan Rus' " are mentioned in the Russo-Byzantine treaty of 945; there is also a reference to a Russian church—that of St. Elias. According to the *Book of Annals* Olga was baptized in Constantinople in the year 955. This information is contradicted by the official record of her reception at the Imperial Palace in Constantine Porphyrogenitus' *De Cerimoniis Aulae Byzantinae*.[45] This document gives the year 957 as the date of Olga's visit to Constantinople; it also makes plain that at the time of her visit she was already a Christian.

Most Russian historians attempt to solve the puzzle by assuming that Olga went to Constantinople twice: in 955, when she was baptized; and once more in 957. The theory seems artificial and hardly tenable, the more so since there is no hint in Constantine's record that her reception at the palace in 957 was not the first one. Moreover, the travel of a princess of Kiev to Constantinople was not an ordinary event and had Olga made two trips thither it would probably have been recorded in her "life." It seems much more probable that the princess was baptized in Kiev in 955, as her grandson Vladimir was to be later on in 988. Her baptism was apparently sponsored by Constantinople, since she accepted the Christian name of Helen, which was that of Emperor Constantine's wife. Similarly, Vladimir later accepted the name of Vasili (Basil) in honor of the then ruling emperor.

While Olga's conversion to Christianity must have strengthened the Christian party among the Kievan Russians, it was not followed by the conversion of the whole nation. The pagan party was still strong, centering as it did around her son Sviatoslav, a lad in his teens at the time of his mother's baptism. In vain Olga tried to instruct him in the Christian faith—he refused to listen.[46]

As in some other cases of conversion of Slavic peoples to Christianity, for example in Bulgaria, the opposition to conversion was partly political. In view of the close connection between church and state in Byzantium, as soon as a foreign people was converted the

---

45. Constantine Porphyrogenitus, De Cerimoniis Aulae Byzantinae, II, chap. xv; *PG*, CXII, cols. 1108–1112.
46. The "Life of St. Olga," in Makarii, I, 269.

Byzantine emperor might be expected to insist that the new converts recognize not only the authority of the Patriarch of Constantinople as head of their church but also the authority of the emperor as their political suzerain.

To forestall subjugation to the emperor each Slavic nation wanted to limit the authority of the Patriarch as well. Therefore the Slavic leaders in each case attempted to have their church organized as an autocephalous institution. As a preliminary step they insisted that it be constituted as a national unit—a diocese of the Patriarchate of Constantinople, with a metropolitan bishop or an archbishop at its head. It was when such a claim of theirs was denied that the Bulgars temporarily changed their allegiance from the Patriarch of Constantinople to the Pope of Rome.[47] Eventually the Bulgarian church received an autocephalous status from the Patriarch.

In Olga's case the pagan party in Russia could not prevent her personal conversion but apparently opposed a national conversion before some kind of autonomy was guaranteed to the Russian church. It was to plead for autonomy that Olga went to Constantinople in 957. Her mission did not bring about the desired results, whereupon she repeated the policy of the Bulgar khan of the eight-sixties by addressing herself to the west—in her case to Emperor Otto I of the Holy Roman Empire.

According to the writer who continued Regino's chronicle, in 959 envoys from the princess came to Emperor Otto requesting that a bishop and priests be sent to Russia, and in 960 a monk of St. Alban's Monastery was ordained bishop for Russia but never reached that country, for he fell ill and died in March, 961. The monk Adalbert of St. Maximin's Monastery at Trier was then consecrated and actually went to Kiev but was not accepted and returned to Trier in 962. M. D. Priselkov believes that his failure must have been the result of a misunderstanding between Olga and Otto.[48] Olga requested that the Kievan church be organized as an autonomous diocese under an archbishop or a metropolitan bishop. Otto sent her only a bishop with limited authority; the church was to be constituted as a mere eparchy under the complete control of the German clergy, an arrangement unacceptable to the Russians. Priselkov's interpretation seems quite plausible.

Olga's failure to secure a national organization for the Russian

47. *Ancient Russia,* p. 362.
48. Priselkov, pp. 12, 13.

church resulted in the ascendancy of the pagan party. Its leader, her son Sviatoslav, now assumed full power in Kiev.

## 5. The Great Adventure: Sviatoslav

The brief period of the reign of Sviatoslav I (962–72) is one of the most dramatic episodes in medieval Russian history. The spadework of building up the inner strength of the Kievan realm which characterized Olga's rule was now over and all the dormant energy of the Russian warriors, their will for imperial expansion, was released as if the gates of a mighty dam had been thrown open all at once. The flood which followed seemed at first irresistible, threatening as it did to affect all the neighboring lands. Mighty blows followed upon each other with lightning speed; Sviatoslav's dread legions struck in various quarters in rapid succession. It is obvious that the Russian campaigns of this period were carefully planned and prepared well in advance under the personal direction of the ruler.

The Russian chronicler likens Sviatoslav to a leopard for the swiftness of his movements. Little did he care for the amenities of life. "Upon his expeditions he carried with him neither wagons nor kettles, and boiled no meat, but cut off small strips of horseflesh, game, or beef, and ate it after roasting it on the coals. Nor did he have a tent, but he spread out a piece of saddle cloth under him, and set his saddle under his head." [49]

An authentic picture of Sviatoslav's appearance and bearing is to be found in the book of the Byzantine historian Leo Diaconus in the passage which describes his meeting with the emperor John Tzimiskes at the Danube River in 971.

The emperor arrived at the bank of the Danube on horseback, wearing golden armor, accompanied by a large retinue of horsemen in brilliant attire. Sviatoslav crossed the river in a kind of Scythian boat; he handled the oar in the same way as his men. His appearance was as follows: he was of medium height—neither too tall, nor too short. He had bushy brows, blue eyes, and was snub-nosed; he shaved his beard but wore a long and bushy mustache. His head was shaven except for a lock of hair on one side as a sign of the nobility of his clan. His neck was thick, his shoulders broad, and his whole stature pretty fine. He seemed gloomy and savage. On one of his ears hung a golden earring adorned with two pearls and a ruby set between them. His white garments were not distinguishable from those of his men except for cleanness. [50]

49. Cross, pp. 170, 171.
50. Leo Diaconus, *Historiae Libri decem*, Pt. 9, chap. xi, pp. 156, 157.

This picture of Sviatoslav is very similar to the portraits of the Cossack hetmans of the sixteenth and seventeenth centuries, including even the lock of hair on a shaven head—the so-called *oseledets*.

Sviatoslav observed strict rules of warfare. He never attacked the prospective enemy without a formal declaration of war. An envoy would deliver his message, which was always very brief: "I am setting forth against you." As with Oleg, Sviatoslav's first objective was to unite the forces of Kievan Russia with those of Tmutorokan Russia in order to extend his control over the Azov region and eventually open the road to the Caspian Sea. For this it was necessary to defeat the Khazars. It so happened that the development of events in the Crimea offered him a suitable pretext to open his offensive.

As we know from our analysis of Igor's treaty of 945, there was even then a dispute between the Tmutorokan Russians and the Khazars for the control of certain towns in the Crimea. In 962 the Khazars attempted to subdue the Crimean Goths, an incident of which we know from fragments of a curious Greek document of the period, the so-called "Report of a Gothic Toparch." [51] Unable to repeal the Khazars by their own forces the Goths sent messengers to their "adherents" (the Crimean Russians, according to A. A. Vasiliev's plausible explanation [52]), asking the latter to come to a conference to discuss the situation. At that conference it was unanimously decided to seek the protection of "the ruler north of the Danube who possessed a strong army and was proud of his military forces and from whose people they did not differ in customs and manner." Although the name of the ruler or the people is not mentioned in the document, it is obvious that the reference is to Sviatoslav and the Kievan Russians. An embassy was then sent to Kiev and a treaty concluded according to which the Crimean Goths and Russians recognized Sviatoslav as their suzerain and he in turn promised to defend them against the Khazars. On their return trip the members of the embassy observed an interesting astronomic phenomenon: "Saturn was at the beginning of its passage across Aquarius, while the sun was passing through the winter signs." According to the astronomical calculations, during the period from the second half of December, 874, to the middle of December, 1021, Saturn had only once held the position among the stars indicated in the toparch's "report": namely, at the outset of Jan-

51. F. Westberg, "Zapiska Gotskogo Toparkha," *VV*, *15* (1908), 71–132, 227–286.

52. A. A. Vasiliev, *The Goths in the Crimea* (Cambridge, Mass., The Mediaeval Academy of America, 1936), pp. 128, 129.

uary, 963. This is one of the rare cases when the date of a historical event may be firmly established with the help of astronomy.[53]

It was in 963, then, and not in 965, the date given in the *Book of Annals*, that Sviatoslav attacked the Khazars. His main blow was directed at Sarkel (Belaia Vezha), the Khazar fortress on the lower Don River. After this was taken, Sviatoslav subdued the Iasy (Ossetians) in the lower Don basin and then proceeded southward to the Kuban area, where the Kosogians (Circassians) pledged their allegiance to him. Undoubtedly this first Khazarian campaign was concluded by his entrance into Tmutorokan. On the grounds of the previous treaty between Sviatoslav and the Crimean peoples, he must have been acclaimed in Tmutorokan as the Russian kagan.

The immediate Khazar danger for the Crimea and the Azov region was now eliminated but the grand prince of Kiev was not satisfied; his intention was to conquer the Khazar Empire altogether. For this he needed to control the whole course of the Volga River, which in its middle section was held by the Volga Bulgars and in its lower section by the Khazars. Access to the realm of the Volga Bulgars was barred by the Viatichians, who at this time were still vassals of the Khazar kagan. Consequently Sviatoslav's next blow was directed against this tribe, which he defeated in 966 according to the *Book of Annals*, the chronology of which needs some correction of this period. Presumably they surrendered in 964, after which Sviatoslav was in a position to attack the Volga Bulgars. Their capital, Bulgar, was stormed and plundered by the Russians around the year 965.

It was only then that Sviatoslav could start preparations for a final attack on the Khazars. However, at this juncture his attention was directed westward toward the Balkans. For the understanding of the Balkan background in this period it is essential to keep in mind the relations between the Byzantine Empire and the Bulgarian tsardom. Constantinople was seriously threatened by the Bulgarians at the beginning of the tenth century and once more in the nine-sixties. Applying its usual method of setting one "barbarian" nation against another, Byzantine diplomacy now decided to approach Sviatoslav with a request for assistance against the Bulgarians. Kalokyras, patrician and chief magistrate of Cherson, was accordingly instructed by the emperor Nicephorus Phocas to negotiate with Sviatoslav.

The choice of ambassador was significant. Cherson was one of the few footholds in the Crimea still controlled by the Empire; Sviatoslav

53. *Idem*, p. 121.

was the recognized ruler of most of the Crimea. Sviatoslav needed no prodding since he must have been as interested in the Balkans as he was in Khazaria. Following the path of his predecessors, he must have contemplated action in both the Caspian and the Balkan areas. While his operations against Khazaria were not as yet completed, the Byzantine offer presented such an excellent opportunity of interfering in Balkan affairs that he could not think of neglecting it. However, being a shrewd politician he asked for a subsidy to prepare for the Bulgarian campaign and obtained it; according to Leo Diaconus, Kalokyras paid him fifteen hundred pounds of gold, presumably as advance payment.[54]

The inside story of these negotiations appears to have been even more involved. There is reason to suppose that Kalokyras played a game of his own, being a secret opponent of the emperor Nicephorus. While "hiring" Sviatoslav against the Bulgarians he must have intimated to the Russian that his campaigns in the Balkans need not be limited to Bulgaria. It is probable that the ambassador hoped to overthrow Emperor Nicephorus with Russian help and seize the throne for himself.[55] In the event of success, the advantages of such a play, not only for Kalokyras but for Sviatoslav as well, would be substantial.

In 967, at any rate, Sviatoslav invaded Bulgaria leading an army of probably no less than forty thousand, with Kalokyras at the head of a Greek auxiliary force of sixteen thousand men. By autumn the whole of northern Bulgaria was overrun by the Russians and Sviatoslav established his winter quarters at Pereiaslavets (Little Preslav), the fortress which commanded the Danubian delta. In despair the Bulgarian tsar turned to the Patzinaks, requesting them to attack the Russians from the rear. It seems probable that by this time new hordes of Patzinaks were let across the Don by the Khazars to invade Russia. Instead of attacking Sviatoslav, the Patzinaks made straight for Kiev and besieged it. Sviatoslav's mother Olga, who with his sons resided at Kiev, succeeded in getting a messenger through imploring him to rescue her and the city. Leaving a strong garrison to hold Pereiaslavets, Sviatoslav led his druzhina back from Bulgaria to Kiev (968). He defeated the Patzinaks without great difficulty, after

---

54. Leo Diaconus, *op. cit.*, Pt. 4, chap, vi, p. 63; Skylitzes = G. Kedrenus, *Historiarum Compendium*, II, 372.

55. Leo Diaconus, *op. cit.*, Pt. 5, chap. ii, p.77; see also Zlatarski, *op. cit.*, I, Pt. 2, pp. 576, 577; N. D. Znoiko, "O posolstve Kalokira v Kiev," *ZMNP, 8* (1897), 253–264.

which he turned his attention to the unfinished task of destroying the Khazar Empire.

There is no information in the Russian sources concerning this second Khazarian campaign; it is mentioned by Ibn-Hauqal, however. According to this writer, in the year 358 A.H. (968–69 A.D.) the Russians plundered both Bulgar, on the Volga, and Khazaria, including the cities of Itil and Samandar. We have seen that Bulgar must actually have been conquered three years earlier; presumably it served as the starting point for the expedition of 968, when the Russians descended the Volga in boats from Bulgar down to Itil, looted that city, and proceeded to Samandar.[56] This was the end of the great Khazar Empire.

There is no indication that Sviatoslav personally participated in the expedition, the conduct of which was probably entrusted to some of his generals. His heart was in Danubian Bulgaria. In 969 he announced to his mother and the boyars: "I do not care to remain in Kiev, but should prefer to live in Pereiaslavets on the Danube, since that is the center of my realm, where all riches are concentrated: gold, silks, wine, and various fruits from Greece, silver and horses from Hungary and Bohemia, and from Russia furs, wax, honey, and slaves."[57] He agreed, however, to postpone his departure until his mother's death: Olga was old and in precarious health. She obliged her son by dying three days later. According to her command no funeral feast was held; a Christian priest performed the last rites over her body.

Soon after the funeral Sviatoslav set forth for Bulgaria. As he intended to leave Kiev permanently, he established his three sons as his lieutenants, Iaropolk in Kiev, Oleg in the land of the Drevlianians, and Vladimir in Novgorod. In the interim the Bulgarians had settled their differences with the emperor. The Russian prince now faced a joint front of Bulgarians and Byzantines. On the other hand, Kalokyras was now openly on Sviatoslav's side, urging the Greeks to revolt against Emperor Nicephorus. A palace revolution indeed took place at Constantinople, but it was not Kalokyras who profited by it. Nicephorus' best and most trusted general John Tzimiskes won the love of the empress and, with it, power. Nicephorus was murdered and his widow married John, who was now proclaimed emperor. The change on the Byzantine throne did not affect the Russian war, however. The new

56. V. V. Grigoriev, *Rossiia i Aziia* (St. Petersburg, 1876), pp. 6–10.
57. Cross, pp. 172, 173.

emperor was ready to proceed with all the energy of which he was capable and Kalokyras lost any chance of obtaining support from within the imperial court.

Meanwhile Sviatoslav advanced swiftly inside Bulgaria and seized the capital, Great Preslav; the young tsar Boris was taken prisoner with all his family. But in 971 the fortunes of war turned in favor of John Tzimiskes. Defeated in several battles, the Russians finally sought refuge in the fortress of Dorostol (Silistria), where they were besieged. Their casualties running high and food running short, they sued for armistice. In July, 971, Sviatoslav concluded a treaty with the Greeks by which he abandoned his claims to both Bulgaria and the Crimea and promised not to wage wars against the Greeks.[58] On these conditions the Russians were allowed to retire. It was after the conclusion of this peace that the meeting took place between John Tzimiskes and Sviatoslav, described by Leo Diaconus.

However, the Bulgars (or was it the Byzantines?) sent word to the Patzinaks to inform them that Sviatoslav was returning to Kiev with rich booty but few troops. The Patzinaks accordingly attempted to sever the path of the retreating Russians by occupying both banks of the Dnieper in the region of the cataracts. Upon receiving news of this move Sviatoslav and his retinue decided to spend the winter at the mouth of the Dnieper. They gained nothing by it, since when they set forth homeward the next spring they were attacked by the Patzinaks as planned. Part of the Russians broke through but Sviatoslav was killed in the skirmish. Kuria, prince of the Patzinaks, ordered a cup to be made of his skull, overlaid with gold, and drank from it.[59] Such was the end of Sviatoslav and with him of the first Russian imperial dream.

58. For the text of the treaty, see the *Book of Annals*, Laur., cols. 72, 73; Hyp., cols. 61, 62; *Kristomatiia*, I, 17. The date of the treaty as well as the chronology of the Russo-Byzantine war at large has been a subject of protracted controversy among scholars of both Russian and Byzantine history. Many accept 972 and not 971 as the treaty date (and consequently 973 and not 972 as the date of Sviatoslav's death). I am not in a position here to review the whole problem but personally I see no reason for changing the date 971, which is given in the Russian text of the treaty (6479 *Anno Mundi*). It is also accepted by F. Dölger ("Die Chronologie des grossen Feldzuges des Kaisers Johannes Tzimiskes gegen die Russen," *BZ, 32* [1932], 275 ff.) and G. Ostrogorsky (*Geschichte des byzantinischen Staates* [München, 1940], pp. 208, 209).

59. Cross, p. 177.

CHAPTER III

# CONVERSION TO CHRISTIANITY

## *1. The Russian Paganism*

OUR knowledge of the religion of the ancient Slavs is far from adequate, due to the paucity of sources.[1] Moreover, it is not easy to differentiate between the beliefs common to all the Slavic tribes and those peculiar to each of them. From this point of view it would be difficult to establish any definite boundaries between Slavic paganism at large and Russian paganism as the religion of the Russian Slavs. In any case it may be said that the Russian paganism undoubtedly possessed some characteristics of its own and presented more variety of beliefs than the religion of any other Slavic tribe, due to the geographic background of Russia. Even more conspicuously than with the religions of the other tribes, the Russian paganism was not a unified system of dogmas but rather a complex body of heterogeneous religious beliefs. There must have been so much diversity in the religion of the Russian Slavs that it would perhaps be more accurate to speak of two, or even three, old Russian religions instead of one.

The worship of clan ancestors constituted what was historically the deepest stratum of Russian religious beliefs. This was connected with a more general idea of propagation as the basic force behind each clan and family. Hence the worship of Rod and Rozhanitsy.[2] The word *rod* means "clan" (i.e., *gens*) but in the early period must also have had a connotation of "generation," in the sense of producing offspring. Grammatically it is a masculine noun. *Rozhanitsa* (singular of *rozhanitsy*) derives from *rod;* grammatically it is feminine. Together, rod and rozhanitsy represent the forces of reproduction inherent in each clan. As late as in the twelfth century many a Russian still offered bread, curd, and mead to Rod and Rozhanitsy, in spite of the admoni-

---

1. On Slavic paganism, see L. Leger, *La Mythologie slave* (Paris, 1901); L. Niederle, *Život starých Slovanů*, II, Pt. 1, Prague, 1916; 2d ed., 1924); A Brückner, *Mitologia Slava* (Bologna, 1923). More bibliographical references in G. Vernadsky, "Svantovit, dieu des Slaves Baltiques," *Annuaire* 7 (1944), 339.

2. See V. J. Mansikka, *Die Religion der Ostslaven* (Helsinki, 1922), pp. 142–147, 162–166, 246, 247, 305–307; Ponomarev, III (St. Petersburg, 1897), 200, 201.

tions of the clergy to abstain from these pagan rites. In the earlier periods the worship of Rod may have had phallic aspects.[3] More specifically, each clan venerated its progenitor (*prashchur*) and each household invoked the protection of its guardian, the *domovoi* ("home sprite," a kind of brownie).

The belief in wood sprites and river nymphs is as old as that in home sprites. Procopius in the middle of the sixth century states that the Slavs reverenced "both rivers and nymphs and some other spirits." [4] The worship of trees is mentioned in pre-Kievan and Kievan sources. After Russia's conversion to Christianity tree worship was forbidden by the clergy but the habit of decorating trees at the time of folk festivals held in the woods was kept in some remote parts of Russia even as late as the nineteenth century. The river and tree nymphs were known in old Russia as *rusalki* (singular, *rusalka*).[5] Festivals in their honor were called *rusalii*. The term is supposed to derive from the Latin word *rosalia*, the ancient ceremony of adorning the tombs of deceased relatives with garlands of roses.

The belief in wood and water sprites was part of the general veneration of forces of nature. The four seasons were understood as so many stages in the struggle between sun and frost, resulting in the yearly revival and death of vegetation as well as the death and reproduction of animals and men.

Generally speaking, the veneration of the forces of nature was adapted to the cycle of labors in both agriculture and cattle breeding, and of it came what may be called the people's agricultural religion of the ancient Russian Slavs with its primitive symbolism and periodic festivals.[6] Many traces of this religion have been preserved in folk-lore. Following Russia's conversion to Christianity, pagan festivities were adapted to, or merged with, the Christian holidays.

The people's religion knew no priests or temples. But above it a more organized pagan cult was established, embodying the worship of the more sophisticated. Socially it must have been the religion of the upper classes. This high church of Russian paganism presumably had a number of temples for its needs, although in the written sources only

3. Brückner, *op. cit.*, pp. 189, 190.

4. Procopius, VII, 14, 23 (H. B. Dewing's translation).

5. According to Zelenin, the *rusalki* represent those women and maidens whose death was "unclean," that is, a result of violence; see D. K. Zelenin, *Russische (ostslavische) Volkskunde*, p. 392.

6. A. S. Orlov, *et al.*, eds., *Istoriia Russkoi literatury*, I, 222–228; N. V. Malitsky, "Drevnerusskie kulty selskokhoziaistvennykh sviatykh," *GA, 11*, No. 10 (1932).

statues of pagan gods are mentioned, erected on hills in the open air. Little is known of the priests (*volkhvy;* i.e., magi) in charge of this pagan worship or of the organization of their caste. Presumably they played a less important role in Russia than among the Baltic Slavs.

The roots of the Slavic religion go deep into the past, being connected with the ancient Indo-European background. According to A. Meillet,[7] the original term for "divinity" which could be deduced from the concordance of old Indo-European languages may be expressed by the symbol *deiwos*. We find *devah* in Sanskrit, *devas* in Lithuanian, *deus* in Latin, *dia* in old Irish. In Avestan there is a similar term *daeva* which denotes, however, not "gods" but "demons." The term *deiwos* is to be compared to the Sanskrit *dyaus*, "sky," "day," which also has parallels in Greek and Latin. The idea of "divinity" is here obviously connected with that of "light." A different connection of ideas is represented by the Sanskrit *bhaga*, to which the Avestan *bagha* and the Slavic *bog* correspond. *Bhaga* has the double connotation of the "wealth which is allotted" and of the "god who allots" it. Similarly in Slavic the term *bog* ("god") corresponds to *bogatstvo* ("wealth"). We have thus before us two categories of deities or two stages in the development of the idea of divinity: that of light and that of wealth.

In Vedic mythology the first of these two principles was represented by Dyaus, the "shining," the sky god. His Greek counterpart is Zeus. In old Slavic texts Zeus is transliterated either as Zeves or as Dii. In the interpolation, by the Russian translator, in the eleventh-century Slavic manuscript of the sermons of Gregory Nazianzen, as well as in the apocryphal "Revelation of the Apostles," the god Dyi is mentioned.[8] I do not think that he could be a mere reflection of Dii— the Greek Zeus. While recognizing the inherent difficulties of the interpretation of the name, I would be inclined to see in Dyi the direct Russian counterpart of the Vedic Dyaus, especially since in the Russian interpolation in Gregory Nazianzen's sermons we also find a feminine name Divia, to be compared with the Sanskrit *diva*, "heaven." It may be added that in the *Lay of Igor's Campaign* we find a demon personified as a gryphon who is called Div. This is to be connected with the old Iranian *daeva* (demons) rather than with the Sanskrit *diva*.

7. A. Meillet, *Linguistique historique et linguistique générale* (Paris, 1921), pp. 323–324.

8. Mansikka, *op. cit.*, pp. 108, 201.

In the epic mythology of the *Mahabharata* period, Dyaus was superseded by Svarga, the sky god. Of this the Russian counterpart is Svarog, presumably also representing the heavens, although in the Russian gloss to the translation of Malalas *Chronography* he is identified with Hephaistus,[9] which would mean that Svarog was likewise looked upon as the fire god. However, in some Russian sources fire is called Svarozhich, that is, son of Svarog.[10] It is probable that Svarog represented the heavens as the highest principle of light, out of which fire emanates.

With Svarog another Russian god, Dazhbog, was closely connected. As we have just seen in the gloss to the Malalas translation, Svarog is identified with Hephaistus; in another gloss the latter's son Helios (the sun god) is likened to Dazhbog. The origin of the first part of the name, *Dazh-*, has been interpreted in two different ways. In 1865 A. Afanasiev suggested the derivation from the Sanskrit *dah*, "to burn." [11] Now the consensus of opinion seems to be that *Dazh-* should be derived from the Slavic verb *dati*, "to give." According to this interpretation Dazhbog is "the giver of wealth." In my opinion, the derivation from *dati*, if valid at all, may be explained as a secondary derivation in popular etymology. All told, Dazhbog appears to have represented the creative and economic function of the sun rather than the cosmic. It is significant that in the *Lay of Igor's Campaign* the Russians are called "Dazhbog's grandchildren." In the Russian folklore Dazhbog was replaced by Iarilo, symbol of sun and fertility.

In the sources of the Kievan period, in addition to Dazhbog we find another sun god, Khors, apparently representing the sun in the astronomical sense. Speaking of a journey of Prince Vseslav to the east— against the sun, as it were—the author of the *Lay of Igor's Campaign* says that Vseslav "cut the path of the great Khors." As to the name Khors, V. F. Miller has suggested its derivation from the Avestan *hvare-khšaeta*, "sun," in modern Persian, *khvarsed*.[12]

Another important old Russian god is Stribog. His element seems to have been the atmosphere; he was supposed to command the winds, which in the *Lay of Igor's Campaign* are called "Stribog's grandchildren." In regard to the name of this god Roman Jakobson has

9. *Idem*, p. 71.

10. *Idem*, p. 150.

11. A. Afanasiev, *Poeticheskie vozzreniia Slavian na prirodu*, I (Moscow, 1865), 65. In Avestan, *dag;* see C. Bartholomae, *Altiranisches Wörterbuch* (Strassburg, 1904), col. 675.

12. Brückner, *op. cit.*, p. 42.

suggested to me the possibility of a parallel between the names Stri-bog and the Indo-Aryan Çri-devi. *Çri* in Sanskrit means "beauty," "fortune"; Çri-devi, the goddess of Fortune. It should be noted that Stribog in Russian is not a feminine but a masculine name. On the other hand, *stri*, both in Sanskrit and in Avestan, means "woman." In the *Mahabharata* woman is, poetically, a divinity: *Çri stri*.[13] Obviously, we have a riddle before us. Could Stribog have been a feminine deity originally? In the epic mythology of the *Mahabharata* certain deities are represented as now male, now female. Thus Dyaus, the sky god, is usually a male god but in his capacity as rain giver "is represented as a female pregnant for nine months and then bearing rain-water conceived of sun-beams." [14]

Dazhbog, Khors, and Stribog seem to have formed a kind of triad emanating from Svarog. Dazhbog, as we already know, was explicitly called son of Svarog. But Khors, representing the sunlight, and Stri-bog, representing the atmosphere (air), must also have been con-sidered an emanation of the heavens, that is, of Svarog. All three may then be called Svarozhichi. It should be noted in this connection that one of the gods of the Baltic Slavs—that of Szczecin (Stettin)—was called Triglav ("Three-headed"). He may be connected with the god, or gods, of Rethra (Radogost') to whom Thietmar of Merseburg refers as Zuarasici. This is obviously another transcription of Svaro-zhich and may easily represent the plural form (Svarozhichi), al-though Thietmar applies the name to one god only—to the first of Rethra deities. However, Thietmar himself says that the pagan temple of Rethra was situated in a "three-horned" castle, that is, a castle with three towers, one over each of the gates.[15] Presumably each gate was guarded by a Svarozhich.

In this connection the name Troian must also be examined. The god is mentioned in the Russian sources at least twice—in the "Revelation of the Apostles" and in "The Holy Virgin's Journey through Inferno." In the *Lay of Igor's Campaign* an adjective form, Troian', is used. This may well derive from Troian but in the opinion of both Henri Gregoire and Roman Jakobson is a derivative not of Troian but of Troy. The problem needs further investigation.

As to the name Troian, a number of scholars have suggested its

13. E. W. Hopkins, "Epic Mythology," *Grundriss der indoarischen Philologie und Altertumskunde*, III, Pt. 1 B (Strasbourgh, 1915), p. 65.

14. *Idem*, p. 78.

15. Brückner, *op. cit.*, p. 245; for the archeological evidence, see C. Schuhhardt, *Arkona, Rethra, Vineta* (Berlin, 1926), pp. 27–63.

derivation from the name of the Roman emperor Trajan. The hypothesis is hardly plausible. In my opinion Troian, like Triglav, must derive from *tri* (three). The connotation is different, however. The latter name must have been applied to the triad of the Svarozhichi. Troian, I believe, may have been an epithet of Svarog, their father; it may be pointed out here that in Ukrainian *troian* means "the father of the three sons" (triplets)[16] and the term may have existed in old Russian as well. It is well fitted to Svarog. The idea of a triad played a considerable role in the Indo-Aryan mythology, and Diva (heaven), a synonym of Svarga, has also a parallel form, Tridiva. Another term of Indo-Aryan mythology may be mentioned here, Tryambaka, an epithet of Siva as of his prototype Rudra. Tryambaka literally means "having three mothers." [17] If an Indo-Aryan deity could be represented as the issue of a triad, why should not a Slavic deity of Indo-Aryan background be thought of as parent of a triad?

In Indo-Aryan mythology Heaven and Earth are considered "universal parents" from whom all other gods emanate.[18] Presumably it was the same in the Indo-Iranian current of the old Slavic mythology. The Svarozhichi may then be thought of as born of the marriage of Svarog and Earth. We know that the cult of the great goddess was widely spread in south Russia in the Scythian and Sarmatian periods. The representation of the goddess is a popular motif in the old Russian folk art.[19] "The Mother Earth," with the epithet "moist" (*mat' syra zemlia*) is constantly referred to in the *byliny*. Even in Christian times we find in Russia some traces of the cult of the Earth, as for example in the habit of confessing one's sins to the Earth.

All this makes it very probable that in the old Russian paganism in addition to the cult of Svarog and the Svarozhichi there was also practiced the worship of the great goddess: the Mother Earth. However, no evidence of such a cult has been preserved in written sources.

Apart from the Svarog group stood a deity of Iranian background, Simargl, to be identified as Senmurv of Iranian mythology and Simurg of Firdausi's *Shah-name*. In the folklore of some Caucasian tribes it

16. B. D. Grinchenko, *Slovar' Ukrainskoi Movy* (Kiev, 1909), II, 798.

17. Hopkins, *op. cit.*, p. 220. In Hopkins' opinion "the simplest explanation of Tryambaka may be that Siva has not three mothers but three Mother-goddesses."

18. A. A. Macdonell, "Vedic Mythology," *Grundriss der indoarischen Philologie und Altertumskunde,* III, Pt. 1 A (Strasbourg, 1897), p. 21; also G. Dumézil, *Ouranos-Varuna* (Paris, 1934).

19. *Ancient Russia,* pp. 53, 90, 94, 99, 100, 113.

is known as Paskudj. Senmurv was represented as a "bird-dog" whose
function was to spread seeds of life over water and earth. In a sense
it was a symbol of fertility and its cult must eventually have degener-
ated into obscene orgies; it is significant that the Russian word
*paskudny*—presumably a derivation from Paskudj—means "odious,"
"filthy," "vile." [20]

We now come to Perun, god of thunder and lightning, who is tradi-
tionally considered the main character in the old Russian pantheon.
The name corresponds to the Lithuanian Perkunas and the Sanskrit
Parjanya.[21]

God, "the maker of the lightning," is mentioned by Procopius in his
description of the Slavs,[22] and although he does not give the name his
evidence may be considered the first statement on Perun in written
sources (sixth century). Later on, the name of Perun was invoked
in the Russo-Byzantine treaties of the tenth century, which shows
that Perun was closely connected with the Rurikide dynasty at Kiev
prior to its conversion to Christianity. Since the princes themselves as
well as many of their retainers were of Scandinavian origin, we may
think that in Perun they worshipped their own Norse god: Thor.
Thor was also known in Russia under his own name, Tur in Russian
transliteration.[23]

The background of Veles (Volos) is not clear. In the *Lay of Igor's
Campaign* the inspired poet Baian is called "the grandson of Veles,"
which seems to indicate that the latter was the god of poetry and
oracles, kin to Apollo. In the resume of Oleg's first treaty with Byzantium (907), Volos is characterized as *skotii bog. Skot* in old Russian
had the connotation of both "money" and "cattle." In this case Volos
was apparently invoked as the protector of commerce. In other sources
he appears as a protector of cattle. Recently Mrs. Chadwick has suggested that the cult of Veles must have developed in Russia under

---

20. K. V. Trever, "Sobaka-Ptitsa: Senmurv i Paskudj," *GA, 100* (1933), 293–328; cf.
*Ancient Russia*, pp. 113, 328. Simargl is mentioned in the *Book of Annals* (*Povest' Vremennykh Let*), A.D. *980*. In some later texts the name has been divided in two (Sim and
Rgl), because of which, prior to the appearance of Trever's study, many scholars were
ready to see in Simargl two deities instead of one. Various derivations have been suggested for the two alleged names, Sim and Rgl. Recently Henri Grégoire has attempted
to restore the theory of two names. Since his study has not yet been published, I cannot
pass any judgment but Trever's article seems quite convincing to me.

21. Meillet, *op. cit.*, p. 333.

22. Procopius, *loc. cit*.

23. See S. Rozniecki, "Perun und Thor," *ASP, 23* (1901), 462–520; Brückner, *op. cit.*,
p. 72.

Norse influence and that even the name Veles itself must be of Nordic origin.[24]

There remains one more Russian deity to be considered: Mokosh. In Sanskrit *mokṣa* means "liberation," "redemption." The term is used to express merging with deity, the state of supreme beatitude of the human soul. This is, however, an abstract philosophical notion and Mokosh appears to have been a concrete deity. Adolphe Gurevitch (in 1943–44) suggested to the members of the seminar on *Slovo o Polku Igoreve* at the Ecole Libre des Hautes Etudes that in Hebrew *mokosh* is a term denoting lesser pagan gods or demons. The derivation of Mokosh from Hebrew would be tempting. However, there is some evidence in Russian sources that this was not a generic term for "demons" but the name of a goddess. According to Grekov, Mokosh must have been a Finnish deity.

From the preceding survey of old Russian deities it must be clear that the Russian pantheon had a very complex origin. At least two different cults were practiced in old Russia—that of Svarog and Khors and that of Perun and Veles. The existence of this religious dualism is corroborated by the archeological evidence. It will be recalled that on the territory of ancient Russia two different funeral rites were practiced: inhumation and cremation. The former was preferred by the Alans, the latter by the Norsemen as well as by that part of the old Slavic tribes which is called Sclavini (Slovene) by Procopius. Procopius' Antes, representing the eastern group of the old Slavic tribes, were, as we know, under considerable Alanic influence and indeed some of these Antian tribes buried their dead instead of cremating them.[25]

It is obvious that the cult of Perun as god of lightning must be connected with cremation. Consequently, Perun must be considered god of the Slovene rather than of the Antes. And in turn the inhumation practiced by the Antes is evidence of the existence among them of a different cult, presumably that of Svarog and Khors.

One of the centers of both Antes and Alans was in the Azov region. And with this region—more precisely, with Tmutorokan—the worship of at least one of the deities of the Svarog group, Khors, may be identified; it was on his way to Tmutorokan that Prince Vseslav "cut the path of the Great Khors," according to the *Lay of Igor's Campaign*. Presumably the cult not only of Khors but of other Indo-

24. Chadwick, pp. 86–89.
25. *Ancient Russia,* pp. 317, 327, 328.

Iranian deities as well found fertile ground in the Azov region and
consequently among all east Russian tribes.

Approaching now the religious geography of pagan Russia from the
political angle we may see that, while the Kievan state grew under the
patronage of Perun, the Tmutorokan kaganate may have depended on
the protection of deities of the Svarog and Khors group. Eventually
Vladimir set up the idols of both groups of gods in Kiev but this attempt at pagan syncretism did not last long, being supplanted by the
new faith, Christianity.

## 2. Vladimir the Saint before His Conversion (972–87)

At the time of Sviatoslav's death his three sons ruled Russia as
his lieutenants. Iaropolk held Kiev, Oleg the Drevlianian land, and
Vladimir Novgorod. It was to Kiev that Sviatoslav's general Sveneld
led the remnants of the slain prince's army.

To the potential political triangle of the conflicting ambitions of
Sviatoslav's three sons a new disturbing element was now added:
Sveneld's arrogant designs. As we have seen, this leader had some
claims to rule the Drevlianian land even in Igor's time. When he returned to Kiev with his veterans of the Bulgarian campaign, he must
have become a coruler with Iaropolk rather than his adviser. He appears to have used his opportunity to intrigue against the latter's
brother Oleg, prince of the Drevlianians. Sveneld's obvious object was
to control the Drevlianian land himself.

A characteristic episode is told in the *Book of Annals*. Sveneld's
son Liut went to the Drevlianian land to hunt. Prince Oleg was hunting, too, and killed Liut as a poacher. "Therefore there sprung up a
feud between Iaropolk and Oleg, and Sveneld was continuously egg-
ing Iaropolk on to attack his brother and seize his property, because
he wished to avenge his son." [26]

In the ensuing war (A.D. 976) Oleg was defeated and perished during the panicky retreat of his druzhina, being pushed from the bridge
in front of his city into the moat "as the soldiery pressed hard on each
other's heels." When his corpse was found, "Iaropolk came and wept
over him, and remarked to Sveneld, 'See the fulfillment of your
wish.' " [27]

There is no mention of Sveneld's name in the chronicle after this
episode. Either he died soon after or fell into disgrace. At the next

26. Cross, p. 177.
27. *Idem,* p. 178.

stage of the fratricidal struggle between Sviatoslav's sons, Blud and not Sveneld appears as Iaropolk's chief councilor.

According to the chronicler, Iaropolk had a Greek wife who had been a nun. Sviatoslav captured her during his Bulgarian campaigns and married her to his son "on account of the beauty of her countenance." Iaropolk himself seems to have been favorably inclined to Christianity and the Christian party was in ascendancy during his brief reign. The violent revival of paganism under Vladimir was apparently a reaction on the part of the pagan party against the rising spirit of Christianity in Kiev.

When the news of Oleg's death reached Vladimir, he understood it as a warning to himself. He fled to Scandinavia and Iaropolk became the sole ruler of Russia. Not for long, however, as Vladimir returned with bands of Varangians hired overseas. True to the spirit of his father, Vladimir sent word to his brother that he was at war with him.

Vladimir's first move was to seize Polotsk, an important point on the way from Novgorod to Smolensk held by a Varangian prince, Rogvolod. Vladimir asked the hand of his daughter Rogneda in marriage. This episode seems to have served as subject matter for an epic poem from which the chronicler must have drawn his information. "Rogvolod inquired of his daughter whether she wished to marry Vladimir. 'I will not,' she replied, 'draw off the boots of a slave's son, but I want Iaropolk instead.' "[28] To draw off the boots of her husband was one of the symbolic acts of the bride in the old Russian marriage ceremony. Enraged by Rogneda's refusal, Vladimir led to Polotsk a strong army consisting of Varangians, Slovenians, Chudians, and Krivichians; stormed the city, killed Rogvolod and his two sons, and married her by force. He then proceeded southward against Iaropolk.

The latter was betrayed by his chief councilor Blud, on whose advice he agreed to negotiate with Vladimir. Vladimir's Varangian supporters treacherously murdered him (977). Presumably Blud belonged to the pagan party in Kiev and welcomed Vladimir as a pagan leader. According to the chronicler, Iaropolk had been warned by a retainer, Variazhko, not to trust his brother but paid no attention. Variazhko (the name is a diminutive of Variag, "Varangian") was very likely a Christian. It is to be noted that Variazhko had advised Iaropolk to flee to the Patzinaks and collect an army there. One may assume that peace between Kiev and the Patzinaks had been restored

28. *Ibid.* It will be recalled that Vladimir's mother, Malusha, was Olga's housekeeper.

not long after Sviatoslav's death. The advice throws some light on the
nature of the fratricidal war. The people as a whole appear to have
remained rather neutral in it and both contesting princes had to rely
on their retainers and hired auxiliary troops. Vladimir's retinue was
reinforced with Varangians and now Variazhko suggested that Iaropolk strengthen his druzhina with Patzinaks.

Following Iaropolk's murder Variazhko actually fled to this tribe,
if we are to believe the chronicler's story. With Patzinak support "he
fought long against Vladimir till the latter won him over only with
difficulty by means of a sworn pledge." [29] It was probably at this time
that Vladimir hired some of the Turkish bands he used a few years
later in his campaign against the Volga Bulgars.

The possibility of hiring Turkish auxiliary troops, one may suppose, allowed him to get rid of his Varangian mercenaries, who behaved in Kiev as in a conquered city. He selected some of their number whom he could trust—"the good, the wise, and the brave men"—
and let the others proceed to Constantinople to offer their services
there. "But in advance of them Vladimir sent couriers bearing this
message [to the emperor] : 'Varangians are on the way to your country. Do not keep many of them in your city, or else they will cause you
such harm as they have done here. Scatter them therefore in various
localities, and do not let a single one return this way.' " [30]

Although in this message Vladimir showed his friendliness to Byzantium, he was strongly opposed to Christianity at home. He set up
idols of pagan deities on the hill outside his palace in Kiev and his
uncle and lieutenant in Novgorod, Dobrynia, acted in a similar spirit.
According to the *Book of Annals* the idols at Kiev represented the following deities: Perun, Khors, Dazhbog, Stribog, Simargl, and Mokosh.[31] Human sacrifices characterized the pagan cult in Vladimir's
time; it was a period of grim pagan reaction.

It has been suggested (by Pogodin [32]) that this revival of paganism
was due chiefly to the pressure on Vladimir of his Varangian retainers.
Indeed, human sacrifices seem better to fit the Norse than the Slavic
paganism. On the other hand, it is known that among Christian martyrs in this period of persecution some were Varangians as well.
Moreover, Perun was not the only god whose worship was promoted

29. Cross, p. 180.
30. *Ibid*.
31. *Ibid*.
32. A. L. Pogodin, "Variazhskii period v zhizni kniazia Vladimira," *Vladimirskii
Sbornik* (Beograd, 1938), pp. 28–30.

by Vladimir. The latter's pantheon was syncretistic and the pagan revival as a whole cannot be explained exclusively by the Norse elements in it.

Vladimir's methods of achieving power suggest him as a cruel and unscrupulous politician, although a very shrewd one. He probably was such a man but it must also be borne in mind that the chronicler tried consciously to paint his portrait—in the first period of his reign, prior to his conversion—in especially dark colors in order to put into bolder relief the magnitude of his moral transfiguration following conversion. Thus, when the chronicler says that Vladimir "had three hundred concubines at Vyshgorod, three hundred at Belgorod, and two hundred at Berestovo," the estimate seems exaggerated unless we assume that the girls he kept at these places in such numbers were not his concubines but female slaves for sale, to be shipped eventually to Constantinople. A few of the best among them he may have kept for himself.

While there is no way to verify the number of Vladimir's concubines, it is known that prior to his conversion he had at least seven wives, including Rogneda and the Greek widow of Iaropolk.[33]

Vladimir never tried to recover his father's Balkan possessions, but seems to have intended from the very beginning of his reign to reestablish contact between Kiev and Azov region. At the same time he paid considerable attention to opening the way westward for the expansion of Russian trade in that direction. Although more limited in scope than those of his father Sviatoslav, his policies in this period were aggressive enough, his western campaigns alternating with the eastern.

Toward the west his first move was made in the Galician triangle at the junction of Ukraine, Czechia, and Poland, with the object of not letting Poland interfere with his direct contact with the Czechs. He marched upon the Poles and took Peremyshl, Cherven, and a number of other west Ukrainian towns (981), since known as the "Cherven cities." The name Cherven was later understood as the old Russian adjective meaning "red" and consequently this region was eventually spoken of as "Red Russia" (*Chervonnaia Rus'*).[34]

Two years later Vladimir undertook a campaign against the Lithuanian tribe of the Iativigians and seized their country in the upper basin of the Nieman River, his intention being obviously to open for

33. Baumgarten, "Généalogies," p. 7.
34. See A. V. Longinov, *Chervenskie goroda* (Warsaw, 1885).

Russia the Nieman riverway to the Baltic. East of the Dnieper River
he had first to reconquer the Viatichians, who had revolted after
Sviatoslav's death. Two campaigns were required (981–82). He then
attacked the Radimichians and overcame them (984). A popular
saying was coined on the occasion of this expedition and recorded by
the chronicler which is interesting evidence of the latter's use of various possible sources. The name of Vladimir's general was Volchi
Khvost, which means "Wolf's Tail." Upon his victory the Kievans
ridiculed the Radimichians, saying that they fled from a wolf's tail.

In 985 Vladimir repeated Sviatoslav's move in attacking the Volga
Bulgars. Presumably he intended in case of victory to descend the
Volga down to its mouth as had his father's warriors. In this campaign the prince with his Russian druzhina set out by boat and his
Turkish allies, the Torks, followed overland on horseback. The campaign ended in victory but a rather indecisive one. Here again a witty
saying is recalled by the chronicler. Vladimir's general, his uncle
Dobrynia, remarked to him, "I have seen the prisoners, who all wear
boots. They will not pay us tribute. Let us rather look for foes with
bast shoes." Accordingly, Vladimir made peace with the Bulgars,
who confirmed it with a characteristic formula: "May peace prevail
between us till stone floats and straw sinks." [35]

## 3. The Story of Vladimir's Conversion (988–89)

The revival of paganism in Kiev in the nine-eighties could not but
meet with strong opposition at home; it was also an anachronism in
the international set-up of the period. As we know, by this time the
Christian faith had already struck roots in Russia. Christian influences had penetrated from various quarters—from Moravia, from
Byzantium, from Scandinavia. The first Russian eparchy was established by Patriarch Photius in 867, one may suppose in Tmutorokan.
From Igor's treaty of 945 we know that a part of his warriors were
Christian and that there was already at that time a Christian church
in Kiev, that of St. Elias. Then, around 955, Princess Olga had been
converted to Christianity.[36]

Thus the ground was well prepared in Russia for conversion. Although in the nine-eighties the Christians were still a minority in Kiev

35. Cross, p. 183.

36. *Ancient Russia,* pp. 345–353, 364; N. Polonskaia, "K voprosu o khristianstve na
Rusi do Vladimira," *ZMNP, 71* (1917), 33–80; V. A. Moshin, "Khristianstvo v Rossii
do sv. Vladimira," *Vladimirskii Sbornik* (Beograd, 1938), pp. 1–18.

and offered no armed resistance to Vladimir's enforcement of paganism, their martyrdom must have attracted much sympathy from the people. Morally, they proved victorious.

As to the international situation, in the tenth century paganism was on the wane everywhere. In the nine-eighties Russia was surrounded by nations of Christian, Jewish, and Moslem faith. The Khazars had been converted to Judaism around 865; the Volga Bulgars accepted Islam in 922. Simultaneously Christianity made rapid progress among Russia's western neighbors. In the period between 942 and 968 several tribes of the Baltic Slavs were converted; in 966 Prince Mieszko of Poland was baptized and in 974 King Harold Blotand of Denmark. Olaf Trygvasson, king of Norway since 995, had become a Christian in 976. In 985 Duke Géza of Hungary accepted the faith.[37]

In view of Vladimir's active interest in the western expansion of Russia, he could not but have been impressed by the spread of Christianity there. And his contact with the Volga Bulgars brought him face to face with Islam. From his intercourse with his neighbors he must have understood before long the necessity of accepting one of the great faiths in order to end Russia's religious isolation.

It appears that the problem of Islam was approached first. According to Marvazi (an Arabic writer of the twelfth century), Vladimir sent messengers to the ruler of Khoresm expressing his people's interest in Mohammedanism. A teacher of the religious laws of Islam was then sent to the Russians.[38] The Russian *Book of Annals* tells a different story. According to it, the initiative in the matter belonged to the Volga Bulgars who sent a mission to Kiev urging Vladimir to accept Islam. The two versions may be reconciled to a certain extent since it is possible that the Volga Bulgars consulted the Khoresmians and a learned man from Khoresm might have taken part in the Bulgarian mission to Kiev. On the whole, however, the version of the *Book of Annals* is more credible. As we know, in 985 Vladimir waged an indecisive war against the Volga Bulgars which ended in a treaty of friendship. It seems quite natural that the Bulgars might like to take advantage of it for religious proselytism. Moreover, Marvazi's story is confusing in many respects. According to him, the Russians first became Christians (A.H. 300; that is, A.D. 912–13), which "blunted their swords, the door of their livelihood was closed to them,

37. Moshin, *op. cit.*, p. 17.
38. Marvazi, pp. 36, 118, 119. Marvazi's story was repeated by Aufi, "Jami al Hikayat," V. Barthold, ed. and tr. *VOZ, 9* (1896), 263–265.

they returned to hardship and poverty, and their livelihood shrank." It was then that they desired to become Moslems. Furthermore, Marvazi asserts that the Khoresmian missionary succeeded in converting the Russians to Islam. In view of such inaccuracies, preference is to be given to the Russian sources in this case. According to the *Book of Annals,* after receiving the Bulgarian envoys, Vladimir convoked his retainers and the city elders to discuss the situation and it was decided to investigate all the religions with which the Russians were acquainted—Islam, Judaism, Greek Christianity, and Latin Christianity—in order to arrive at a conclusion.

The story of Vladimir's listening to the preachers of the various faiths and sending Russian envoys to the countries where they were practiced accurately summarizes the actual historical trends. The envoys were most impressed by the Greek worship of God. After attending the service at St. Sophia in Constantinople they are said to have reported: "We know not whether we were in heaven or on earth." After hearing all the reports, Vladimir's retainers added one more argument in favor of Greek Orthodoxy: "If the Greek faith were evil, it would not have been adopted by your grandmother Olga, who was wiser than all other men." [39]

It so happened at this juncture that the turn of events in the Byzantine Empire made a rapprochement between Russia and Byzantium imperative for the young Byzantine emperor Basil II (976–1025). Toward the end of his reign he became one of the mightiest rulers Byzantium ever had but during the first thirteen years he was faced with almost insurmountable obstacles in the effort to restore the international prestige and internal stability of the empire. His predecessor John Tzimiskes had succeeded in throwing the Russians out of Bulgaria. Within a few years it became clear that the Bulgarians were profiting more by Tzimiskes' victory over Sviatoslav than the Byzantines, for Bulgaria rapidly acquired strength, asserting its independence from Byzantium. In 986 the tsar Samuel of Bulgaria administered a severe defeat to Basil's troops.

Simultaneously, the new emperor had to fight for his throne and his life against powerful rivals representing the aristocratic reaction in Byzantium. The center of the opposition was in Anatolia. First Tzimiskes' relative Bardas Skleros revolted against him (976–79); the revolt was crushed with the help of another Anatolian aristocrat Bardas Phokas, nephew of Emperor Nikephorus Phokas, who had been slain

39. Cross, p. 199.

by Tzimiskes. However, eight years later Bardas Phokas himself assumed leadership of the opposition (987). Gradually he established control over all of Anatolia and early in 988 approached Constantinople. The position of Emperor Basil seemed desperate and he was saved only by the timely help received from Prince Vladimir of Kiev.

Basil's envoys arrived in Kiev in January or February, 988. The purpose of their mission was to ask Vladimir to send a detachment of Varangians to Constantinople to support Basil's small army. For this help Basil was prepared to pay a high price. The envoys were authorized to promise Vladimir the hand of the Byzantine princess Anna, Basil's sister. Vladimir, on his part, had of course to agree to be baptized.[40]

In order fully to understand the significance of the honor shown him by the offer of Princess Anna in marriage we must recall the strictness of the Byzantine court ceremonial, which forbade marriage ties between the members of the imperial house and foreigners. In his book *De Cerimoniis Aulae Byzantinae*, Constantine Porphyrogenitus severely condemns Emperor Constantine V (748–75), who allowed his son to marry a Khazar princess, as well as Emperor Roman I (920–44), who gave his granddaughter in marriage to Tsar Peter of Bulgaria.

Those members of the imperial house who were "Porphyrogenetes" ("born in the purple")—that is, born in the imperial palace—were considered especially sacred. Now, Princess Anna was a "Porphyrogenete." It is characteristic that, when in 968 Bishop Liutprand of Cremona came to Constantinople as envoy of the German emperor Otto I to ask the hand of a "Porphyrogenete" Byzantine princess (presumably this same Anna, then a girl of five) for the emperor's son Otto II, the Byzantine emperor Nikephorus Phokas haughtily refused. Four years later the new ruler John Tzimiskes, a much subtler politician than Nikephorus, agreed to marry Princess Theophano to the younger Otto. She was not a "Porphyrogenete," however.

Because of this honor and because of the existence of a strong Christian party at his court, Vladimir accepted Basil's offer and was baptized, apparently in February, 988. He was given the Christian name of Basil in honor of the emperor.

Vladimir faithfully fulfilled his part of the bargain by sending to Constantinople a division of Varangians six thousand strong. They

40. The best outline of the Byzantino-Russian negotiations of 988 is that by G. Ostrogorsky, "Vladimir Sviatoy i Vizantiia," *Vladimirskii Sbornik*, pp. 31–40.

arrived at the imperial city in the summer of 988 and with the help of these troops Basil defeated the opposing army. Bardas Phokas had to retreat hastily; the Varangians pursued him and finally destroyed his forces in the battle of Abydos, April 13, 989, in which Bardas himself perished.[41]

As the danger waned, Emperor Basil felt less and less inclined to send his sister to Russia. This of course could not but irritate Vladimir. Presumably with this personal question a more general problem was connected—that of the organization of the future Russian church. This must have been discussed by Vladimir with the Byzantine envoys as early as in February, 988. Each ruler of a pagan nation about to be converted might be expected to insist on certain autonomy of the future Christian church in his country and, as we know, Princess Olga's failure to Christianize Russia must have been partly the result of her inability to solve the problem of church autonomy. It is highly probable that the Byzantine envoys promised in 988 not only Anna but also a bishop with sufficient authority to organize the Russian church as an autonomous eparchy. Neither promise was kept and Vladimir decided to put pressure on Byzantium by attacking the Byzantine possessions in the Crimea.

In the Crimean campaign of 989 his purpose must have been partly strategic and partly ecclesiastical. To begin with, the Russians had controlled part of the Crimea under both Igor and Sviatoslav; the latter had been compelled to renounce all claims on the area after his defeat by John Tzimiskes in 971. Now Vladimir laid claim to the land as his patrimony. Strategically it was of great importance to the princes of Kiev as a link between their possessions and Tmutorokan. Moreover, it could be attacked overland, thus avoiding the danger of naval war, in which the Byzantines had the advantage of the "Greek fire."

The ecclesiastical implications of the campaign are no less obvious.[42] By conquering the Crimea Vladimir could hope to obtain control over several episcopal sees: Kherson (Korsun), Doras, Phullae, Sugdaea (Surozh), and Bosporus (Kerch), not to mention Tmutorokan, where we have assumed the first Russian eparchy was established in 867.

Vladimir set forth for the Crimea in the spring of 989. By July

41. Ostrogorsky, *Geschichte des byzantinischen Staates,* pp. 214–215.
42. See G. Vernadsky, "The Status of the Russian Church during the First Half-Century Following Vladimir's Conversion," *SEER, 20* (1941), 294–314.

Korsun had surrendered. In the story of its siege, inserted into the *Book of Annals*, it is told that he was advised by Anastasius, a man of Korsun, to dig down and cut off the pipes which supplied the city with water from springs outside.[43] When the water supply was cut off the inhabitants had no alternative but to surrender. The story shows characteristically that there were pro-Russians in Korsun. In the eastern Crimea, which Igor and Sviatoslav had controlled, part of the population was Russian and the pro-Russian party there must have been even stronger than in Korsun itself.

After the capture of Korsun the emperor had finally to agree to marry his sister to the conqueror; the princess came to the defeated city and there the wedding was celebrated. Vladimir then returned the city to the emperor as *veno*—the bridegroom's gift.

However, Byzantium was apparently still reluctant to make concessions in the matter of the autonomous organization of the Russian church. In this connection it is highly significant that after the fall of Korsun the Pope's envoys visited Vladimir there. Since no agreement was concluded, we may suppose that either the envoys lacked authority to make definite promises or the conditions they offered concerning the proposed organization of the church did not satisfy Vladimir.

The prince now turned to the Crimean bishops to obtain priests and church books for Russia. The presence of his bride Anna, a "Porphyrogenete" princess, must have greatly enhanced his prestige with the bishops and clergy of the Crimean cities. From the story of Anna's illness and miraculous healing which is an appendix to the "Life of St. Stephen of Surozh" we know that she undertook a voyage from Korsun through Phullae to Kerch.[44] Undoubtedly Vladimir also went to Kerch and we may likewise conjecture that on this occasion he visited Tmutorokan, across the strait, where he must have assumed the title of kagan. From Ilarion's "Eulogy" (see sec. 5, below) we know that he bore that title and was thus considered the heir of the Russian kagans of Tmutorokan. The city must likewise have been important to him as the site of the oldest Russian eparchy, if such indeed it was.

In the spring or summer of 990 Vladimir returned to Kiev bringing with him not only his bride but also a number of Crimean priests as well as relics of saints, sacred vessels, and icons. He was now ready to start Christianizing Russia in earnest.

43. Cross, p. 199.
44. V. G. Vasilievsky, *Trudy*, III (Petrograd, 1915), 96, 97.

## 4. Laying the Foundations of the Russian Church
### (990–1037)

Following his return to Kiev, Vladimir ordered the statues of pagan deities to be thrown down and destroyed. The idol of Perun was bound to a horse's tail and dragged to the Dnieper. The whole population of Kiev was instructed to betake itself to the river to be baptized, rich and poor alike. Similar orders were issued by his lieutenants in Novgorod and in the other cities.[45]

Pagan sanctuaries were replaced by Christian churches. Most of the latter must at first have been hastily built wooden chapels but Vladimir lost no time in starting Kiev's first magnificent cathedral of stone —that of the Dormition of the Holy Virgin,[46] also known as the "Church of the Tithe." Its construction was begun in 990 and completed by 996.

The church received its name—"of the Tithe"—because the prince granted to it a tithe from all over Russia, to be paid from the princely treasury: "from [the revenues] of the princely courts, the tenth *veksha;* from the customs duties, [the proceedings] of each tenth week; and from the landed estates [the tithe of the offspring] of each flock and [the tithe of the yield] from each crop." In 996 he issued his important "Church Statute," later revised at some time between 1007 and 1011.[47] Besides the decree of the tithe, this statute also laid the foundation of the church courts.

As more and more churches were built, bishoprics were also established. By the end of Vladimir's reign there were seven, to wit: Novgorod, Chernigov, Vladimir in Volynia, Polotsk, Turov, Belgorod, and Rostov. With these new eparchies we must include also that of Tmutorokan, which existed even before Vladimir.

The moot question in the study of the initial organization of the Russian church has been its relation to Byzantium. It is known that the first metropolitan of Kiev to be ordained by the Patriarch of Constantinople was Theopemptus, who arrived in Kiev around 1037.

45. Golubinsky, *Istoriia*, I, Pt. 1 (2d ed. Moscow, 1901), pp. 163–182. See also A. H. Krappe, "La chute du paganisme à Kiev," *RES, 17* (1937), 206–218.

46. The Greek Orthodox speak not of "Assumption" of the Holy Virgin but of her "Dormition" (in Greek, *Koimisis;* in Russian, *Uspenie*).

47. The best edition of Vladimir's Church Statute is that by V. N. Beneshevich, *Pamiatniki drevne-russkogo kanonicheskogo prava*, Pt. 2 Fasc. 1, *RIB, XXXVI* (Petrograd, 1920). For the history and criticism of the text, see S. V. Iushkov, *Ustav kniazia Vladimira* (Novouzensk, 1926); for the English translation of the four basic articles of the Statute, see Vernadsky, "Status of the Russian Church," *SEER, 20* (1941), 306.

Prior to this, there seem to have been no direct relations between the Patriarchate of Constantinople and the church of Russia.

In 1913 the late M. D. Priselkov suggested that Vladimir, unable to come to terms with Byzantine authorities, addressed himself to Bulgaria and placed the Russian church under the authority of the archbishop of Ochrida.[48] The theory seems at first glance very ingenious, and for a number of years I was prepared to accept this view. However, after giving more attention to the problem I have been obliged to reject it. Priselkov was not, in fact, able to produce any direct evidence for his Bulgarian theory. There is no mention of the dependence of the Russian church on the archbishop of Ochrida in any of the sources, either Russian or Bulgarian.

In my opinion, Vladimir himself gives a definite clue to the solution of the problem. In the preamble to his church statute he says that he received holy baptism "from the Greek emperor [Michael] and from Photius the Patriarch of Constantinople." The reference is obviously to the first conversion of the Russians, in 867. It is known that at this time the first Russian eparchy was already established but unfortunately there is no mention in the sources of the location of the see of the first Russian bishop. According to Golubinsky's surmise, this must have been in Tmutorokan. The theory is more than plausible and in my opinion should be universally accepted.[49]

Photius' successor Ignatius raised the title of the Russian prelate from bishop to archbishop. There were two classes of archbishop in the Byzantine hierarchy: the majority were subordinated directly to the Patriarch, the position of each being thus equal to that of a metropolitan; there were, however, a number who enjoyed wider authority and were recognized as autocephalous. The authority of an autocephalous archbishop was practically equal to that of the Patriarch. To this class the archbishop of Ochrida belonged and, according to Golubinsky, the archbishop of the first Russian eparchy—that of Tmutorokan—was in the same class.

From this point of view Vladimir's reference to the first baptism of the Russians becomes quite understandable. What he meant, ap-

---

48. Priselkov.

49. Recently Ernest Honigmann in his learned article, "Studies in Slavic Church History," *Byzantion*, 17 (1945), 128–162, has voiced his opposition to Golubinsky's theory as well as to my interpretation of Vladimir's church policy. Honigmann even denies that there was any break between Vladimir and Byzantium in church affairs. While realizing the complexity of the question, I am unable to accept Honigmann's conclusions and intend to review the whole problem once more in the near future.

parently, was that the Russian church already had a primate with autocephalous authority. Assuming that his see was in Tmutorokan, we have now to consider the position of the Tmutorokan eparchy. The see is mentioned (under the Hellenized name of Tamatarcha) in some of the Byzantine lists of eparchies of the tenth century, and in the late eleventh century (1078–88) Tmutorokan is mentioned in Russian sources as one of the Russian eparchies.

Now, the only possible time when the eparchy of Tmutorokan could have been transferred to Russia was the period of Vladimir's victorious campaign in the Crimea (989).

The assumption that the archbishop of Tmutorokan was the primate of the Russian church during the reign of Vladimir fits well into the general picture of the church in this period as we have it from other sources. No eparchy of Kiev is ever mentioned in the contemporary sources. Presumably the archbishop of Tmutorokan visited the capital from time to time and in the intervals the bishop of near-by Belgorod officiated in Kiev whenever need arose. It is characteristic that the prelate Ioann, mentioned as the primate of the Russian church in the period 1008–24, bore the title of archbishop and not of metropolitan. Priselkov for this reason identifies him as the archbishop of Ochrida. In my opinion it is much more likely that his see was that of Tmutorokan.

We have now to examine the position of the eparchy of Tmutorokan during the reign of Vladimir's successors. The prince's viceroy there was his son Mstislav. In the later internecine struggle between Vladimir's other son, Iaroslav, and Mstislav, the latter not only succeeded in keeping Tmutorokan but even enlarged his principality by conquering Chernigov. In 1026 he made a deal with his brother by which control over Russia was divided between them, Iaroslav receiving Novgorod, Kiev, and presumably Rostov.

Considering this division of power as to its ecclesiastical implications, we see that, of Russia's eight eparchies, five bishoprics were located in Iaroslav's portion (Novgorod, Belgorod, Turov, Vladimir-in-Volynia, and Rostov): one in the neutral district of Polotsk; and two in Mstislav's portion (Tmutorokan and Chernigov).

It is obvious that ecclesiastically Iaroslav had an advantage over his brother as to the number of bishoprics. On the other hand, the leading see of Tmutorokan remained in Mstislav's territory. The only way open to Iaroslav to make his realm independent of his brother's interference in church affairs was to come to terms with Constantinople.

We know that in the year 1037 he accepted a metropolitan for Kiev from the Patriarch (see Chap. IV, sec. 3). Negotiations must have started much earlier. The matter was delicate, since Mstislav might be expected to object to any attempt on the part of his brother to undermine the authority of Tmutorokan. But in 1036 Mstislav died leaving no male descendants and his principality went to Iaroslav, who was now free to act as he pleased. The agreement with Constantinople was finally approved: the metropolitan of Kiev became primate of the Russian church and Tmutorokan was reduced to the position of just one of the Russian eparchies.

### 5. The Significance of Conversion: An Early Appraisal

The conversion to Christianity is one of the most important land-marks in the history of the Russian people. It was not a purely religious event: Christianity, for Russia, meant at that time a higher civilization. In the eyes of the Russians themselves the conversion made them part of the civilized world.

By the time of Vladimir's son Iaroslav, the new faith was already firmly entrenched in Russia. And a contemporary of his, the metropolitan Ilarion, expressed the views of educated Russians on the significance of the conversion with a force and eloquence hardly surpassed since. In his famous "Discourse on Law and Grace" Ilarion drew a contrast between the Old and the New Testament, giving a broad historical picture of the rise of Christianity. "Faith of grace spread over the earth and finally reached the Russian people. . . . We build no pagan sanctuaries any more, but are erecting Christian churches instead. . . . The gracious God who cared for all the other countries now does not neglect us; he has desired to save us and to lead us to reason." In his "Eulogy" of Vladimir Ilarion praises him for his own baptism as well as for the baptism of the whole Russian nation. "He ruled not over a small and unknown country but over the Russian land which is [now] known and heard all over the earth." He praises Vladimir for his ability—after his conversion—to love the invisible and heavenly values more than the material ones.

The prelate concludes his "Eulogy"—which he must have recited in the Cathedral of St. Sophia—with an appeal to the deceased prince: "Rise, oh honored ruler, from thy tomb, shake off thy sleep, since thou art not dead but only sleeping until the general resurrection. Rise, since thou art not dead, and it does not become thee to die because of thy faith in Christ, the life of the whole world." Ilarion then invites

Vladimir to look upon the progress of Christianity in Russia and to
rejoice over it with the living.[50]

It may be recalled that seven centuries later, and under different
circumstances, Ilarion's appeal to a dead ruler, urging him to rise,
was repeated by the renowned Russian rhetorician of the eighteenth
century—Archbishop Feofan Prokopovich—in his famous funeral
oration on Peter the Great.

In view of the veneration of Vladimir's memory by men of the first
generation after him and by the following generations of Russians,
it might be expected that Vladimir, as baptizer of Russia—a prince
"equal to the apostles" (*isapostolos*)—would be recognized as a saint
soon after his death. He was not canonized, however, until the thirteenth century. One may suppose that the reason for this delay was
Byzantine opposition to the Russian demands for his canonization.
The Byzantine authorities could not so easily forgive the prince his
independence in handling church affairs. But if the Greeks refused
to praise him personally, they could not but praise the church of
Russia, to the building of which, after all, he contributed more than
any other Russian ruler. And the Russians, formerly referred to by
the Byzantines as the "barbarians of the north," were recognized by
the Greeks two centuries after Vladimir's death as "the most Christian nation."

50. The best edition of Ilarion's discourse, "On Law and Grace," and his "Eulogy"
of Vladimir is that in Ponomarev, I (St. Petersburg, 1894), 59–76. For interesting comment, see D. S. Likhachev, *Natsionalnoe samosoznanie drevnei Rusi* (Moscow and
Leningrad, 1945), pp. 24–33.

# Chapter IV

# THE KIEVAN REALM, 990-1139

## *1. Vladimir as Christian Ruler (990-1015)*

VLADIMIR's motives in his conversion may have been predominantly political. Once baptized, however, he accepted the new faith with all possible sense of responsibility. We have seen Ilarion's philosophical appraisal of the significance of the prince's work. A more personal approach and more detailed account of Vladimir's labors is to be found in the monk Iakov's essay, "The Memory and Eulogy of Prince Vladimir," written in the middle of the eleventh century, as well as in the *Book of Annals*.

These eulogies emanating from monasteries cannot be considered objective evidence; they are necessarily partial. Iakov's study follows the pattern of lives of saints. The chronicler—also a monk—may naturally be expected to idealize the person of the "Baptizer of Russia," just as he was inclined to stress the negative features in Vladimir's character while he was still a pagan. Yet these monkish accounts of the prince's life are not stilted panegyrics. Under the mantle of official luster many a trait of reality may easily be discerned and in some cases the information given by Vladimir's early biographers is corroborated by other available evidence.

Vladimir's program of Christianization of Russia may be summarized under three headings: the building of churches, education, and charities. Immediately after his return from the Crimean campaign and the baptism of the Kievans, he "ordained that churches should be built and established where pagan idols had previously stood." [1] The first church built under these orders was that of St. Basil, Vladimir's patron saint, on the hill where the idol of Perun had presided. Then a more elaborate cathedral was built: the Church of the Holy Virgin in Kiev, the so-called "Tithe Church" which I have mentioned, whose foundations still exist.

In regard to education, Vladimir ordered that children of best families be sent to schools for instruction in book learning. "The

1. Cross, p. 205.

mothers of these children wept bitterly over them, for they were not yet strong in faith, but mourned as for the dead." [2] An illustration to this passage of the *Book of Annals* may be found in the "Life" of St. Feodosi, who attended a school in Kursk in the early eleventh century—obviously one of the schools organized under Vladimir's orders. While his mother did not object to his going to school, she became worried when the boy was carried away by the new Christian ideas he learned there and decided to enter a monastery. She tried in vain to dissuade him—even beating him did not help—and he finally became a monk, whereupon, her will broken, she herself entered a nunnery.

Vladimir's extensive charities are described in the *Book of Annals* in a vivid and concrete manner which leaves no room for doubt.

He invited each beggar and poor man to come to the Prince's palace and receive whatever he needed, both food and drink, and money from the treasury. With the thought that the weak and the sick could not easily reach his palace, he arranged that wagons should be brought in, and after having them loaded with bread, meat, fish, various vegetables, mead in casks, and kvas, he ordered them driven out through the city. The drivers were under instruction to call out, "Where is there a poor man or a beggar who cannot walk?" To such they distributed according to their necessities.[3]

The monk Iakov adds that this was done not only in Kiev but in other cities as well.[4]

Banquets—an important feature of Russian social life from time immemorial—now assumed a new significance, becoming an expression of Christian brotherhood and love. As Vladimir's banquets were a kind of agapes of primitive Christians, the chronicler mentions them immediately after recording the prince's charities. "Moreover, he caused a feast to be prepared each week in his palace for his subjects, and invited the boyars, the court officers, the centurions, the decurions, and the distinguished citizens, either in the presence of the prince or in his absence. There was much meat, beef, and game, and an abundance of all victuals." [5]

The prince's hospitality seems to have struck the popular imagination more than anything else and in all of the earlier bylinas his

2. Cross, p. 205.
3. *Idem,* p. 210.
4. Iakov, "Life of Prince Vladimir," in Makarii, I, 255.
5. Cross, p. 210.

entertainment of the valiant knights (*bogatyri*) and the people at large are glorified. It is as a genial host that Vladimir is chiefly referred to in Russian folklore; in the memory of the Russian people he remained forever the "Bright Sun" (*Krasnoe Solnyshko*).

How honest Vladimir was in his desire to apply the new faith to Russian life may best be seen from a story in the *Book of Annals* concerning his hesitation to chastize robbers. He must have understood Christ's command, "Resist not him that is evil," literally and in all seriousness. So did many other Russians in the Kievan period and so did Leo Tolstoy in modern times. The Byzantine-trained clergy had a hard time to convince him that the Church does not deny state discipline:

While Vladimir was thus dwelling in the fear of God, the number of bandits increased, and the bishops, calling to his attention the multiplication of robbers, inquired why he did not execute them. The prince answered that he feared the sin entailed. They replied that he was appointed by God for the chastisement of malefactors and for the practice of mercy toward the righteous, so that it was entirely fitting for him to punish a robber condignly, but only after due process of law. Vladimir accordingly set out to execute the brigands.[6]

Incidentally, the new method of dealing with robbers did not last long and capital punishment was soon replaced by money fines.

Vladimir's foreign policy in this period was not aggressive. As the chronicler has noted, "he lived in peace with the neighboring princes, Boleslaw of Poland, Stephen of Hungary, and Udalrich of Bohemia, and there was unity and friendship among them." [7] Except for one expedition against the Galician Khorvats—presumably to quell a revolt—he concentrated his attention on the defense of Russia's southern frontier against the Patzinaks, who raided Russia at least three times (in 992, 995, and 997) but were each time repulsed, although with great difficulty.

In order to protect the country from the nomads Vladimir built several lines of forts along the northern banks of the steppe rivers. In this he set a model for generations of Russian rulers to come, and "fortified lines" as a protection against the nomads were still built by the Russians in south and east Russia as late as in the eighteenth

6. *Ibid.*
7. *Ibid.*

century, and in Turkestan even in the nineteenth century. In Vladimir's time fortified cities were founded on the banks of the Desna, Oster, Trubezh, Sula, and Stugna rivers. Immigrants from the north and northeast—Slovenes, Krivichians, Chudians, and Viatichians— were settled there. The largest of these new or restored cities was Pereiaslav, which became the capital of the land of the same name, the border land (*ukraina*, hence Ukraine) par excellence.

Following the example of his father, Vladimir ruled distant cities and lands through his sons as viceroys. In the latter part of his reign his son Iaroslav was viceroy of Novgorod; Sviatopolk of Turov; Boris of Rostov; Gleb of Murom; Sviatoslav of the Drevlianian land; Iziaslav of Polotsk; and Mstislav of Tmutorokan. The end of Vladimir's life was darkened by the incipient revolt of his ablest son, Iaroslav of Novgorod, who refused to continue payment of the Novgorodian tribute to Kiev. The amount of the annual tribute to be collected in Novgorod was three thousand *grivna*, of which two thirds were to be sent to the Kievan treasury and the remaining third was to be disposed of by the viceroy of Novgorod for local expenditure. In 1014 Iaroslav stopped all payments to his father, no doubt under the pressure of the Novgorodians, who objected to their subordinated position in the Kievan realm.

Vladimir's answer was to start preparations for a campaign against Novgorod. In the midst of them he fell ill and was not long after saved by death from the tragedy of an armed conflict with his son (1015).

## 2. The Struggle between Vladimir's Sons (1015–36)

The aftermath of Vladimir's death was a bloody feud between his sons. The lack of brotherly ties between them may be partly explained by the fact that they were not all of the same mother. Prior to his conversion the great prince had been a polygamist and there must have been much tension in the relations between his several family establishments. Of his various progeny, Iaroslav, Mstislav, and Iziaslav are said to have been his sons by Rogneda. Sviatopolk was of dubious parentage, the son of Iaropolk's widow, whom Vladimir married when she was already pregnant if we are to believe the chronicler. Sviatoslav's mother was Vladimir's Czech wife; Boris and Gleb were sons by a Bulgarian woman according to the *Book of Annals*. However, as described in the "Tale" of the sufferings of these two, later known as saints, Gleb was a mere child at the time of his assassination (1015). If so, he must have been the son of the prince's first Christian wife, the Byzantine Princess Anna.[8]

It appears that Vladimir intended to bequeath his realm to Boris, one of the youngest of his sons, to whom, during his last illness, he entrusted the command of the troops sent against the Patzinaks. Boris was on his way back from the expedition and had just reached the banks of the Alta River when he received news of his father's death and of the seizure of the Kievan throne by Sviatopolk. His retainers urged him to march against the latter, warning that otherwise Sviatopolk would have him killed. Boris' attitude was characteristic of that thin upper layer of the Russian people who had accepted Christianity in all seriousness. He was not willing to resist evil with evil and abhorred the idea of fighting his elder brother; he therefore dismissed his retinue and calmly waited for the assassins. He was murdered but by his death remained forever alive in the popular memory as a symbol of brotherly love. Boris and his brother Gleb, likewise killed by Sviatopolk's agents, were the first two Russians to be canonized by the Church. Another brother, Sviatoslav of the Drevlianian land, fled westward but was caught by Sviatopolk's emissaries on his way to Hungary. Iziaslav of Polotsk remained neutral and was not molested, nor did Mstislav of Tmutorokan consider himself threatened by Sviatopolk. One may suppose that there was some kind of agreement between them, possibly a nonaggression pact. At any rate, Mstislav was busy rounding out his possessions in the Azov region. In 1016 he fought the remnants of the Khazars in the Crimea with the assistance of Byzantine troops.[9]

The only brother who dared to oppose Sviatopolk was Iaroslav of Novgorod, whose cause the Novgorodians identified with their aversion to Kiev's predominance over them. The war between the two men was a struggle between Novgorod and Kiev rather than the personal feud of brothers. It lasted for four years (1015-19) and both adversaries used auxiliary troops from outside Russia. Iaroslav hired Varangian troops and Sviatopolk the Patzinaks. After his first defeat, the latter fled to Poland and concluded an alliance with King

8. Princess Anna died in 1011. According to Baumgarten, Vladimir married once more after her death (Baumgarten, "Généalogies," pp. 7-8).

9. The Khazar expedition is not mentioned in Russian sources but was briefly described by the Byzantine historian Ioannes Skylitzes. See Kedrenus, *Historiarum Compendium*, II, 464. Kedrenus gives the name of the Russian prince as Sphengus and considers him Vladimir's brother. Presumably it is a mistake, since Mstislav (Vladimir's son) was at that time the only Russian prince in position to fight the Khazars.

Boleslaw I. Together they were able to recapture Kiev from Iaroslav (1018), who in turn fled to Novgorod once more. Thinking that the danger was over, Sviatopolk quarrelled with his Polish allies and Boleslaw returned home, taking with him Iaroslav's two sisters and those of the Kievan boyars who sympathized with Iaroslav, apparently as hostages. He also reannexed to Poland the Cherven cities.[10] Sviatopolk's triumph proved of short duration, however, since Iaroslav after a while attacked him again. Once more Sviatopolk hired Patzinak troops to assist him and once more he lost. This time his defeat was final and he died (1019), apparently somewhere in Galicia, as he was fleeing westward.

Iaroslav had now to face another opponent, his brother Mstislav. By this time the latter was firmly established in eastern Crimea and Tmutorokan. In 1022 the Kosogians (Circassians) recognized him as their suzerain after he had killed their prince Rededia in a duel; this episode must have been described in an epic poem on the basis of which it was recorded in the *Book of Annals*.

Reënforcing his retinue with Khazar, Kosogian, and presumably Iasian warriors, Mstislav set forth to the north and occupied the land of the Severians, apparently by agreement with the population, since they supplied him with troops. As he reached Chernigov, Iaroslav retired to Novgorod once more and issued another call to the Varangians for help. Haakon the Blind responded, bringing along a strong band of Varangians to Novgorod.[11]

The decisive battle of the campaign took place at Listven (near Chernigov), the victory falling to Mstislav (1024). Iaroslav decided to compromise and the two brothers agreed to divide Russia in two parts along the course of the Dnieper River. Although Kiev was thus included in Iaroslav's half, he preferred to remain in Novgorod. Mstislav, meanwhile, established his throne in Chernigov (1026). It must be noted that one of the Russian lands, north of the headwaters of the Dnieper—Polotsk—was not affected by the agreement. From that time it remained somewhat aloof.

Iaroslav and Mstislav maintained a close alliance and in 1031, taking advantage of King Boleslaw's death and the ensuing troubles in Poland, they recaptured the Cherven cities and ravaged the Polish

---

10. On the Polish intervention, besides the Russian literature, see S. Zakrzewski, *Boleslaw Chrobry Wielki* (Lwow, Warszawa, and Krakow, 1925), pp. 297–311.

11. Cross, p. 224. In the Russian original of the Laurentian version the name is spelled Iakun; in the Hypatian version, Akun; in Old Norse, Hakun. See Thomsen, pp. 131–132.

countryside. According to the *Book of Annals*, "they also captured many Poles and distributed them as colonists in various districts. Iaroslav located his captives along the Ros River." [12]

It is interesting to note that in this period of coöperation between the brother princes the city of Kiev seems temporarily to have lost its predominance in Russian politics. Novgorod and Chernigov now emerged as the two leading political centers. Behind this political change a shift in the direction of the main commercial highways may be surmised. Novgorod controlled, as before, the northern entrance for goods shipped from the Baltic southward but from Chernigov these were now sent via steppe rivers and connecting portages to the Azov region instead of being carried down the lower Dnieper to the Black Sea and Constantinople. It is possible that the lower Dnieper riverway was in this period barred by the Patzinaks. But the shift in the southern route may also have been the result of a conscious policy of Mstislav, representing in this case the interests of Tmutorokan merchants. The Azov region lay at the junction of several commercial ways: to Turkestan, to Transcaucasia, and—by way of the Crimea—to Constantinople.

It was, no doubt, to obtain full control of the Azov region that Mstislav undertook his expedition against the group of Iasians who lived in the lower Don area north of the Sea of Azov. They recognized his authority in 1029.[13]

The chronicler describes Mstislav as "corpulent and red-faced, with large eyes, bold in battle, merciful, and a great lover of his retainers, begrudging them neither treasure nor food nor drink." [14] As the ruler of Tmutorokan, Mstislav must have held the title of kagan. It is interesting to note that in the *Lay of Igor's Campaign* Prince Oleg of Chernigov, who had also controlled Tmutorokan for some time, is referred to as kagan. The reign of Mstislav is, then, in a sense, an attempt to replace the predominance of Kiev in Russia by that of Tmutorokan and to revive the old Russian kaganate of pre-Kievan times. Presumably Tmutorokan was likewise the ecclesiastical capital of Russia in this period.

Mstislav was an enthusiastic builder. During his duel with Rededia he made a vow in case of victory to build in Tmutorokan a church

---

12. Cross, p. 225.

13. In the Nikon chronicle, *PSRL*, IX, 79, it is said that the Iasians were conquered by Iaroslav in 1029. The mention of the name Iaroslav is, in this case, the result of a copyist's mistake. The reference is obviously to Mstislav.

14. Cross, p. 225.

dedicated to the Holy Virgin, and he kept his promise to the Mother of God. When he shifted his capital to Chernigov he began to build a sumptuous cathedral there, dedicating it to Christ the Savior. The chronicler records that at the time of Mstislav's death the church was built "to a point higher than a man on horseback could reach with his hand." [15] It is significant that in their architectural style Mstislav's churches follow the pattern of eastern Byzantine art— that of Transcaucasia and Anatolia. In this case, as in many others, artistic influences spread along the lines of commercial intercourse.

Some exchange of the populations between the Tmutorokan region and the Severian land may also be supposed. Mstislav brought along to Chernigov a strong body of Kosogian retainers. Some of them were probably settled in that part of the Severian land which later became known as the Pereiaslav land. While there is no mention of it in the chronicles, the name of a river in that region, Psiol, is indirect evidence, since it is of Kosogian origin: in Circassian, *psiol* means "water." The river Psiol discharges into the Dnieper from the east. On the western bank of the Dnieper at some distance there is a town called Cherkasy, which in old Russian means "Circassians" (the modern Russian form is Cherkesy). The name does not appear, however, in the sources of the Kievan period and is first mentioned in the sixteenth century. At that time, not only the Circassians (old Kosogians) were known in Russian as Cherkasy but the Ukrainian Cossacks as well, which means that in the opinion of the Russians of the Muscovite period there was some connection between the Kosogians and the Cossacks. And indeed, Ukrainian scholars of the seventeenth century derived the very name Cossack (*Kozak*) from that of the Kosogians. On the other hand, the word *kozak* (now usually spelled in Russian *kazak*) is supposed to derive from the Turkic word *kazak* which denotes a free frontiersman. The problem is thus very complex and cannot be given full attention here. [16] Suffice it to say now that Mstislav's Kosogians were presumably settled in about the region where, five centuries later, the Zaporozhie Cossacks emerged as a mighty military commune.

Turning now to Iaroslav's policies as ruler of Novgorod, we have first of all to mention the charters he granted to the northern metropolis in 1016 and 1019 to recompense the Novgorodians for their support in the civil war. Unfortunately the originals of these charters

15. *Ibid.*
16. See W. E. D. Allen, *The Ukraine*, pp. 68–70.

have not been preserved and not even a transcript of either of them is known. In some copies of the Novgorodian chronicles the text of the *Russian Law* (*Pravda Russkaia*) is inserted instead of the charters. And indeed, the compilation of the Iaroslav's *Pravda*, so-called, was in some way connected with the issuing of the charters. In its opening article the equality of the wergeld [17] of a Novgorodian Slav with that of a Kievan Russian is proclaimed. This must have been an important point in the Novgorodian demands.

Iaroslav's expedition against the Chudians in Estonia must likewise have been dictated by Novgorodian interests. It represented an attempt to extend westward the Novgorodian control of the southern shores of the Gulf of Finland and adjacent territories. In the conquered territory, in the year 1030, Iaroslav founded a new city, called Iuriev for his patron saint (Iuri is the old Russian form of the name George). After the German conquest of the Baltic provinces in the thirteenth century the city became known as Dorpat (now Tartu).

### 3. The Age of Iaroslav the Wise (1036–54)

In 1036 Mstislav fell sick and died while on a hunting expedition. His only son had passed away three years earlier. Iaroslav now remained the indisputable sovereign of the whole of Russia except for the Polotsk land. As the ruler of Tmutorokan he could now claim the title of kagan. That he actually assumed it is indicated by Ilarion's "Discourse," in which Iaroslav is so addressed.

His first move after his brother's death was to ward off a Patzinak attack on Kiev. By the time he arrived from Novgorod with an army of Varangians and Slavs the nomads had penetrated the outskirts of the city. They were crushed, however, by Iaroslav's warriors and the victorious prince decided to remain in Kiev, making it his capital.

It was at this juncture that the relations between the Russian church and the Patriarchate of Constantinople were normalized. According to the agreement reached between Iaroslav and Constantinople, the Russian church was to be headed by a metropolitan of Kiev ordained by the Patriarch of Constantinople. In other Russian cities bishops were to be ordained, nominally by the metropolitan, but it was understood that the prince's wishes as to the nomination of suitable candidates would be considered. Not later than 1039 the first metropolitan of Kiev, Theopemptus, arrived in Russia from Constantinople.

17. Wergeld, the value set on a man's life.

Having made Kiev the country's political and ecclesiastical capital, Iaroslav put forth every effort to make that city Russia's artistic and intellectual center, taking Constantinople as a pattern. A sumptuous cathedral dedicated to St. Sophia and several other churches were built by imported Byzantine masters, as well as a new citadel and the so-called Golden Gate. Great attention was paid to learning. According to the chronicler, Iaroslav "applied himself to books and read them continually day and night. He assembled many scribes to translate from the Greek into Slavic. He caused many books to be written and collected, through which true believers are instructed and enjoy religious education. . . . Thus Iaroslav, as we have said, was a lover of books and, as he had many written, he deposited them in the Church of St. Sophia." [18] Taken together, the ambitious translation project and the library at St. Sophia amounted to the establishment at Kiev of an important institution of learning and research. It is hardly an exaggeration to call this institute, as M. Hrushevsky does, Russia's first learned academy. [19]

A delicate problem in Iaroslav's internal policy was that of regulating the position of Novgorod, since many a Novgorodian might be expected to oppose the shifting of Iaroslav's throne to Kiev. When he did so, in 1036, he had once more to confirm his charters to the city. The *Russian Law* was also revised and an ordinance added to it limiting the amount of food deliveries to the collectors of bloodwite [20] on the part of the local population. A new bishop was appointed to Novgorod, Luka Zhidiata, a Novgorod man, presumably of Jewish extraction. As viceroy in the northern city Iaroslav appointed his eldest son Vladimir. Novgorod's main sanctuary was the Church of St. Sophia, whose first edifice was of wood. When it was destroyed by fire, Vladimir built a new one of stone, still considered one of the most remarkable monuments of the old Russian architecture (1045).

In his foreign policy of this period Iaroslav paid considerable attention to the expansion of Russia's western frontier. In 1038 he attacked the Iatvigians, a Lithuanian tribe, and two years later invaded Lithuania once more. In 1041 he led a campaign by boat against

18. Cross, p. 226.

19. M. Hrushevsky, "Tri Akademii" ("Three Academies"), *Kyivs'ki Zbirnyky*, I (Kiev, 1931 [1930 on the title page]), 1–14. The three academies in question are Iaroslav's institute of learning; the Kievan Theological Academy (founded in the seventeenth century); and the Ukrainian Academy of Sciences (founded in 1918).

20. Bloodwite (in Russian, *vira*), the fine paid to the prince for murder.

the Polish tribe of Mazovians. In the following year his son Vladimir conquered the Finnish tribe of Iam to secure Novgorod's control of the Gulf of Finland. Friendly relations were eventually established between Iaroslav and King Kazimierz of Poland; in 1043 the prince married one of his sisters to Kazimierz and "as a wedding gift Kazimierz surrendered eight hundred captives whom Boleslaw had taken when he overcame Iaroslav." [21] In 1047 Iaroslav helped Kazimierz to subdue the Mazovians.

Meanwhile Russia's relations with Byzantium went through a period of acute crisis. Around 1042 a disagreement occurred between the Greeks and the Russian merchants in Constantinople and a number of Russians were killed. [22] The Russians apparently demanded satisfaction but were denied it, and in 1043 "Iaroslav sent his son Vladimir to attack Greece and entrusted to him a large force." [23] The chiliarch Vyshata [24] was appointed commander of the troops. He was the father of Ian, one of the informants of the chronicler, and the story of the *Book of Annals* is apparently based on Ian's narrative.

It must be noted that the realization of a Russian expedition to Byzantium presupposes control by the Russians of the whole course of the lower Dnieper, and especially of the region of the cataracts. This region must have been held by the Patzinaks from the death of Sviatoslav but apparently they lost it following Iaroslav's victory over them in 1037. Vladimir's expedition of 1043 was a naval one; the Russian fleet suffered severely both from a storm and the "Greek fire," after which most of the Russian troops were landed somewhere in Bulgaria. Vyshata went ashore with them. The war then took a different turn from the previous expeditions against Byzantium. Although damaged by the storm the remnants of the Russian fleet scored a victory over the Greek squadron. The overland troops, on the other hand, surrendered to the Byzantines, who blinded many of their captives. Vyshata himself was brought to Constantinople but was released and sent back to Kiev later on. There followed a truce for three

21. Cross, p. 229.

22. There are two Russian versions of the story of the Russo-Byzantine war of 1043: that of the *Book of Annals* (Cross, pp. 227–228) and that of the Voskresensk Chronicle (*PSRL*, VII, 331); and three Byzantine narratives: Skylitzes, see Kedrenus, *op. cit.*, II, 551–555; M. Attaliates, *Historia*, pp. 20–21; and M. Psellus, *Chronographia*, C. Sathas, ed., pp. 129–132; E. Renauld, ed., II, 8–12. See also Hrushevsky, II, 35–37 and 559–560; M. Levchenko, *Istoriia Vizantii* (Moscow and Leningrad, 1940), p. 190; Chadwick, pp. 104–111.

23. Cross, p. 227.

24. Chiliarch, *tysiatsky*, "commander of the thousand," i.e., of city militia.

years, after which the relations between Kiev and Constantinople were severed once more but apparently without actual war.

Then, in 1051, Iaroslav made a bold attempt to assert the independence of the Russian church from Constantinople. On his initiative an assembly of Russian bishops elected a Russian, the famous Ilarion, as Metropolitan of Kiev. He was not recognized by Patriarch Michael Cerularius of Constantinople. The Russian move must have caused considerable anxiety in Constantinople, since this was a period of great tension between the Patriarch and the Pope of Rome. The Russians might be expected to profit by it and to shift their allegiance from Constantinople to Rome. In a sense, then, the move became a factor in the great schism between the Greek and the Roman Church.[25]

We do not know how the Russo-Byzantine conflict was settled, but settled it must have been as early as 1052, since we find the following note in the *Book of Annals*, dated 1053: "A son was born to Vsevolod [son of Iaroslav] by the Greek Princess, and he named him Vladimir." [26] Apparently Vsevolod married the princess in 1052 and this would scarcely have been possible without the reëstablishment of friendly relations between Byzantium and Russia. But the marrying of a princess to Iaroslav's son would hardly be enough to compensate the Russians for abandoning the idea of making their church independent. Presumably a new trade agreement was simultaneously concluded between Kiev and Constantinople on conditions favorable to Russia.

What became of Ilarion following his demotion is not known. M. D. Priselkov suggested that he must have assumed the highest monastic orders and eventually entered the Monastery of the Caves under the name of Nikon. This is only a surmise, ingenious as it is. By a coincidence which seems full of inner significance, the death of Iaroslav and the final rupture between the Eastern and the Western Church occurred in the same year, A.D. 1054.

For the characterization of Iaroslav's personality we possess not only the evidence of the literary sources but also an anthropological and anatomical analysis of his skull and skeleton, as mentioned earlier, which corroborates the data of the literary sources on at least one important point. Thus in the *Book of Annals* it is mentioned that the prince was lame and in another contemporary source it is said that

25. Priselkov, pp. 93–95, 109–111.
26. Cross, p. 231.

in childhood he had difficulty in walking. By the anatomical analysis it has been established that as a child he had an illness which hampered his walking and that he later broke his leg.[27]

## 4. The Triumvirate (1054–93)

Iaroslav's eldest son Vladimir had died two years before his father. As we know, he occupied the important position of viceroy of Novgorod. He was also twice entrusted with independent military command—against the Finnish tribe of Iam in 1042 and against Byzantium in 1043. It is probable that had he been alive at the time of his father's death the latter would have bequeathed the realm to him; none of the five other sons seems to have been sufficiently prepared for the task. Toward the close of his life, if we are to believe the *Book of Annals*, Iaroslav favored his fourth son Vsevolod over the others. To leave him the throne was, however, out of the question, for his elder brothers would have objected and also Vsevolod himself lacked the essential qualities of leadership.

Shortly before his death Iaroslav came to the decision to entrust the power to all his sons as a family group, under certain conditions. The text of his testament is recorded in the *Book of Annals*. It is so important for the understanding of following political developments that it will not be amiss to quote it here in full.

My sons, I am about to quit this world. Love one another, since ye are brothers by one father and mother. If ye dwell in amity with one another, God will dwell among you, and will subject your enemies to you, and ye will live in peace. But if ye dwell in envy and dissension, quarreling with one another, then ye will perish yourselves and bring to ruin the land of your ancestors, which they won at the price of great effort. Wherefore remain rather at peace, brother heeding brother. The throne of Kiev I bequeath to my eldest son, your brother Iziaslav. Heed him as ye have heeded me, that he may take my place among you. To Sviatoslav I give Chernigov, to Vsevolod Pereiaslav, to Viacheslav Smolensk, and to Igor Vladimir [in Volynia].[28]

Note that, while Iaroslav distributed various cities among his sons, there was no formal division of realm, since the senior prince's throne, that of Kiev, was the only one invested with full political authority. On the basis of this testament the scale of political seniority of Rus-

---

27. D. G. Rokhlin, "Itogi anatomicheskogo i rentgenologicheskogo izucheniia skeleta Iaroslava"; V. V. Ginzburg, "Ob antropologicheskom izuchenii skeletov Iaroslava Mudrogo, Anny i Ingigerd"; M. M. Gerasimov, "Opyt rekonstruktsii fizicheskogo oblika Iaroslava Mudrogo." These articles appear in *IIM*, 7 (1940), 46–66 and 72–76.
28. Cross, pp. 231, 232; see also Presniakov, *Kniazhoe pravo*, pp. 34–42.

sian cities was established, to be coördinated with the genealogical seniority of princes.

Actually, instead of Iziaslav's chairmanship in the princely family, a triumvirate was formed by the three elder brothers—Iziaslav, Svia-toslav, and Vsevolod. Together they attempted to rule all Russia. This proved to be not so easy a task, however. The major disturbing factor proved to be the prince of Polotsk, Vseslav, grandson of Iziaslav and great-grandson of Vladimir the Saint. Iziaslav had been established in Polotsk by Vladimir and, as we saw earlier, remained neutral in the struggle of his brothers following Vladimir's death. As a result, the land of Polotsk had remained an autonomous unit during the whole reign of Iaroslav. Belonging to Vladimir's clan, if not to Iaro-slav's family, the Polotsk princes resented Iaroslav's testament as excluding them from any participation in the joint rule of Russia. On the other hand, they were not bound by it and reserved complete freedom of action.

Vseslav's weird personality adds a sinister touch to the picture. Restless and ambitious, he was considered a sorcerer and was apparently an adept in the magic arts. We find in the *Book of Annals* the following note on the occasion of his accession to the throne of Polotsk (1044): "Him his mother bore by enchantment, for when his mother bore him, there was a caul over his head, and the magicians bade his mother bind this caul upon him, that he might carry it with him the rest of his life." [29] In the *Lay of Igor's Campaign* Vseslav is portrayed as a man endowed with supernatural power and as a were-wolf.

Besides the Polotsk princes Iaroslav's own grandson Rostislav, son of Vladimir of Novgorod, who had died before the prince his father, likewise received no share in the common rule of Russia by Iaroslav's sons and had even more reason to object than Vseslav of Polotsk. It would be natural for the two outcasts—Vseslav and Rostislav—to come to an agreement for combining their efforts against the triumvirate and apparently they did so, although there is no direct evidence of it in the chronicles.

Rostislav made the first move by seizing the city of Galich, from which he was, however, expelled by the triumvirs. He then rushed to Tmutorokan, which belonged to the share of Sviatoslav of Chernigov and was held by the latter's son Gleb as his lieutenant—the same Gleb who later measured the width of the Kerch Strait and recorded

29. Cross, p. 229.

it on the so-called "Tmutorokan stone." Rostislav ousted Gleb from Tmutorokan but when Sviatoslav himself came to his son's assistance the intruder withdrew, being reluctant to take up arms against his uncle, as the chronicler explains. This is a typical attitude, showing the strength of the principle of seniority among the descendants of Iaroslav. As soon as Sviatoslav returned to Chernigov, however, Rostislav fell upon Gleb once more and again established himself in Tmutorokan, "receiving tribute from the Kosogians and from other regions" (1064).[30] It was at this juncture that Vseslav began hostilities against the triumvirs. Presumably Rostislav's dash to Tmutorokan had been made on the former's advice. In the *Lay of Igor's Campaign* it is said that Vseslav knew how to reach Tmutorokan from Polotsk miraculously in one night. As Vseslav seems never to have visited the city personally, the author of the *Lay* apparently has Rostislav in mind as his agent.

One may suppose that, with Rostislav as his ally, Vseslav dreamed of repeating the political combination of 1026, when two princes held the northwest and southwest of Russia, thus controlling the commercial highway from the Baltic to the Sea of Azov. The plan failed because of the interference of an outside force—Byzantine diplomacy. The Greeks became worried by Rostislav's aggressive action in the region of the Crimea where the city of Kherson was still under Byzantine control. Under the pretext of negotiations the Greek governor (*katepano*) of Kherson came to Tmutorokan and at a state banquet poisoned Rostislav's drink. The prince died a week later. It is typical of Rostislav's popularity in the Crimea that on the governor's return to Kherson he was stoned by the infuriated populace.[31]

Meanwhile Vseslav was engaged in a fierce struggle with the triumvirs but, being defeated, agreed to negotiate. He was treacherously arrested during the meeting of truce and brought to Kiev as a captive (1067). This broken oath on the part of the triumvirs is considered by the chronicler the main cause of their ensuing troubles; in his opinion they provoked God's wrath by their action. It is the steppe nomads who appear as the tool of God for the punishment of the sinful Russian princes. It will be recalled that in the late tenth and the first half of the eleventh century the south Russian steppes were controlled by the Patzinaks who harassed Russia on many occasions and even caused the death of one of Russia's mightiest rulers—

30. *Idem*, p. 234.
31. See Hrushevsky, II, 53.

Sviatoslav I. But toward the end of Iaroslav's reign the Patzinak danger was overcome by the victorious Russians.

Their success was partly due to the fact that the Patzinaks at the time were subject to pressure from the east by another Turkish horde, the Cumans (Polovtsi), whose abode was originally in Kazakhstan. The victory over the Patzinaks thus proved futile, since the Cumans who replaced them in the Pontic steppes were a stronger and fiercer enemy, who began to harass the border districts of the Pereiaslav land in 1061. In 1068, encouraged no doubt by the news of dissensions among the Russian princes, they attacked in force and defeated the Russians. Each of the triumvirs fled to his own city but, while Sviatoslav was able to defend Chernigov and Vsevolod kept Pereiaslav, Iziaslav was faced with a popular revolt in Kiev. The rioters freed Vseslav from prison and proclaimed him prince of Kiev (1068). This episode is poetically reflected in the bylina on "Volkh Vseslavich." Iziaslav escaped to Poland and asked King Boleslaw II for assistance, which he received. Forgetting his magic Vseslav fled to Polotsk, making no attempt at a stand against the advancing Polish army. The Kievans had no alternative but to surrender to Iziaslav on condition that he would not wreak vengeance on the leaders of the revolt. He personally did not do so but before he entered the city his son, who preceded him, executed a number of prominent Kievan citizens, both guilty and innocent (1069). After recovering his throne Iziaslav got rid of the Poles at the first opportunity.

The triumvirate was now reëstablished, but not for long. In 1072 the three brothers attended the festivities in Kiev on the occasion of the transportation of the relics of Ss. Boris and Gleb. About the same time they confirmed a collection of ordinances known as the *Pravda* of Iaroslav's sons. But already in 1073 the triumvirate was broken by the conspiracy of two of its members—Sviatoslav and Vsevolod—against the third, Iziaslav. The latter fled again to Poland but this time received no help. He then addressed himself to Emperor Henry IV of Germany and finally to Pope Gregory VII, expressing his willingness to make Russia "St. Peter's fief." He had no success, however, since his brother Sviatoslav, now ruler of Kiev and Chernigov, was not only a powerful prince but a skillful diplomat as well and himself showed an inclination toward ecclesiastical compromise with Rome. Sviatoslav further entertained friendly relations with both the Holy Roman Empire and Poland and in 1076 Russian troops aided the Poles against the Czechs.

Sviatoslav's death in 1076 made possible Iziaslav's return to Kiev. As soon as he was back he forgot all about his commitments to the Pope. Of his brother Vsevolod, to whom he promised Chernigov, he was more considerate and joined him in the expedition against Sviatoslav's sons, who refused to surrender the city, which they considered their patrimony. The uncles won the battle against the nephews but Iziaslav fell in that battle (1078) and, in the chronicler's opinion, by his faithfulness to his younger brother expiated his sins.

Vsevolod was now the only surviving member of the former triumvirate. He remained established in Kiev, appointing his able son Vladimir Monomach as viceroy of Chernigov. Vsevolod's reign (1078–93) was full of interprincely feuds caused chiefly by Sviatoslav's sons, who resented their loss of Chernigov. The ablest of them, Oleg, a haughty aristocrat and a daring warrior, finally succeeded in establishing himself at Tmutorokan. In their despair the Sviatoslavichi (Sviatoslav's sons) turned for assistance to the Cumans, who were more than glad to have the opportunity to plunder Russia posing as allies of Russian princes. It is understandable that the chroniclers spare no words in condemning the Sviatoslavichi for thus bringing misfortune on the Russian land. But in his own mind Oleg was only trying to defend his rights to his patrimony.

Not fortunate in his external policies, Vsevolod was no more successful in his internal administration. According to the chronicler, "the people had no longer access to the Prince's justice, justices became corrupt and venal." [32] The chronicler tries to excuse the prince by referring to his illness and old age and puts the blame on his young councilors, whose advice he sought instead of that of his old retainers.

## 5. The Reign of Sviatopolk II (1093–1113)

Following the death of his older brothers, Vsevolod had concentrated in his weak hands the whole authority of the triumvirate. The principle of genealogical seniority was not forgotten, however, and immediately after Vsevolod's passing, Iziaslav's son Sviatopolk occupied the Kievan throne, allowing his cousin, Vsevolod's son Vladimir Monomach, to keep Chernigov. This was an infringement of the principle of seniority, since that city had been held by the second member of the triumvirate, Sviatoslav, and the latter's sons now claimed it. In 1094 one of them, Oleg, arrived at Chernigov from Tmutorokan with a band of Cumans and Vladimir decided to com-

32. Cross, p. 265.

promise. He made peace with Oleg and leaving him Chernigov moved to Pereiaslav. In a sense the original triumvirate of Iaroslav's sons now seemed restored by his grandsons. There was, however, even less cohesion in the second triumvirate than in the first, especially because of Oleg's attitude of suspicion and aloofness. Although he had recovered Chernigov, he could not so easily forget his earlier misfortunes and expected his cousins to use the first suitable pretext to drive him away once more. He gave them the pretext himself by his ambiguous policy toward the Cumans.

Upon receiving the news of Vsevolod's death, the latter sent proposals of peace to Sviatopolk but he ignored them and arrested the envoys. Although he later released them, the Cumans were enraged and attacked Russia in force. Defeating the combined forces of Sviatopolk and Vladimir in a fierce battle, they pierced the Russian rampart at Tripolie and scattered marauding expeditions throughout the countryside. After a brief siege the fortified town of Torchesk surrendered to them, the inhabitants being weakened by hunger. As nomads ravaged the southern districts of the Kievan and Pereiaslav lands they led away droves of Russian captives, men and women. A striking picture of the sufferings of the population is given in the *Book of Annals*.

A multitude of Christian people were thus reduced to dire distress: sorrowing, tormented, weak with cold, their faces ravaged with hunger, thirst and misfortune, their bodies black with blows, as they made their painful way, naked and barefoot, upon feet torn with thorns, toward an unknown land and barbarous races. In tears they made answer one to another, saying, "I was of this city," and others, "I came from that village." Thus they tearfully questioned one another, and spoke of their families, as they sighed and lifted up eyes to the Most High, who knoweth all secrets.[33]

In 1094 Sviatopolk made peace with the Cumans and took to wife the daughter of Khan Tugorkan. Vladimir, however, was no party to the agreement and when in 1095 Cuman envoys came to Pereiaslav he ordered them killed. The chronicler relates that he did so at the insistence of his retainers. The war began anew, Sviatopolk joining his cousin against the invaders despite his connection by marriage. Both urged Oleg to help them but he remained neutral. The war went badly for the Russians. Several more towns in the Kievan land were destroyed and the environs of Pereiaslav plundered. The Cumans attacked the city itself but were beaten off, and Sviatopolk's father-

33. *Idem*, p. 270.

in-law, Khan Tugorkan, lost his life in the battle. Simultaneously, however, another Cuman khan, Boniak the Mangy, dashed to Kiev and burned several churches and palaces.

Worried by Oleg's neutrality, Sviatopolk and Vladimir sent him an ultimatum either to join them or to face their enmity. Oleg "assumed an attitude of arrogance" [34] and disregarded the ultimatum. His cousins then ousted him from Chernigov. He went to Smolensk, which was ruled by his brother David, and gathering troops there set forth for Murom on the lower Oka River, a city held by Vladimir's son Iziaslav. The latter refused to surrender and made a stand before the city but was killed in the battle, and Oleg entered Murom. When news of his son's death reached Vladimir the latter wrote a remarkable letter to Oleg, permeated by a spirit of forbearance.[35] Accepting Iziaslav's death as God's judgment, he implored Oleg to cease hostilities and to come to a mutual understanding. Oleg's answer was to seize the city of Rostov in Suzdalia. At this juncture Vladimir's eldest son Mstislav, the powerful viceroy of Novgorod, took the matter in his own hands and, attacking Oleg, chased him from one town to another until he retired to Riazan. Mstislav then sent him the following message: "Flee no more, but rather approach your brethren with the request that they may not expel you from Russia. I shall intervene with my father in your behalf." [36] Oleg accepted the proposal and the feud was over.

It may be remarked that in the entire episode both Vladimir and his son Mstislav showed a high degree of moderation and sense of constructive statesmanship. Peace, not revenge, was their goal. As soon as Oleg agreed to negotiate they proposed the convocation of an interprincely conciliation conference to eliminate any discord. The meeting took place at Liubech in 1097 and the following princes were present: Sviatopolk II; Vladimir Monomach; David, son of Igor of Volynia; Vasilko, son of Rostislav; and two sons of Sviatoslav II, David and Oleg. The conference thus represented all branches of Iaroslav's descendants. Note that even the sons of Rostislav were represented in the parleys, despite the fact that their father during his lifetime was denied a share in the common heritage. It may be remembered that before his Tmutorokan venture Rostislav attempted to establish himself in Galicia; here each of his three sons eventually

34. *Idem,* p. 272.
35. *Idem,* pp. 310–312.
36. *Idem,* p. 278.

succeeded in carving out a small principality for himself. The eldest, Riurik, died in 1092, so that by the time of the Liubech conference only two remained: Volodar and Vasilko. Of these, only Vasilko was present at the conference.

The decisions of the conference are recorded in the *Book of Annals* in the following form. The princes "said to one another":

Why do we ruin the Russian land by our continued strife against one another? The Cumans harass our country in divers fashions, and rejoice that war is waged among us. Let us rather hereafter be united in spirit and watch over the Russian land, and let each of us guard his own domain: with Sviatopolk retaining Kiev, the heritage of Iziaslav, while Vladimir holds the domain of Vsevolod [i.e., Pereiaslav], and David, Oleg, and Iaroslav between them possess that of Sviatoslav [their father—i.e., Chernigov]. Let the domains apportioned by Vsevolod stand, leaving the city of Vladimir [in Volynia] in the hands of David [son of Igor], while the city of Peremyshl belongs to Volodar, and Vasilko holds Terebovl.[37]

This important declaration introduced a new element into inter-princely relations. While the principle of seniority was not abrogated, that of the special rights of each princely branch to its patrimony was now recognized. Thus the conference tried to be realistic in its approach to the claims of each member and it could be hoped that at least some degree of stability had been reached.

It was not easy, however, for all the princes to abandon the attitude of greediness and mutual distrust. This time David of Volynia was responsible for the breach of the peace. He suspected Vasilko of Galicia of intending to expand his authority to Volynia (David's own appanage) and decided to seek Sviatopolk's protection, warning the latter that, according to his information, Vladimir Monomach was conspiring with Vasilko against Sviatopolk and himself. Sviatopolk finally believed him and, inviting Vasilko to Kiev, treacherously arrested him and turned him over to David, whose agents blinded the unhappy Galician prince.

Blinding political rivals, especially potential candidates to the throne, was an established practice in Byzantium but until the Vasilko case the Russian princes had never used this method in their mutual struggles. The news of the crime shocked all Russia. "When Vladimir learned that Vasilko was captured and blinded, he was horror-struck, and bursting into tears declared, 'Such a crime as this has never been perpetrated in Russia in the time of either our grandfathers or our

37. *Idem*, p. 279.

fathers.' " The Sviatoslavichi (sons of Sviatoslav), David and Oleg, were likewise deeply troubled, saying, "Such a thing never before happened in our family." [38] Vladimir and the Sviatoslavichi immediately got together to discuss the situation. Apart from the terrible injury inflicted on Vasilko, Sviatopolk's separate action was a breach of the Liubech agreement. This was emphasized in the joint message they sent to Sviatopolk: "If there was any charge against Vasilko, you should have accused him before us." [39] Sviatopolk tried to evade responsibility by putting all the blame on David of Volynia.

Not satisfied by the explanation, Vladimir and the Sviatoslavichi decided to punish him and marched on Kiev. The Kievans were perturbed and, fearing the seemingly inevitable civil war, sent Vsevolod's widow (Vladimir's mother-in-law) and the metropolitan to Vladimir with the plea, "We beseech you, oh Prince, and your brethren not to ruin the Russian Land." [40] Vladimir was faced with a moral dilemma: to let the breach of the Liubech agreement and the blinding of Vasilko go unpunished or be responsible for new bloodshed. In this spiritual conflict he obeyed his mother-in-law, "as he was bound to obey his mother, and he respected the metropolitan as well (for he revered ecclesiastical rank), and did not disregard his plea." [41] Calling the war off, Vladimir and the Sviatoslavichi imposed on Sviatopolk the task of punishing David.

Threatened by both Sviatopolk and Volodar (Vasilko's brother), David released Vasilko. This, however, did not satisfy his opponents and he was obliged to face a war, which was further aggravated by a conflict between Sviatopolk and the Rostislavichi (sons of Rostislav). Finally, a new interprincely conference was held at Uvetichi which settled the conflict by depriving David of the throne of Volynia. He was granted the town of Buzhsk for his sustenance (1100).

In the following year there was another meeting of the interprincely conference, at which peace was concluded with the Cumans. It was not of long duration, for in 1103, in the chronicler's words, "God inspired a noble project in the hearts of the Russian princes, Sviatopolk and Vladimir," [42] and they resolved to attack the Cumans in force and invade their territory. They invited the Sviatoslavichi to join them. Oleg refused, referring to his illness, but David accepted. The

38. *Idem*, p. 282.
39. *Idem*, pp. 282–283.
40. *Idem*, p. 283.
41. *Ibid.*
42. *Idem*, p. 292.

campaign was highly successful: twenty Cuman princes were slain and one taken prisoner. Huge booty was seized—sheep and cattle, horses and camels, tents and slaves.

It took four years for the Cumans to recover. In 1107 two of theii Khans—the old Boniak and Sharukan—raided the Pereiaslav land. They were, however, repulsed with great losses. Four years later came the climax. In 1111 the three allied Russian princes, Sviatopolk, Vladimir, and David, penetrated deep into the steppes, reaching as far as the Don River. The city of Sharukan surrendered and its inhabitants offered gifts of fish and wine to the Russians. The main Cuman army was then crushed on the banks of the Salnitsa River. The Russian triumph was unprecedented and, as the leading role in the campaign had been played by Vladimir Monomach, his popularity increased immensely.

While Sviatopolk participated in the campaigns against the Cumans, his attention was focussed mainly toward the west. He married one of his daughters to King Boleslaw II of Poland (1102) and another to the son of the king of Hungary (1104). These diplomatic marriages were meant to strengthen the friendly relations between Russia, Poland, and Hungary, but Sviatopolk seems to have been interested even more in promoting trade relations than in diplomacy as such. The Cuman attacks must have severed for several years the Dnieper riverway to Byzantium and Russian merchants were eager to intensify their commercial connections with the western countries. As Sviatopolk was attempting to monopolize the salt trade in Russia, he must have coveted the Galician salt mines but the Rostislavichi could not be expected to yield them. He could, however, buy salt from the Wieliczka mines in Poland.

While the Russians had won an overwhelming victory over the nomads by the close of Sviatopolk II's reign, the devastation wrought by the Cumans prior to the campaign of 1111 was serious enough to upset the economic and social life of Russia's southern regions. The population losses must have been tremendous. Even those who escaped death or captivity were ruined. Many had to borrow money from the Kievan capitalists or from wealthy landowners and, not being able to repay their loans, had to agree to work for their creditors on conditions dictated by the latter.

Thus, while part of the population suffered, the owners of the large estates in unmolested sections of the country profited by the supply of cheap labor, and the Kievan capitalists by collecting interest at exorbitant rates. High prices on salt, which resulted from Sviatopolk's monopoly, added to the general discontent. The resounding victory over the Cumans distracted public opinion for a while but drastic internal reforms were needed to eliminate the abuses of the financiers. No such reforms could be expected from Sviatopolk, since he himself was deeply involved in financial speculations.

### 6. A Social Legislator: Vladimir Monomach

Sviatopolk's death on April 16, 1113, released the forces of the opposition. The violent outburst which followed was dubbed by the late M. N. Pokrovsky a "social revolution"; because of the wholesale rejection of Pokrovsky's views in recent Soviet historiography, however, the Kievan events of 1113 are now called just "riots." No matter what we call them, they amounted to a serious political and social crisis.

On April 17 the Kievan city assembly (*veche*) met in an emergency session. Under normal conditions such a meeting after a prince's death would be convoked by the metropolitan and the boyars but their authorization is nowhere mentioned in the chronicles for this meeting. Presumably it was an assembly of democratic elements only and its spirit was revolutionary. The assembly resolved to invite Vladimir Monomach, Prince of Pereiaslav, to ascend the Kievan throne. As recorded in the Hypatian Chronicle, "on hearing this message, Vladimir wept, and refused to accept, mourning for his brother [i.e., cousin]." [43]

The motives for his refusal are understandable. First of all, he must have been reluctant to accept the Kievan throne from the hands of the democratic elements of the population only, since this would entail his taking repressive measures against the late Sviatopolk's boyars. Furthermore, Vladimir must have been expected officially to repudiate the policies of his late cousin, with whom he had maintained friendly relations. Finally, he hesitated to accept the Kievan throne without being authorized to do so by an interprincely conference, since otherwise he might be faced with a stubborn opposition on the part of the princes of senior branches—both of Sviatopolk's brothers and the Sviatoslavichi.

Whatever his motives, he refused to come to Kiev. Then it was that

43. *Idem*, p. 319.

the riots started "The men of Kiev plundered the palace of the chiliarch, Putiata, and attacked and robbed the Jews." [44] As the dis-
orders became more and more violent, both the church authorities
and the men of the upper classes were alarmed and, though they
seem previously not to have approved the veche decision to offer
Vladimir the throne, they now sent him frantic messages imploring
him to save order in the state.

"Come, oh Prince, to Kiev; and if you do not come, know that
much evil will befall. For it will not be merely a matter of robbing
the palace of Putiata, of the hundreders, or the Jews, but they will
attack your sister-in-law [i.e., Sviatopolk's widow], the boyars, and
the monasteries, and if they plunder the monasteries, you will be
responsible for it." [45]

Now that the aristocratic elements of the population seconded the
democratic in inviting him to the throne, it was apparent that only
through Vladimir's mediation could a social revolution be averted.
He did not flinch from the responsibility but went to Kiev, where, in
the chronicler's words, "he was met with great honor by the metropolitan Nicephorus, the bishops, and all the inhabitants. He thus
assumed the throne of his father and his ancestors, and all the people
rejoiced, and the rioting was quelled." [46]

In analyzing these April events we must differentiate between the
immediate actions of the Kievan revolutionaries and their general
program. Their first moves were directed against the agents of Sviatopolk's administration (the chiliarch and the hundreders) and against
his financial advisers (the Jews). The plundering of the houses of high
officials and capitalists was apparently a spontaneous action of the
revolutionary mob. It is obvious, however, that the leaders contemplated a more radical move—the confiscation of the wealth of the
upper classes at large, that is, of the boyars and the merchants, and
also of the monasteries. Incidentally, one should not suppose that
the movement was anti-Semitic. There was no general Jewish pogrom.
Wealthy Jewish merchants suffered because of their association with
Sviatopolk's speculations, especially his hated monopoly on salt.

Vladimir's first move was to replace the chiliarch of Kiev by a man
he trusted. He then gathered a conference of the highest officials to
revise legislation in regard to loans and indentured labor. Besides the

44. *Ibid.*
45. *Ibid.*
46. *Idem*, p. 320.

new chiliarch of Kiev, the chiliarchs of Belgorod and Pereiaslav participated in the conference, as well as two other retainers of Vladimir and a retainer of Prince Oleg of Chernigov. The presence of the latter is evidence of Oleg's acceptance of Vladimir's rule in Kiev. To take personal part in a conference held for the benefit of the lower classes was, however, too much for Oleg and he sent a retainer instead.

The conference resolved to prevent the abuses connected with short-term loans and to limit the interest on long-term loans. Further, the authority of the lord over indentured laborers was somewhat limited and their enslavement forbidden. To legalize the self-selling of impoverished men into slavery certain formalities were now required as a guarantee against fraud.

These measures could hardly satisfy the radical wing of the opposition. They proved sufficient, however, to restore public confidence in the princely power.

It should be borne in mind that Vladimir's interference in favor of the lower classes was not only the result of his enlightened statesmanship but an evidence of his deep Christian spirit. Social legislation was for him an extension of Christian charity. In his famous "Testament" he instructs his sons: "Give to the orphan, protect the widow, and permit the mighty to destroy no man." And he describes his own policies in a similar vein: "I did not allow the mighty to distress the poor peasant (*smerd*) or the poverty-stricken widow." [47]

Vladimir's "Testament" (instruction to his sons), besides being a precious piece of old Russian literature, is also a human document of great significance.[48] It reveals an old Russian prince at his best. The two pillars of Christianity for Vladimir are the fear of God and love of fellow men, of which charity is an essential expression.

He has a strong feeling of responsibility and emphasizes the importance for the prince of keeping his word. "Whenever you kiss the Cross to confirm an oath made to your brethren or to any other man, first test your heart as to whether you can abide by your word, then kiss the Cross, and after having given your oath, abide by it, lest you destroy your souls by its violation." [49] It may be seen from the chonicles that Vladimir actually followed this rule in his relations with other Russian princes.

47. *Idem*, pp. 305, 309.
48. On the "Testament" ("Admonition," *Pouchenie*) of Vladimir Monomach, see Chap. IX n. 74.
49. Cross, p. 305.

A true Christian, Vladimir was not, however, an ascetic. He admired nature and loved life in all its aspects. Work and not ascetic retirement was his advice to his sons. In his brief autobiography, which constitutes an important part of the "Testament," he relates his chief military campaigns as well as his hunting expeditions. He does not boast of his military victories and there is no vanity in the narrative. The feudal spirit of knightly glory is entirely alien to him. All he sets down of his Cuman campaign of the year 1111 is the following laconic note: "With Sviatopolk and David, I later went as far as the Don, and God granted us his aid." [50] While he is more outspoken about his hunting achievements, war and the hunt are for him part of his princely labors. He speaks of his fatigues more than of his exploits, which perfectly agrees with his favorite maxim, "Laziness is the mother of all evil."

Vladimir attributes a high value to education and learning: "Forget not what useful knowledge you possess, and acquire that with which you are not acquainted, even as my father, though he remained at home in his own country, learned five [foreign] languages." [51] Vladimir was well educated himself and fond of reading. As with many of his contemporaries, his favorite religious books were the Psalter and the Prophets.

Vladimir was Vsevolod's son by his first wife, a Greek princess presumably of the Monomach family, hence his surname. Family ties must have been influential in his friendly attitude toward Byzantium. Among other things, this attitude was revealed in his support of Grecophile tendencies in the Russian church, for which he has been blamed by some modern Russian historians of nationalistic spirit.

## 7. The First Two Monomashichi (1125-39)

The popularity of Vladimir Monomach is evidenced by the fact that after his death (1125) his eldest son Mstislav assumed the Kievan throne without opposition either on the part of the people of Kiev or that of other princes. Even the Olgovichi of Chernigov did not object, in any case not openly.

Mstislav I (1125-32) proved to be as strong and conscientious a ruler as his father. He was Vladimir's son by his first wife, Princess Gyda of England, daughter of Harold II. His Nordic connections

50. *Idem*, p. 308.
51. *Idem*, p. 305.

were further fortified by marriage to Princess Christina of Sweden, daughter of King Ingue. In Norse sources Mstislav is referred to as Harald. During his father's life he was at first prince of Novgorod, then titular prince of Belgorod. In leaving Novgorod, Mstislav left there his son Vsevolod, whom the Novgorodians gladly recognized as their prince (1117). Thus he did not actually sever his connection with the northern metropolis and it is significant that after the death of his first wife he married a daughter of the mayor of that city (1122).

His popularity in Novgorod greatly helped him when he became prince of Kiev. Being the most powerful of the Russian princes he succeeded in keeping the whole clan of Monomashichi in good order. His brothers ruled as follows: Iaropolk in Pereiaslav, Viacheslav in Turov, Iuri in Suzdalia, and Andrei in Volynia. Mstislav also intervened in Galicia, held by the Rostislavichi, and Chernigov, the patrimony of the Olgovichi. In both principalities there was a strife between the older and younger princes of the same branch. Mstislav supported the older in each case. However, the younger won in both instances. The energetic Vsevolod, son of Oleg, seized Chernigov in 1127 and the crafty Vladimirko, son of Volodar, was recognized prince of Peremyshl (then the capital of Galicia) around 1130. But, while opposing Mstislav's attempts to interfere with their family affairs, both the Olgovichi and the Rostislavichi had to recognize him as the senior Russian prince.

Mstislav's closest assistant was his brother Iaropolk, prince of Pereiaslav. Together they shaped the course of Russian foreign policy with the obvious objective of keeping open the commercial highway between the Baltic and the Azov areas. Iaropolk, a brilliant warrior, assumed the task of clearing the way to the lower Don. His first campaign against the Cumans took place in 1116. He took many captives, among them an Ossetian princess whom he married. Ten years later he administered another crushing defeat to the Cumans. He did not succeed, however, in establishing his control over the Azov area permanently.

Mstislav's own attention was focussed on the Baltic area. In order to eliminate any obstacles to his power among the princes of Polotsk, he seized their land and exiled all members of the Polotsk princely family to Constantinople (1130). He also waged a successful war against the Lithuanians (1131). Meanwhile his son Vsevolod of Novgorod imposed his authority on the Finnish tribes in eastern Estonia.

After Mstislav's death the people of Kiev invited his brother Iaropolk to occupy the throne. As prince of Kiev he is known as Iaropolk II (1132–39). He attempted to continue Mstislav's policies but was less fortunate; the only achievement of his foreign policy was the further success in Estonia of his nephew Vsevolod, who reoccupied Iuriev in 1133.

The major cause of Iaropolk's troubles was his inability to keep in check his own clan, that of the Monomashichi. One of his brothers, Iuri of Suzdalia, revolted against him and invaded the land of Pereiaslav. While Iaropolk was able to recover it, the Olgovichi of Chernigov lost no time in taking advantage of the inner strife in the Monomashichi clan. Prince Vsevolod of Chernigov, who had kept quiet during the reign of Mstislav, now presented his claims for some border lands between the Chernigov and the Pereiaslav principalities. Not trusting his own forces, he concluded an alliance with the Cumans, who were certainly glad to have an opportunity of raiding Russia once more. Iaropolk hastened to make peace with Iuri but it was already too late. Defeated by Vsevolod and his Cuman allies he had to satisfy the former's claims (1135).

As soon as the Pereiaslav problem was settled a new crisis arose in Novgorod. In 1136 the people revolted against their prince, Vsevolod, son of Mstislav, who was put under arrest in the bishop's palace and then exiled. On this occasion the Novgorod city assembly passed a resolution reserving the right of acquiring landed estates in Novgorod to Novgorodian citizens only. For any grants of state land in Novgorod a specific approval of the assembly was required besides. The new law was probably the reinstatement of an old custom; it was primarily directed against the prince and his retainers and it may be assumed that the reason for issuing it was some abuse on the part of Vsevolod. The latter must have recognized the validity of the new law, since in 1137 he was invited again to reign in Novgorod. He died, however, before he could assume office.

Following Vsevolod's death the Novgorodians accepted as their prince a candidate recommended by Iuri of Suzdalia. For this price the latter gave Iaropolk active support against Vsevolod of Chernigov, who had profited by the Novgorodian troubles to present more claims, but, receiving little help this time from the Cumans, had to sue for peace (1139). In the same year Iaropolk II died. Although he had succeeded in holding the throne of Kiev until his death, in his reign both the supremacy of Kiev and the unity of Russia were shattered almost beyond recovery.

# Chapter V

# ECONOMIC FOUNDATIONS OF KIEVAN RUSSIA

## *1. Introductory Remarks*

IN THE three preceding chapters I have outlined the main trends of Russian political development from the late ninth century through the first third of the twelfth century. In Chapter VIII I shall continue that outline down to the Mongol invasion of 1237 but we have now to pause for a systematic assay of the fundamentals of Russian economics as well as of social and political organization in the Kievan period.

There are two schools of thought in modern Russian historiography as to what was the main factor in the economic development of Kievan Russia: the "traditional" school and the "revolutionary." According to the former, of which the late V. O. Kliuchevsky was the outstanding spokesman, foreign trade must be considered the foundation of early Russian economics as well as the main formative factor in the progress of the Kievan state. According to the latter school, of which B. D. Grekov is the best-known representative, in the Kievan period just as later in the Muscovite period agriculture and not trade was the mainstay of both state and society.

Kliuchevsky went so far in expounding his theory that he all but denied to agriculture any important role in the economic life of Kievan Russia. Grekov cannot completely deny the role of foreign trade in the Kievan period: that role is too obvious. He tries, however, to minimize its importance and questions its vitality.

Says Kliuchevsky:

The history of our people would have been substantially different if, in the course of some eight or nine centuries [i.e., in the Kievan and Muscovite periods], our economics had not presented an historical contradiction to the nature of our country. In the eleventh century the mass of the Russian population centered around the black-soil middle Dnieper region, while toward the middle of the fifteenth century it moved to the Upper Volga region. It would seem that in the former region agriculture should have become the foundation of the national economy, and in the latter, foreign trade as well as the forest and other industries. However, the concurrence of external events resulted in the fact that so long as the Russians sat on the Dnieper region black soil, they traded in products of the forest and other industries, and started ploughing only when they moved to the upper Volga region argillaceous soil.[1]

And says Grekov:

It seems to me that there is no evidence in our sources to prove any of the main statements of Kliuchevsky, Rozhkov, and their followers. In Kievan, Novgorodian, and Suzdalian Russia agriculture was the main occupation of the people.[2]

What stand shall we take in the controversy?

It must be said first of all that Kliuchevsky's basic idea—that of an almost wholesale migration of the population of the middle Dnieper region to the upper Volga, which allegedly took place in the period between the eleventh and the fifteenth centuries and to which he ascribes the rise of Muscovite Russia—this very idea is unacceptable.

We know that the Slavs appeared in the north of Russia centuries before the establishment of the Kievan state; that they penetrated into the Novgorod region as early as in the fourth century; that the upper Volga-Oka region was colonized by them—from Smolensk and Novgorod, and not from Kiev—not later than the seventh century. We likewise know that, according to the archaeological evidence, not only Slavs but Lithuanians and Finns as well practiced agriculture in the north long before the eleventh century, not to speak of the fifteenth.

In his remarkable study, of which I was unable to make full use in my volume, *Ancient Russia,* P. N. Tretiakov has shown convincingly that the inhabitants of the upper Volga region, whom he considers proto-Slavs, were acquainted with agriculture from at least the third century; and that in the seventh century the people in those parts, by this time undoubtedly Slavs, passed from primitive agricultural methods (*podsechnoe zemledelie*) to regular plowing of the land.[3]

Thus even in northern and central Russia agriculture played an important role in the economic life of the people long before the eleventh century. And very much so, of course, in the Ukraine.

It is known that as early as in the Scythian era some of the tribes

1. V. O. Kliuchevsky, *Boiarskaia Duma drevnei Rusi,* p. 13.
2. B. D. Grekov, *Kievskaia Rus',* p. 35.
3. P. N. Tretiakov, "K istorii plemen verkhnego Povolzhia," *MIAS,* V (1941).

subject to the Scythian kings—such, for example, as the "Scythian-Agriculturists" and the "Scythian-Plowmen"—raised a variety of crops. According to Byzantine sources the Antes in the sixth century cultivated lands and stored grain in their settlements. According to Oriental sources the Slavs in the eighth century supplied the Khazars and the Magyars with grain. It is known from the Russian *Book of Annals* that one of the east Slavic tribes, the Viatichians, paid to the Khazars as their tribute one coin for each plow, which implies that the plow was their main tool for subsistence.

In the written sources of the Kievan period there is an abundance of reference to agriculture and grain. And all this evidence is strongly corroborated by archaeological data.[4] Thus there cannot be any doubt that agriculture was one of the mainstays of Russian national economy in the Kievan period. The "historical paradox" to which Kliuchevsky refers was but the product of his own brain.

However, from admitting the value of agriculture for Kievan Russia it does not follow that we should deny the role of foreign trade or even minimize it, as does Grekov. As in the case of agriculture, there is evidence enough to assert the vitality of commerce in the economics of western Eurasia from time immemorial. Foreign trade, moreover, was undoubtedly the primary factor in shaping the policy of all the empires in the Pontic steppes, from the Scythian down to the Khazar.

What is even more important for our problem, by the time of the establishment of the Kievan state, trade in grain played but a minor role—if any—in Russian foreign commerce. The bulk of it consisted of the products of hunting and forest industries, including furs, wax, and honey. Even Grekov cannot deny this. While we cannot accept Kliuchevsky's views on agriculture, therefore, we have still to follow his lead in regard to the importance of nonagricultural products in the foreign trade of Kievan Russia, in any case in the tenth century.

This is a very important point in view of the use made of the data on agriculture by partisans of the school to which Grekov belongs to interpret the sociological foundations of Kievan Russia. Since, generally speaking, agriculture constituted the basis of feudalism in western Europe, it is argued that its growth in Kievan Russia is irrefutable proof of a thorough feudalization of Russia in that period. To admit a paramount importance of foreign trade would, from the point of view of Grekov and his school, endanger the whole scheme.

One may say, roughly, that in its early stages European feudalism

4. See Grekov, *op. cit.*, pp. 26–31.

was based on a closed economy; any very substantial development of foreign trade, by contrast, presupposes a considerable growth of money economy. There is here, then, a potential contradiction and a new problem. We shall return to it in Chapter VI and must turn now to a survey of the data on various aspects of Kievan economics.

## 2. Natural Resources and Population

The Russian expansion of the seventeenth, eighteenth, and nineteenth centuries resulted in providing the peoples of Russia—now the Soviet Union—with a vast territory well stocked with mineral deposits and natural resources of various kinds. The country is all but self-sufficient in regard to raw materials.

In the Kievan period the Russians controlled only the western part of the modern U.S.S.R., and not even all of that, since the middle and lower basin of the Volga River was occupied by Turkish peoples, as were likewise the southern steppes. The south—Ukraine and the Donets Basin (Donbas)—is today one of the two main metallurgical and mining centers of what is known as the European part of the Soviet Union; the Ural region is the other. In the Kievan period small parties of Russian explorers penetrated into the Ural region only in its northernmost part and, as I have just said, the Russians were likewise excluded from the south. They were thus deprived of the richest mining areas. It must be added that, even if they had not been, they could hardly have made proper use of any deep mineral deposits since they were not sufficiently acquainted with the techniques of mining.

However, even in the Kievan period the Russians were not altogether deprived of access to mineral deposits. There were at their disposal vast areas containing plenty of near-surface iron ore, chiefly in swamps and on lake shores. Such deposits were available both in western Russia (Volynia) and in the north. In many archaeological sites of Slavic settlements, dating even from the early Kievan period, evidence of the extraction and smelting of iron has been found. In the north the swamp iron deposits at Ustiuzhna were exploited by neighboring peasants as late as in the nineteenth century.[5]

When all is said, however, the main natural resources of Kievan

5. See N. Ia. Aristov, *Promyshlennost' drevnei Rusi*, pp. 111–112; M. D. Khmyrov, *Metally, metallicheskie izdeliia i mineraly v drevnei Rossii* (St. Petersburg, 1875), pp. 18–33, 51–52, 63; M. V. Dovnar-Zapolsky, *Istoriia Russkogo narodnogo khoziaistva*, I, 248–249; S. G. Strumilin, *Chernaia metallurgiia v Rossii i S.S.S.R.* (Moscow, 1935), pp. 113–114; G. Vernadsky, "Iron Mining and Iron Industries in Medieval Russia," *Études dédiées à la mémoire d'André Andreadès* (Athens, 1939), pp. 361–366.

Russia consisted not in her mines but in her forests, her tillable lands, and—for fishing—her lakes and rivers. And of course her outstanding asset was the people themselves: a sturdy and healthy race according to all we know of them.

There are no statistics concerning the population of Kievan Russia. It is only by considering that of neighboring countries and by analyzing the data on the Russian population in later periods that we may venture to offer a tentative estimate of the Russian population in the Kievan period. As a starting point, let us first examine the figures available for computing the population of the Near East and of central and western Europe in late antiquity and the Middle Ages. The population of the Roman Empire in the period of its greatest expansion was around eighty million. Within the boundaries of the Byzantine Empire, in the age of Justinian I in the sixth century, there lived not less than twenty-five million persons. The population of the Ottoman Empire in the sixteenth century was not less than fifteen million.

In western Europe the population of England in the first half of the fourteenth century—that is, prior to the "Black Death" epidemics—was from four to five million. In France and western Germany, Charlemagne in the late eighth and early ninth century must have had around eight million subjects. In the first half of the fourteenth century the population of France was close to twenty million.

The estimates for Germany run from three million for the tenth century to six million for the eleventh century. In the twelfth century, according to Kötschke, it reached a figure between seven and eight million; in the first half of the fourteenth century, according to Schmoller, around twelve million. The population of Hungary in the late fifteenth century was around four million.[6]

Let us now turn to Russia. In the *Entsiklopedicheskii Slovar'* published by Brockhaus and Efron the population of Russia is estimated at 2.1 million for the late fifteenth century.[7] M. V. Dovnar-Zapolsky's estimate is two million for the middle of the sixteenth century.[8] These figures are mere guesses and are undoubtedly the result of some misunderstanding. Much more reliable is P. N. Miliukov's computation.[9]

6. For Germany, see P. A. Sorokin, *Social and Cultural Dynamics* (New York, American Book Company, 1937), III, 343–344. For Hungary, see S. Szabo, *Ungarisches Volk* (Budapest and Leipzig, 1944), pp. 50–53.

7. *ES*, Half-Volume XL (1897), 631.

8. Dovnar-Zapolsky, *op. cit.*, I, 57–58.

9. P. N. Miliukov, *Ocherki po istorii russkoi kultury*, I (7th ed. Moscow, 1918), 27–28.

He starts his argument with the figure of thirteen million for the population of the Russian Empire in the year of Peter the Great's death. This is based on a census and thus is fairly reliable, although we may suppose that a number of people managed at the time to avoid being counted in order to escape taxation, since the purpose of the census was to establish a national list of taxpayers. Moreover, the constant wars of Peter's reign resulted in heavy casualties and must have depleted the population. Therefore, Miliukov argues, Russia's population must have been more numerous in the late seventeenth century than in 1725. He offers the figure sixteen million for the year 1676 and fifteen million for the late sixteenth century.

P. P. Smirnov considers the latter estimates too high.[10] On the other hand, we must bear in mind that Miliukov's figures refer to the tsardom of Muscovy only. According to Polish historians the Ruthenian (Ukrainian and Belorussian) population within Poland and Lithuania was around two and a half million in the sixteenth century.[11] Thus, even if we considerably lower Miliukov's figures for the latter part of the century, we cannot estimate the total population of Russia in that period at less than twelve million, which is probably still too low. Due to constant wars and Tartar raids there was hardly any marked increase in population between the late fifteenth and late sixteenth centuries. Thus for the late fifteenth century we may conjecture a figure of ten million, or perhaps nine, but no less.

In the middle of the fourteenth century Russia, together with all Europe, was stricken by the great plague. In the mid-thirteenth century she was devastated by the Mongols. On the eve of the Mongol invasion, therefore—that is, in the early part of the thirteenth century—the population can not have been much smaller than in the late fifteenth century. It appears, then, that a figure of between seven and eight million for the twelfth century would be a rather conservative estimate.[12]

Any attempt to calculate the proportion of urban population in Kievan Russia must be only tentative. Around three hundred cities are mentioned in the sources for this period. Most of them must have been rather small towns but there were also large cities among them

10. P. P. Smirnov, "Dvizhenie naseleniia Moskovskogo gosudarstva," *Russkaia istoriia*, M. V. Dovnar-Zapolsky, ed., II, 67–69.

11. J. Rutkowski, *Histoire économique de la Pologne* (Paris, 1927), p. 90.

12. G. Vernadsky, *Zvenya Russkoi kultury*, I, 25–30. A. I. Iakovlev, using a different method of computation, has arrived at similar conclusions; see his book, *Kholopstvo i kholopy v Moskovskom gosudarstve*, I (Moscow and Leningrad, 1943), 298.

if we judge by the standards of the time. The combined population of the three major cities—Kiev, Novgorod, and Smolensk—was probably no less than four hundred thousand. The urban population of Russia as a whole in the late twelfth and early thirteenth centuries can hardly have been less than one million. If we assume the figure of 7,500,000 for the whole population, the proportion of urban population to the total will be around thirteen per cent, which is a much higher proportion than in the Muscovite period and corresponds to the situation in the late nineteenth century.

### 3. Hunting, Apiculture, and Fishing

Hunting was the favorite sport of the Russian princes of the Kievan period. In his "Testament" Prince Vladimir Monomach recalls his main hunting exploits with obvious pride and warmth of feeling in the following words:

At Chernigov, I even bound wild horses with my bare hands or captured ten or twenty live horses with the lasso, and besides that, while riding along the Ros River, I caught these same wild horses barehanded. Two bisons tossed me and my horse on their horns, a stag once gored me, one elk stamped upon me, while another gored me, a boar once tore my sword from my thigh, a bear on one occasion bit my kneecap, and another wild beast jumped on my flank and threw my horse with me. But God preserved me unharmed.[18]

Speaking of the animals and birds which populate the forests and fields of Russia, Vladimir says: "All these blessings God has bestowed upon us for the delight, sustenance, and pleasure of mankind." [14]

Even with the princes, hunting was not merely a sport but an essential industry; much more so with the commoners, especially in the forest zone of northern Russia. First, it supplied food to a considerable section of the population; second, it provided furs which were needed for warm clothing, for the payment of taxes (instead of money), and for commerce; in the third place, it was one of the means of obtaining hides for leather work.

Animals and birds were killed with either arrows or spears or caught alive with nets and snares of various kinds. Small snares were used for catching birds. Huge nets were hung between trees in the forests to entrap animals, which were roused and driven into them by beaters. Hunting with hounds was also popular. Some of the princes

13. Cross, pp. 308–309.
14. *Idem*, p. 304.

even had hunting leopards. While commoners hunted by themselves or formed hunting associations, the princes and boyars employed professional huntsmen of various sorts, such as whips, falconers, and so on. A prince's hunt was more often than not a very elaborate establishment.

Because of the importance of hunting as an industry, preserves were protected by law. Each prince had his own places for hunting but preserves belonging to persons of other classes as well as to the churches and monasteries are also mentioned in the sources. In the *Russian Law* severe penalties were prescribed for trespassing in another's preserve as well as for the theft or destruction of a hunting net and for the killing of a hound.

Apiculture was another popular branch of forest industries. It was rather primitive: the bees were kept in the hollow trunks of forest trees. Such a hollow (*bort'*) might be natural but mostly they were specially cut in the trunk for the purpose. The trunk was then marked with the apiculturist's mark (*znamia*). The section of the forest containing marked beehive trees was preserved and the rights of the owner protected by law. A fine of three grivna was established by the *Pravda* for cutting another's beehive and of twelve grivna for deleting the owner's mark from the tree. Beehive preserves of both princes and commoners are mentioned in the sources of the period. Monks practiced apiculture as well and the princes used to grant some of their preserves to bishops and monasteries. Thus in 1150 Prince Rostislav of Smolensk gave to Bishop Manuel of the same city a beehive forest with the services of an apiculturist (*bortnik*).

The products of apiculture—wax and honey—were in great demand both within the country and outside it. Wax was needed for church candles, among other things; it was exported in great quantities both to Byzantium and to the west and, following the conversion of Russia, Russian churches and monasteries made demands upon it.

The Christianization of Russia should have raised the demand for fish as well, since a fish diet was now prescribed for fasting periods, especially for Lent. However, even in the twelfth century the Russians were poor observers of fasts and the princes on many occasions tried to obtain dispensation from them. Only in the monasteries was fasting a rigid rule. While the religious motive for preferring the fish diet produced fewer results than might be expected, fish was consumed in Russia both before and after the conversion and fishing consequently played a not inconsiderable role in Russian economics. Commercial fishing was developed chiefly on lakes and larger rivers. Fishing establishments in north Russia, as at the Volkhov River and at White Lake (Beloozero) are mentioned in the sources of the twelfth century. In the same period fishermen from Galicia established themselves on the lower Danube River. Sturgeon was considered the most valuable kind of fish.

Angling was practiced by individual fishermen in smaller rivers and ponds but for the commercial fisheries seines and dragnets of diverse kinds were chiefly used. In northern Russia a popular device was that of barring a small river with pales. In such a case several holes were made in the paling, at which creels were placed for the fish to be driven into. While this method of fishing is not mentioned in the sources prior to the fourteenth century, there can hardly be any doubt that it was applied in the earlier period as well.[15]

Banks of rivers and lakes convenient for fishery could be owned privately. Monasteries were especially anxious to have their own fishery establishments to secure the necessary supply of fish for the brethren for Lent.

In connection with fisheries, walrus catching in the Arctic Ocean and the White Sea may be likewise mentioned. Walrus were sought chiefly for their tusks, known in old Russian as "fish teeth." The Novgorodians dealt in them as early as the twelfth century.

## 4. Agriculture and Cattle Breeding

The basic geographic feature of "European Russia" (western Eurasia)—the division of the country along landscape zones—predetermined, as we have seen, the development of forest industries in the region north of the steppe border. With agriculture the situation was different, since it was, and indeed still is, possible to raise crops in both the steppe and forest zones. Nevertheless, the existence of different landscape zones exerted a profound influence on agricultural methods and techniques, resulting in a marked difference between the north and the south. The steppe zone with its rich black soil (*chernoziom*), is open to the farmer throughout and the only major technical problem which confronts him is the occasional one of irrigation in border regions between the steppe and arid desert zones.

In the forest zone man had to clear the woods before using any

15. Aristov, *op. cit.*, pp. 22–23.

part of the land for crops. In the intermediate forest-steppe zone it was possible to use the islands of treeless land for agriculture even before the cutting of trees in the forest enclaves.

Both in the north and in the south of Russia, agriculture—steadily but slowly evolving as it did from primitive conditions—passed through many stages. On the whole it may be said that the earliest stage was that of breaking up the soil with a hoe or primitive tool of similar sort and sowing seeds in the same operation. At this stage each plot of land was used only temporarily for raising crops. Gradually the next stage was reached, when fields were assigned for agricultural use on a permanent basis and were regularly tilled.

In the forest zone the work had to be started by cutting down trees and burning the underbrush. Such burned-out patches of woodland made fit for agriculture were known as *liada* (plural from *liado*). The operation as a whole is spoken of as *podseka* (cutting), or *liado* (burning out). In the first two or three years the yield was high, since wood ashes is a good fertilizer. After three or four years, however, the land on a given patch ceased to yield enough and new patches, prepared well in advance, were used. Meanwhile the previously tilled patch rapidly covered itself with young growth which had to be burned anew when the tiller needed it once more. Such an overgrown patch in the woods was known as a *liadina*. On the whole, the task of clearing and keeping up *liada* entailed hard work on the part of a considerable number of laborers and was above the forces of a single peasant family. Thus the practice of primitive agriculture in the forests presupposed the existence of coöperative guilds in the form of "greater family" communes (*zadruga*—see Chap. VI, sec. 1).

In the steppe zone the original system of using land was that of *perelog*—letting the land, after the first harvests, lie fallow for a number of years, without keeping any regular intervals or establishing any rotation of crops. In the steppes the virgin soil was so rich that after being plowed once it secured good harvests for a number of seasons, even without new tilling. When weeds spread and stifled the crops, the agriculturist would plow another strip of the steppe and return to the first only after some years. It may be noted that perelog agriculture was practiced by the Kazakhs (Kirghiz) as late as in the nineteenth century.[16]

---

16. On Russian agriculture in the Kievan period, see *idem*, pp. 48–64; A. Petrov, *Drevneishie gramoty po istorii Karpato-russkoi tserkvi* (Prague, 1930), pp. 79–84; J. Kulischer, *Russische Wirtschaftsgechichte*, pp. 86–88; Grekov, *op. cit.*, pp. 36–50.

Such lavishness in the use of the countryside is possible only so long as land is plentiful and population scarce. Wherever and whenever the supply of land becomes limited and private ownership is established, perelog agriculture has to be abandoned and the land can be allowed to lie fallow at regular intervals only. Historically this resulted in the appearance of the two-field, and later three-field, crop rotation system. That stage had already been reached in the Kievan period both in the south and in the north, in any case in the more thickly populated parts of each principality. In the backwoods and border regions of the steppes, podseka and perelog were, of course, still practiced. The liada system was in use in some regions of northern Russia even as late as the middle of the nineteenth century.

At the stage of regularly tilled fields, less work was needed for cultivating than at the podseka stage. Thus from an economic point of view there was no obstacle to the separation of each family from the zadruga; hence the appearance of small farms. On the other hand, large landed estates could also be profitably exploited with the use of slave or hired labor.

In the written sources of the Kievan period there is ample evidence of the existence of regularly tilled fields in private possession. Copies of deeds are known in which the boundaries of each estate are described with great precision. In the *Russian Law* (*Pravda Russkaia*) fines are established for plowing beyond the boundary of one's land.

As to tools, in the primitive stage of agriculture in the forest zone, as Grekov rightly remarks, the ax may be called the chief agricultural implement, without the help of which the hoe would be useless. At that stage there was no need even for animal power and, indeed, according to Tretiakov, in the upper Volga region the horse was originally used, like cattle, for meat and not for work, and it was only from about the fifth century that it was adapted to agricultural operations.

The original north Russian plow (*sokha*) was a kind of wooden hack with three teeth. It was later made more effective by the addition of an iron plowshare (*lemekh*). In the south a real plow (*ralo*) was used from Scythian times. The sokha was driven by a horse or horses, the ralo by either horses or oxen.

As the kind of grain raised, spelt (*polba*), wheat, and buckwheat were the staple crops in the south; rye, oats, and barley in the north.

In the three-field system only these standard crops were used; fiber plants for textiles (flax and hemp), legumes (peas and lentils), and turnips were cultivated on separate patches.

Little is known of gardening in Kievan Russia.[17] Presumably apple
and cherry orchards existed in Ukraine from the Iranian age. There
probably was not much variety in native fruit production, since fruits
constituted one of the items of import from Byzantium. From the
*Paterikon* of the Monastery of the Caves at Kiev it is known that
the monks there cultivated some fruit trees. Commercial vegetable
gardens existed around Kiev and other cities, usually on low swampy
ground covered by the spring floods (*bolon'e*). Cabbages, peas, turnips, onions, garlic, and pumpkins were planted. Vegetable gardens
were also cultivated by the monks on monastery grounds, and vegetable gardeners are mentioned among people living and working on
private landed estates.

Horse and cattle breeding had been practiced in south Russia from
time immemorial and constituted an important branch of Russian
national economy in the Kievan period.[18] Special attention was paid
by the princes to horse breeding, partly because of war needs, and
huge droves of horses were kept on the princely estates. As an example an episode in the clash between the Davidovichi and Olgovichi
princes in 1145 may be cited here: according to the Hypatian Chronicle the Davidovichi, raiding the Olgovichi cattle range at Rakhna,
seized three thousand mares and one thousand stallions.

The *Russian Law* (*Pravda*) contains a great number of clauses
dealing with trading in cattle or stealing of cattle. In the so-called
Karamzin copy of the Expanded Version of the *Pravda* there is an interesting computation of the cumulative increase of cattle stock which
a good ranger may expect.[19] Horses and cattle of various kinds, including camels, were also imported from the Turkish nomads—from
the Patzinaks and later from the Cumans. Hungarian amblers are
mentioned in Igor's *Lay*.

Since hunting played a considerable role in Kievan Russia and the
prince more often than not was a passionate sportsman, it may be
mentioned that breeding of hounds was given considerable attention,
in any case on princely estates. Poultry was likewise an important
item of husbandry, both for home consumption and commercially.

While farms of various size existed in Russia in the Kievan period,
the bulk of agricultural production must have been on the larger

17. Aristov, *op. cit.*, pp. 64–68.
18. *Idem*, pp. 40–48; Kulischer, *op. cit.*, pp. 88–89.
19. *Pravda Russkaia*, B. D. Grekov, ed., I, 352–354.

estates. These were of three kinds: those belonging to the princes, those owned by the boyars and persons of other classes, and those belonging to the church.

Evidence on the management and inner organization of the large landed estates is scarce for the Kievan period.[20] Of the management of the boyar estates we know only the title of the steward (*tiun*). The prince's estate was under the general management of a bailiff (*ognishchanin*); each unit of the estate (*selo*, corresponding to *villa* in Carolingian France) was under the authority of the "villa elder" (*starosta selsky*); a special agent known as the "plowmen's elder," (*starosta ratainy*) supervised the field work. The master of stables (*tiun koniushi*) was in charge of horses and horse breeding; the shepherd (*ovchar* or *ovchiukh*) in charge of sheep. Grooms and herders were often of Turkish extraction. Whippers-in, in charge of princely kennels, are mentioned in the chronicles. Most of the prince's grooms and herders, as well as the whips, were probably his slaves. Princely lands were likewise at least partly tilled by slaves (*kholopy*) and indentured laborers (*zakupy*). However, free contract laborers (*riadovichi*) as well as freedmen (*izgoi*) were also used.

Presumably some of these tenants on both princely and church estates received for their use special plots of land which they tilled. In such cases they had to furnish a certain share of the harvest to the lord or pay some rent in cash.

The boyar estates must have been organized on the pattern of the princely, except of course that in most cases they were smaller. Some of the church estates, especially of the monasteries, must have been as great economic units as the princely but there were some differences as to both production and organization. War horses were not raised on the church estates, nor were hounds. Moreover, because of the opposition of the church to slavery as an institution slave labor was rarely used.

## 5. Metallurgy

As I have already mentioned, iron was the only metal ore to be extracted within the boundaries of Kievan Russia. It was used chiefly for the production of weapons and tools of every possible kind; it may be said that iron formed the backbone of the material culture of the country, for both peace and war.

20. See Grekov, *Kievskaia Rus'*, pp. 86–93.

Copper and tin were imported from the Caucasus and Asia Minor. Lead came chiefly from Bohemia. Of copper, church bells were made. With lead, or occasionally tin sheets, church roofs were covered. Copper was also used for kitchen and household utensils such as kettles, wash basins, candlesticks, and so on; and lead, for seals.

Silver was imported from various quarters: from Bohemia, from beyond the Urals, from the Caucasus and the Byzantine Empire. Gold was obtained, whether by commerce or war, from the Byzantines and the Cumans. Gold and silver were used for coinage, seals, and the making of vessels of various kinds, such as dishes, bowls, and goblets. Naturally only princes and wealthy people could afford them. The church was, however, a permanent customer for gold- and silverware. Besides chalices and other church vessels the clergy placed demands for gold and silver crosses as well as for covers for the icons and for the copies of the Gospel used in the church service. Some of the cathedral churches had gilded domes and certain parts of the inside walls and partitions were occasionally covered with sheets of gold or silver.[21]

Though the supply of metals other than iron was scarce in Kievan Russia, the art of metallurgy attained a comparatively high level. In the earlier period, as we know, the Antes were known as skillful armorers and in the ninth and tenth centuries the Polianians kept up their tradition. Foundries and smithies as well as founders and smiths are mentioned in a number of sources of the period on various occasions. In Kiev in the twelfth century a special section of the city was occupied by smithies and the near-by gate was known as the Smiths' Gate. In Novgorod in the early thirteenth century there were skillful founders, nailers, shield makers.

Salt may also be mentioned here. It was mined in the Carpathian Mountains in Galicia. Kiev depended chiefly on this source for the commodity and, when, during one of the interprincely wars, in 1097 the Galician princes forbade its export, there was an acute shortage of salt in the whole Kievan region. Another important source of salt supply was in the Crimea, where deposits were formed through a natural process in the shallow bays between the peninsula and the mainland. In the north the Novgorodians produced salt from sea water by artificial evaporation. The water was boiled either in large iron frying pans (*tsren*) or in huge kettles (*salga*).[22]

21. Aristov, *op. cit.*, pp. 117–131.
22. *Idem*, pp. 68–73.

## 6. Building Industries

The severity of the Russian climate made indispensable the building of houses which would offer man sufficient protection for the winter season, especially in northern Russia. Since excellent timber was abundant in the whole forest zone—that is, in northern and central Russia—houses there were made of wood. In the steppe zone the wooden frame of the walls was filled with stucco or clay. The north Russian *izba* and Ukrainian *khata* thus represent the two traditional types.

With the accumulation of wealth among the upper classes and the rise of princely authority, more elaborate mansions were built, most of them of wood. However, the prince's palace in Kiev had a stone hall as early as 945. The sumptuous palaces of the Suzdal princes of the late twelfth century were all stone. Fortified castles and city walls were, in the Kievan period, mostly of wood; however, Bishop Efrem of Pereiaslav built a stone wall around that city in 1090 and a century later Prince Riurik erected another around the St. Michael Monastery at Vydubichi near Kiev, which served as a section in the system of Kievan fortifications (1190). Altogether, only in the church architecture was stone extensively used. By the twelfth century all the cathedrals and most of the churches in major cities were of stone or brick. In minor towns and rural districts, especially in northern Russia, wooden churches prevailed.

In the oldest times there can hardly have existed a class of trained builders. Each man or, rather, each family commune built a house for himself or themselves. However, with the growth of the upper classes and the demand for larger homes and mansions, and especially with the growth of the church, specialization became unavoidable. Novgorod, the great metropolis of the north, was known as the home of the wooden building crafts in the Kievan period. An episode in the struggle between Sviatopolk of Kiev and Iaroslav of Novgorod (1016) is characteristic in this connection. When the two opposing armies were ready to fight, Sviatopolk's general scoffed at Iaroslav's Novgorodians, shouting: "You carpenters! We shall put you to work on our houses." [23]

A section of Novgorod was known as the "Carpenters' Borough." As the city was situated on both banks of the Volkhov River and as its streets were paved with timber, Novgorodian bridge builders were

23. Cross, p. 220.

known for their skill; the *Russian Law* contains an interesting table of fees for the work of bridge builders. Presumably Novgorodian master builders were invited to work in other cities whenever necessary. However, native carpenters must have been trained there as well.

The building and repairing of city walls, as for example in Kiev, was another important task for which master builders were required. This type of work is also mentioned in the *Pravda*. The position of chairman of the builders' association in Kiev in the late eleventh century was considered of such importance that he was one of the prince's closest associates and even took part in the codification of the *Pravda* of Iaroslav's sons, around 1072.

The ax was the old Russian carpenter's master tool and in handling it he achieved a high degree of skill. The saw is mentioned in the sources occasionally but was not in general use in Russia until the sixteenth century. Other tools mentioned are the chisel, the drill, and the adze.

An important branch of old Russian carpentry was shipbuilding. The construction of Russian boats of the tenth century, of the monoxylon type, has been already described (Chap. II, sec. 3). The boats used by the Novgorodian merchants in the Baltic Sea were of a different type (known as *nasad*) and seem to have been much more seaworthy. Similar boats, probably smaller, were used on the rivers both in north and south Russia. Even smaller was the *strug*, a river freight boat; it could carry over thirty tons of goods. In the *Russian Law* the value of a strug is given as one grivna; that of a larger river boat, two grivna; of the seagoing boat, three grivna.

While the art of carpentry grew on Russian soil and developed in connection with local needs and traditions, that of masonry was transplanted to Russia from Byzantium in the course of the tenth and eleventh centuries. Gradually native craftsmen were trained and in the late twelfth century the city of Vladimir in Suzdalia became the most important center of the Russian stone and brick-building industries. Vladimir men were commonly dubbed "masons" just as the Novgorodians were called "carpenters."

## 7. Textile Arts, Furriery, Tanning, Ceramics

The art of weaving had been known to the eastern Slavs and before them to the proto-Slavs for ages past. Both hemp and flax yarn served for fabrics. In Kievan Russia, with the growth of population and the development of handicrafts and commerce, the demand for textile products increased rapidly. Linen of both hemp and flax fibers was used for the garments of both men and women. The increase in wealth among the upper classes resulted in a certain refinement of life and taste for luxury. Finer linen had now to be procured. The new demands were partly satisfied by imported goods but must also have led to improvement in the methods of domestic handicraft.

In addition to the making of garments, hemp and flax yarn were needed for technical uses. Huge supplies of cordage were required for hunting and fishing nets. Of burlap, and also of canvas, army tents were made. Quantities of sailcloth and cordage were needed to equip the boats of the yearly commercial flotillas plying between Kiev and Byzantium, as well as for the Novgorodian boats in the Baltic Sea.

Woolen fabrics and cloth were also produced in Kievan Russia, being used chiefly for winter garments and overcoats. For hats and winter shoes, felt was used. No silk industry existed in Russia in the Kievan period—in fact, not before the seventeenth century. In the Kievan time silk fabrics were imported from both Byzantium and the Orient.

Originally most of the burlap and linen was homespun, and woolen cloth home-fulled. Each family commune was a shop. The women spun and wove, the men fulled cloth and twisted rope. When, after the conversion of Russia, monasteries and convents were founded, the monks and nuns made their own linen and cloth. In the cities more and more professional weavers and fullers must have been trained but unfortunately very little is said of them in the contemporary sources available.

The art of furriery must have been highly developed at the time, since fur coats were a necessity, especially in north Russia, in view of the severity of the climate. Furs were also worn as adornment. There is no doubt that there were expert furriers in Russia at this period but there is little evidence concerning the technique of old Russian furriery.

On tanning there are but few indications in our sources. In the satirical story of the visit of St. Andrew to Novgorod, where a north Russian bathhouse is described (see Chap. X, sec. 5), it is mentioned that the Novgorod Slavs anointed themselves with tannic acid (*kvas usniannyi*). The story of the duel between a Russian and a Patzinak wrestler, told in the *Book of Annals* under the year 992, has it that the Russian hero was a tanner.

Pottery was as old an art with the Russian Slavs as spinning. Pots and vases of diverse kinds were produced, some of them artistically ornamented. On the other hand, there is no definite evidence that glass was produced in Kievan Russia.

## 8. Commerce

Foreign commerce has traditionally been considered the mainstay of Kievan economy and, even if, as we have seen (sec. 1, above), reservations must be made with regard to the traditional view, the importance of foreign trade cannot be denied. However, the role of domestic trade in the Kievan period should not be neglected, either; while the wealth of the upper classes depended to a large extent on foreign trade, the well-being of the masses of the population was even more closely connected with the functioning of domestic commerce. Historically, in many cases domestic commercial intercourse—between the cities and outlying regions of Russia—preceded the expansion of foreign trade or in any case developed even in regions not directly affected by outside commerce. Thus, in regard to the Dnieper riverway, trade between Smolensk and Kiev existed before the opening of regular commercial relations between Novgorod, Kiev, and Constantinople.

The main reason for the growth of domestic commerce, in Kievan Russia as in other countries, may be seen in the diversity of the natural resources of the country. For Russia the fundamental contrast was that between the north and the south—the forest zone and the steppe zone. The difference between the grain-producing provinces of the south and the bread-consuming provinces of the north goes through the whole of Russian history and is valid even for our own times. And indeed, the history of the relations between Novgorod on one hand and Kiev and Suzdalia on the other cannot be properly understood without taking into account the dependence of the northern city on southern grain supplies. The trade in iron and salt was likewise the result of divergencies in Russia's economic geography.

Another reason for the development of domestic commerce—sociological rather than geographical—lies in the contrast between the cities and the rural districts. Here we have before us the case of the dependence of city dwellers on the agricultural products supplied to them by the farmers and the latter's demand for the tools and other manufactured goods produced by the city artisans.

The sociological importance of domestic trade in Kievan Russia may best be appreciated by examining the role of the market place in the life of both the cities and the surrounding rural districts. The market place was usually a very large square surrounded by storehouses and shops. Booths and stands filled part of the space between. Scales approved by city officials were at the disposal of buyers and sellers for a small fee paid to the attendant. Once a week, usually on Fridays, farmers brought their produce for sale and the market place was turned into a fair.[24]

All this belongs to the commercial nature of the market place as such. But in Kievan Russia it was also associated with political life and administration. It was in the market place that all official announcements were made. According to the *Russian Law,* if a theft occurred either in the city or in the vicinity, the claimant had first of all to announce it at the market place—the first step in any litigation of this kind, without which the judges would not let proceedings be started (see Chap. VII, sec. 10).

In the city market, likewise, meetings of the city assembly (*veche*) were sometimes held, especially in cases where the citizens were not pleased with their prince and the meeting was called by oppositional elements. It was to prevent the veche opposition from gathering strength that Prince Iziaslav I moved the main Kievan market place from a downtown location to the hill, closer to his palace (1069).

To go back to the commercial functions of the market place in the Kievan period, goods of every possible kind were bought and sold in the markets of the major Russian cities. In a number of contemporary sources the following items are mentioned: weapons, metal ware, metals, salt, clothes, hats, furs, cloth, pottery, timber, wood, wheat, rye, millet, flour, bread, honey, wax, frankincense, horses, cows, sheep, meat, geese, ducks, and game. In the smaller towns presumably only local merchants operated, while the merchants of the major cities transacted business on a national scale. There is much evidence in the sources as to the presence of out-of-town merchants in almost any large Russian city. Novgorodian merchants were especially active in establishing their agencies throughout Russia.

Let us now turn to the foreign trade.[25] As we know, in the eighth and ninth centuries the Norsemen opened a through trade route across Russia from the Baltic to the Azov and Caspian seas. In the tenth

24. Aristov, *op. cit.,* pp. 170–172; Kulischer, *op. cit.,* pp. 103–105.

25. Aristov, *op. cit.,* pp. 183–258; Kulischer, *op. cit.,* pp. 118–157; see also M. Berezhkov, *O torgovle Rusi s Ganzoiu do kontsa XV veka;* L. K. Goetz, *Deutsch-russische Handelsgeschichte des Mittelalters.*

century the Russians organized their trade on a national scale but continued to benefit from the transit trade. The Dnieper riverway soon became the main artery of Russian commerce, whose main southern outlet was now in Constantinople. Thus the Black Sea came to play a more important role in Russian trade than the Caspian; however, the Russians tried desperately to keep the road to the Caspian open as well, and it is from this point of view that we may best understand the interest of the Russian princes of the tenth and eleventh centuries in Tmutorokan and the importance of that city in Russian history of the early Kievan period. By the late eleventh century the road to the Azov and the Caspian seas was barred to the Russians by the Cumans, who now—in periods of peace—served as intermediaries between Russia and the Orient. A similar role was played by the Volga Bulgars.

Important changes which occurred in Mediterranean commerce after the First Crusade (1096-99) seriously affected both the Byzantine and the Russian Black Sea trade, undermining both, and the sack of Constantinople by the knights of the Fourth Crusade (1204) administered a *coup de grâce* to Kievan Black Sea commerce. However, the development in the twelfth century of overland trade between Kiev and central Europe to a certain extent attenuated the unfavorable results of the loss of Byzantine markets. In the north the Baltic trade continued to grow and with it the importance of the north Russian city-republics, Novgorod and Pskov. There was also an overland trade route from Germany to these centers; Bremen merchants used it in the middle of the twelfth century.

A brief survey of the main items of the Russian import and export trade may best be arranged by regions. To Byzantium, in the tenth century, the Russians exported furs, honey, wax, and slaves; what the situation was in the eleventh and twelfth centuries is not clear. Christian slaves were no longer sold abroad by the Russians; whether any pagan slaves, such as Cuman prisoners of war, were sold to the Greeks we do not know but it is well known that the Cumans sold Russian prisoners as slaves to overseas merchants. It is possible that grain was exported from Russia to the Byzantine Empire in the twelfth century. Meanwhile, from Byzantium during these three centuries Russia imported chiefly wines, silk fabrics, and objects of art, such as icons and jewelry; also fruits and glassware.

To the Oriental countries she exported furs, honey, wax, walrus tusks, and—in some periods at least—woolen cloth and linen, while the

Oriental trade brought her spices, precious stones, silk and satin fabrics, also weapons of Damask steel, and horses. It is noteworthy that some goods bought by the Russians from Oriental merchants, such as precious stones, spices, rugs, and so on, went on through Novgorod to western Europe. In the tenth and eleventh centuries Byzantine goods, especially silk fabrics, likewise went to northern Europe via the Baltic. The Novgorodian trade was thus partly a transit trade.

Another peculiarity of the Baltic trade consisted in the fact that similar categories of goods were on different occasions exported or imported, depending on the constellation of the international market. Staple goods exported from Novgorod and Smolensk to western Europe consisted of the same three leading items as in the Russo-Byzantine trade—furs, wax, and honey. To this may be added flax, hemp, tow, burlap, and hops; as well as tallow, suet, sheepskin, and hides. From Smolensk, also, silver and silverware were exported. From the west a number of manufactured goods were imported, such as woolen cloth, silk, linen, needles, weapons, and glassware. In addition, such metals as iron, copper, tin, and lead came to Russia via the Baltic; also herring, wine, salt, and beer.

Examining the list of products in Russia's foreign trade we may see that she sent abroad mostly—although not exclusively—raw materials and received from the foreign countries chiefly manufactured goods and metals.

As might be expected from our knowledge of this lively commercial intercourse, Russian merchants were accustomed to travel abroad and foreign merchants visited Russia. Russian merchants appeared in Persia and Bagdad as early as the ninth and tenth centuries. In Constantinople, as we know, there was a regular settlement of Russian merchants. Novgorodian merchants regularly visited the island of Visby as well as a number of cities along the southern shore of the Baltic Sea—the Pomeranian coast. It will not be amiss to point out here that until the middle of the twelfth century a number of these cities, such as Volyn and Arkona, were still Slavic.

In their turn, foreign merchants came to Russia in droves. In Novgorod there were two foreign settlements: the Gotlander and the German. A sizable German merchants' colony thrived in Smolensk. In Kiev Armenian, Greek, and German merchants resided. Jewish merchants living in Kiev are also mentioned in the sources but most of them were not foreigners. In Suzdalia Volga Bulgar, Khoresmian and Caucasian merchants represented the foreign element.

Some Russian and foreign merchants traveled individually but the bulk of trade, whether overland or maritime, was by commercial caravans-flotillas of boats or trains of wagons. This mode of travel was preferred because of the difficult conditions of the period. At sea, if a single ship of a flotilla was wrecked, its crew could obtain help from their companions on other ships; similarly on land, a broken wagon could be more easily repaired by the combined efforts of many than by a mere few. In river travel the hauling of boats over portages likewise required coöperation. Then, also, travel by caravans offered better protection against theft and robbery, especially in the overland trade, when crossing the no man's land of frontier regions.

Caravan travel was conducive to the forming of merchant associations, useful in many other respects—for instance, in the general protection of merchants' rights and in regulating taxes and customs duties. Associations of merchants were formed early in Kievan Russia. From the Russo-Byzantine treaties of the tenth century we know that the Greeks had to allow funds for the sustenance of Russian merchants according to cities. Presumably the merchants of each city represented a kind of joint stock company. It is known that in Novgorod they were organized in guilds known as "hundreds." Wealthy merchants dealing in overseas trade formed there an exclusive corporation of their own, known as the "St. John's Guild." Its admission fee amounted to fifty silver grivna plus an unspecified quantity of Ypres cloth.[26]

In addition to the formal associations there were also private combinations. Two or three or more would coöperate, pooling their capital or services, or both. Credit transactions were highly developed. A merchant could borrow money either from the prince or from other merchants. In traveling through various Russian cities he often needed storage services, which were accordingly made available. To cover every possible eventuality in case of a misunderstanding between members of a commercial combine or between the merchant and his creditors, as well as between him and the depository, a well-balanced system of commercial law came into existence through princely legislation. The Expanded Version of the *Russian Law* contains provisions which may be called a bankruptcy statute. An interesting feature of it is that in satisfying creditors the law gives preference to foreign creditors as against the native.

26. See Prince Vsevolod's charter to St. John's Church (around 1135), *Khristomatiia*, I, 212–215.

Russian commercial law of the Kievan period had its international aspects, since the relations between Russian and foreign merchants were regulated by a number of international commercial treaties and agreements, starting with the Russo-Byzantine treaties of the tenth century. In the early eleventh century a commercial convention between the Russians and the Volga Bulgars was concluded (1006).[27] In the course of the eleventh and twelfth centuries a number of peace agreements were made with the Cumans, each presumably containing commercial clauses as well.

In 1195 a commercial treaty was concluded between Novgorod, on the one hand, and the Germans, the Gotlanders, and "every Latin [i.e., Roman Catholic] nation" on the other. Even more important and elaborate is the treaty between the city of Smolensk, on one part, and Riga, Gotland, and a number of the German Pomeranian cities on the other (1229).[28] Both treaties contain not only commercial clauses but likewise a number of penal norms for cases of injury or murder of Russians by foreigners and vice versa. Complete reciprocal equality is an outstanding feature of both treaties.

## 9. Money and Credit

In pre-Kievan Russia furs were used as currency in the north and cattle in the south. Hence the two terms denoting money: *kuny* ("marten skins") and *skot* ("cattle"). Both were used in the Kievan period, although actually silver bars and coins were by then the tokens of exchange. Gold was rare.

Foreign coins, both Oriental (Sasanian and later Arabic) and Western (Roman and later Byzantine), circulated in pre-Kievan Russia in considerable quantities. They still did in the Kievan period but domestic coinage was also introduced in the reigns of Vladimir and Iaroslav.

In view of the variegated origin of the old Russian currency, the definition of the value of each monetary unit is not an easy task.[29]

27. Tatishchev, II, 88–89; M. Martynov, "Dogovor Vladimira s Volzhskimi Bolgarami 1006 goda," *Istorik-Marksist*, 1941, No. 2, pp. 116–117 (inaccessible to me); S. L. Peshtich, "O dogovore Vladimira s Volzhskimi Bolgarami," *Istoricheskie Zapiski, 18* (1946), 327–335.

28. *Khristomatiia*, I, 93–108; L. K. Goetz, *Deutsch-russische Handelsverträge des Mittelalters*, pp. 14–72, 231–304.

29. On Russian money and monetary systems, see I. Prozorovsky, *Moneta i ves v Rossii;* Count I. I. Tolstoy, "Drevneishie Russkie monety," *RAO, 6* (1893), 310–382; see also Sources, I, 2.

Broadly speaking, there were three monetary standards in Russia in the Kievan period: (1) gold, (2) silver, and (3) what was known as "furs" (*kuny*), although actually this was also silver but of lesser value. The basic unit of each of the three systems was known as a *grivna*. This term originally denoted a torque (neck ring). Golden torques were worn by Iranian and Gothic chieftains and because of the predominance of Alans and Goths among the Byzantine palace guards in the fifth century the torque (in Byzantine Greek, *maniak*) became the sign of a guard officer in Byzantium. The grivna as a monetary unit was not a ring but a bar of gold or silver.

The gold grivna presumably corresponded to one half a troy pound of gold. The silver grivna must have equaled approximately one troy pound of silver. The first was seldom used but the silver grivna was a standard unit in all commercial transactions and particularly in foreign trade. In everyday specie transactions the reckoning was in grivna of kuna.

Fractions of grivna were known as *nogata* and *rezana:* there were 20 nogata and 50 rezana in one grivna of kuna. The lowest unit was known as *veksha* (literally, "squirrel"); in Smolensk one nogata was equal to 24 veksha.

Somewhat later the term *kuna* in the specific sense of a fraction of a grivna was introduced. There is no consensus of scholarly opinion as to the exact relative value of one kuna and the original one grivna of kuna. According to Prozorovsky there were 50 kuna in a grivna, which would mean that kuna was equal to a rezana. However, according to Mrochek-Drozdovsky there must have been 25 kuna in one grivna of kuna, making one kuna equal to two rezana. As to the relation between the silver grivna and the grivna of kuna, it is known that in Smolensk one silver grivna was considered equal to four grivna of kuna. It may be further mentioned that in chronicles as well as in some other sources one more term for money occurs: *bela*. It is hard to say whether this was a general word for a silver coin or a term denoting a specific monetary unit. Bela also denoted fur, presumably ermine; in modern Russian, *belka* means squirrel.

As we have seen (sec. 8, above), credit transactions played a prominent role in the growth of the Russian commerce of the Kievan period, especially in relation to foreign trade. It is therefore not at all surprising that considerable attention was paid in Kievan legislation to loans and interest on them. According to the *Russian Law* the rate of interest on loans depended on the term of the loan. The "monthly" rate, which was the highest, was allowed for short-term loans of not over four months; for loans of a term between four months and one year the "third-of-the-year" rate was legal; for long-term loans the "yearly" rate, which was the lowest. It was only for this last category that a ceiling on the rate of interest was established: 10 kuna on each grivna loaned. It is usually considered that the grivna in this case was a grivna of kuna. If we assume, with Prozorovsky, that one grivna of kuna consisted of 50 kuna, then 10 kuna on a grivna would represent an interest rate of 20 per cent; if we prefer Mrochek-Drozdovsky's computation, 25 kuna in one grivna of kuna, the interest rate would be 40 per cent. This last figure was accepted by Kliuchevsky.

However, one may doubt that the grivna mentioned in this clause of the *Pravda* was a grivna of kuna.[30] In large-scale commercial loans and other transactions of the period the count was almost always in silver. Thus in this case the grivna must mean the silver grivna. As one silver grivna was equal to four grivna of kuna, for computing the real interest rate we have to divide the above-mentioned figures, 40 per cent and 20 per cent, by four in each case. Accordingly, we may think of an interest rate of either 10 or 5 per cent. It will not be irrelevant to point out in this connection that under Byzantine law of the eleventh century the approved rate of interest on loans varied from 5.5 to 8 per cent, depending on the terms of the loan.[31]

## 10. Capital and Labor

Capital in Kievan society materialized in land, money, slaves and cattle, apiaries, hunting and fishing preserves, and so on. Initial accumulation of capital was chiefly the result of commercial transactions, especially in foreign trade. In this sense and with due reservations we may speak of the Kievan economic regime as one of commercial capitalism.

Since commerce and war were closely connected in the early Kievan period, it will not be inappropriate to mention here that both war booty and indemnities paid to the Russians by conquered enemies constituted another important source of capital accumulation. In the funds obtained by war each army officer and man participating in

30. Article 53 A of the Expanded Version (G. Vernadsky, tr. *Medieval Russian Laws,* p. 45).

31. C. E. Zachariä von Lingenthal, *Geschichte des griechischrömischen Rechts* (3d ed. Berlin, 1892), p. 311. See also G. Ostrogorsky, "Löhne und Preise in Byzanz," *BZ, 32* (1932), 293–333.

the campaign had his share in proportion to his rank; the prince's share was of course the largest.

Treasure hoards consisting of jewelry and coins, a large number of which have been found in various parts of Russia, give an interesting indication of the wealth accumulated by people of the upper classes in Russia in this period.[32] As an example, the treasure hoard found in Riazan in 1828 contained more than seventy pounds of silver coins. Precious jewels have likewise been excavated in both Riazan and Kiev, as well as in other places.

The princes of the major Russian principalities were perhaps the greatest capitalists of the period since they were owners of the largest landed estates and also held controlling shares in the foreign trade. The boyars' wealth was mostly in land and that of the merchants chiefly in money and goods. The church with its tithe rights and land grants was well on its way to enter the rank of capitalists, although the real growth of church wealth occurred later on, in the Mongol period. As an indication of the wealth of some of the princes: Sviatoslav II, when he was prince of Chernigov and not yet of Kiev, donated one hundred gold grivna to the Monastery of the Caves. Vladimir II, when still a minor local prince, on one occasion gave his father three hundred gold grivna; on another, one thousand two hundred silver grivna. In 1120 Vasilko of Terebovl paid the Poles two thousand silver grivna as ransom money for the release of his brother Volodar. In speaking of the princes it is not always possible to differentiate between their private means and their disposal of state funds. Generally the prince was entitled to a third of the revenue collections. But one must not forget that he could, on many occasions, use his administrative discretion for the support of his commercial enterprises. Thus, as we know, Sviatopolk II of Kiev attempted to monopolize the trade in salt for his own benefit.

The combined wealth of a rich prince, like this same Sviatopolk, must have mounted to a high figure if expressed in monetary units but it would be hard to say even tentatively what that figure was. From the report on the *Book of Annals* on the visit of Emperor Henry IV's ambassadors to Sviatoslav II in 1075 it is clear that the Russian prince's amassed treasures were greater than Henry's, since the only comment the ambassadors made was that he would make better use of his riches by distributing them among his vassals instead of letting them lie dead. Some of the merchants, especially the Novgorodians,

32. N. P. Kondakov, *Russkie klady*, I.

likewise must have been very wealthy but again there is no way properly to appraise their capital. The building of churches by some of them out of their own purses may give an idea of the means at their disposal. From the Novgorodian chronicles we know, for example, that in 1050 Sadko the Wealthy built a church in Novgorod (probably of wood); in 1115 an anonymous Novgorodian merchant founded a stone church; in 1192 the daughter of the merchant Shirozhkin likewise built a stone church.

While there were many wealthy merchants in Novgorod, no one of them was rich enough to monopolize the market. The story of the competition between Sadko and other leading Novgorodians, told in one of the byliny, is characteristic in this respect. While no merchant individually wielded sufficient political or administrative power to promote his commercial interests as did the princes, collectively the merchants of Novgorod were able to influence the decisions of the city assembly in their favor more often than not. Merchant associations like the St. John's Guild mentioned above must likewise have helped the capitalistic interests. Similar associations probably existed in other cities as well and the merchants of those cities also had their voice at the meetings of the city assembly. Moreover, merchants and merchant associations were often in a position to influence the course of princely policies. To return to the case of Sviatopolk II, the idea of salt monopoly was suggested to him by the leading salt merchants, who formed a kind of cartel under his chairmanship.

Let us now turn to labor. In its modern connotation the term is hardly applicable to medieval conditions or may be applied, in any case, to only a small proportion of the workers of the period. The bulk of agriculturists were peasants and the bulk of manufacturers small artisans, each owning his shop. In the west what may be called industrial labor did not appear before the thirteenth or fourteenth centuries. In Kievan Russia hired workers were employed both in agriculture and handicraft but the number of those permanently employed appears to be small. On certain occasions, however—as for the building of the larger churches or palaces—additional workers were engaged. Thus when Iaroslav the Wise undertook the building of the St. Sophia Cathedral in Kiev he ordered that announcements be made calling for wagon drivers and other workers. The story has it that at first there was no response, people being apparently under the impression that they would not be paid for their work. Iaroslav then made an additional announcement that everybody would be paid one nogata a day and that payments would be made daily; to assure which, wagons with money were placed at the Golden Gate. The value of a nogata was at the time around $0.18 (gold).[33]

This was a case of unskilled labor. From the provisions of the clause of the *Russian Law* on bridge and city wall building it has been calculated that the carpenter's daily wage was $0.25 (gold) plus living expenses. The wages of an agricultural laborer must have been much smaller. According to a late version of the *Russian Law* a female laborer with a daughter was paid two grivna a year for both.[34] As to the wages of a male laborer there is reference in the *Russian Law* only to the indentured laborer, whose yearly wages are estimated at half a grivna. This was not, however, the amount actually paid him but that credited for repayment of his debt. Obviously no conclusion should be drawn from this evidence as to the amount of the yearly wages of a hired worker not handicapped with indenture. The wages of a free male worker must have been superior to those of female workers in any case.

The rights of workers were protected by custom, if not by law. From the Kievan *Paterikon* we know that if an employer after hiring a worker changed his mind and decided not to have the work done, he had nevertheless to satisfy the employee even if the latter had not actually begun working. If an employer handed the worker's wages to a third party (presumably his steward) and the latter failed to pay the employee, the employer was held responsible.[35]

It should be noted that there was one kind of work which was not supposed to be done by free employees and was thus more or less reserved to the slave. This was household service—not only that of a footman or a maid but likewise that of a housekeeper (*kliuchnik*) and of a steward (*tiun*). If a man or woman entered such service with the understanding that he or she remained free, a special contract had to be signed (see Chap. VI, sec. 7). As to labor organizations, there undoubtedly existed associations of carpenters and masons but there is little information about them in the sources for this period.

## 11. National Income

An accurate appraisal of Russia's national income in the Kievan period is impossible because of the lack of statistical data. However,

33. Hrushevsky, III, 344.

34. *Pravda Russkaia*, Grekov, ed., I, 354.

35. V. Iakovlev, ed., *Pamiatniki russkoi literatury XII i XIII vekov* (St. Petersburg, 1872), pp. clxx, clxxviii.

even tentative speculation on the problem may not be out of place as a means to round out our understanding of the Kievan background. No census of population was ever taken in Kievan Russia. Nor was there any census of real estate, except for the princely domains and the estates of the church, the management of which must have had pretty accurate tabulations of both income and expenses. Unfortunately, except for a few fragments, no such records have been preserved.

Generally speaking, any evaluation of the annual income of a nation is conditioned by the following factors.[36]

(1) The gross output of the country, comprising the total volume of materials produced and reproduced within a year.

(2) The net output, to calculate which we have to deduct from the gross output that part of the materials produced which is used for further reproduction of the capital of the country. This final total is the nation's income.

(3) The income of individuals which results from the distribution of net output among all the citizens: the producers, the middlemen, and members of what are usually called the "leisure classes."

In the Middle Ages the relation between the first two factors (gross and net output) differed greatly from that of the modern period, for in the absence of complicated machinery fewer materials were required for the reproduction of the nation's capital. Kievan Russia was certainly no exception in this respect and its net output must have been much closer to gross output than in the case with modern Russia.

In regard to the income of the people, the majority of the population consisted of small producers (farmers and artisans) and a considerable number of them were provided with at least a minimum of food and consumer goods except in periods of national calamity.

As to Kievan Russia's gross output, four branches of it may be considered of particular importance: (1) hunting and fishing, (2) agriculture, (3) cattle breeding, and (4) crafts and industries.

(1) The gross output of the first category was considerably higher than the consumer needs of the people engaged in producing it. It was even higher than the needs of the internal market and supplied the main items of Russian export, especially in the earlier part of the Kievan period.

(2) Agriculture covered consumer needs in south Russia and its

36. S. N. Prokopovich, *Narodnyi dokhod zapadnoevropeiskikh stran* (Moscow and Leningrad, 1930), pp. 11–12.

output was, except for the lean years, high enough for export requirements—chiefly to north Russia, where local output was below the needs of the population.

(3) Cattle breeding as a branch of Russian national economy satisfied the needs of the domestic market and there were enough hides for export. On the other hand, a number of horses and cattle were imported from the steppe nomads.

(4) In regard to industries and crafts, small-shop artisan production covered the local consumer needs. Larger establishments in the cities as well as in the princely domains and monasteries produced some surplus goods which were absorbed mostly by the internal market, though partly by export.

It may be added that a comparatively numerous class of merchants and middlemen derived their livelihood from commerce, both internal and foreign. In the latter, as we know, the princes were interested as well. To sum up, it may be said that according to the standards of the Middle Ages the gross output of Kievan Russia's economy must have been quite impressive. Its net output, moreover, was apparently sufficient to cover the consumer needs of the bulk of the population as well as to satisfy the demands for luxury of the wealthy minority, at least in part.

## 12. Prosperity and Depression

The problem of the study of business cycles in Kievan Russia has been only recently posed by Peter Savitsky.[37] In view of the fact that exact statistical data for this period are practically unavailable, this scholar suggested an indirect approach to the problem by considering "groups of indices" of prosperity cycles. He then analyzed the chronicles and other sources to obtain evidence of the presence, in any given subperiod, of all or some of the groups of indices, or categories of economic facts. By this method he was able to extract from the sources evidence for twenty-seven categories, such as commercial transactions, accumulation of individual capital, the flourishing of agriculture, technical devices, the building of new cities, colonization, and so on.

On the basis of these considerations he has offered the following chronological table of business cycles in Russia in the Kievan period.

37. P. N. Savitsky, "Pod'em i depressiia v drevne-russkoi istorii," *EK, 11* (1936), 65–100.

981–1015 Prosperity (evidence for the presence of fourteen "groups of indices")
1015–1026 Depression
1026–1061 Prosperity (fourteen groups)
1061–1071 Depression
1071–1073 Trend toward prosperity
1073–1086 Period of transition
1086–1092 Prosperity (six groups)
1092–1101 Depression
1101–1123 Prosperity (thirteen groups)
1123–1129 Depression
1129–1133 Prosperity (eleven groups)
1133–1137 Period of transition
1137–1144 Depression
1144–1146 Prosperity (five groups)
1146–1150 Depression

For the period from 1150 to 1178 Savitsky fails to perceive any coördination of business cycles on a national scale and analyzes regional trends only, examining the three separate regions of Kiev, Novgorod, and Suzdalia. For the period from 1178 to 1237 he again speaks of national cycles, to wit:

1178–1202 Prosperity (eleven groups)
1202–1218 Depression
1218–1227 Prosperity (thirteen groups)
1227–1232 Depression
1232–1237 Period of transition

It is evident from the table that according to Savitsky most of the periods of prosperity may be coördinated with the fluctuations of Russian political history. The reigns of Vladimir I, Iaroslav I, Vladimir II, and Mstislav I in the eleventh and first half of the twelfth centuries and the periods of reign of Sviatoslav III and Riurik in Kiev (1178–1202) and of Vsevolod III's sons in Suzdalia (1218–27) are those of greatest prosperity.

It is obvious—as Savitsky himself recognizes—that his method can give tentative results only, since the chroniclers made no effort to record systematically the facts of economic life, their main object being to describe political and ecclesiastical events. Thus the evidence in the sources for each category of the prosperity study is only casual. On the other hand, the number of categories involved in each case presents a certain corrective and while Savitsky's findings cannot be considered conclusive they are certainly of great interest to the student of the period.

CHAPTER VI

# SOCIAL ORGANIZATION

## *1. The Basic Social Units*

THE *Book of Annals* contains the following statement concerning the social organization of one of the leading Russian tribes at the dawn of their history: "The Polianians lived in clans, each clan (*rod*) controlling the locality roundabout." [1]

This famous passage served as the starting point for building up the so-called theory of "clan manner of life" (*rodovoy byt*) which dominated Russian historical thought throughout the nineteenth century. This theory may be called the leading generalization or most popular "working hypothesis" of that stage of Russian historiography, intended as it was to unveil the origins of the social order in the early stages of Russian history.

J. P. G. Ewers, an outstanding student of Russian legal history— a German by birth—was its originator [2] and S. M. Soloviev made it the cornerstone of his magnum opus, *The History of Russia from Ancient Times.*[3] The jurist K. D. Kavelin further elaborated the conception.[4] According to Ewers, Russian society passed from the clan stage to the stage of being a state almost without any transitional period. For him the early Kievan state was but a combination of clans. According to Soloviev the very fact that the princely clan of the Rurikides enjoyed exclusive control of state machinery in the Kievan period is a decisive argument in support of Ewers' theory.

The theory met strong objections from the outset on the part of the Slavophile historian K. Aksakov, in whose opinion not the clan but the commune (*obshchina, mir*) was the foundation of the old Russian social and political order.[5] Aksakov's point of view was not then generally accepted, however, partly because of some vagueness in his definition of the commune.

1. Laur., col. 9.
2. J. P. G. Ewers, *Das älteste Recht der Russen* (St. Petersburg, 1826).
3. Soloviev, I, 46–55, 88–89, 210–212; II, 1–9.
4. K. D. Kavelin, *Sobranie Sochinenii*, I, cols. 5–66.
5. K. S. Aksakov, *Sochineniia*, I (Moscow, 1889), 63–123.

For further discussion of the problem the comparative study of the social organization of various branches of the Slavs, as well as of other peoples, was of much value. That brilliant student of comparative jurisprudence and economic history, M. M. Kovalevsky, collected important materials bearing on the organization of the Ossetians and other Caucasian tribes; he also examined the problem as a whole in the light of comparative ethnology.[6] Simultaneously F. I. Leontovich studied the social institutions of the Slavic peoples, emphasizing some parallel trends in the history of the Russians and the southern Slavs and introducing the term *zadruga* into Russian historiography.[7] Among the names of the younger generation of Russian historians who have given the problem much attention that of A. E. Presniakov should in any case be mentioned.[8] And recently some Soviet historians, especially B. D. Grekov, have reconsidered the problem as a whole, using —as might be expected—Friedrich Engels' writings as their theoretical base.[9]

What, then, is the present state of the problem? It seems to be the consensus of learned opinion that the Russians as well as most other peoples must have passed through the stage of patriarchal clan organization but that in the Kievan period that stage was already far behind. No immediate historical connection between the clan and the state can be recognized. Clan combinations resulted in the formation of tribes but tribal organization was never strong on Russian soil; moreover, in the time of the migrations not only tribes but some of the clans themselves were broken up. In any case, the component parts of Kievan Russia—the city-states and principalities—only partly coincided with former tribal divisions and in some cases did not coincide at all. Thus the old Russian state did not directly grow out of the Russian tribes, which were merely an intermediate type of social and political organization. More often than not a tribe was but a dead end, politically.

But if the clan cannot be considered the basic social unit of old Russia, what, then, was that unit? Surely not the family in the modern sense of the term. This would be too small and weak a group to

---

6. M. Kovalevsky, *Pervobytnoe pravo* (Moscow, 1876); *Sovremennyi obychai i drevnii zakon* (Moscow, 1886); *Zakon i obychai na Kavkaze* (Moscow, 1887); *Rodovoi byt, 1* (St. Petersburg, 1905).

7. F. I. Leontovich, "O znachenii vervi," *ZMNP, 134* (1867), 1–19.

8. A. E. Presniakov, *Lektsii po russkoi istorii*, I, 51–61.

9. Grekov, *op. cit.*, pp. 51–67; F. Engels, *The Origin of the Family, Private Property and the State* (London, Lawrence and Wishart, Ltd., 1941).

cope with the hardships of primitive economy, especially in the period of migrations. And thus we come to the problem of the *zadruga*, that is, the "greater family" commune—a social unit more or less intermediate between the clan and the family, based on a coöperation of three or more generations.[10] The term is taken from the Serbian language; it means "friendship," "agreement," "harmony." In Yugoslavia, the zadruga commune is still a living institution, or was so until the last war. According to the Code of Law of the Principality of Serbia (1844) the zadruga "is the community of life and property originated from and asserted through blood relationship and natural increase."[11] The average Yugoslav zadruga numbers from twenty to sixty members (including children). Occasionally the membership may reach the figure of eighty or even a hundred.

Among the Russian peasants a smaller unit of this type, known simply as the "family," survived almost to the revolution of 1917. In a report from a town elder (*volostnoi starshina*) of Orel province in the late eighteen-nineties, the institution is described as follows:

The peasant family in our town consists of several kinsmen, their wives and children, from fifteen to twenty persons in all, who all live in the same house. The elder wields great authority over the family. He keeps the family in peace and order; all of the members are subordinated to him. He assigns the work to be done to each member, manages the farm, and pays the taxes. After his death his authority goes to his eldest son, and if none of his sons is of age, then to one of his brothers. If there are no men of age left in the family, the elder's widow assumes his duties. When several brothers live thus in one house, keeping the family in unity and order, they consider all of the belongings the common property of the family, except for women's clothes, linen and canvas. This is exempt from the commune. Except for these, everything else is managed by the elder—either the oldest man in the family or any other member of the family chosen by the agreement of all others. The elder's wife supervises the work of the women-folk; however, if she is not fit for the task a younger woman may be selected for it. All the work is distributed among the men and women according to the strength and health of each.[12]

10. On *zadruga*, besides the works of Leontovich, Kovalevsky, and others quoted above, see K. Kadlec, *Rodiný nedíl čili zádruha* (Prague, 1898); V. Popović, *Zadruga* (Sarajevo, 1921), and "Zadruga: teorija i literature," *SZM, 33–34* (1921–22); Z. Vinski, *Die Südslavische Grossfamilie* (Zagreb, 1938); P. E. Mosely, "The Peasant Family: The Zadruga," *The Cultural Approach to History*, C. E. Ware, ed. (New York, 1940), pp. 95–108.

11. H. Jireček, *Svod zákonův slovanských* (Prague, 1880), p. 448.

12. Kovalesky, *Rodovoi byt*, I, 32–33.

In the *Russian Law* there is no mention of the zadruga. Instead, the term *verv* is used to denote the local community. The same word also means "rope," "cord." It has been argued that *verv* in the sense of "commune" must have emphasized the blood relationship or, rather, lineal descent of generations. Another term may be mentioned in this connection: *uzh'*, "cord," to which *uzhika*, "kin," "member of a family commune," corresponds. Even admitting that the word *verv* may originally have denoted a greater family commune of the zadruga type, we may note that in the eleventh and twelfth centuries the term had already changed its original meaning. From the *Russian Law* it is obvious that *verv* at that time was similar to the Anglo-Saxon guild. It was a community of neighbors bound by the responsibility of its members to pay the bloodwite for murder committed within the boundaries of the commune in cases where the murderer could not be identified. Membership in the verv was on a voluntary basis. Men could join the guild or refrain from joining. In the later periods of Russian history the guild was superseded by the peasant commune, *obshchina*, also spoken of as *mir*. In the *Russian Law* the term *mir* is used to denote a wider community—a city with the rural district around it. A peculiar form of the old Russian land system was that of coöperative ownership of an estate by several co-owners (*siabry*). Like the verv, the siabry association must have developed from a family commune. *Siaber* or *seber* is an archaic word, the original connotation of which seems to have been that of a "member of a family working, together with other relatives, on the family land." There are parallel terms in Sanskrit: *sabha*, "kin," "village community"; and *sabhyas*, "a member of a village community." Consider likewise the Gothic *sibja* and the German *Sippe*, "relatives" (collectively).[13] In its structure the word *seber* (note the final "r") is similar to the basic terms of kinship in Indo-European languages, like *pater* and *mater* in Latin; "brother" and "sister" in English; *bratr* and *sestra* in Slavic. More specifically, *seber* is to be connected with the reflexive pronoun *sebe* ("to himself"). Incidentally, in the opinion of some modern philologists the Slavic word *svoboda* ("liberty") comes from the same root.[14]

Other types of social unit originated in old Russia for the promo-

13. Preobrazhensky, II (Moscow, 1916), 266–267. On the coöperative associations among the Slavs, see K. Kadlec, "O trudovykh assotsiatsiakh u Slavian," *SVB*, pp. 125–141.

14. G. Ilyinsky (Il'insky), "Slavianskie etimologii," *RFV*, 69 (1913), 18–22; see also G. Bonfante, "Sabadios-Svoboda le libérateur," *Annuaire*, 7 (1944), 41–46.

tion of commerce and industry. There existed coöperative associations of artisans and workers similar to those which later on became known as *artel* (the old Russian term is *druzhina,* from *drug,* "friend"). Merchants, as we have seen, formed various kinds of companies or guilds of their own.

## 2. Social Stratification

A society consisting solely of family communes may be thought of as basically homogeneous. All members of the zadruga have an equal share both in the communal work and in the products of that work. It is a "classless" society in miniature.

With the breaking up of the zadruga and the emancipation of the family from the clan; with the similar emancipation of the individual from the commune and the formation of territorial communes of a new type; with all this the social structure of a nation becomes more complex. Gradually various social classes constitute themselves.

The process of social stratification had started among the eastern Slavs long before the formation of the Kievan state. We know that the Sclaveni and the Antes in the sixth century turned prisoners of war— even of their own race—into slaves. We also know that there was an aristocratic group among the Antes and that some of their chieftains gathered much wealth.[15] Thus we have elements of at least three social groups already in existence among the eastern Slavs as early as the sixth century: the aristocracy, the common people, and slaves. Subjugation of some of the east Slavic tribes to foreign conquerors must likewise have resulted in a political and social differentiation of various tribes. We know that the eastern Slavs paid tribute in grain and other agricultural products to the Alans, Goths, and Magyars, as each of those peoples succeeded in turn in establishing control over a part of the east Slavic tribes. While some of the Slavic groups eventually asserted their independence or autonomy, others remained under foreign control for a longer period. Peasant communes originally dependent on foreign overlords later recognized the authority of native Slavic princes but their status did not change and they continued to pay the former duties. Thus a difference was established in the position of various Slavic groups. Some were self-governing, others subordinate to the princes.

It is with this complex social and historical background in mind

15. *Ancient Russia,* pp. 158, 159, 169, 170; Grekov, *op. cit.,* p. 174.

that we must approach the study of Russian society in the Kievan period. As may be expected, that society was complex enough, although there were in Kievan Russia no such high barriers between single social groups and classes as existed in feudal Europe of the same period. In a general way it may be said that Russian society of the Kievan period consisted of two main groups: freemen and slaves. Such a statement, however, while correct, is too broad adequately to characterize the composite structure of Kievan society.

To fully realize that complexity one must note that there were different groups among the freemen themselves: while some were full-fledged citizens the legal status of others was somewhat limited. In fact, the position of some classes of freemen, owing either to legal or to economic restrictions, was precarious to such a degree that some of them preferred voluntarily to sell themselves into slavery. Thus, between freemen and slaves an intermediate group which might be called that of the half-free must be discerned. Moreover, some groups of freemen proper were better off economically and better protected by the law than others. Consequently, one may speak of the existence of upper-class and middle-class freemen in Kievan society.

Our basic juridical source for the period is the *Russian Law* (*Pravda Russkaia*) and to that code we must turn for legal terminology in regard to the social classes. In the eleventh-century version of the *Pravda*—the so-called "Short Version"—we find the following basic terms: *muzhi* for upper-class freemen, *liudi* for the middle-class, *smerdy* for the freemen of somewhat limited status, and *cheliad'* for slaves.

In the eyes of the legislator a man had a different value depending on the class to which he belonged. The old Russian criminal law knew no capital punishment. Instead there was a system of money payments imposed on the murderer. The latter had to pay both the amends to the relatives of the murdered man (known as *bot* in Anglo-Saxon) and a fine to the prince ("bloodwite"). This system was common to the Slavs, the Germans, and the Anglo-Saxons in the early Middle Ages.

In the earliest *Pravda* the wergeld, or value set on a freeman's life, amounted to 40 grivna. In the *Pravda* of Iaroslav's sons the prince's men (*muzhi*) were protected by a double bloodwite of 80 grivna, while the bloodwite for a *liudin* (singular form of *liudi*) remained on the original level of 40 grivna. The fine to be paid to the prince for the murder of a *smerd* (singular of *smerdy*) was set at 5 grivna—one eighth of the normal wergeld. Slaves, being unfree, had no wergeld whatever.

From the philological angle it is interesting that all the above terms belong to the old Indo-European background.[16] The Slavic *muzh* (*mǫži*) corresponds to the Sanskrit *mánuh, mánuṣah;* the Gothic *manna;* the German *mann* and *mensch*. In old Russian *muzh* has the connotation of "man of noble origin," "knight," and besides it also means "husband." *Liudi* means "people" or "men" collectively, to be compared with the German *leute*. It appears that the root of the term is the same as in the Greek adjective *eleutheros* ("free").[17] *Smerd* may be considered in connection with the Persian *mard*, "man"; in Armenian likewise *mard*. The disappearance of the initial "s" in the combination "sm" is not unusual in Indo-European languages.[18] According to Meillet, *mard* denotes man as a mortal being (in contrast to the "immortals," i.e. gods).[19] From this point of view it is also interesting to compare the Persian *marg* and the Slavic *smert'* (both meaning "death").

In the social development of Russia each of the above terms had its own story. The term *smerd* acquired a derogatory connotation in connection with the verb *smerdeti*, "to stink." The term *muzh* in the sense of a specific social category gradually disappeared and from the *muzhi* the boyar class eventually developed. In its diminutive form, *muzhik* ("little man"), the term was applied to the peasants subjected to boyar authority. Hence *muzhik*, "peasant." The term *liudin* (in singular) likewise disappeared, except in combinations like *prostoliudin* ("commoner"). The plural form *liudi*, is still used; to it corresponds in modern Russian the word *chelovek* ("man," "human being") used in the singular only. The first part of this word (*chel-*) represents the same root as that in the old Russian word *cheliad* ("household slaves"). The original connotation of the root is "clan": consider the Gaelic *clann* and the Lithuanian *keltis*.[20]

## 3. The Upper Classes

The upper classes of Kievan society were of heterogeneous origin. The backbone consisted of the prominent men (muzhi) of the leading Slavic clans and tribes. As we know, even in the period of the

16. Meillet, *Linguistique historique et linguistique générale,* pp. 272–278.
17. Preobrazhensky, I, 493–494.
18. H. Hirt, *Indogermanische Grammatik,* I (Heidelberg, 1927), 277.
19. Meillet, *op. cit.,* p. 275.
20. E. Berneker, *Slavisches etymologisches Wörterbuch,* I (Heidelberg, 1913), 141.

Antes a kind of tribal aristocracy was in existence: "the elders of the Antes" (ἄρχοντες ᾿Αντῶν). Some of those elders must have been of Alanic origin. With the rise of princely power in Kiev the prince's retinue (druzhina) became the main catalytic agent for the formation of the new aristocracy, that of the boyars. The druzhina in the Kievan period was a melting-pot in itself.[21] Under the first Kievan princes its core consisted of the Swedish Rus'. More Norse elements joined it whenever the princes hired new bands of Varangians from "overseas," i.e., from Scandinavia. However, the prince's retinue likewise absorbed some of the Slavic muzhi, as well as every possible kind of alien adventurer. Ossetians, Kosogians, Magyars, Turks, and others are mentioned on various occasions as belonging to the druzhina. By the eleventh century it was already Slavicized.

Socially it consisted of diverse elements. Some of its members were prominent even before joining it; others were of low origin and some had even been the prince's slaves. To these, service in the druzhina not only opened the way to lucrative office but also presented an opportunity to climb the social ladder to its very top.

The retinue consisted of two groups which may be called the senior and junior druzhina, respectively. Among the senior retainers in the eleventh century the bailiff (ognishchanin), the master of the horse (koniushi), the steward (tiun), and the adjutant (podiezdnoi) are mentioned. All were originally merely the prince's agents for the management of his own court and estates but were later used in the state administration as well. The term ognishchanin is derived from ognishche, "hearth." Thus the ognishchanin is a member of the prince's "hearth," that is, of his household. The term tiun is of Norse origin; in old Swedish, thiun means "servant." In Russia it denoted at first a steward but later came to be used chiefly with the connotation of "judge." It may not be inappropriate to remark that a similar process of transformation of prince's servitors into state officials took place in England, France, and Germany in the early Middle Ages.

The junior retainers were known collectively as grid', a term of Norse origin, the original meaning of which is "domicile," "home."[22] Hence the old Russian word gridnitsa, "house," or "hall." They were originally the prince's pages and lesser household servitors, also at-

21. On the boyars and the princely retinue, see the following: Vladimirsky-Budanov, Obzor, pp. 25–31; Kliuchevsky, Boiarskaia Duma drevnei Rusi, chaps. i–ii; I. A Malinovsky, "Drevneishaia russkaia aristokratiia," SVB, pp. 256–274; Sergeevich, Drevnosti, I, 364–373; Diakonov, Ocherki, pp. 74–80.

22. Thomsen, Origin, p. 128.

tendants to the major druzhina officers. A member of the grid' is sometimes called in the sources *otrok* ("boy"), *detskii* ("adolescent"), or
*pasynok* ("step-son"), which seems to indicate that they were considered members of the prince's family, as it were. In Suzdalia in the
late twelfth century a new term appeared to denote the junior retainers: *dvorianin*, literally a "courtier," from *dvor*, "court" (also
"yard"). In imperial Russia of the eighteenth and the nineteenth
centuries the term *dvorianin* acquired the connotation of "nobleman."

From the year 1072 the senior members of the prince's druzhina
were protected by a double bloodwite. For offending the honor of a
senior retainer the offender had to pay a fine to the prince four times
as large as for injury of a smerd. This qualified protection for offenses
against prince's retainers also existed in the German law of the period.

Far from all of the Russian upper class served in the druzhina. In
Novgorod, where the prince's authority and the duration of his office
were limited by the provisions of his contract, his retainers were
even expressly prevented from settling permanently on Novgorodian
land. Thus, in addition to aristocracy of service, there existed in
Kievan Russia an aristocracy in its own right. Its members are
variously called in the sources of the earlier period; for instance,
"the prominent men" (*muzhi narochitye*), or "the best men" (*luch-
shie liudi*), also in many cases "city elders" (*stareishiny gradskie*).
Some were the descendants of the old tribal aristocracy; others, especially in Novgorod, must have come to prominence because of their
wealth, more often than not derived from foreign commerce.

Eventually both the princely and the local aristocracy became
known as the boyardom. While some of the local boyars must have
been descendants of merchants and the princely boyars originally
derived their wealth from the sustenance and bonuses received from
the prince and from their share in the war booty, in the course of time
all the boyars became landowners and it was on the large landed
estates that the strength and social prestige of the boyardom as a
class was built.

It may be added that by the early thirteenth century, because of
the rapid propagation of the House of Riurik, the number of princes
had increased and the domains of each prince—except those reigning in the major cities—decreased to such an extent that for all practical purposes the lesser princes of the period themselves were no
longer socially distinguished from the boyars. Thus the princes by

that time may be considered as socially and economically merely the upper crust of the boyar class.

Actually some of the major boyars enjoyed more wealth and prestige than the lesser princes, a fact especially evident if we consider that each of the wealthier boyars had a retinue of his own and some tried to emulate the princes by establishing courts of their own. As early as in the tenth century, Igor's general Sveneld had his own retainers (*otroki*) and boyars' retainers are mentioned in the sources of the eleventh and twelfth centuries on several occasions. The life of the boyar's tiun (steward or judge) was protected by law along with that of the prince's tiun.

With all the political and social prominence of boyardom, the latter did not constitute in the Kievan period any distinct order from the legal point of view. First of all, it was not an exclusive group, since a commoner could join it through his service in a prince's retinue. Secondly, it had no legal privileges as a class. Thirdly, while the boyars together with the princes were the owners of large landed estates par excellence, they were not the only landowners in this period in Russia, since land could be bought and sold without restriction and a person of any social group could acquire it. Moreover, it was quite usual for a boyar of this period not to sever his ties with the city. Each of the major boyars of the prince's retinue had a residence in the city where that prince reigned. All the Novgorodian boyars were not only residents of the city of Novgorod but also took part in the meetings of the city assembly.

## 4. The Middle Classes

The underdevelopment of the middle classes is usually considered one of the basic traits of Russian social history. It is true that in both Muscovite and Imperial periods, down to the late nineteenth century, the proportion of people engaged in industry and commerce, and of city dwellers at large, as compared to villagers was low. However, even for those periods any sweeping generalization as to the absence of the middle classes in Russia would call for reservation. In any case, such a generalization would not hold for the Kievan period. As we have seen (Chap. V, sec. 2), the proportion of city population to total population must have been, in Kievan Russia, not lower than thirteen per cent. To appreciate the significance of this figure one must approach it not from the point of view of the social stratification of modern times but by comparison with contemporary conditions in central and western Europe. While no exact demographic data for Europe of this period exist, it is generally accepted that, until the fourteenth century at least, the proportion of city population in Europe as compared to the total was very low.

The bulk of the urban population of Russia undoubtedly belonged to what may be called the lower classes; we have no data which would enable us to determine with a safe degree of precision the relative proportion of the middle classes in the total. However, knowing as we do of the expansion of the merchant class of Kievan Russia, we may be sure that, in Novgorod and Smolensk at least, the *bourgeoisie* as a social group was proportionately larger than in the cities of western Europe at the time.

While in our thinking the term "middle classes" is usually associated with an urban *bourgeoisie*, it is also possible to speak of the middle classes in rural society. Prosperous farmers possessing enough land to make them comfortable may be said to form the rural middle class by contrast with the owners of large estates on the one hand and the landless or land-hungry peasants on the other. The question therefore confronts us, whether such a rural middle class existed in Russia at this time.

There is no reason to doubt its existence in the pre-Kievan and early Kievan periods. The men (liudi) organized in guilds (verv) who are mentioned in the *Russian Law* seem to have constituted such a middle class.[23] It is significant that the wergeld of a liudin was forty grivna—i.e., equal to that of a man of the upper classes (muzh) unless the latter belonged to the prince's retinue, in which case his bloodwite was doubled (eighty grivna).

While the existence of the liudi organized in guilds cannot be denied for the tenth and the eleventh centuries, it is usually contended that in the course of the twelfth century the old social regime of rural Russia was upset by the rapid growth of the large estates of the princes and the boyars on the one hand and by the proletarization and feudal subjugation of the liudi on the other. The argument is valid to a certain extent only. It is true that the princely and boyar domains expanded rapidly in the twelfth century but this was as much the result of exploitation of land hitherto untouched by cultivation as of the absorption of already existing small farms.

It is equally true that a process of proletarization of small landholders had been going on since the late eleventh century, in the

23. Vernadsky, *Zvenya Russkoi kultury*, pp. 111–112.

course of which formerly free and independent men became indentured laborers. Again, however, it may be asked whether this part of the argument should be applied to our case without reservation. There is no evidence in the sources to show from what original social group the indentured laborers of the twelfth century came. Some may have been former members of the liudi group but certainly not all. As to the peasants more or less attached to large landed estates, as were the *smerdy* and *izgoi* (see sec. 8, below), there seems to be little connection if any between them and the liudi. Already in the eleventh century the smerdy existed as a separate group, and probably even much earlier. Most of the izgoi were freedmen.

Thus there is no direct evidence of the alleged total disappearance of the liudi in the course of the twelfth century. Their number may have decreased, especially in south Russia, for various reasons. A considerable number of them must have been ruined by the Cuman raids and interprincely wars, following which they no doubt had either to move to cities or become agricultural laborers; either remaining personally free as hired laborers or accepting indenture. In many cases, also, the rural guilds must have disintegrated. We know from the provisions of the *Russian Law* that a liudin was allowed to leave the guild under certain conditions. But even in the case of the dissolution of a guild its former members may each have kept his farm in his own right or they may have formed smaller associations of the siabry type.

Altogether, the liudi doubtless suffered individually and may have lost their previous form of social organization but surely a number of them continued to exist as an economic group, that of free landowners, especially in the north. Following the conquest of Novgorod by the Moscow grand dukes in the late fifteenth century a census of the rural population on all kinds of lands was ordered. It revealed the existence of a numerous class of so-called *svoezemtsi* ("owners of land in their own right"). These must have been the descendants of the liudi class.

Turning back now to the cities, we find the same term, *liudi*, originally applied to the bulk of the city population.[24] Later, in Novgorod in any case, two groups were discernible: the *zhit'i liudi* ("well-to-do men") and the *molodshie liudi* ("younger men"), who are sometimes also called in the Novgorodian sources *chernye liudi* ("black men"). The zhit'i liudi formed a sizable part of the Novgorodian middle class.

24. On the merchants and burghers in the Kievan period, see Vladimirsky-Budanov, *Obzor*, pp. 31–33; Sergeevich, *Drevnosti*, I, 335–338; Diakonov, *Ocherki*, pp. 89–93.

The scale of group distinctions in Novgorodian society may best be seen from the table of fines for contempt of court inserted in one of the clauses of the charter of the city. According to this table the boyar had to pay 50 rubles, the zhit'i 25 rubles, and the molodshi 10. This Novgorod charter was approved in 1471 but for its compilation old rules and regulations were partly used and the interrelation of classes indicated in it presumably represents an old tradition. The merchants (*kuptsy*) are mentioned in the Novgorodian sources as a group separate from the zhit'i but on the same social level. It appears that the zhit'i were not merchants. What, then, was the source of their income? Some probably owned landed estates outside the city. Others may have been owners of industrial enterprises of some sort, such as carpenter's shops, smithies, and so on.

The composition of the middle classes in other Russian cities must have been very similar to that in Novgorod.

## 5. The Lower Classes

As we have just seen, people of the lower classes in Russian cities of the Kievan period were called "younger men" (*molodshie liudi*). They were chiefly workers and artisans of various kinds: carpenters, masons, smiths, fullers, tanners, potters, and so on. Men of the same profession usually lived in the same section of the city, which was named accordingly. Thus for Novgorod the Potters' District and the Carpenters' District are mentioned; in Kiev the Smiths' Gate, etc.

There is for this period no evidence of the existence of artisans' guilds as such but each section of a larger Russian city of the time constituted a guild of its own (see Chap. VII, sec. 6) and a "street guild" or a "row guild" in the artisan section must have been not only a territorial commune but in a sense a professional association as well.

To the lower classes of Kievan society the hired workers or laborers also belonged. In the cities, artisans possessing no shop of their own and junior members of artisan families would offer their services to any who needed them. If many workers were engaged together for a major job, such as the building of a church or a large house, more often than not they would form a coöperative association.

As to hired laborers in rural districts little is known for this period. They are, however, mentioned in some contemporary sources; presumably the need for their help was at its peak in harvest time.

We now come to the smerdy, who constituted the backbone of the lower classes in rural districts.[25] As I have already mentioned, the term *smerd* must be compared with the Iranian *mard* ("man"). It is most likely that it originated in the Sarmatian period of Russian history.

The smerdy were personally free but their legal status was somewhat qualified since they were subject to the special jurisdiction of the prince. That they were free may be best seen by comparing article 45A of the Expanded Version of the *Russian Law* with the following article, 46.[26] In the former it is said that the smerdy may be fined by the prince for offenses committed by them. In the latter, slaves are exempted from these payments "because they are unfree."

That the prince's authority over the smerdy was more specific than with other freemen is made clear by the *Russian Law* as well as by the chronicles. In the *Pravda* of Iaroslav's sons the smerd is mentioned among men dependent on the prince in one way or another. According to the Expanded Version of the *Russian Law* a smerd could not be arrested or otherwise abused without the prince's authorization.[27] After a smerd's death his sons inherited, but if no sons were left the property went to the prince—who, however, had to assign a share for the unmarried daughters, if such were left. This is similar to mortmain in western Europe.

It is significant that in the city-states of northern Russia, Novgorod and Pskov, the supreme authority over the smerdy belonged not to the prince but to the city. Thus, for example, in 1136 Prince Vsevolod of Novgorod was criticized by the veche ("city assembly") for oppressing the smerdy. In Novgorod's treaty with King Kazimierz IV of Poland it is stated expressly that the smerdy are within the jurisdiction of the city and not of the prince. This treaty is a document of a later period (signed around 1470) but its provisions were based on old traditions.

Taking into account the status of the smerdy in Novgorod we may suppose that in the south, where they were subject to the prince, the latter exercised his authority as the head of the state rather than as lord of the manor. The smerdy, then, may be called state peasants, with due reservations. Bearing in mind that the term *smerd* originated, in all probability, in the Sarmatian period, we may surmise that to

25. On the smerdy, see Vladimirsky-Budanov, *Obzor*, pp. 33–35; Sergeevich, *Drevnosti*, I, 203–214; Diakonov, *Ocherki*, pp. 93–99; Iushkov, *Narysy*, pp. 73–95; Grekov, *op. cit.*, pp. 122–142; G. Vernadsky, "Three Notes," *SEER*, 22 (1944), 85–88.

26. *Medieval Russian Laws*, p. 42.

27. *Idem*, p. 49, Article 78.

this same era the origin of the smerdy as a social group must be referred. Presumably the early smerdy were Slavic "men" (*mardan*) paying tribute to the Alans. Later on, with the emancipation of the Antes from Iranian tutelage, authority over them may have passed to the Antic chieftains. In the eighth century the smerdy must have been subject to the authority of the Khazar and the Magyar voevoda; with the emigration of the Magyars and the defeat of the Khazars by Oleg and his successors, the Russian princes finally assumed control of them. This outline of the history of the smerdy is, of course, hypothetical but it seems to be in agreement with the facts; in any case it does not contradict any of the known facts.

Whether the land they tilled was their own or belonged to the state is a moot question. It appears that in Novgorod in any case the smerdy occupied state lands. In the south a sort of condominium must have existed on the part of the prince and the smerdy over the latter's land. At the conference of 1103 Vladimir Monomach mentions "the smerd's farm" (*selo ego*—"his farm").[28] As we have already seen, the smerd's sons inherited his estate—that is, his farm. Granted, however, that a smerd possessed the land he cultivated, it must be admitted this was not a full ownership, since he was not free to will the land even to his daughters; when no sons were left after his death, as we have just seen, the land reverted to the prince. Since the smerd might not bequeath his land he probably was not free to sell it, either. The land was for his perpetual use and that of his male descendants; it was not his property.

The smerdy had to pay state taxes, especially the so-called "tribute." In Novgorod each group of them was registered at the nearest *pogost* (center of a tax collection district); apparently they were organized into communes to make the collection of taxes easier. Another obligation of the smerdy was that of supplying horses to the city militia in case of a major war.

At the princely conference of 1103, mentioned above, a campaign against the Cumans was discussed and Prince Sviatopolk II's retainers remarked that it was not advisable to open hostilities in the spring since by taking their horses they would ruin the smerdy and their fields, to which Vladimir Monomach replied: "I am surprised, comrades, that you concern yourselves for the horses with which the smerd plows. Why do you not bear in mind that as soon as the smerd begins his plowing, the Cuman will come, shoot him down with his

28. Laur., col. 277.

bolt, seize his horse, ride on into his farm, and carry off his wife, his children, and his property? Are you concerned for the horse and not for the smerd himself?" [29]

The low level of the smerd's social position is best shown by the fact that in case of his murder only five grivna—that is, one eighth of the normal bloodwite—was to be paid to the prince by the murderer. The prince was entitled to receive the same amount (five grivna) in the case of murder of a slave. However, in the latter instance the payment represented not bloodwite but compensation to the prince as owner. In the case of the smerd a compensation to his family was to be paid by the murderer in addition to the bloodwite but the amount is not specified in the *Russian Law*.

In the course of time the term *smerd*, as I have mentioned, acquired a derogatory connotation, that of a man of the lowest class. As such, it was applied by haughty aristocrats to denote the commoners at large. Thus, when Prince Oleg of Chernigov was summoned by Sviatopolk II and Vladimir Monomach to attend a conference in Kiev at which the clergy, the boyars, and the Kiev citizens were to be present, he answered in an attitude of arrogance that "it was not proper for him to submit to the judgment of a bishop, of priors, or of smerdy" (1096).[30]

In the early thirteenth century the term *smerdy* was occasionally used to denote the rural population at large. Describing one of the battles in Galicia in 1221, the chronicler remarks: "A boyar would take a boyar as his prisoner; a smerd, a smerd; and a city-man, a city-man." [31]

## 6. The Half-free

Serfdom as a legal institution did not exist in Kievan Russia. In the technical sense of the word, serfdom is a product of feudal law. The subjection of the serfs was not the result of a free interplay of economic forces but rather that of "non-economic" pressure. Feudalism may be defined as a fusion of public and private law, and the nature of the seignorial power in feudal Europe was dual. The seignior was both landlord and ruler. As lord of the manor he exercised a dual authority both over his serfs and over other tenants on his estate.

Potentially the prince in Kievan Russia wielded the same kind of

29. Cross, p. 292.
30. *Idem*, p. 272.
31. *PSRL*, II, 163.

power over the population of his domains. However, the sociopolitical regime of the country at the time was not conducive to the development of feudal institutions and the process of consolidation of the manorial authority of the princes—not to speak of that of the boyars —never went as far as in western Europe in the same period. In spite of all encroachments on the part of the princes, the smerdy, as we have seen, remained freemen.

In addition there also existed a social group of what may be called half-free people. These were not serfs, either, in the technical sense, since there was no element of "noneconomic pressure" in the process of their loss of freedom. The tie between them and their lords was purely economic, since it was the relation between creditor and debtor. If and when the debt was paid with interest, the debtor became a full-fledged freeman once more.

The peculiarity of the relation lay in the fact that a debt of this kind was supposed to be paid not in money but in work, although there was no objection to paying it in money if the debtor unexpectedly obtained a sufficient sum to do so.

The obligation might be incurred in various ways and for various reasons. The debtor might be a farmer (an impoverished liudin), or merchant, or artisan, who, having borrowed money for the purpose of improving his business was unable to obtain funds to repay it in money and thus had no alternative to paying it by his own work. But he might also happen to be a hired laborer by calling and being in need of money might ask and receive his seasonal or yearly wages in advance; the transaction would be formulated as a loan to be repaid by work, with interest. Such a debtor (*zakup*) was in fact an indentured laborer and such a laborer could be employed by his creditor for every kind of work, but the greater number of them appear to have become agricultural workers (*roleinyi zakup*). The group as a whole must have been fairly numerous, since they were held responsible—in part at least—for the abortive social revolution of 1113, after which special laws were enacted, on the initiative of Vladimir Monomach, to improve their position. These laws, some of them bearing on loans at large and some specifically referring to the *zakupy* (which is the plural form of *zakup*), were included in the Expanded Version of the *Russian Law*.[32]

32. On the *zakupy*, see M. N. Iasinsky, "Zakupy Russkoi Pravdy i pamiatniki zapadno-russkogo prava," *SVB*, pp. 430–465; Sergeevich, *Drevnosti*, I, 215–225; Diakonov, *Ocherki*, pp. 101–103; Iushkov, *Narysy*, pp. 53–61; Grekov, *op. cit.*, pp. 113–121.

The provisions of the *Russian Law* concerning the zakup had as their object to establish a fair balance between the rights and the duties of the indentured laborer on the one hand and those of the creditor—"the lord" (*gospodin*)—on the other. Thus if a zakup attempted to flee from his lord he became the latter's slave; but, if the lord fraudulently sold him into slavery, not only was the zakup's freedom automatically restored but his obligation to the lord was terminated. The indentured laborer was entitled to sue the lord for any unprovoked offense on the latter's part; the lord, however, might punish the zakup even by beating him, if there were "a good reason for it"—that is, if the zakup neglected his work.

Under the new clauses in the *Russian Law* the lord could not compel the indentured laborer to do every kind of work; only such work as was suited to the type of laborer he was could be expected from him. Thus if a zakup ruined his lord's war horse he could not be held responsible, and for obvious reasons: the tending of the war horse of a prince or boyar—a magnificent steed more often than not—required the services of a specially trained man. Moreover, a grandee's groom was usually chosen from among his slaves and a freeman— even one of the half-free—could object to performing the work. If, however, the horse ruined by a zakup was a work horse—one "to work with plow and harrow," as the *Russian Law* explains it—the zakup had to pay for it. That is, the term of his work was prolonged according to the extent of the damage done.[33]

Besides the indentured laborers there was another social group which may also be listed as consisting of the half-free, although not in any strict juridical sense. These were the so-called *vdachi,* men or women who "gave themselves" (the Slavic word for "give" is *dati*) into a lord's temporary service. This was done chiefly in periods of distress—during a famine or after a devastating war. In this case the transaction was couched in terms of charity rather than of juridical obligation. The people in distress received a "favor" (*milost'*) from the lord; the money or grain they obtained from him was considered not a loan but a "gift." However, they had to work for it for at least a year. The institution of *dacha* was likewise known among the Baltic Slavs; there, especially in the thirteenth century, it assumed an entirely different character, approaching slavery.[34]

---

33. *Medieval Russian Laws,* p. 46.

34. On the *vdachi,* see Grekov, *op. cit.,* pp. 121–122; Vernadsky, "Three Notes," pp. 83–85.

In concluding this section one more category of the half-free should be mentioned: the "freedmen" (*izgoi*). Their position was closest to serfdom of any Russian social group of the period. Since they were under the protection of the church, they will be dealt with in connection with the other "church people" (sec. 8, below).

## 7. The Slaves

The oldest Russian term for "slave," as we have seen, is *cheliadin;* collectively, *cheliad'*. This term is found in the old Church Slavonic texts and is also used in the Russo-Byzantine treaties of the tenth century.[35]

Another old term is *rob* (otherwise *rab;* feminine *roba,* later *raba*), to be connected with the verb *robotati,* "to work." In this sense the slave is a "worker" and vice versa.

In the mid-eleventh century a new term appears: *kholop,* to be compared with the Polish *khlop* (in Polish spelling *chłop*), "peasant," "serf." The proto-Slavic form was *kholp;* in the transcription used by most Slavic philologists, *cholpŭ*.[36] In Russian the term *kholop* denoted a male slave. A female slave was continuously called *raba*.

Slavery in Kievan Russia was of two kinds: temporary and permanent. The latter was known as "full slavery" (*kholopstvo obelno*—literally, "round slavery"). The main source of temporary slavery was war captivity. At first not only soldiers of enemy armies but even enemy civilians seized during the war were subject to slavery. In the course of time more concern was shown for civilians and finally, by the treaty between the Russians and the Poles signed in 1229, the inviolability of the civilian population was recognized.

At the close of a war, captives were released for ransom if it was offered. In the Russo-Byzantine treaties a ceiling on ransom was established to prevent abuses. If the ransom could not be collected, the captive remained at the disposal of his captor. According to *Zakon sudnyi liudem,* in such cases the captive's work was credited to the payment of the ransom and after the full amount was covered the captive was to be released. The rule must have been duly observed in regard to nationals of states with which the Russians signed specific treaties, such as Byzantium. In other cases it may have been disre-

35. On slavery in old Russia, see Vladimirsky-Budanov, *Obzor,* pp. 391–408; Sergeevich, *Drevnosti,* I, 105–159; Diakonov, *Ocherki,* pp. 104–113; Iushkov, *Narysy,* pp. 48–53; Grekov, *op. cit.,* pp. 104–110; Vernadsky, "Three Notes," pp. 81–83.

36. Berneker, *op. cit.,* I, 394; G. Ilyinsky (Il'insky), "Zvuk *ch* v slavianskikh iazykakh," *ANORI, 20,* Pt. 4 (1916), p. 141.

garded. In any case, it is significant that the *Russian Law* does not mention war captivity as a source of full slavery.

According to Article 110 of the Expanded Version, "full slavery is of three kinds." Man becomes a slave: (1) if he voluntarily sells himself into slavery; (2) if he marries a female slave without previously making a special agreement with her lord; (3) if he enters the service of a lord in the capacity of steward or housekeeper without a specific agreement that he should remain free.[37]

As to self-selling into slavery, two conditions had to be observed to make the transaction legal: (1) a minimum price (not less than half a grivna); and (2) a fee to the town clerk (one nogata). These formalities were prescribed by law in order to prevent the enslavement of a man against his will. Nothing is said about female slaves in this section of the *Russian Law* but it may be assumed that a woman could sell herself into slavery just as a man did. On the other hand, a woman was not given the privilege of preserving her freedom by agreement with the lord in the case of marrying a male slave. Although the point is not mentioned in the *Russian Law,* from later codes as well as by inference from various sources we know that such a marriage automatically made the woman a slave. It must have been an old custom and therefore not considered worth mentioning in the *Russian Law.*

In addition to the main sources of slave population just mentioned, the transaction of sale may be said to constitute a derivative source. Apparently the same formalities as in the case of self-selling had to be observed in the case of selling a slave. In this way a minimum price was established on full slaves. There was no minimum price on war captives. After the victory of the Novgorodians over the Suzdalians in 1169, captive Suzdalians were sold at two nogata each. In the *Lay of Igor's Campaign* it is said that if grand Duke Vsevolod had taken part in the campaign against the Cumans, the latter would have been defeated and then female captives would have been sold for one nogata and males for one rezana.

No ceiling price on slaves was set but public opinion—at least that of the clergy—was against speculation in the slave trade. It was considered sinful to buy a slave for one price and then resell him for a larger sum; this was called "usury" (*izgoistvo*).

The slave had no civil rights. If one was murdered a compensation was to be paid by the murderer to his owner and not to the slave's kinsmen. There is no provision in the laws of the period as to the

37. *Medieval Russian Laws,* p. 52.

murder of a slave by his owner. Obviously the lord was held responsible if he murdered a temporary slave. In the case of a full slave he was subject to church penance but this was apparently the only sanction in such cases. The slave could not sue in the courts and was not accepted as a full-fledged witness in any litigation. Legally, he might own no property except his clothes and other personal accessories, known as *peculium* in the Roman law (*otaritsa* is the old Russian term); nor might a slave enter upon any obligation or sign any contract. Actually, many a slave in Kievan Russia possessed property and entered obligations but in each case it was in the name of his owner. If in such a case the slave failed to meet his obligation his owner had to pay the damages, provided the man with whom the slave dealt was not aware that the other party was a slave. If he was aware of the fact, he acted on his own risk.

Slaves were used by their owners both as household servants of various kinds and as field hands. They might also happen to be men and women skilled in handicrafts, or even pedagogues. They were valued according to their skill and the services performed. Thus, according to the *Russian Law*, the amount of compensation to the prince for the murder of his slaves varied from five to twelve grivna, depending on what sort of slave the victim was.

As to the termination of slavery, aside from the death of the slave, temporary slavery could be ended by a sufficient amount of work performed. The termination of full slavery might occur in two ways: either the slave would redeem himself (which, of course, only a few could afford to do) or the lord could emancipate his slave, or slaves, by his own will. This he was constantly encouraged to do by the church and many a wealthy man followed the advice by freeing his slaves posthumously through a special provision in his testament.

There also existed, of course, an illegal way for a slave to free himself—by running away. Many slaves appear to have tried this way to freedom, for there are several articles in the *Russian Law* dealing with runaway slaves. Any person who gave shelter to such a slave or helped him in any way was liable to a fine.

## 8. The Church People

In old Russia not only the clergy and members of their families came under church jurisdiction but likewise certain other categories of people who either served the church in one way or another or needed its protection. They were all known as the "church people" (*tserkovnye liudi*).[38]

The Russian clergy may be divided into two groups: the "black clergy" (i.e., monks) and the "white clergy" (priests and deacons). Following the Byzantine pattern, it is an established custom in the Russian church that only monks are ordained bishops and, contrary to the practice of the Roman Church, Russian priests are chosen from among married men.

Throughout the Kievan period the office of Metropolitan of Kiev was occupied by Greeks, with only two exceptions (Ilarion and Kliment). About half the bishops were, however, of Russian origin. The bishops were head and shoulders above the regular clergy in authority, prestige, and wealth. In the later periods it became common to speak of them as "princes of the church."

Let us now examine the position of the other "church people." The first category among them comprises those who in some way participate in the church service but do not belong to the clergy: such are the church singers, the man who takes care of extinguishing the candles after service (*sveshchegas*), and the woman who bakes the wafers (*proskurnitsa* or *prosvirnia*, from *prosvira* ["prosphora"], "wafer"). Incidentally, it may be recalled that the poet Pushkin advised those who wanted to familiarize themselves with racy Russian language to learn it from the Moscow *prosvirni* (plural from *prosvirnia*).

The second category of church people consists of those connected with the charity institutions supported by the church, such as the physician (*lechets*) and other personnel of the hospitals, homes for aged, inns for pilgrims, and so on, as well as the people who are cared for in those institutions.

The third category is the so-called *izgoi*.[39] The characteristics of this group as well as the origin and the connotation of the term have been the subject of protracted controversy among scholars. The main difficulty is that the term is used in one sense in the sources of the twelfth century and apparently in quite a different sense in Iaroslav's *Pravda* of the eleventh century. In my own opinion the only way to

---

38. On the clergy and church people in old Russia, see Golubinsky, *Istoriia*, I, Pt. 1 (2d ed. Moscow, 1901), pp. 444–502, 557–588; I, Pt. 2 (Moscow, 1904), pp. 603–689.

39. On the *izgoi*, see Vladimirsky-Budanov, *Obzor*, pp. 390–391; Sergeevich, *Drevnosti*, I, 298–302; Diakonov, *Ocherki*, pp. 113–116; M. Szeftel, "La Condition juridique des déclassés dans la Russie ancienne," *Archives d'histoire du droit Oriental, 2* (Brussels and Paris, 1938), 431–440; Iushkov, *Narysy*, pp. 103–106; Grekov, *op. cit.*, pp. 142–147; Vernadsky, "Three Notes," pp. 88–92.

untie this Gordian knot is the proverbial one: to cut it—that is, to admit that the *Pravda* of the eleventh century and the sources of the twelfth century, while using the same word, speak of two entirely different social groups. This is not the only known case of such divergency between the *Pravda* and later sources. For example, the term *ognishchanin* in the *Pravda* denotes the prince's bailiff but in Novgorodian sources the term is applied to a special group of Novgorodian citizens who have no connection with the princely court.

The *izgoi* of the *Russian Law* will be dealt with in another section (11, below); here we shall examine only the "church people," so-called. The classical definition of this social group is found in Prince Vsevolod's "Statute of the Church Courts" (1125–36): "There are three kinds of izgoi: the priest's son who has remained illiterate; the slave who has redeemed himself from slavery; and the bankrupt merchant." Then follows a gloss by a later copyist: "And may we add the fourth kind of izgoi: the orphaned prince." [40]

The common characteristics of all these men was that each had lost his former status and needed adjustment to new conditions, for which the church offered him its protection. The very term *izgoi* may be explained in this sense if we agree to derive it from the old Slavic verb *goiti*, which means to "live," also to "let live," "supply means of existence," "care for." From this point of view the izgoi is a man deprived of care, hence to be "cared for." In this connection we must recall that the term *izgoistvo* or *izoistvo* ("izgoyism") had also the connotation of undue profit derived from the trade in slaves and especially from the redemption price of a slave. Because of this, in a wider sense *izgoistvo* was sometimes used as a synonym of "usury." Bearing in mind the connotation of this term, we may guess that the largest group among the izgoi were freedmen and that the term was originally applied to them alone, and only later other similar groups were included in it by analogy.

According to custom, the freedman might not stay with his former master. The obvious purpose of this rule was to prevent any possibility of his reënslavement. More often than not, he had no means of subsistence and no place to go. The church offered him both, by employing him in one way or another or by settling him on church land. Thus we find a group of izgoi in Novgorod under the jurisdiction of the bishop of that city. Most of them, however, were settled in rural districts. In his charter of 1150 Prince Rostislav of Smolensk granted

40. *Khristomatiia*, I, 209.

to the bishop of the same city, among other things, two localities, one "with izgoi and land" and the other "with land and izgoi." [41] It appears in this case that the izgoi were considered an appurtenance of the estate. Were they in the rural districts permanently attached to the land? Hardly. Presumably they were expected to reimburse the church by money or work for the assistance given them in their settling but afterward they must have been free to move elsewhere if they so chose.

From Rostislav's charter the conclusion may be drawn that the izgoi mentioned there had been previously connected with one of the prince's estates. And yet we know that the izgoi as a group were under the church jurisdiction. It may therefore be surmised that the izgoi mentioned in the charter had a rather complex history: originally, we may suppose, they had been cared for by the church—probably settled on church land, had then moved to the prince's estates, and finally found themselves on church land once more.

If we admit that the rural izgoi retained freedom of movement, we may guess that they were allowed to move only once a year, after the end of the agricultural season and after having paid their rent.

## 9. Woman

The position of woman in old Russia is often represented as that of complete subjugation to man. Women are supposed to have been deprived of any freedom and to have been compelled to live in Oriental seclusion. It is true that the Muscovite queens and princesses of the sixteenth and seventeenth centuries led a retired life in their private apartments (*terem*) in the tsar's palace and that the same custom was also practiced in boyar and merchant families, although less strictly. With the commoners, however, it was different, and thus, even for the Muscovite period, the traditional view on the subjugated position of woman in Russia cannot be accepted without reservations.

For the Kievan period such a view would be absolutely untenable. Russian women in that time enjoyed considerable freedom and independence, both legally and socially, and showed a spirit of self-reliance in various aspects of life. We see a woman ruling Russia in the mid-tenth century (Princess Olga), another starting a school for girls at the convent she founded in the eleventh century (Ianka, Vsevolod I's daughter). Princesses send their own envoys to foreign nations (as we know, two members of the Russian peace delegation

41. *Idem*, I, 222–223.

to Constantinople in 945 represented women). It is to a woman (step-mother of Vladimir Monomach) that the people of Kiev appeal to restore peace among the princes (in the case of the incipient conflict between Sviatopolk II and Vladimir Monomach in 1097).

If we turn to the folklore, the woman warrior is a popular heroine of the old Russian epic poems. The *polianitsa* ("adventuress of the steppes") of the Russian bylina reminds us of the Amazon of classical tradition. And indeed, from the geographical point of view, there is a complete parallel, since both performed their exploits in the same region—the lower Don and Azov area. As we know, the myth of the Amazons reflects an important fact in the social history of the Don and Azov tribes in the Scythian and Sarmathian periods: the prevalence of a matriarchal form of clan organization.

The possibility that a matriarchate was the basis of social organization in some of the proto-Slavic tribes and especially some of the Antian clans should not be disregarded. If so, the comparatively independent position of woman in Kievan Russia may be explained at least partly as a remnant of matriarchal tradition. It is perhaps not accidental that in the earliest version of the *Russian Law*, among the relatives who have the right—and duty—to avenge the murder of their kinsman, "sister's son" is mentioned together with the "brother's son."

On the whole, the old Russian clan as described in the *Russian Law* and other sources was clearly of the patriarchal type. At the same time, however, a woman was guaranteed certain rights. To begin with the wergeld—that symbol of the social value of a human being in those times—a woman *had* a wergeld but the amount of the bloodwite paid for her murder was only one half that paid for the murder of a man of the middle classes: twenty grivna instead of forty.[42]

A woman, even a married one, had the right to own property in her own name. Following the Byzantine pattern, Russian civil law recognized both the dowry, in the sense of the money which a woman brings to her husband in marriage, and the "prenuptial gifts" (*propter nuptias donatio*)—i.e., a gift of property by a man to his bride, which is also called "dowry" in English. In Russian two different terms are used, to wit, *pridanoe* in the first sense and *veno* in the second. Besides this, a married woman might own any other kind of property, whether bequeathed to her by her parents or acquired by her. A com-

42. On the Russian marriage law and the legal position of woman in old Russia, see Vladimirsky-Budanov, *Obzor*, pp. 411–468.

mon source of income for a woman, including the married woman, were the products of her handicraft. According to the so-called "Church Statute" of Iaroslav the Wise, (actually compiled not in the eleventh but in the thirteenth century), a man stealing hemp or flax raised by his wife, or any kind of linen and fabrics made by her, was subject to a fine. According to the *Russian Law*, after her husband's death, if he died first, the wife was entitled to the property he had given her and to any other property she might happen to own. Moreover, the widow was recognized as head of the family, if there were children, and was entrusted with the management of her late husband's estate. When children came of age each had the right to claim his or her share in the estate but if they did so they were obliged to give a certain part of the estate to their mother "for the conclusion of her life" (*prozhi-tok*). Speaking of the children, the daughters inherited together with the sons, except in the smerdy families (see sec. 5, above).

Following Russia's conversion to Christianity, marriage and family life were put under both the protection and the supervision of the church. Here again, in the Kievan period the rights of women were not forgotten. According to the above-quoted church statute, the husband was subject to a fine in case of adultery. The rights of the daughter were also protected, to a certain extent at least. If the parents compelled their daughter to marry against her will and she committed suicide, they were held responsible for her death.

In a broader sense, Christianity affected the attitude of Russian society toward woman in a twofold way. On one hand the Christian doctrine—in its Byzantine interpretation, at least—held woman responsible, through Eve, for the original sin. In the synopsis of Biblical history, which, according to the *Book of Annals*, was taught to Vladimir by a Greek missionary, it was explained that "the human race first sinned through woman . . . for it was through woman that Adam fell from Paradise." [43]

On the other hand, one of the cardinal points of Byzantine Christianity was the worship of Our Lady, the Holy Virgin, who vindicated womanhood by giving birth to the Saviour, hence her name, "Mother of God" (Μήτηρ θεοῦ) or Θεοτόκος (literally, "Birthgiver to God"). As explained to Vladimir by the Greek missionary, "after being incarnate by a woman, God made the faithful enter into Paradise." In this way, God "avenged himself on the devil."

43. Cross, p. 196.

Thus the church doctrine both humiliated and glorified woman and in this sense supported both the negative and the positive attitudes toward woman in Russia. Ascetic monasticism saw in woman the main source of temptation for man. For the monks and those influenced by them, woman was the "devil's vessel" (*sosud diavola*) rather than anything else. And yet the church, including these same monks, also spread the worship of Our Lady all over the Russian lands and not women alone but men as well offered constant prayers to Her.

Spiritual life defies weighing or measurement and religious influences are intangible. It may be argued whether the positive or the negative aspect in the Christian doctrine about woman left a deeper impression on the Russian soul. It seems likely, however, that the Russian woman gained more than she lost in the final count. It was the old Russian literature, as we shall see (Chap. IX, sec. 8), which suffered most from the degradation of Eve.

### 10. The Steppe Frontiersmen

From the appearance of the Patzinaks in the late ninth century and even more with that of the Cumans in the mid-eleventh century, the steppes were closed to Slavic agriculture. It was only in the intermediate forest-steppe zone and in the northern fringe of the steppes that land could be regularly tilled. That fringe the Russian princes tried to protect from nomadic inroads by lines of fortifications, which frequently did not present insurmountable barriers to the Cumans but at least offered some security to the Russian population. Beyond that fortified line no agriculturist ventured to establish any kind of farm and few Russians penetrated at all, except either as soldiers in a campaign or as war captives of the Cumans.

In a sense, the steppe may be likened to the sea. With sufficient forces it could be blockaded but it was impossible for either the Russians or the Cumans to control or guard every section of it. The Cuman horde made yearly rounds of the steppe, men following their grazing horses and cattle; the section in the vicinity of the nomad tents could not be entered by any outsider but the rest of the steppe was practically no man's land, at least periodically.

This was the *pole* ("prairie") of the old Russian epic poems, the scene of the heroic deeds of Ilia Muromets and other Russian legendary *bogatyri* ("valiant knights"); also that of actual battles—of the exploits of thousands of real Russian warriors, whether victorious, like Vladimir Monomach, or vanquished, like Igor of Novgorod-Seversk. Covered with *kovyl* (a special kind of grass peculiar to south Russia) and abundant in animal life, but also in Cuman archers, the steppe held out a strong attraction to the adventurous, while repelling the weak. It is poetically, if tersely, described in the *Lay of Igor's Campaign* of the late twelfth century and hardly less poetically but with much more elaborate verbosity in Nikolai Gogol's *Taras Bulba* seven centuries later.

In the course of the fifteenth and sixteenth centuries this no man's land became the abode of the Ukrainian and Russian Cossacks, who eventually organized themselves in strong military communes ("hosts"), of which the Zaporozhie—beyond the Dnieper cataracts—and Don hosts—the latter in the lower Don region—were the most important two.

In the Kievan period a similar commune was established in the lower Don area. Its members were known as *brodniki*.[44] The term *brodnik* (which is the singular form) is to be connected with the verb *broditi* ("to rove"), the original meaning of which in old Russia is "to wade" (in water); hence *brod*, "ford." From the economic point of view, the purpose of wading is to catch fish by dragging a net. Thus, *brodnik* means "fisherman."

The brodniki were outside the pale either of the Kievan state or of the Cuman, although possibly at times they recognized the authority of certain Cuman khans as a temporary political device. Little is known of the organization of their commune. It may have started as a fishermen's association and later acquired some military features. Presumably similar communes existed also in the regions of the lower Dniester and lower Danube rivers.

The preference of the frontiersmen for rivers may be explained partly by the fact that the river provided them with ample food and partly by the element of protection it gave them against the nomads. In their campaigns nomad armies tried to follow the watersheds.

## 11. National Minorities

From time immemorial proto-Slavic and Antian tribes lived in contact with other national groups. Never once, prior to the Kievan period, were the Slavs able to colonize the whole extent of the territory of western Eurasia, and even in the Kievan period the Russians

44. On the *brodniki*, see P. Golubovsky, "Pechenegi, Torki i Polovtsy," *KU*, 1883 (November), 586–604; 1883 (December), 707–708.

failed to populate the whole area politically subject to them. Moreover, the "Russians" of the ninth and tenth centuries themselves represent a mixed group because of the Swedish element.

However, new bands of Norse warriors hired from time to time by the Russian princes constantly increased the Scandinavian element and their stream died out only in the late eleventh century. Some of these Varangians stayed in Russia only temporarily and must thus be considered aliens rather than minority nationals. Others who settled in Russia permanently followed the path of the old Swedish Rus' and rapidly dissolved in the Slavic sea. Thus, while there were a considerable number of men of Norse extraction in Kievan Russia, no Norse national minority was ever constituted by them.

The largest minority group in Russia of the Kievan period was the Finns. Various Finnish tribes had occupied the northern and eastern regions of Russia from time immemorial.[45] Some were dislocated by the process of Slavic colonization, others completely Russianized. Suzdalia in particular became the Slavo-Finnish melting pot and out of the mixture of Slavs and Finns the nucleus of the so-called "Great Russian" branch of the eastern Slavs was formed, to assume leadership over the Russians in the Muscovite period. Many national characteristics of the Great Russian are to be explained by the Finnish strain in his blood.[46]

While some Finnish tribes disappeared during the Slavic expansion, many others were able to hold their ground, although one by one they had to join the Russian federation, except for the western Finns in Finland, eventually conquered by the Swedes.

According to the story of the "calling of the Varangians,"[47] the latter were invited jointly by the "Russians" (Rus'), the Slovenians, the Krivichians, and by three Finnish tribes: the Chudians, the Merians, and the Vesians. At that time, in the mid-ninth century, there existed a strong Slavo-Finnish federation in north Russia. The Chudians and Merians are also mentioned as participants in Oleg's Byzantine campaign of 907. This is the last mention of the Merians, who were completely Russianized in the course of the tenth century.

With Russia's conversion to Christianity the Finnish tribes who lived in closest proximity with the Russians were eventually baptized;

45. See *Ancient Russia*, pp. 233–239.
46. See Kliuchevsky's famous analysis of the background of the "Great Russians" in his *Kurs Russkoi istorii*, I, 361–391.
47. *Ancient Russia*, p. 336.

other, mostly smaller, tribes in more remote districts remained heathen for a long time, some being unconverted even at the time of the Russian revolution of 1917. Because of the authority wielded among the Finnish tribes by the shamans, it was in the mixed Finno-Slavic regions of northern Russia that Christianity met with the strongest opposition. As a result of the conversion of the eastern Finns to Greek Orthodox Christianity and the eventual conversion of the western Finns to Roman Catholicism (later, to Lutheranism), a religious and cultural barrier was erected between the two branches of the Finns, which has lasted up to the present time.

The Lithuanians must be mentioned here after the Finns.[48] As late as the eleventh century a Lithuanian tribe, Goliad' (Galindi), had its abode in central Russia, in the basins of the Ugra and Protva rivers, both of them tributaries of the Oka River. According to the *Book of Annals*, the Goliad' were conquered by Iziaslav I in 1058. After that they gradually merged with the Russians. In the tenth and eleventh centuries the Russians also came in contact with the Iatviagians (Iatvingi), one of the main Lithuanian tribes, who lived between the Russians and the Poles. Some of the Iatviagians were conquered by Vladimir I and Iaroslav I; others were subdued by Roman of Volynia in the late twelfth century. It seems, however, that even those Iatviagian clans which had to recognize the supremacy of the Russian princes succeeded in keeping their national identity.

While the Finns and the Lithuanians formed an important part of the ethnic and historical background of northern, northwestern, and eastern Russia, the Jews, although much less numerous, played a significant role in the life of south Russia. Jewish colonies existed in Transcaucasia, in the Taman peninsula, and in the Crimea from at least the fifth century A.D., if not earlier. In the eighth and ninth centuries Jewish missionaries were active in Khazaria and around 865 the Khazar kagan and many of his grandees were converted to Judaism. Thus a considerable number of Jews settled in south Russia in this period must have been of Khazar extraction.

Not counting the Taman peninsula, from which the Russians had to withdraw in the late eleventh century, and the Crimea, from which they had withdrawn a century before, the main center of Judaism in old Russia was Kiev. A Jewish colony existed there [49] from the Khazar

---

48. See *idem*, pp. 229–233; A. Brückner, *Dzieje Kultury Polskiej* (Krakow, 1930), I, 405–413.

49. *Ancient Russia*, p. 333.

period. In the twelfth century one of the city gates in Kiev was known as the Jewish Gate—evidence that the Jews occupied the section of the city close to it and that there were a considerable number of them in Kiev.

The Jews played a prominent role in both the commercial and the intellectual life of Kievan Russia.[50]

At least one of the Russian bishops of this period, Luka Zhidiata of Novgorod, was, as we may think, of Jewish extraction. Judaism appears to have had a strong appeal for the Russians of this time, as a result of which Russian bishops such as Ilarion of Kiev and Kirill of Turov in their sermons paid considerable attention to Judaism in its relation to Christianity.

While the presence of the Jews in south Russia was, partly at least, the result of the Khazar expansion, the Russians were in direct contact through Tmutorokan with the peoples of the Caucasus, especially the Iasians (Ossetians) and Kosogians (Circassians). As we know, both these peoples recognized the suzerainty of Sviatoslav I and later that of Mstislav of Tmutorokan in the tenth and eleventh centuries, respectively. The Kosogians constituted an important element in Mstislav's druzhina and he settled some of them in the Pereiaslav area. Undoubtedly, some of the Iasian warriors likewise joined his retinue. It is against this background that we may best interpret the term *izgoi* in Iaroslav's *Pravda*.[51] The term occurs in the opening section of the code, in the list of people worth normal wergeld. It is obvious that the izgoi mentioned here belongs to the upper or middle classes and has nothing in common with the freedman under church protection, although the latter is also called izgoi. Vladimirsky-Budanov considers the izgoi of the *Russian Law* a member of the prince's druzhina and he is certainly right, only he does not explain the origin either of this category of princely retainer or of the term itself. The only key to the meaning of the term is its place in the list. The izgoi is mentioned between the [Kievan] Russian and the [Novgorodian] Slav. The term must then have had an ethnic meaning

---

50. On Judaism and Jews in old Russia, see S. M. Dubnow, *History of the Jews in Russia and Poland*, I. Friedlaender, tr., I (Philadelphia, The Jewish Publication Society, 1916), 13–38; I. Berlin, *Istoricheskie sud'by Evreiskogo naroda na territorii Russkogo gosudarstva* (Petrograd, 1919); G. M. Barats, *O sostaviteliakh Povesti Vremennykh Let i ee istochnikakh, preimushchestvenno evreiskikh* (Berlin, 1924), reviewed by A. Brückner, *ASP, 40* (1926), 141–148; I. Brutskus (J. Brutzkus), "Pershi zvistki pro Evreev u Polshchi ta na Rusi," *Naukovyi Zbirnyk, 24* (1927), 3–11.

51. Vernadsky, "Three Notes," pp. 88–92.

and, since there was no Slavic tribe of this name, the izgoi must have been of non-Slavic origin.

So far we are on firm ground; what follows is only my hypothesis. In my opinion the term *izgoi* should be derived from the Ossetian word *izkaei,* which means "alien," "hireling," and also "hired laborer." If so, the izgoi must have been a prince's "hireling"—a member of the druzhina—of Ossetian or Kosogian extraction. Following Mstislav's death in 1036 his principality was inherited by Iaroslav and presumably most of Mstislav's retainers were included in Iaroslav's retinue, on which occasion they were guaranteed equal wergeld with the other members of the druzhina. Precisely in 1036 it is supposed that Iaroslav's *Pravda* was revised and it is at this time that the term *izgoi* must have been inserted in it.[52]

From the late eleventh century bands of Turkish warriors and whole Turkish tribes were hired by the Russian princes as auxiliary troops against the Cumans. Some of these Turkish groups, such as the Chernye Klobuki ("Black Caps"), the Berendei, the Koui, and several others, settled permanently in south Russia. They were usually referred to as "those pagans of ours" (*svoi poganye*).[53]

Of them all, the Chernye Klobuki, settled in the region of the Ros River south of Kiev, came into closest contact with the Russians. In the middle of the twelfth century they even played an important political role, supporting Prince Iziaslav II against his opponents. Presumably all these Turkish tribes kept their traditional clan organization.

In addition to the "loyal Turks," small groups of independent Turkish peoples—the Patzinaks and the Cumans—were also, on several occasions, brought to Russia either as prisoners of war or as hirelings and slaves. Both Patzinak and Cuman settlements are mentioned in Russian sources and also left traces in toponymics. It is in this connection that the term *khop* in the *Pravda* of Iaroslav's sons may be considered.[54] The term is mentioned in the list of various categories of men subject to the prince's jurisdiction, for whose murder or injury fines were to be paid to the prince. Article 26 of the

52. M. N. Tikhomirov, *Issledovanie o Russkoi Pravde,* pp. 28–29, 49, 51, 54, 55, 61.

53. See D. A. Rasovsky, "O roli Chernykh Klobukov v istorii drevnei Rusi," *SK, 1* (1927), 93–109; *idem,* "Pechenegi, Torki i Berendei na Rusi i v Ugrii," *SK, 6* (1933), 1–66; *idem,* "Rus' i kochevniki v epokhu Vladimira Sviatogo," *Vladimirskii Sbornik,* pp. 149–154; *idem,* "Rus', Chernye Klobuki i Polovtsy v XII veke," *BID, 16/18* (1940), 369–378.

54. G. Vernadsky, "Three Notes," pp. 85–88.

Short Version of the *Russian Law* reads as follows: "And for the smerd and the khop, five grivna." [55] In the corresponding section of the Expanded Version of the *Russian Law*, *kholop* ("slave") is read instead of *khop*, and therefore the reading *khop* is usually considered merely a copyist's error. The explanation is hardly acceptable. This section of the *Pravda* obviously deals with the standard social pair mentioned in Byzantine law manuals: the peasant (*smerd*) and the herdsman (*khop*).

Khop is the name of a Patzinak tribe and it is known from Constantine Porphyrogenitus that Russians used to buy horses and cattle from the Patzinaks.[56] When large herds were bought, Patzinak herders must have been hired—or bought—by the Russians to tend the beasts both on the march and after arriving at their destination. Presumably most of the Patzinak herders so employed were of the Khop tribe, hence the term *khop*, which at first must have denoted "a herder of Patzinak extraction," then a herder in general.

As we know, in the course of the eleventh century the Patzinaks were driven away and replaced by the Cumans. Cuman herders were likewise hired by the Russian princes. In the twelfth century the term *khop* was no longer in use and at the time of the final revision of the *Pravda* in the late twelfth century it was replaced by the somewhat similar *kholop* ("slave"). Incidentally, a prince's herders were usually his slaves; thus between *khop* and *kholop* there is an inner connection through the social connotations of the two terms.

## 12. Concluding Queries: on "Economic and Social Feudalism" in Kievan Russia

Having examined both the economic foundation and the social organization of Kievan Russia, we now may ask ourselves to what stage of social and economic development—or, to borrow a term from geology, to what sociopolitical formation—Kievan Russia belongs.

Chronologically, as we know, the Kievan period included the tenth, eleventh, and twelfth centuries. Those three centuries witnessed the rise and blossoming of feudal institutions in western and central Europe; they represent what may be called the feudal age par excellence. It seems only natural that one should be inclined to place

55. See *Medieval Russian Laws*, p. 32.

56. *Khop*, in Greek transcription Χοπόν, *De Adm.*, chap. xxxvii, col. 13. See K. H. Menges, "Etymological Notes on Some Päčänäg Names," *Byzantion*, *17* (1945), 263–264.

Kievan Russia in the same category and characterize its sociopolitical regime as feudal. Yet until recently the Russian historians have been reluctant to do so. They did not raise any definite objections to the study of feudalism in Russia: they simply ignored the problem.

Such an attitude on the part of not only the leaders of Russian historical science, such as S. M. Soloviev and V. O. Kliuchevsky, but also the rank and file historians may be partly explained by the guiding idea—consciously or subconsciously entertained—of a basic difference in the historical development of Russia on one hand and Europe on the other. Each scholar had his own explanation of the causes at the root of this difference. Some emphasized the important role of the clan in Russian social structure (Soloviev, Kavelin); others that of the *mir*, or commune (K. Aksakov); still others the overgrowth of central state authority (Miliukov) or the expansion of foreign trade (Kliuchevsky). While the Slavophiles extolled Russia's uniqueness as a historical asset, the Westernizers deplored it as a liability and—as we have seen—cited the "retardation" of the historical process in Russia as the main reason for her "backwardness."

An important contributing cause of the neglect shown by Russian historians of the nineteenth century in regard to the problem of feudalism was the concentration of their attention—for the Mongol and post-Mongol periods—on study of the eastern, or Muscovite, Russia where the development of feudal institutions, or those similar to the feudal, was less marked than in western, or Lithuanian, Russia. From this angle the appearance of M. K. Liubavsky's work on the *Provincial Division and Local Administration of the Lithuanian-Russian State* (1893) constituted an important historiographical landmark, which opened new vistas to historical research.

N. P. Pavlov-Silvansky was the first to put the study of the problem of feudalism on the order of the day in Russian historiography but he dealt chiefly with feudal institutions of the Mongol period, making no attempt to assert their development in Kievan Russia. It is only in the Soviet period that the problem of feudalism in Kievan Russia has been given full attention.[57]

Since "feudalism" is a rather vague term and since the Marxist definition of it differs from that more or less generally accepted in western historiography, we must clarify the meaning of the term itself before accepting or rejecting the conclusions arrived at by Soviet

57. See G. Vernadsky, "Feudalism in Russia," *Speculum, 14* (1939), 300–323.

scholars. The term "feudalism" may be used in both a specific and in a wider sense. In the specific sense it is used to denote the social, economic, and political system characteristic of the countries of western and central Europe—chiefly France and Germany—in the Middle Ages. In a wider sense it may be applied to certain social, economic, and political trends in any country at any time.

In the specific sense, any definition of a developed feudal regime would include the following three items: (1) "political feudalism"— mediatization of supreme political authority, existence of a scale of greater and lesser rulers (suzerain, vassals, subvassals) bound by personal contact, reciprocity of such a contract; (2) "economic feudalism"—the existence of a manorial regime with a restriction of the legal status of the peasants, also the distinction between the right of ownership and the right of use in regard to the same landed estate; and (3) the feudal nexus—an indissoluble fusion of personal and territorial rights, the control of the land by the vassals being stipulated by the service rendered to their seignior.

The essence of feudalism in the specific sense is the complete fusion of the political and economic authority in the class of noble owners of large landed estates. To this may be added the fact that in the early feudal age European society in its economics depended chiefly upon agriculture. And in spite of A. Dopsch's objections it may be said, in a general way, that in the initial stages of European feudalism there was a prevalence of the so-called "natural economy," as contrasted with "money economy."

If only some of the trends referred to above are present and others not and if there is no harmonious connection between them, there is no "feudalism" in the specific sense before us and one should speak in such a case of a feudalizing process only, rather than feudalism.

Let us now turn to the Marxist approach to the problem. According to the *Small Soviet Encyclopedia* (1930), feudalism is a "socio-economic formation through which many of the countries of the new and ancient world have passed." The essence of feudalism is the exploitation of the peasant masses by the lord of the manor. This is characterized by the "non-economic pressure" of the lord as applied to his serfs in order to obtain the "rent," which is one of "precapitalistic nature." The feudal state of both lay and church seigniors is but a political superstructure above the economic foundations of a feudal society and thus does not belong to the essentials of feudalism.[58] In

58. *Malaia Sovetskaia Entsiklopediia, 9* (Moscow, 1931), cols. 291–292.

other words, what is called "feudalism" in the Marxist interpretation corresponds rather to "economic feudalism" in popular parlance.

For the peculiar conditions of scholarly work in the Soviet Union— the party's setting forth of rules for historical terminology—it is characteristic that the publication of critical notes of Stalin, Zhdanov, and Kirov on the project of a standard textbook on the history of the U.S.S.R. (1934) is considered in Soviet historiography as a landmark of tremendous importance (*ogromnoe znachenie*) for the development of the Soviet historical science. "In these 'notes' the historians of the Soviet Union have received the most important advice on principles, to the effect that it is the establishment of serfdom which must be considered the boundary line dividing the feudal period from the pre-feudal." [59]

In numerous "discussions" by Soviet historians, a series of which was inaugurated by B. D. Grekov's report on "Slavery and Feudalism in Kievan Russia" presented in 1932 to the Academy of the History of Material Culture, the conclusion was reached that Kievan society was not a "slave-owning" but a "feudal" one. The origin of the Kievan state is now considered by Soviet historians a manifestation of the Pan-European historical process—that of transition from the slavery regime of classical antiquity to medieval feudalism.

As a result of all this the two leading contemporary students of the history of Kievan Russia, B. D. Grekov and S. V. Iushkov, consider the Kievan regime as a feudal one, albeit with some reservations.

Terminology, after all, is not a matter of paramount importance. One has only properly to understand what is meant by such and such a term. We may call a tiger a big cat, or a cat a little tiger; it will make no difference so long as the person whom we address knows what we mean by "cat" or "tiger." But if we see a cat crossing the street and start shouting "tiger" we may easily create panic.

As a matter of fact, my own objection to the stand of the recent Soviet school in discussing the problem of feudalism in Kievan Russia is not from the terminological angle only. In a sense the growth of the manor may be called an evidence of the growth of feudalism. And one may agree with Soviet historians that the manorial authority of the princes and boyars was steadily increasing in Kievan Russia. I am quite ready, moreover, to give Soviet historians full credit for

59. I. I. Smirnov, "Problemy krepostnichestva i feodalizma v Sovietskoi istoriche-skoi literature," *Dvadtsat' piat' let istoricheskoi nauki v SSSR* (Moscow and Leningrad, 1942), p. 96.

the novelty of their approach to the study of the economic and social development of Kievan Russia, as well as for important achievements in their research.

Nevertheless, the question remains whether they have not unduly exaggerated the sociological implications of the growth of the manorial system and minimized the role of slavery in the Kievan period. One may admit that the manor was an important institution in Kievan Russia and that some tenants were on a semiserf level but still doubt that manor and serfdom were the two leading sociopolitical institutions and the foundation of the Russian national economy of the period.

In order properly to determine the specific importance of the manor in Russian social and economic life of the time we have to consider— or reconsider—the following points: (1) the degree of expansion of large landed estates in Kievan Russia; (2) their types; (3) the status of land from the juridical point of view; (4) the degree of manorial authority over the tenant farmer; (5) the social standing of the landowners; (6) the general pattern of national economy in the Kievan period.

(1) There is no doubt that large landed estates existed in Russia in the Kievan time. However, side by side with them there existed also estates of a different type, such for example as the farms of the commoners (liudi) organized in guilds. It is characteristic that the Expanded Version of the *Pravda* deals with such guilds in more detail than the Short Version. This is an important evidence of the fact that the liudi still owned land in the twelfth century. We also know of the existence of a numerous class of small-scale landowners (*svoezemtsy*) in the Novgorod region.

(2) In regard to the large-scale landed estates the question may be asked whether all were of the manorial type (using that term in the specific sense of feudal estates). The existence of large landed estates per se does not necessarily imply that a feudal regime prevailed. Large landed estates existed in the nineteenth and the beginning of the twentieth century in England, France, and Germany under democracy, or at any rate under capitalism.

Large estates existed in the Roman Empire and, although they are sometimes considered one of the causes of its eventual downfall (*latifundia perdidere Italiam*), their growth did not at once change the "capitalistic" economy of the Romans into feudalism. In that medieval extension of the Roman Empire which is known as the

Byzantine, likewise, in spite of the gradual growth of "economic feudalism" the land regime, being based upon Roman law, did not stifle the functioning of "money economy." In Kievan Russia the situation was similar.

(3) From the juridical point of view, land in Kievan Russia was just one kind of private property. Deals in land were not hampered by any feudal injunctions. It could be bequeathed, donated, bought and sold, and otherwise disposed of without restriction.

The Byzantine law—that is, basically the Roman law—served as pattern for Russian practice in any deals concerning land. Two Byzantine law manuals, the *Ecloga* of the eighth century and the *Procheiron* of the ninth, were available in Slavic translation. Law codes in the original Greek may have been used, besides.

In Russian practice certain modifications of Byzantine law were introduced, such as the right of the seller or his relatives to redeem the land sold, at least within a certain term. But such reservations sprang not from feudal law but from the remnants of clan mentality, as well as from general notions of law and justice peculiar to the Russian mind.

(4) While it is true that the lord of the manor in Kievan Russia, as in feudal Europe, had a certain authority over his tenants, this authority was less marked in the former case than in the latter. And, whatever legal authority the lord may have had, it was originally delegated to him by the prince. We know that the peasants (smerdy) were originally on the princely estates; some of them may subsequently have happened to find themselves under the authority of a boyar through the grant of the estate to that boyar on the part of the prince but there is no positive evidence for this. The izgoi, or freedmen, were settled chiefly on the church estates. The indentured laborers (zakupy) as well as the "grantees" (vdachi) were dependent on the lord of the manor to a considerable extent but the origin of their subjugation was financial—that is, "capitalistic"—rather than feudal. Their plight was not a result of "noneconomic pressure."

And—a very important point—even if we agree to call izgoi semi-serfs (which we cannot without proper reservations), they supplied only part of the agricultural labor needed. In addition, hired free laborers (*naimity, riadovichi*) were used. And, whatever the objections of Grekov and the historians of his school against the concept of Kievan society as a "slave-owning" one, slaves were in fact indispensable to Kievan economics. The indentured laborers (zakupy) and grantees (vdachi) were actually half-slaves and their role should be connected with a slave economy rather than with serfdom.

When all is said, there was no universal serfdom in Kievan Russia and the sociological importance of this fact cannot be overemphasized, since it is serfdom and not slavery which is peculiar to feudalism according to Soviet historians themselves.

(5) From the social angle, the owners of the large landed estates in Kievan Russia cannot be identified without reservation as feudal barons. As a social group they did not present in the Kievan period as exclusive a unit as the feudal lords in western Europe. A lord in his manor, the Russian boyar of the Kievan period, was but a plain citizen outside his domains. He was subject to the same laws as other freemen and in city-states like Novgorod had officially at least, no more voice in the city assembly than any other burgher. It must be conceded that the life of some boyars was protected by a double wergeld but this was set on the persons of princely servitors only and not all the owners of large landed estates were princely servitors in this period.

Moreover, for his income a Russian boyar of the Kievan period depended not only on agriculture but on trade—chiefly foreign trade—as well. Not only might the forefathers of such a boyar have acquired their wealth as members of the druzhina of the old prince-adventurers but he himself, more likely than not, would own a considerable share in Kievan commerce even in the twelfth century. In this respect the Kievan boyars did not differ from Kievan princes. The two groups coöperated—or at times competed—with the regular merchant class and had as much stake in the river caravans as the merchants proper.

(6) In western Europe feudalism originated in conditions of so-called "natural economy" as opposed to "money economy." In a sense and with due reservations one also may characterize the economic regime of the feudal countries of western and central Europe, at least in the tenth and eleventh centuries, as "closed economies," each manor being economically self-sufficient. Agriculture was the main source of national income and trade as a source of subsistence and supplies played, for the bulk of the populations, but a minor role. We know that in Kievan Russia, too, agriculture was an important branch of the economic life and that agricultural production was organized partly on the manorial plan. However, we also know that there were other trends in agricultural management. There existed smaller, non-feudal farms; and, I repeat, on large farms labor was supplied to a con-

siderable degree by both hired laborers and slaves and not exclusively by semiserfs. Thus a large landed estate in Kievan Russia had, perhaps, a closer similarity to a Roman *latifundium* than to a feudal *seigneurie*. An important point also is that grain was raised on the large estates of the Kievan period not only for the consumption of the inhabitants of the estate but for the market as well. To sum up these remarks, while agriculture was highly developed in Kievan Russia, this does not necessarily imply that a "natural" or "closed" economy prevailed in the nation's life.

Agriculture, moreover, constituted, as we have amply seen, only one important source of Russia's national income in the period. Trade, and especially foreign trade, was a no less significant factor in Russian economic life. Here many of Kliuchevsky's brilliant generalizations still stand firm in defiance of recent criticism. The commercial expansion of a nation is in itself an important evidence of the spread of "money economy" (as opposed to "natural economy") in the life of that nation. In regard to Kievan Russia we know that money and commerce played a very important role. Foreign trade was the original source of the wealth of her upper classes, even if later they settled on the land. Money was available for commercial and other transactions at a comparatively low rate of interest.

Credit, trade, storage of goods, bankruptcy—to each of these the Kievan legislation of the period paid considerable attention. And in the province of commerce and credit as in that of land turnover Kievan legislation drew on Byzantine (that is, essentially Roman) sources.

What then should be the answer to the question we put at the beginning of the section? To what sociopolitical formation shall we refer Kievan Russia? Surely she was not a feudal state, in any case not a typical feudal one. But if not this, then what?

We have seen that the first Kievan rulers dreamed of the creation of a vast commercial empire which would pick up the tradition of the Huns and the Khazars and simultaneously take over the accumulated wealth of Byzantium. In a sense the Kievan realm grew from the same soil as all these nomadic and seminomadic empires, which controlled, each in turn, the area of the Pontic steppes beginning with the Scythian age. Each tried to build up a link between the northern and oriental commerce on one hand, and the Mediterranean trade on the other. Chronologically, the last of those west Eurasian commercial empires prior to the formation of the Russian state was that of the Khazars. It was in the bosom of the Khazar kaganate, so to speak, that the first Russian kaganate—that of Tmutorokan—came into being. The Kievan realm was built up by Oleg and his successors with the intention of continuing and expanding the commercial and political tradition of the first kaganate.

It is against this historical background that the origins of Kievan "commercial capitalism" may best be understood. But there was also a considerable difference between the early nomadic and seminomadic states and the Kievan realm, the bulk of the population of the latter being firmly settled irrespective of whether agriculture or forest industries constituted their chief pursuit.

Also, Kievan Russia even prior to the conversion of her people to Christianity was under considerable Byzantine influence, and is naturally increased after Russia's conversion.

On several occasions we already have emphasized the dependence of the Kievan regime on Roman law. The national economy of the Roman Empire may be called, in a sense, capitalistic; the peculiarity of Roman capitalism consisted in the fact that it was—partly at least —based upon slave labor. The Roman economic system as well as Roman law continued to exist, under different historical circumstances and with considerable modification, in the Byzantine Empire. As time went on, feudalizing tendencies became more and more marked in the Byzantine imperial regime. But until its first downfall, at the time of the Fourth Crusade (1204), the Byzantine economy was essentially a "money economy."

Culturally under considerable Byzantine influence, Kievan Russia had economically as well many similarities to Byzantium. It goes without saying that we may not identify the Kievan economy with that of the Roman Empire or even that of the Byzantine, without reservations. Kievan "capitalism" was not as well established as the Roman and Kievan civilization, although brilliant in many ways, was not on the level of the Roman. For one thing, it was much younger, if we may use this expression here. As a result there were many more primitive elements left in Kievan civilization than in the Roman. Leaving aside the fact that in the Kievan period Russian country life as a whole was culturally on a much lower level than life in the cities, many a remote district in Kievan Russia was not touched by new civilization at all. On the whole, the elements of the older cultural strata, including the clan and the zadruga mentality and habits, were still easily discernible immediately beneath the superimposed strata of new commercial civilization.

Industrially, and technologically too, Kievan Russia was certainly on a lower level than the Roman Empire. Kievan capitalism may be called commercial par excellence.

Russia always has been and still is a land of contrasts and Kievan civilization with its combination of refinement and primitiveness presents an interesting case. Yet, when all is said, we are obliged to connect Kievan Russia sociologically not only with the type of commercial empire of the nomads but, in a sense, also with a type of which the highest manifestation in classical antiquity was the Roman Empire—that of a "capitalistic" formation based on slavery.

To be sure, elements of feudalism were present and increased steadily from the middle of the twelfth century. But, in spite of a certain curtailment of the legal status of some of the peasants, no universal serfdom was established in the Kievan period. This process of "retardation" of serfdom was certainly one of the characteristic facets of the social and economic regime prevailing in Kievan Russia.

We thus come to the conclusion that in the tenth and eleventh centuries there was a basic difference, as regards social and economic foundations, between Kievan Russia on one hand and western and central Europe on the other. That difference was the result partly of different historical backgrounds, partly of different social and economic factors at play in the Kievan period—also of the Byzantine influence in the shaping of Kievan institutions.

# Chapter VII

# GOVERNMENT AND ADMINISTRATION

## *1. Introductory Remarks*

The *Book of Annals* opens with its author's promise to describe "the origin of the Russian land—who first began to reign in Kiev, and from what source the Russian land had its beginning." The term "land" (*zemlia*), is used here not as a geographical term but in the sense of "nation" or "state." The term "to reign" (*kniazhiti*) refers to the form of government. The terminology of the *Book of Annals* is typical of the Russian mentality of those times.

"Land" was the common term for "state" throughout the Kievan period. The notion of government was expressed by the term *volost'* ("power"), in Church Slavic, *vlast'*; it is in this latter form that the word, in this connotation, is used in modern Russian. The term *kniazhenie* ("principate") denoted the government in its executive aspects; it more or less corresponded to the notion of "supreme executive power." It must be noted that all three terms, *zemlia, volost'* and *kniazhenie*, were used not only in the abstract sense but also to denote a given state with its government. In this concrete sense the three are almost synonymous.

To this list of basic old Russian political terms that of *gospodin* ("lord") may be added. It was used in various senses—to denote the owner of land or the owner of slaves, or the lord of the manor; also the sovereign, the bearer of sovereignty. In the latter sense it could be applied not only to a prince but also to a free commonwealth, like Novgorod.

The variety of terms denoting "state" and "government" in the Kievan period is not accidental. It corresponds to the heterogeneous nature of the Kievan state, which consisted of several "lands," at first united under the authority of the prince of Kiev and later ruled each by a prince of its own. Each "land" centered around its capital city (*gorod*). All other cities in the land were considered mere "by-towns" (*prigorod*)—"junior cities," so to say. Rural districts were known as *volosti*, which is the plural of *volost'*. This term, in its abstract sense denoting "power" and "government," and more concretely the state, or rather a given state, a country, was used for a rural district because it was ruled by the capital city. *Volodeti*, a verb of the same root, means both to "rule" and to "own."

Essentially, then, each old Russian land was a city-state in the classical sense of the term. It is significant that in Scandinavian sources Russia is called Gardariki, "the Realm of Cities." Since the old Slavic word *grad* (in Russian, *gorod*) meant both a city and a fort, the Scandinavian name for Russia is often understood as "the Realm of Castles." The interpretation is hardly valid. It was not the "castles" of Russia that must have impressed the Norse visitors but her cities. Surely the Normans saw more castles in western Europe than they did in Russia, and more impressive too, since they were built of stone. But nowhere in the central or western Europe of that period could they see so many cities as in Russia and, especially, nowhere in the west could they find cities so influential in a political sense.

With the coming of Riurik to Novgorod, and later of Oleg to Kiev, the princely authority was superimposed on this system of city-states. This brought the element of personal power into the government, but not only that. The strength of each prince lay in his private army, the druzhina. With the assistance of the druzhina he was able to protect the city from any attack from outside. Simultaneously, however, as the cities were soon to find out, it could be used by the prince to enforce his authority over the city itself.

The prince's court, supported by his private army, gradually became the nucleus of the new administration. This represented an encroachment of the patrimonial idea upon the state and in a sense resulted in a degree of fusion of the public "land" law and the private "princely" law. It would be a mistake, however, to suppose that the princely power was of demesnial nature exclusively. It also had its statehood aspects, especially after Russia's conversion to Christianity and the blessing of the princely authority by the church. But the notion of the prince's being the head of the state and not merely the lord of his household was not entirely alien to the Russians even before the conversion. The idea of the sovereign power of the prince must have been partly the result of the Khazar influence and it is significant that the Khazar title of the supreme ruler, kagan, was first assumed by the Russian ruler of Tmutorokan and later used by those Kievan and Chernigovan princes who controlled, or attempted to control, that city.

In the late twelfth and early thirteenth century the Byzantine imperial title, "autocrate" (αὐτοκράτωρ; in Slavic translation, *samoderzhets*), was applied by the chroniclers to Prince Vsevolod III of Suzdalia and Prince Roman of Galicia, but there is no evidence that either of them assumed it officially.

## 2. The Lands and the Principalities

The original "lands" of which the Kievan realm was composed partly coincided with the tribal groups. Thus the Kievan land was populated chiefly by the Polianians, the Novgorodian by the Slovene, and the Riazanian by the Viatichians. The Khorvatians and Dulebians constituted the ethnic foundation of Galicia and Volynia, respectively. In other cases a tribe was divided between two or more lands. The Severians constituted the bulk of population in both the Chernigov and the Pereiaslav lands; the Krivichians, in the Smolensk and Polotsk lands; the Dregovichians, who originally centered around the city of Turov, were later distributed between the Kievan, Polotsk, and Chernigovan lands. The Suzdalian land had been originally colonized by the Slovene and the Krivichians. The Drevlianians were incorporated into the Kievan land by the close of the eleventh century.

The identity of each land, except the Drevlianian, was not lost after its inclusion in the Kievan realm. The Kievan land was under the immediate authority of the ruling prince; in each of the others the prince was represented by his lieutenant, usually one of his sons, less frequently a boyar.

Following Iaroslav's death the lands were grouped and regrouped among his descendants and, with the decrease in authority of the prince of Kiev, first each group of lands and then each land became a distinct principality. By the late twelfth century ten lands were finally formed: the Kievan, the Novgorodian, Suzdalia, the land of Riazan, the land of Pereiaslav, the land of Chernigov, the land of Smolensk, and the lands of Polotsk, Volynia, and Galicia. In each of them a separate branch of the house of Riurik entrenched itself, except Novgorod, where the prince was elected from the members of the princely family at large.

Even after the dismemberment of the Kievan realm, not all the links between the lands were severed and it may be said that in their totality they constituted a kind of loose federation—the Russian federation (see below, Chap. VIII, sec. 1).

It will not be out of place to examine here the gradual expansion of the name Rus' (Russia). Its origin has already been discussed in detail elsewhere.[1] Suffice it to repeat here that in the author's opinion it was a derivation from the Iranian word *rukhs* ("light"), hence the name of the people Rukhs-As, or Roxolani ("the Brilliant Alans"), as one of the Iranian tribes was known. This name was later assumed by a group of the Slavic Antes. Still later the name was taken over by the group of Swedes who established themselves in the Azov-Tmutorokan region in the eighth century.

Thus the Russian kaganate in that region came into existence. Since settlements of the Rus'-Antes also existed in the Kievan region (consider the name of the river Ros) and since the descendants of the old Swedish Rus' constituted the bulk of the druzhina of the first Kievan princes, the name Rus' became identified with the Kievan land and in the eleventh century the term Rusin ("a Russian") became synonymous with "a Kievan" or "a Polianian."

With the extension of the authority of the Kievan princes over all the Antian and Slovenian lands, the name "Russia" spread beyond the boundaries of the Kievan land and came to be applied, likewise, first to the land of Chernigov and that of Pereiaslav and then to all other lands. It is characteristic that, in the treaty of 1229 between Smolensk and the German cities, "Russians" and not merely "Smolensk men" are mentioned throughout.

Since Novgorod elected her princes from among the members of the house of Riurik, she was also considered a part of Russia in the larger sense of the word. However, the Novgorod men always spoke of themselves as "Novgorodians" and not "Russians," even in international treaties, as for example that of 1195.

As we have seen, each Russian land consisted originally of the capital city, "junior cities," and rural districts. In most instances the same capital city kept its seniority intact from the ninth century down to the Mongol invasion; in some cases, however, a competition developed between two or more cities within the same land, being usually aggravated by interprincely rivalry, as a result of which the capital was shifted from one place to another. Thus in Suzdalia the old city of Rostov eventually lost its seniority to Suzdal, which, however, was not able to keep it for long and had to yield it to the much younger Vladimir.

With the multiplication of the princely family in each principality and the habit of reigning princes of assigning a city to each of their

1. *Ancient Russia*, pp. 276–278.

sons as his share in the common patrimony, some of the principalities were by the early thirteenth century divided into a number of appanages, the unity of the land being preserved by the submission of the junior princes to the senior and of the "by-towns" to the capital city. The whole structure was not very stable, however, and in this way the parcelling of principalities, which reached its climax in the Mongol period, was prepared.

## 3. The Three Elements of Government

Plato, in his *Republic* and *Statesman* postulated two higher forms of government—monarchy and aristocracy; and three lower forms—tyranny, oligarchy, and democracy. In his last work, *The Laws,* approaching the problem from a different angle, he suggested two basic forms, monarchy and democracy, from which all the others derive.

Aristotle in his *Politics* speaks of three basic forms of government—kingship, aristocracy, and "citizenship" (*politeia,* perhaps best translated as "constitutional democracy"); and three deviations—tyranny, oligarchy, and democracy. Generally speaking, in the political thought of the Hellenistic and Roman periods, monarchy, aristocracy, and democracy were considered the three main forms of government.

The government of the Russian lands of the Kievan period represented a mixture of the three. Historically, as we know, the old Russian government was a combination of the city-state with princely power. Since, however, the prince's strength depended on his druzhina, the latter proved before long to be an influential factor in itself.

The prince may be said to represent the monarchic element in Kievan Russia, the druzhina the aristocratic, and the veche the democratic. In the government of each Russian land all three elements were present but the specific gravity of each was different in various cases. In the late twelfth century the monarchic element came into prominence in Suzdalia and the aristocratic in Galicia. In Novgorod, on the other hand, democracy became paramount in the same period. Whether the Novgorodian government was actually a politeia or a democracy from the point of view of Aristotelian terminology is another question.

Let us now examine the three elements of government one by one, starting with the monarchic.

## a. The Monarchic Element: the Prince

The old Slavic word for "prince" is *kniaz'*. It derives from the old German *kuning* (in old Norse, *koningr*), meaning "king." [2] Presumably the Antian and Slovenian princes of the sixth and seventh centuries, as well as the Drevlianian prince Mal of the tenth century, were clan and tribal elders. The nature of the princely power changed with the appearance of the Norsemen in Russia. Oleg and his descendants represented a foreign element dominating over the old tribes and cities. By the middle of the tenth century the new princes were firmly entrenched in Kiev and gradually the house of Riurik became an integral part of Russian political life at large. [3]

Justice and military defense were the two main provinces in which the prince was expected to be useful to the people. In carrying on both these tasks he was assisted by his druzhina but it was on the prince that the supreme responsibility rested.

The prince was also the head of the executive power at large and following Russia's conversion became the protector of the church in a general way, although he did not enjoy in this period any specific prerogatives in church administration, since the Russian church was not autocephalous and the metropolitan of Kiev came under the authority of the Patriarch of Constantinople. Some of the princes, however, were ready to give their support to the party in the Russian clergy which strove for more independence from Byzantium. Thus Iaroslav the Wise took upon himself the initiative of gathering a council of Russian bishops, which elected Ilarion metropolitan of Kiev without previously securing the approval of the Patriarch (1051), and a century later Iziaslav II made a similar move (1147).

The first Kievan princes seemed to consider Russia as their patrimony, their right, which they could bequeath and pass on to the next of kin. From the death of Iaroslav the Wise, however, the succession to the throne was regulated by two seemingly opposite principles: genealogical seniority and popular election. [4] Of the two, the second factor remained dormant as long as the first worked smoothly, which was the case until the middle of the twelfth century. The accession

2. Preobrazhensky, I, 324.

3. On the prince and princely power in Kievan Russia, see Vladimirsky-Budanov, *Obzor*, pp. 36–44; Sergeevich, *Drevnosti*, II (1908), 150–240; Presniakov, *Kniazhoe pravo*.

4. On the rights of succession to the throne, see S. M. Soloviev, *Istoriia otnoshenii mezhdu Russkimi kniaziami Riurikova doma* (Moscow, 1847); Kliuchevsky, *Kurs Russkoi istorii*, I (1918), 203–211; Presniakov, *Kniazhoe pravo*, pp. 25–157.

to the throne of each of the Kievan princes in this period of political peace was approved *par acclamation* by both the notables and the city population as a matter of formality.

However, even in this period the population raised its voice every time the reigning prince led the country to a disaster or offended the people in one way or another. Thus, when Prince Iziaslav I proved incapable of organizing the city's defense against the Cumans, the Kievans revolted against him and elected Vseslav of Polotsk as their prince (1068). When the latter did not live up to their expectations, however, they were compelled to admit Iziaslav to the throne once more.

From the eleven-forties the Kievan veche played a more active role in the princely succession, promoting and demoting various candidates to the throne. On the whole, the Kievans showed preference for the Monomashichi (descendants of Vladimir Monomach) as against the Olgovichi (descendants of Oleg of Chernigov) but in some cases they were ready to accept an Olgovich on their own conditions.

Each Kievan prince, in this period, had to come to terms with the veche. Both parties then "kissed the cross," promising to abide by the provisions of the agreement. Unfortunately, no copy of any such contract has been preserved and the chronicles contain only brief notices of the provisions. One chronicler records that Prince Sviatoslav, son of Oleg, who signed the contract for his sick brother Igor in 1146, agreed to make the office of *tiun* (chief justice) elective.

Let us now turn to consideration of the principle of genealogical seniority as a factor in succession to the throne. It was based upon Iaroslav's will (see Chap. IV, sec. 4) and behind it lay the notion of dynastic interests. The right to rule Russia was considered the prerogative not of any single prince, however mighty, but of the house of Riurik as a whole. Each member of the house was entitled to a share in the common patrimony and thrones of single principalities were distributed among the princes according to the place of each on the genealogical tree.

The higher a prince's genealogical position, the more important and lucrative a throne he could claim. The senior prince was entitled to the throne of Kiev; Chernigov was rated second best; next came Pereiaslav, Smolensk, and Vladimir in Volynia, in that order, as suggested in Iaroslav's will. By the late twelfth century some old cities, like Pereiaslav, had lost their former importance and some new ones, such as Vladimir in Suzdalia, had come in, to prominence, as a result of which adjustments became necessary.

The death of any prince affected those who held lesser cities and the death of the prince of Kiev affected them all, being the signal of a general redistribution of thrones, each prince moving one step up the political ladder; the prince of Chernigov was supposed to move to Kiev, that of Pereiaslav to Chernigov, and so on. With the multiplication of princes and the ramification of the house of Riurik the system gradually broke down, since with each new generation it became more and more complicated to establish the genealogical seniority, especially in view of the fact that a nephew could be, and often was, older than some of his uncles. The rule that the elder son of the first brother in a princely generation was genealogically equal to his third uncle (i.e., the fourth brother)—a rule formulated to prevent discord—actually made the situation even more delicate.

While it was still possible in the late twelfth century to determine seniority for each branch of the house of Riurik, to decide which of the branch seniors was genealogically the head of the house as a whole became an extremely difficult task and in the end a futile one, since genealogical leadership often did not coincide with political strength.

The house of Riurik which under Vladimir, and again under Iaroslav, had consisted of one family, now became a populous clan. Sociologically the consolidation of single princely branches may be described as the disintegration of the clan and its dismemberment into single families. In regard to the house as a whole the process was a protracted one, not completed until after the Mongol invasion. In spite of the actual emancipation of single families, the notion of the unity of the clan as a whole did not disappear.

All told, by the late twelfth century the principle of general genealogical seniority played hardly any role in the succession of the Kievan throne and even in the other principalities it was replaced by patrimonial instincts and the desire of each powerful prince to secure the principate for his descendants. The complexity of princely claims and counterclaims was conducive to discord and, indeed, internecine strife and fratricide wars were endemic in Kievan Russia, seriously sapping the vitality of the nation.

As a remedy against the curse of civil war, as we saw earlier, inter-princely conferences met from time to time with the object of clearing up mutual claims and pretensions. The earliest meetings of this kind were due to the initiative of Vladimir Monomach (1097 and 1100).

In the late twelfth century several such conferences took place at Kiev. While the interprincely conference never became a regular institution on a permanent basis, the very fact that such meetings were held is an evidence of constructive tendencies in the princes' attitude toward reality.

Besides the conference method another approach was tried in Suzdalia in the late twelfth century: that of organizing interprincely relations on the basis of political instead of genealogical seniority. Both Andrei Bogoliubsky and his brother Vsevolod III considered the lesser princes, at least in Suzdalia, their subordinates. Such a subordinate (*podruchnik*, literally "one who is under the arm," i.e., under the protection of his superior) had to promise to obey his senior. At first this tendency met with revolt on the part of the lesser princes but some of them had later to accept the new notion.

Vsevolod III, in fact, aimed at becoming the suzerain of the lesser princes, whom he treated as his vassals. It is significant that he assumed the title "grand duke" (*velikii kniaz'*), of which the princes of Moscow were to make full use in the fourteenth and fifteenth centuries.[5] As has been already mentioned, Vsevolod seemed ready even to assume the title of "autocrate." This was the beginning of the end of the social and political equality to which originally every member of the house of Riurik considered himself entitled.

At this juncture it may be well to mention that, while the name "house of Riurik" has been used above to denote the princely clan and is generally used by historians in this sense, the name does not belong to the Kievan period. The princes of Kievan Russia liked to emphasize the unity of their clan, saying that they were "grandsons of the common grandfather," but the name of Riurik was never mentioned in this connection. Usually Iaroslav the Wise was considered the forefather of the clan. It was only in the early Muscovite period that Riurik was recognized as the founder and name-giver of the dynasty.

The Russian princes of the Kievan period had a common heraldic emblem: the trident. It is represented on the coins of both Vladimir I and Iaroslav I and was kept in use by all branches of the house except the princes of Suzdalia, who replaced the trident by the lion.[6]

5. *Velikii kniaz'*, literally "grand prince." In English and French this Russian title is traditionally rendered as "grand duke," which term will be used here as well as in the following volumes of this work. I have preferred, however, to call the Kievan princes of the tenth century (Chap. II) "grand princes" since their title belongs to an earlier epoch and has no immediate connection with the title of the Moscow rulers.

6. See Baron M. A. Taube, "Zagadochnyi rodovoi znak sem'i Vladimira Sviatogo,"

## b. The Aristocratic Element: the Boyar Council

It is an established tradition in Russian historical writings to call the council of the boyars the "Boyar Duma." The term is indeed convenient and there is no reason why it should not be used but at the same time it should be made clear that it was not in use in old Russia and is in that sense artificial. In modern Russia the term Duma has been officially applied to the city councils as well as to the House of Representatives of the prerevolutionary period. The counterpart of the noun *duma* is the verb *dumati,* which in modern Russian means "to think" and in old Russian had the special connotation of "deliberate," especially to discuss affairs of state or any serious matter. One of the prince's functions was to deliberate with his boyars and *dumaiushchii* (literally "deliberating") became the habitual epithet of such a boyar who was a member of the council.

The Boyar Council was an essential supplement to the princely power.[7] No decision of importance could be taken by the prince, or executed, without the concurrence of the boyars. It was by the opposition of the druzhina to the new faith that Sviatoslav motivated his refusal to accept Christianity. On the other hand, Vladimir's conversion was approved by the boyars. The boyars likewise participated in current legislation as well as in the codification of laws. It is significant that the names of leading boyars along with those of the princes are mentioned in the preamble to the *Pravda* of Iaroslav's sons. Boyar approval was also required for the conclusion of international treaties; for example, in Igor's treaty with Byzantium of 945 the boyars are expressly referred to. The Boyar Council was also consulted by the prince in the matters of domestic administration.

In certain cases the council acted as a supreme court. Thus, when Vladimir's wife Rogneda made an attempt on his life, he convoked the boyars and left the decision to them. Incidentally, they advised clemency. In 1097 Prince Sviatopolk II consulted the boyars concerning the alleged treason of Prince Vasilko. The boyar element was likewise represented in the interprincely conferences of the late eleventh and twelfth centuries.

While the Boyar Council was a permanent institution, its com-

---

*Sbornik statei posviashchennykh P. N. Miliukovu* (Prague, 1929), pp. 117–132, and "Rodovoi znak sem'i Vladimira Sviatogo," *Vladimirskii Sbornik* (Beograd, 1938), pp. 89–112; A. V. Artsikhovsky, "Miniatiury Kenigsbergskoi Letopisi," *GA, 14* (1932), No. 2, 31.

7. Vladimirsky-Budanov, *Obzor,* pp. 44–51; Kliuchevsky, *Boiarskaia Duma drevnei Rusi,* chaps. i–ii; Sergeevich, *Drevnosti,* II, 371–504.

petence as well as its functions were determined by custom rather than by law. However, when a prince was elected by the veche the boyars were usually a party to the agreement and when a contract between the prince and the veche was signed the boyars also were sworn. Whether a separate contract was signed between the prince and the boyars on such occasions is not clear.

On other occasions princes are known to have concluded special agreements with the boyars. Following the death of Prince Sviatoslav of Chernigov (1164) his widow wanted to arrange that their son should succeed him. Accordingly, she conferred with the bishop and the senior members of Sviatoslav's druzhina. An agreement was reached and an oath taken. The very fact that such special agreements between the prince and the boyars were needed is evidence of the lack of any standard charter by which the prerogatives of the Boyar Council had been secured once and for all.

The composition of the Boyar Council was as indefinite as its competence. Custom required that the prince should consult the old and experienced men only. If a prince broke this rule he was severely criticized by what may be called public opinion. The compiler of the *Book of Annals* ascribes the troubles of the latter part of Vsevolod I's principate to the fact that Vsevolod "began to take pleasure in the opinions of young men and consulted with them. They induced him to withdraw his favor from his older retainers." [8] While the chronicler is indignant with Vsevolod, whom he excuses only by referring to his old age and sickness, he sees no break of any contract in his behavior. Apparently there was none in this period.

In the functioning of the Boyar Council an inner circle and a wider assembly may be discerned. In the inner circle only the leading members of the druzhina (*muzhi perednie*, literally "foremen") took part. This inner council consisted of three to five members, including the chiliarch, who must have been an ex officio member. This body was in permanent session. Vladimir Monomach instructs his children to "sit and deliberate" with their retainers every morning and it is obviously the inner council that he means in this case. In a sense this institution was the prince's cabinet.

While the cabinet was considered competent to dispose of current matters of both legislation and administration, for any discussion of major state affairs the plenary session of the council had to be convoked. In it not only the members of the princely druzhina but out-

8. Cross, p. 265.

side boyars as well participated. This latter group consisted of descendants of former clan and tribal chiefs and of the new commercial aristocracy of the cities. In those cities which preserved their self-government, the elected elders were also invited to the plenary session and in the tenth and eleventh centuries this group of the council as a whole was known under the name of "city elders" (*startsi gradskie*).

In the twelfth century the two groups merged under the common name of "boyars." Presumably each boyar connected with the capital city of a land was entitled to sit at the plenary session of the council but whether all were always called is not known. There is no evidence that the number of members of the council was limited by law but it might have been by custom.

It should be noted that, contrary to the princes, the boyars did not form an exclusive order. Through service in the princely druzhina access to boyardom was open to any able man, theoretically at least. Actually it must have been easier for a boyar's son to achieve a high position in the druzhina than for that of a commoner.

A boyar had no obligation to serve the prince and was free to leave him and enter the service of another prince at any time. Even if he were recompensed by a land grant for his service, the landed estate he received—except in Galicia in the thirteenth century—became his personal property and entailed no obligation of service. Thus a boyar, whether a prince's councilor or a prince's servitor, was not his vassal. This is an important point of difference between the social regime of Kievan Russia and that of the west in the same period.

Only in western Ukraine did certain feudal customs and institutions develop, partly as a result of foreign influences. It is recorded in the Hypatian Chronicle that, at the time of his visit to Volynia in 1149, Prince Boleslaw of Poland "girdled many boyars' sons"—that is, knighted them.

In Galicia the boyars strove to achieve political equality with the princes and in 1212 the boyar Vladislav even proclaimed himself Prince of Galicia, the only known case in pre-Mongolian Russia of a person not belonging to the house of Riurik assuming the title of prince. About the same time some of the boyars were appointed governors of Galician cities, with full princely power although not assuming the princely title. Cases of land grants to the Galician boyars as fiefs (*derzhanie*) are also mentioned in the sources. All this is a clear evidence of the process of feudal dismemberment of the principality of Galicia in the period. The Galician boyars tried to assert themselves as a feudal aristocracy.

## c. The Democratic Element: the Veche

The town meeting was a universal institution in old Russia, both in the cities and in the rural districts. In large cities the population of each of the district communes met to discuss their communal affairs and besides that there were also meetings of the whole city population. In this sense each old Russian city had its own veche. However, the assembly of the capital city of the land constituted the veche in the technical sense of the term, that of a full-fledged political institution.[9]

The word *veche* corresponds to the French word *parlement*, literally a place where people speak (about state affairs). The Russian word *soviet* derives from the same root as *veche*. All the city freemen were entitled to participate in the meetings of the veche. While the assembly met always in the capital city, residents of the "by-towns" had the right to attend it and to vote. Actually few of them were able to do so for reasons of distance and the fact that no advance notice of meetings was sent to the "junior towns." A meeting was called whenever need arose, by announcing it in the market place of the capital, through heralds or by pealing the city bell.

For practical reasons, then, with few exceptions the veche may be defined as a general assembly of the population of the capital city only. Men alone had the right to vote, and only heads of families. This does not mean that bachelors were excluded on principle but the vote of unmarried sons living in their father's house was not counted. A bachelor living by himself was a member of the assembly.

Custom required that the decision be unanimous. A small minority had to bow before the majority. Where there was no distinct majority, two divergent parties argued for hours and often came to blows. Either no decision at all was passed in such cases or finally one side prevailed and the minority had grudgingly to accept the inevitable.

The city mayor usually presided over the meeting but occasionally the metropolitan (as in Kiev in 1147) or local bishop was asked to take the chair, presumably in cases when an influential group of citizens was in opposition to the mayor. The prince might be present at the meeting and usually was so when the meeting was called by himself. Not infrequently, however, it would be called by a group of citi-

9. Vladimirsky-Budanov, *Obzor*, pp. 51–60; Sergeevich, *Drevnosti*, II, 1–118.

zens dissatisfied with his policies. In such cases the prince abstained from any participation in the meeting. Such meetings of protest usually gathered in the market place. In normal times the veche met either in the square before the princely palace or in that before the cathedral church.

As we have already seen the veche had its voice in the succession to the throne by supporting or opposing a candidate from the point of view of the city's interests and on certain occasions even demanded the abdication of a prince already in power. In normal times it concurred with the prince and the boyar council in all major matters of legislation and general administration. Less often, it acted as a supreme court. In cities in which the administration was not absorbed by the authority of the prince, the veche elected the mayor and other city officials, as well as the mayors of the by-towns.

The degree of authority enjoyed by the veche varied in the various cities. It was in Novgorod that the institution reached the height of its power.

## d. The Problem of Representative Government

Russian democratic institutions of the Kievan period belong to the classical Greek type—that of immediate democracy. All citizens were supposed to take part in the assembly, which resulted in the fact that citizens of the capital city were in a privileged position, since they alone were physically able to participate in the veche. The capital city thus dominated the by-towns politically. The population of the latter met for the discussion of their local affairs but such meetings had no political importance. There was no attempt to organize the veche on a representative basis through delegates from both the capital city and the by-towns. Nor was there any effort to improve the functioning of the veche of the capital city by creating a city house of representatives.

The method of immediate democracy is fit for small communes only. Aristotle considered a population of around five thousand normal for a well-ruled city. The population of Novgorod was many times larger and the inconvenience against which Aristotle warned was felt acutely, especially in times of serious political crisis.

If we turn to the aristocratic institutions of Kievan Russia we shall find the same inability to use the representative method. The prince's cabinet—that inner circle of the Boyar Council—was not elected by the plenary session. In the plenary session not all the boyars of a given land participated but only those connected with the capital city.

It is only in the monarchic division of the government that some experiment with the idea of representation may be observed. In 1211 Vsevolod III, in order to stabilize interprincely relations in Suzdalia, convoked a gathering which some Russian historians consider the prototype of the future consultative assemblies of the tsardom of Muscovy, the so-called *Zemsky Sobor*. According to the chronicler the prince called into consultation "all of his boyars, both residing in the cities and those residing in the rural districts; Bishop Ioann and the abbots, and the priests; and the merchants, and the *dvoriane*, and all the people." [10] The text is rather vague but it may be argued that "the merchants, and the *dvoriane*, and all the people" were not invited to participate *in corpore* but only through representatives chosen by them. Otherwise the conference would have included the male population of all Suzdalia, which of course is unthinkable. Still, the chronicler's statement is too vague to permit any definite conclusion from it.

## 4. The Princely Administration

Because of the heterogeneous origin of the old Russian government, the administration of each principality was of a twofold nature.[11] Some officers derived their authority solely from the prince, while others were supposed to represent the people even though actually appointed by the prince. Originally, officers of the second category had been elected by the people. Such officers were graded according to a mathematical principle. They were: the chiliarch (*tysiatsky*, head of a thousand); the hundreder (*sotsky*, head of a hundred); and the decurion (*desiatsky*, head of a unit of ten). The origin of this system and its relation to clan and tribal authority is a moot question.

The decimal system in the grouping of population and in territorial division existed among many peoples, including the Anglo-Saxon. It must have originated in connection with primitive military organization. In a campaign involving the coöperation of many clans and several tribes it may have been preferable, from a military point of view, to divide the army into units of standard size. Under such an arrangement the task of planning and executing military operations

---

10. *PSRL*, VII (1856), 117; A. E. Presniakov, *Obrazovanie velikorusskogo gosudarstva* (Petrograd, 1918), p. 44.

11. On the princely administration, see Vladimirsky-Budanov, *Obzor*, pp. 75–80; Presniakov, *Lektsii po russkoi istorii*, I, 197–207.

was much easier than it would have been otherwise. Moreover, to make war mobilization easier it was expedient to keep the division of manpower in decimal units in times of peace as well. Such units then became territorial divisions, which were also useful when it came to taxation.

In Russia the decimal system of units may have originated in the Sarmatian era but it seems more probable to connect its beginnings with the Hunnic Empire. The Huns were Turks, with some admixture from the Mongols, and the decimal system seems to have been an old tradition with both the Turks and the Mongols. The name of the city of Tmutorokan may be used as a pertinent illustration. This name must be derived from the title of the Turkish commander who presumably pitched his tent on the Taman peninsula in 568. *Tma-Tarkhan* means the chief of ten thousand. Later on, Chingis Khan's army was organized according to the same decimal system. Still later, the Cossacks organized themselves by units of tens and hundreds.

Both the Khazars and the Magyars must likewise have applied the decimal system of division in ruling their Aso-Slavic subjects—in drafting them as auxiliary troops as well as in collecting tribute from them. It is not clear how the system was adjusted to the clan and tribal divisions of the Slavs. Presumably a tribe counted as a thousand, a clan as a hundred, and a family commune (*zadruga*) as a unit of ten.

In the Kievan period there was a tysiatsky in each major city, that is, in each capital of a principality. While the office was originally an elective one, eventually the prince assumed the prerogative of nominating the candidate for it, except in Novgorod. Usually an influential boyar held the position and the tendency among them was to make it hereditary. Thus under Iaroslav the office for Kiev was held first by Vyshata and then by his son Ian. As a general rule, however, the hereditary system of holding office failed to strike firm roots in Kievan Russia.

Even though the chiliarch became the prince's appointee, he always was considered the commander of the city militia ("thousand") as contrasted to the prince's retinue. On some occasions he acted as the people's mouthpiece to voice their opposition to the prince. For example, when Prince Vsevolod II of Kiev, who belonged to the Olgovichi branch of the Kiev family, planned to bequeath the Kievan throne to his brother, the tysiatsky Uleb protested in the name of the Kievans that the latter did not want the house of Olgovichi to continue in power and insisted on a Monomachovich as their next ruler to succeed Vsevolod after his death (1146).[12]

If the chiliarch neglected the people's opinion and interests, the citizens held him responsible for acting against their interests and on some occasions expressed their displeasure rather violently. During the Kievan uprising of 1113 the populace looted the house of the chiliarch. Incidentally, on this occasion the houses of the hundreders likewise were looted, which indicates that the rioters considered them the chiliarch's agents. These city hundreders under the chiliarchs should not be confused with the hundreders of rural districts, who were always elected.

The prince's court was the center of princely administration proper. Any steward (*tiun*) of the princely estate was entitled to hold an office in the state administration as well. The major-domo (*tiun dvorsky*) eventually became the head of the financial administration of each principality. Other stewards served as judges and the very term *tiun* eventually assumed the connotation of "judge."

In the provincial administration the prince was represented by his lieutenant (*posadnik*). It should be noted that the term *posadnik* also meant "city mayor"; the two kinds of posadnik should not be confused. The prince's lieutenants were chosen either from the junior members of the house of Riurik or among the boyars. They were entitled to a share in the taxes collected by them for the prince, as well as to special contributions on the part of the population of the province for their sustenance. Later, in the early Muscovite period, this system of remuneration of the provincial governors became known as *kormlenie* ("feeding")—"feeding off the land," as it were. There was some irony in the term, because in old Russian it also had the connotation of ruling; a case of two identical words derived from different roots.

Under the supervision of the posadnik the local communes, both urban and rural, managed their own affairs through a number of elected officers.

## 5. Branches of Administration

### a. Finance

As we have seen, the princely court in Kievan Russia was closely bound up with the state administration and the prince's major-domo performed the duties of a minister of finance. In spite of this there

12. See Vladimirsky-Budanov, *Obzor*, p. 77.

was no complete fusion of princely funds with the public finances and wherever possible a distinction was made between the two. It appears that the prince was entitled to one third of the revenue or in any case of the tribute paid by conquered tribes. Thus Princess Olga appropriated one third of the tribute paid by the Drevlianians; Iaroslav, at the time he was his father's lieutenant at Novgorod, was entitled to keep one third of the revenue, sending the balance to Kiev, and so on.

As a matter of fact it was the princely family as a whole, the house of Riurik, which had to be provided for out of the state revenue, each member of the family claiming his or her share of the income. For example, from Prince Rostislav of Smolensk's charter granted to the bishop of that city (1150) we know that a certain part of the "tribute" (direct taxes) collected in the land of Smolensk belonged to the prince's wife. Undoubtedly similar arrangements were made in other principalities as well.

The usual method of satisfying the claims of members of the princely family was to assign to each a certain district or city for his or her sustenance (*kormlenie*, "feeding"; or *uteshenie*, "comfort"). All, or a certain part, of the revenue collected in that district was at the disposal of its holder. It is in this sense that we must interpret the chronicler's remark that Vyshgorod was Princess Olga's own city and similar statements about other princes. In addition to the estates thus used by members of the princely family, each could, and most of them did, own private landed estates in his or her own right.

There were three main sources of state revenue in this period: direct taxes, court fees and fines paid by offenders for committing crimes, and custom duties and other taxes on commerce.[13]

The direct taxes evolved from the tribute (*dan'*) imposed on the conquered tribes by the first Kievan princes. As we know, in the tenth century the prince with his retinue used to visit the conquered territories yearly to collect tribute. This was known as *poliudie*. Princess Olga replaced this military way of collecting state funds by establishing a network of local collecting agencies. The tribute thus was turned into a regular tax but the old Russian term for it (*dan'*) was retained and I shall continue to call it "tribute," accordingly.

The tribute was collected in nonagricultural regions from each homestead (*dym*, literally, "smoke"—i.e., "hearth") and in agricultural regions from each tilling unit (*ralo*, "plow"). Gradually the

13. On taxation, see *idem*, pp. 82–85; Sergeevich, *Drevnosti*, III (1911), 164–313, and *Lektsii i issledovaniia*, pp. 335–349; Presniakov, *Lektsii po russkoi istorii*, I, 205–207.

original connotation of both terms faded and either was used in the conventional sense of a unit of taxation. It will not be amiss to note here that in the Mongol and post-Mongol periods the term *dym,* in the technical sense of a unit of taxation, was widely used in western (Lithuanian) Russia. In Muscovy the unit was called *sokha* (the word for a wooden plow).

In the twelfth century the sum total of the tributes due was tabulated for each taxation district (*pogost*), and within it the people themselves, through their selectmen, calculated the amount to be collected from each "hearth."

The tribute was imposed on the rural population only. Larger cities were exempt from any direct taxes. The residents of the smaller towns paid a much lighter tax than the tribute, known as *pogorodie* ("town collection"). There were further exemptions from tribute, of a social nature: men of the upper classes (*muzhi*) paid no tribute no matter where they happened to live. The same seems to have been true of men of the middle classes (*liudi*).

On the other hand there was no exemption, either territorial or social, for the payment of court fees and penal fines. These fines, especially the bloodwite (*vira*), constituted as important a source of state revenue as the tribute. The bloodwite payments and other penal fines were collected by a special official, *virnik* ("bloodwite collector"), who with a few assistants rode around the district assigned to him at least once a year. The local population had to provide these officials with food and fodder for their horses. A table of the delivery of such supplies was included in the *Russian Law.*

The taxes on commercial transactions were manifold. First there was the *myto* (to be compared with the Gothic *mōta*),[14] which may be called "customs duty" in a sense, although it was collected not at the state frontier but at the approaches to each city, especially on the bridges for goods carried in wagons and on the river embankments for goods transported in boats. Apparently no distinction was made between foreign goods and merely out-of-town goods.

Secondly, there was the *perevoz,* a toll for crossing a river in a ferry or for transporting goods over a portage between two rivers. There was also a tax on storehouses used by foreign merchants at the market place (*gostinnoe*) and a general tax on merchants using the market place for the upkeep of the latter (*torgovoe*). In addition, special fees were collected for weighing and measuring goods in the

14. Preobrazhensky, I, 574–575.

market place. In connection with commercial taxes, the tax on taverns (*korchmita*) may also be mentioned here.

## b. The Army

The Russian army of the Kievan period consisted of two separate bodies: the druzhina of the princes as well as that of the major boyars, and the city militia.[15] The druzhina was not numerous but very effective, since it was a highly mobile corps consisting of able-bodied, well-armed, and well-trained horsemen.

The city militia was mobilized only for major campaigns or for emergencies, such as the necessity of warding off a sudden inroad of enemies coming in force, as the Cumans in south Russia may always have been expected to do in spite of existing peace treaties. City men had not enough weapons and horses and it was the duty of the prince to provide them with both. As to horses, each major prince kept herds of them but they were used mostly for equipping his own retainers. For the needs of the city militia, horses were requisitioned from the rural population, especially from the smerdy.

There was no definite contingent of militia troops. Presumably every able-bodied youth who could be provided with weapons and a horse was expected to serve, especially in case of emergency. According to information available in the twelfth century, the militia corps of a major city numbered from fifteen to twenty thousand men. In some of the major campaigns peasants (smerdy) also participated.

The druzhina was supposed to serve as a shock brigade in the battle and upon its maneuverability and tactical skill the issue of the campaign often depended. On the other hand, there was a tendency among some princes to use the city militia as cannon-fodder, if such an expression may be applied to the pre-cannon era of military technique, and to spare his retainers. Prince Mstislav of Tmutorokan's comment after the battle of Listven, in which he defeated the forces of his brother Iaroslav, is typical. As he inspected the battlefield on the following day he exclaimed in exultation, "Who does not rejoice at this spectacle? Here lies a Severian, here a Varangian, and my retainers are unharmed." [16]

Since the Russians' main enemies in the eleventh and twelfth cen-

---

15. On the organization of the army, see Vladimirsky-Budanov, *Obzor*, pp. 85–86; Sergeevich, *Drevnosti*, I (1909), 595–618, and *Lektsii i issledovaniia*, pp. 319–331; A. I. Nikitsky, "Voennyi byt v Velikom Novgorode," *Russkaia Starina*, *1* (2d ed. 1870), 5–33; Grekov, *Kievskaia Rus'*, pp. 187–222.

16. Cross, 224.

turies were such splendid horsemen as the Cumans and in view of the nature of steppe warfare, cavalry was considered the main branch of the Russian army. However, the city men, even if provided with horses, were poor riders, and the druzhina was numerically small. It therefore became necessary to use Turks as auxiliary cavalry troops. Several groups of various Turkish tribes who for one reason or other were in hostile relations with the Cumans were settled in south Russian lands. The best organized and the most reliable among them were the so-called "Black Caps" (*Chernye Klobuki;* in Turkish, *Karakalpak*) settled in the Ros River region in the Kievan principality (see Chap. VI, sec. 11).

As to the equipment of the Russian warrior of the period, his armor consisted of a helmet, a cuirasse, and a shield; and his standard weapons were the sword and the spear; bows and arrows were also used, especially by auxiliary troops.

The commissariat was not very elaborate. Troops on the march were followed by a train of wagons on which tents, standards, heavy armor, and weapons were loaded; also food supplies—these, however, were not ample, since the army as a rule lived off the country it passed through.

### c. The Police

There was no regular police force in Kievan Russia. Order in and around the princely palace was maintained by junior members of the druzhina; on the manors of the princes and boyars, by stewards and watchmen. In the major cities presumably the chiliarch and his agents were entrusted with preventing any major crimes and riots. In the rural districts local officials were too few to be of any use and the task of preventing crime and of apprehending criminals therefore rested with the people themselves. According to the *Russian Law,* if the members of the local guild (*verv'*) were not able to identify or apprehend a murderer, they had collectively to pay the bloodwite he owed to the state for his crime.

### d. Means of Communication

The lack of good roads has always been, and to a certain extent still is, a sore spot in Russian life and public economy. Enormous distances, severe climatic conditions, and the scarcity of stone account for the fact that ballasted roads appeared in Russia only shortly before the railroads. In northern Russia it was easier to travel in winter, by sleigh or sledge, than in summer on a road deformed by ruts and holes. In the spring and autumn the notorious Russian *rasputitsa* ("roadlessness") makes traveling, for at least a month in either season, almost impossible whether in northern Russia or in Ukraine. Commercial and other travelers in Kievan Russia therefore preferred, in summer, to travel by boat on the rivers. Here, however, on many occasions rapids and cataracts presented a problem of their own and the portages connecting one riverway with another had all the hardships of overland traveling.

What little the princes of the Kievan period could do in regard to improving the roads and riverways they honestly attempted. Bridges were built and repaired when needed, and portages paved with timber. As we know (Chap. V, sec. 6), bridge building and road paving were considered such an important state business that a special section in the *Russian Law* was devoted to them.

With the low technical standards of the period the Kievan princes could hardly hope to make the Dnieper cataracts navigable. They offered, instead, military protection to the commercial caravans crossing the cataract region. In north Russia, however, some efforts were made to improve the riverways. In 1133 the Novgorod mayor Ivanko Pavlovich undertook to dig a canal near Lake Sterzh to improve the navigation in the upper Volga basin. In the second half of the twelfth century the Polotsk princes dredged the Western Dvina River and eliminated a number of rocks interfering with navigation.[17]

Public postal service was nonexistent in Kievan Russia. Princes sent their orders and letters by special messengers whenever the need arose.

### e. Public Welfare

Education, as well as the care of the sick and the poor, was considered in the Kievan period the concern of both the princes and the church. Hardly anything was done in this field prior to Russia's conversion. It was Christianity that supplied the driving motives for such activities: the ideas of Christian enlightenment and charity.

The educational policies of the princes and the church will be dealt with in another connection (Chap. IX, sec. 9). Here we shall deal briefly with social care. It should be noted first of all that there was

17. Orlov, *Bibliografiia*, pp. 12, 14; V. Semenov, *Rossiia*, IX (St. Petersburg, 1905), 311, 397, 497, 505.

much more cohesion in Kievan society, and in medieval society at large, than in modern society, as a result of which the need for assistance on the part of the state to individuals was less marked than it is now. Each family commune (zadruga) and each guild (verv') customarily took care of its own members whenever they needed care. In their turn the prince's retainers could always count on the prince for assistance in any emergency, and so with the members of a boyar's household. However, with the gradual dissolution of the guilds and the separation of the family from the zadruga, that new social unit—the family—being smaller, was more vulnerable in the face of elemental disasters such as war or famine and consequently afforded less protection to its members. Simultaneously, the growth of the cities and the gradual proletarization of small landowners likewise resulted in the appearance of men and women deprived of regular means of subsistence. All of them needed aid and to a certain extent such assistance was given to them by the princes.

As we know, Vladimir the Saint was the pioneer in this field as in many others. Even granting that both the chronicler and the biographer exaggerated the neophyte prince's Christian zeal, we must admit that he laid the foundation of public charities in Kievan Russia. At least some of his descendants followed his lead and the distribution of food to the poor became an essential feature of every important state and religious festival, even if not made continuous. As an example, on the occasion of the transportation of the relics of the martyr princes Boris and Gleb (1072) the sick and the poor were fed for three days. In 1154 Prince Rostislav of Kiev distributed all of the estate of his uncle, which the latter had bequeathed to him, among the churches and the poor.

That the princes generally considered the care of the poor as part of their duties may be seen from the words of Vladimir Monomach's "Testament," already mentioned, in which he advises his children: "Above all things, forget not the poor, and support them to extent of your means. Give to the orphan, protect the widow, and permit the mighty to destroy no man." From the last phrase it may be seen that a new idea is here expressed: not of mere charity but of a social policy having as its object the protection of the underprivileged. As we know, Vladimir Monomach himself entered upon such legislation.

The church in its turn contributed much to social care by founding hospitals, homes for the aged, and hostels for pilgrims. It is significant that in Kievan Russia the physician (*lechets*) was considered one of the "church people," which means that he enjoyed the protection of the church (see Chap. VI, sec. 8).

## 6. The City-State

Every Russian principality of the Kievan period was, in its political essence, a combination of a city-state and of the princely system of administration. In most cases the princely authority, superimposed upon the city, gradually took the lead. In Novgorod, however, the historical process went in the opposite direction, with the prince's role eventually reduced to that of a mediator or magistrate engaged by the city.[18] If the story of the "calling of the Varangians" is to be credited, the role originally assigned by the Novgorodians to Riurik was exactly of this kind. However, both he and his immediate successors obviously overstepped their bounds. For some time Novgorod became subject to princely power.

With the shifting of the princely throne to Kiev the position of Novgorod deteriorated even more. The Novgorodians obviously objected to the predominance of Kiev, hence their eagerness to help Iaroslav wage war against his brother Sviatopolk. The Novgorodian assistance proved invaluable to Iaroslav and after his victory he had to recompense the Novgorodians by granting them certain charters, one of which seems to have been the original version of the *Russian Law*. It is significant that in the very first article of this code the equality of the wergeld of a Slav (i.e., Novgorodian) with that of a Russian (i.e., Kievan) is proclaimed.

Following Iaroslav's death it became customary for the prince of Kiev, as head of the Russian state, to appoint his eldest son as his lieutenant in Novgorod. Since the latter was apparently bound by Iaroslav's charter, the Novgorodians did not at first object to such an arrangement. Later on, however, with the decline of the authority of the prince of Kiev and the growing rivalry between the different branches of the house of Riurik, the Novgorodians found themselves in a position to make their choice among several princely candidates and they knew how to use their opportunity.

In 1095 a disagreement arose between the Novgorodians and their

18. For a general outline of Novgorodian government and history, see N. I. Kostomarov, *Severnorusskie narodopravstva;* Ikonnikov, *Opyt,* II, Pt. 1, chap. viii; see also Bibliography, XVII.

prince David, son of Sviatoslav, as a result of which David temporarily left the city. The Novgorodians bade him never return and themselves invited another prince from Rostov to take his place. Seven years later, when Prince Sviatopolk II of Kiev proclaimed his intention of appointing his son to the Novgorodian throne, the Novgorodian emissaries appeared before him with the following blunt message: "We were sent to you, oh Prince, with positive instructions that our city does not want either you or your son. If your son has two heads, let him come." [19] In 1136, as we know (see Chap. IV, sec. 7), the Novgorod veche took a decisive step toward asserting the sovereign rights of the city: both the prince and his non-Novgorodian retainers were deprived of the right to own landed estates within the boundaries of the Novgorodian state.

By the middle of the twelfth century the office of the prince of Novgorod became in fact an elective one and in 1196 the privilege of the Novgorodians to elect their prince of their own will was formally recognized by a congress of Russian princes, with the understanding that they would choose their candidates from among members of the house of Riurik only.

Four years later, however, being severely defeated by Prince Vsevolod III of Suzdal, the Novgorodians, addressing him as the "Lord Grand Duke" (*Gospodin Velikii Kniaz'*), asked him to send his son as their prince and, if the statement of the Suzdalian chronicler is to be credited, even agreed to recognize Novgorod as his patrimony (*otchina i dedina*). At any rate, from this time on most of the Novgorodian princes were chosen among Vsevolod's descendants. This fact, however, did not impair the Novgorodian independent rights, which by this time were firmly secured, and in 1211 Vsevolod himself confirmed their old liberties.

Each new incumbent, upon assuming the principate, had to sign a special contract with the City of Novgorod. Unfortunately no copy of such a contract for the Kievan period has been preserved; the earliest known text is that of 1265. From the evidence of the chronicles of the Kievan period at least four important clauses of a typical contract may be reconstructed, however. One was the prohibition (from 1136 on) of the owning of landed estates in the Novgorodian state by the prince or his retainers. The second important point was the freedom of the Novgorodians to elect city officials without interference

19. Cross, p. 291.

on the part of the prince (confirmed by Vsevolod III in 1211). With this the third provision was connected: the prince had no right to dismiss city officials without a veche decision or a court trial. According to the chronicles, in 1218 Prince Sviatoslav announced at a meeting of the veche that he had decided to dismiss the mayor, Tverdislav. He was immediately asked what his accusation was against the mayor. The prince could only say that he did not like him. The veche accordingly resolved that if no fault could be laid to the mayor he should not be removed. He stayed. Fourth, the supreme judicial authority of the veche was guaranteed; in the words of Vsevolod III, the Novgorodians were free to punish criminals.

The state sovereignty of Novgorod rested with the city and not with the prince. The city was spoken of as the Lord Novgorod the Great (*Gospodin Velikii Novgorod*). The supreme organ through which the sovereignty materialized was the city assembly (veche). It had its own chancellery, housed in the city hall (*izba*), and its own seal.

As in Kiev, the Novogorod city assembly usually met either in the square before the prince's palace ("Iaroslav's Courtyard") or in that before the St. Sophia Cathedral. The meeting was called by the pealing of the city bell, which thus became the symbol of Novgorodian liberties. After the conquest of the city by the grand duke of Moscow in the late fifteenth century, the latter's first order was to remove the veche bell.

The city assembly combined the supreme executive, legislative, and judiciary power. Actually only major problems of the executive were submitted to the consideration of the veche, current administration being dealt with by the prince and the mayor. Similarly, the courts were given sufficient latitude for their current work and the veche acted as the supreme court in major cases only, such as the trial of the prince or of a high city official. Broadly speaking, then, the city assembly was chiefly a legislature.

As in other Russian cities of the period every Novgorodian citizen had the right to vote at meetings of the city assembly and—as elsewhere—unanimous approval was required for all decisions of the veche. To prevent the recurrence of violent conflicts between two parties when there was no overwhelming majority, a special council came to being in Novgorod, whose chief concern was to prepare bills for the consideration of the veche. This council met under the chairmanship of the archbishop and consisted of three hundred members, to wit: the prince's lieutenant, the senior city officials, and the boyars. The German merchants called this council *Herrenrath* ("Council of Lords"). In Russian it was known as *Gospoda* ("the Lords").[20]

From the strictly legal point of view this institution was not an upper chamber, since the veche's authority was indivisible, but a committee of the city assembly. For practical purposes the Gospoda exerted the moderating influence of an upper chamber but its advice could always be overruled by the veche.

The constitution of the Novgorodian state may be characterized as a democracy limited to a certain extent by the interests of the upper classes—*de facto*, if not *de jure*. Furthermore, it should not be forgotten that certain categories of the population, such as the smerdy and, of course, the slaves, were disfranchised altogether.

The two major city officials were the mayor (*posadnik*) and the chiliarch (*tysiatsky*). Both were elected by the city assembly for a brief term, not precisely specified, and could be reëlected. It is noteworthy that any former posadnik, even if not reëlected, was considered a notable and continued to have some part in directing Novgorodian affairs. All were members of the Gospoda. It has been observed that from the early twelfth to the middle of the thirteenth century, five generations of the same family held the office of posadnik in Novgorod, with some intervals. It was a certain Giuriata who occupied the post in the early twelfth century. From 1126 to 1134 the position was held by his son Miroslav; from 1137 to around 1175, by the latter's son Iakun; from 1211 to 1219, by Iakun's son Dimitri; and for several years after 1220, by Dimitri's son Ivanko.[21]

The duties of the posadnik consisted mainly in the general supervision of the city administration. He was also the chief justice for litigation about land. As to the tysiatsky, he was the commander of the city militia and the chief justice for commercial litigation.

The City of Novgorod may be called a commonwealth consisting of five autonomous communes, each in one of the five boroughs (*konets*, literally "end") into which the city was divided. These boroughs were called as follows: Slavensky (Slovenian), Plotnitsky (the "Carpenters' Borough"), Zagorodsky ("Beyond the City Walls") Goncharsky (the "Potters' Borough"), and Nerevsky. Each

20. A. I. Nikitsky, "Ocherki iz zhizni Velikogo Novgoroda, I. Pravitelstvennyi Soviet," *ZMNP, 145* (1869), 294–309.

21. Vladimirsky-Budanov, *Obzor,* p. 67.

borough commune elected its own mayor, known as the *starosta* (elder); each consisted, in turn, of "street" guilds (*ulitsa*), and each of the latter, of "rows" (*riad*).

Novgorod was, however, not merely a city; it was the metropolis of a state commanding a vast territory stretching from the Gulf of Finland to the Urals and from Lake Ilmen to the White Sea and the Arctic Ocean. This was a territory rich in natural resources, except grain, and able to provide the metropolitan merchants with many an item for their export trade.

The metropolis itself was favorably located from the commercial point of view. A junior partner in the Novgorodian commerce was the city of Pskov, which attained independence in the Mongol period. In the Kievan period Pskov was considered only a dependent town (*prigorod*). Like every other Novgorodian by-town, Pskov enjoyed local self-government under the supervision of a mayor appointed by the Novgorod veche. Pskov residents were entitled to Novgorodian citizenship. Actually, as usual in the period, it was hard for them to attend the meetings of the chief city assembly of their land and few were able to do so.

The population of other by-towns of Novgorod was in the same position. In the rural districts there were few people holding Novgorodian citizenship and even those who did—especially those living in remote provinces—usually failed to exercise their right to vote. The majority of the provincial population were not granted citizenship. For practical reasons, then, the people of the city of Novgorod ruled not only the city but the whole Novgorodian empire as well. In Novgorod, as in Rome of the republican period, the city *was* the state.

In regard to administration the territory of the Novgorodian state was divided into two distinct parts. Its western section, closest to the capital, consisted of five provinces (*volost'*), which in a later period became known as "fifths" (*piatiny*, from *piat'*, "five"). The northern and eastern area of the state, consisting of vast and thinly populated territories with many native tribes of Lapp and Finno-Ugrian extraction living on them, was the Novgorodian colony.

The pentamerous organization of the Novgorodian provinces was not accidental. Each of the five provinces was ascribed to one of the boroughs, to wit: Bezhetskaia to Slavensky, Obonezhskaia to Plotnitsky, Shelonskaia to Zagorodsky, Derevskaia to Goncharsky, and Vodskaia to Narevsky. Among the duties of the population of each province was that of repairing the street paving in the borough to which the province belonged. For this task either workers were drafted (which seems to have been the original method) or money collected.

The northern and eastern area subject to Novgorod consisted of several colonies of which the richest and the most important was the Dvina land north of the city of Vologda; it was also known as Zavolochie ("Beyond the Portage"—i.e., the area beyond the portage by which the Northern Dvina River could be reached). This colonial part of the Novgorodian empire was ruled not by the boroughs but by the City of Novgorod as a whole, through governors and other agents appointed by the prince in concurrence with the mayor. These officials were assisted in their task by hundreders representing the local Russian population and the tribal chiefs of the native peoples.

At times the population of the colonies would be aroused by the ruthless exploitation of their wealth by the metropolis as well as by the arbitrary behavior of the Novgorodian agents. In the second half of the twelfth century the colonial city of Khlynov (later known as Viatka; now Kirov) seceded from Novgorod. The opposition in the Dvina land was kept in check until the late fourteenth century.

Novgorod was not the only Russian city-state of the period. Polotsk seems to have been another. According to Narbutt the sons of Prince Vseslav of Polotsk (reigned 1044–1101) willed their authority to the city, which after their death became a republic ruled by the veche and the council of boyars. Unfortunately, Narbutt fails to refer to the source of his information.[22] In the case of Khlynov it is positively known that after seceding from Novgorod it became a city-state in its own right. It was organized as a democratic republic.[23]

## 7. The Local Commune

The local commune (*mir*) was the basic cell in the system of the old Russian government and administration, both in the city and the rural districts. As we have seen above, it was of such local communes ("street guilds") that each Novgorod borough consisted and even the street guild was not the primary cell, since it in turn was composed of "rows." Each Novgorodian street commune elected its own elder (*starosta*). In Pskov the local city district guild was known as a "hundred," with an elected "hundreder" at the head of it. Presumably such local communes existed in each major Russian city of

22. See *idem,* pp. 64–65.
23. Kostomarov, *op. cit.,* I, 241–251.

the Kievan period. Smaller towns constituted each a single commune.

The organization of the local commune in the rural districts is less well known, since pertinent information for this period is scarce. Such communes appear to have been of various types. In the *Russian Law* the verv' is mentioned. This type presumably represented a combination of two or more neighborhood family communes (zadrugi— see Chap. VI, sec. 1).

With the gradual disintegration of both the family commune and the verv', new types of rural associations must have been formed, some of them based on economic coöperation (the siabry guild), others being formed for the allotment and collection of taxes, for which elected officials such as selectmen (*dobrye liudi*, literally "good men"), hundreders, and decurions were responsible.

## 8. The Manor

In feudal Europe the manor was not only an economic unit but an important sociopolitical institution at large, since the lord of a manor —the seignior—wielded both administrative and judiciary authority over the population of his domains. In Kievan Russia, where the city played such an important role in political life and the prerogatives of the prince, except in western Ukraine, precluded any attempts on the part of the boyars to seize political power, the role of the manor was much more restricted than in either central or western Europe.

However, Russia's political life in the Kievan period was complex and its nature heterogeneous, some elements of feudalism being present there alongside of institutions of an entirely different order. Although the manor never became the basic institution in Russian sociopolitical life of the period, it cannot be denied that by the late twelfth and early thirteenth centuries the manorial authority of the lord, especially in western Ukraine, must have assumed greater proportions than it had enjoyed earlier.

In the case of the princely domain, the seignorial authority of the lord may be considered but a reflection of the princely power at large. Therefore, in order better to understand the growth of the manor as such it will be expedient to examine first the case of the boyar manor.

An important boyar's household was a replica of the princely court on a lesser scale. Boyars' officials, such as stewards (*tiun*), are mentioned in the sources of the period. We have seen that the princely tiun eventually assumed administrative and judiciary authority even outside the court. Similarly the boyar's tiun became, in the course of time, an agent or judge appointed by the boyar to administer justice to the residents of the domain.

The full development of the manorial administration belongs, however, to the Mongol period when grants of immunity were issued by the grand dukes to many a petty prince, boyar, and monastery. The recipient of such a grant was given judicial and administrative authority over the population of his domains and the grand duke's agents were not allowed to interfere with the manorial courts. According to S. V. Iushkov, boyar estates might have enjoyed such immunity even in the Kievan period.[24] No copy of any grant of this kind made to a boyar in the Kievan period is known, however. A few examples of grants to bishops and monasteries have been preserved but they can hardly be called full immunity grants. One of them is Prince Mstislav I's grant of a certain locality—Lake Buitsy, presumably with the adjacent strip of land—to the St. George Monastery in Novgorod (1130). The property is granted "with the tribute and the bloodwite and fines." [25]

The meaning of the phrase needs elucidation. The question is whether the monastery was given the right to impose bloodwites and fines, i.e., to judge the people living in that locality, or was merely entitled to collect the income derived from that source. In my opinion the second interpretation is the one which must be accepted. Indeed, "tribute" is mentioned in the document in the same connection and surely the monastery was not given the right to impose tribute on the population. The grant was obviously of a financial nature and Mstislav's charter should be compared with Prince Rostislav's charter issued to the Bishop of Smolensk (1150), which confirms the grant of a tithe of the income in various localities in the land of Smolensk. A lengthy list of such localities is included in the charter and the precise amount of the bishop's share of income from each locality is indicated. The source of income is mostly the tribute but at least in one case it is the bloodwite.[26]

All told, it may be assumed that the manorial authority of a boyar over the population of his domains was very restricted. Legally, it extended to his slaves only. It is true that, according to the *Russian Law*, the lord was not to be held responsible for beating a half-free laborer (*zakup*) working for him if there was some good reason for

24. Iushkov, *Narysy*, pp. 191–197.
25, *Khristomatiia*, I, 112–113.
26. *Idem*, I, 219–224.

the punishment. This might be interpreted as the right of the lord to judge his indentured laborers. The law adds, however, that "if the lord, being drunk, beats the indentured laborer without any fault on the part of the latter, he [the lord] has to pay for the offense against the *zakup* the same amount as for that against a freeman." [27]

Free hired laborers were obviously outside the lord's manorial jurisdiction altogether. Turning now to the prince's manor we find a different picture, since the whole population of the princely domain was under the jurisdiction of the prince and of the judges appointed by him. However, in this case the prince exercised his authority not merely as lord of the manor but as a prince.

The two sources of authority seem to have been indissolubly interwoven in the person of the prince and it would be hard to determine in any case in what capacity he acted. The nature of his domination over his slaves was obviously the same as the boyars'—that of property owner. In the case of the mistreatment of indentured laborers by the prince's agents, the laborers had nobody to appeal to except perhaps the prince himself, so that their position on princely estates was, from the legal point of view, more precarious than on the boyars' estates.

The prince's authority over the smerdy emanated, as we have already seen (Chap. VI, sec. 5), from his position as head of the state, but in practical application this governmental authority merged with the manorial and the stewards of princely estates must have cared little for legal subtleties. For practical reasons, then, not only the slaves and the half-free but also a category of freemen were subject to the manorial authority of the prince.

## 9. The Church

From the year 1037 the Russian Church was organized as a diocese of the Patriarchate of Constantinople. While some Russians objected to this situation, it was in a way advantageous to the Church, making it less dependent on the local state government and local politics.

From this local angle the Russian Church in the Kievan period was an autonomous body, a state within the state, as it were; as we know (Chap. VI, sec. 8), the Church even had its own "subjects," since certain categories of the people were under its exclusive jurisdiction. At the same time, not only as a result of the Byzantine theory of "symphony" between church and state but as a living body, the Church was

27. *Medieval Russian Laws*, p. 47.

an important factor in the development of the Russian state and nation at large, as well as in Russian economics.

To a certain extent the Church administration, based as it was on the principle of strict subordination, served as a model for strengthening the princely administration, as for example in Suzdalia. The Church sponsored the spread of Byzantine law in Russia and, being interested in securing its property rights on the lands granted to it, contributed to a clearer definition of the notion of property. On the other hand, it introduced some feudalizing elements into the Russian social organization by objecting to outright slavery and sponsoring a new social group of freedmen, the *izgoi,* whose position had some similarity to that of serfs (see Chap. VI, sec. 8).

Last, but not least, the Church through its leaders—bishops and priors—wielded a moderating influence in political life, aiming at the peaceful settlement of interprincely discords and, especially in Novgorod, at a reconciliation of antagonistic popular parties.

The metropolitan of Kiev was the head of the Russian Church in that period. As a rule, he was a Greek appointed by the Patriarch of Constantinople.

Bishops were nominally appointed by the metropolitan. Actually the prince of Kiev, and later the prince of each land in which a bishop's see was situated, exerted considerable influence on the nomination of the bishop.[28] In Novgorod the veche likewise had to be consulted every time the Novgorodian see became vacant. Under Vladimir eight eparchies were organized in Russia (see Chap. III, sec. 4). As the authority of the Kievan prince decreased, each of the local princes tried to have a bishopric established in his own principality. On the eve of the Mongol invasion there were already fifteen eparchies in Russia. From 1165 the bishop of Novgorod bore the title of archbishop. Each bishop wielded considerable authority over the priests and other clergy within his eparchy. However, the parish priest was usually nominated by the congregation and the bishop usually approved the nominee.

Russian monasticism followed the Byzantine pattern.[29] In Russia, as in Byzantium, there was no specialization in the monks' activities and all the monks formed but one order. As to their organization, some of the Byzantine monasteries were of communal type. The

28. See *Golubinsky, Istoriia,* I, Pt. 1, pp. 344–363.

29. On Russian monasticism and monasteries in the Kievan period, see *idem,* I, Pt. 2, chap. vi.

brothers lived in the same building, received clothes from the monastery, ate together, and worked under the supervision of the prior. In other monasteries each monk lived in his own cottage (*kelia*, cell).

The first Russian monasteries were apparently of this latter type and a communal statute—that of the Studion Monastery in Constantinople—was first introduced in Russia in the Monastery of the Caves at Kiev in the eleventh century. This monastery played an important role in sponsoring Christian morals and learning and within its walls the first Kievan chronicle was written. Under the patronage of the princes, monasteries spread rapidly in Russia in the Kievan period, by the end of which their number had reached the figure of fifty-eight, to which we have to add twelve nunneries. With one exception, all the monasteries and convents were located in cities. This is a marked contrast to the situation in the Mongol period (thirteenth to fifteenth centuries), during which most of the new monasteries were founded "in the wilderness"—that is, in the virgin woods —and were thus destined to play an important role in the colonization of northern Russia.

As to the church judiciary, the bishop was the supreme judge in each eparchy. To his jurisdiction all church people were subject in all matters of court action. Litigation between church people and outsiders was tried by a mixed court of the bishop and the prince or their respective agents.

There were, further, specific cases in which even non-church people were subject to the bishop's jurisdiction. To this category belonged offenses against the Church and religion; family conflicts; and cases of moral delinquency. Lists of such cases were included in the so-called "Church Statutes," of which most are known in late and unofficial copies only.[30] We find in these lists mention of such crimes as robbing a church; cutting of crosses (presumably in cemeteries or on crossroads); stealing clothes from the bodies of the dead; and also, what to a modern reader may seem a rather minor offense, bringing a dog or any other animal into a church, and so on. As to family conflicts and offenses against morality, such incidents as the following are listed: brawl between husband and wife about property; beating of the parents by their children (but not vice versa); adultery; rape of a woman or girl (that of a nun called for the highest fine); calling names, especially calling a woman a "whore," and so on.

---

30. On the early Russian church statutes, see Vladimirsky-Budanov, *Obzor*, pp. 93–94; Golubinsky, *Istoriia*, I, Pt. 1, pp. 399–409; Iushkov, *Ustav Kniazia Vladimira*.

## 10. *The Judiciary*

In the preceding sections some aspects of the organization of the judiciary in Kievan Russia, such as the manorial authority of the prince and the boyars, as well as the bishop's court, have been briefly discussed. We have now to examine the old Russian jurisprudence at large (see also Chap. IX, sec. 10e).

An important factor in the development of the old Russian law was its inherent dualism.[31] Each Russian tribe maintained definite rules of social behavior long before the establishment of the princes of the Riurik dynasty in Kiev. The princes in their turn tried to impose on the people certain new legal provisions which suited them. The social unit—guild, clan, city—on the one hand and the prince on the other are thus two main factors in the development of Russian law and legislation. With Russia's conversion to Christianity a third factor appeared: the Church, which by that time already had an elaborate system of canon law for its guidance.

The influence of these three factors may be felt, each in different degree, both in the organization of the courts and in the court procedure. In the oldest part of the *Russian Law*, Iaroslavs' *Pravda*, we find some coöperation between the prince's courts and the people's institutions. In the *Pravda* of Iaroslav's sons, as well as in the Expanded Version of the *Pravda*, the princely court is obviously the dominant institution. In Novgorod and Pskov, as evidenced by the charter of either city issued at a later date, the prince's judicial authority was limited by that of the city officials. The competence of the church courts has already been described above.

In Russian court procedure of the Kievan period the element of the individual will of the litigants played a very important role, while that of the judge was limited to supervision of the contest and to equalizing the means and chances of the contestants. There was no inquisitorial system of procedure.

The state authorities did not interfere with the investigation of the case prior to its hearing. The local community, or guild, was of more assistance to the plaintiff in cases where it was difficult for him to establish the identity of the defendant. Anyone who lost something, or from whom something was stolen, could make an announcement at the market place of his town. If the item in question was not

---

31. On old Russian courts and court law, see Vladimirsky-Budanov, *Obzor*, pp. 610–629; *Medieval Russian Laws*, pp. 9–12.

declared within three days, anyone found holding it after the expira-
tion of this term was considered the defendant in the case. If the
owner found the object in somebody else's house the holder of the
object could reject the accusation of theft by stating that he had
bought it in good faith from a third party. He was obligated, however,
to assist the owner in establishing the identity of the seller. This was
done by means of the so-called *svod* ("confrontment"), an important
feature of medieval Russian precourt procedure. The plaintiff and
the defendant, accompanied by reliable citizens, went to the seller; if
the latter could not explain how he obtained the object in question,
he was recognized guilty and had to pay for it. If he insisted that he
himself obtained the object in good faith from still another man, they
all went to examine that other man, and so on, until they would find
the guilty party. If, however, the investigation was to be transferred
to other towns, the plaintiff had to go to the third "confrontment"
only: that third party had to pay the damages and could then continue the examination by himself.

The modes of proof at the disposal of the contestants at the court
trial were threefold: witnesses, appeal to God's judgment, and—in
civil litigation—deeds, notes, and other documents.

(1) According to the *Russian Law* there were two kinds of witnesses: the eyewitness (*vidok*) and the witness claiming to have full
knowledge of the case (*poslukh*). Later texts deal with the second
kind of witness only.

(2) There were several means by which people in the Middle Ages
—not only in Russia—believed they could have God's will revealed
to them. The habitual approach to God in court procedure was to have
one of the contestants, or the witness, take the oath (in old Russian,
*rota*). Another way of appealing to God's judgment was by ordeal:
by water or by iron. The oath as well as ordeals was known not only
to Russian but to German law as well. In addition, the German law
in certain cases recommended the judicial duel (*Zweikampf*). This institution is not mentioned in the *Pravda Russkaia*. It constituted,
however, an important feature of the Novgorod and Pskov law in the
later period. It is first mentioned on Russian soil in the treaty concluded between Smolensk and the German cities in 1229. Presumably
the institution was borrowed from German law. A judicial duel may
not necessarily end in the death of either contestant; once either is
knocked to the ground he is recognized as the loser.

(3) As to deeds and other documents, they were considered abso-

lutely valid only when certified by public authorities. In Pskov, copies of deeds and other acts had to be filed with the office of archives at the Holy Trinity Cathedral.

A few words may be added concerning old Russian penal law. In the *Pravda Russkaia* the transition from blood revenge to the punishment of a criminal by the state has been recorded. That punishment, in the period of the *Pravda,* consisted in the imposition by the prince of a "composition" (money fine) on the criminal. It is noteworthy that the *Pravda* does not impose any capital punishment and recommends corporal punishment only once, and only for slaves. Presumably the introduction of capital punishment into Russian legislation of the fourteenth century was the result of the influence of German law on one hand, in western Russia, and Mongol law on the other, in eastern Russia.

## 11. Concluding Queries: on "Political Feudalism" in Kievan Russia

We have already come to the conclusion (see Chap. VI, sec. 12) that there was in Kievan Russia no developed feudalism in the western sense of the term, and could not be, since Russia in that age belonged to a different socio-political formation: that of commercial capitalism partly based upon slavery.

I have admitted, however, that even in the Kievan period there were in Russia certain elements of what may be called "economic feudalism" and that the growth of the manor was one of the most important manifestations of it. In the course of this chapter we have examined the role of the manor in the local government and administration of the Kievan period. We have seen that, in this regard, it likewise may be called a manifestation of the feudalizing process.

We have now to consider the problem of "political feudalism" at large in the Kievan period. Was there any mediatization of supreme political authority in Kievan Russia? Was there a scale of rulers (suzerain, vassals, subvassals)? Was there a reciprocity of contract between greater and lesser rulers?

As we know, Russian political history of the Kievan period may be divided into two periods: that of the predominance of the prince of Kiev over all others and that of the dismemberment of the Kievan realm. At the beginning of the first period—to be more exact, in the first half of the tenth century—certain features of political feudalism may be recorded in Russian political history. The Russo-Byzantine treaties of 911 and 945 were concluded, on the Russian side, in the name of the grand prince of the Russians and of all the "illustrious princes under his arm." Some of these subordinate princes may have been tribal chieftains who recognized first Oleg and then Igor as their suzerains. Later their authority was reduced and from the reign of Vladimir I we do not hear of the existence of any local princes except for Vladimir's descendants. Obviously the original local princes disappeared from the historical stage in the process of the consolidation of the authority of the one prince of Kiev.

As we know, Iaroslav I before his death divided the princely authority between his sons but tried to prevent a complete dismemberment of the realm by introducing in his "Testament" the principle of seniority to be observed by his descendants. This was a genealogical rather than a feudal principle. Actually at first, instead of the personal seniority of the oldest brother, a triumvirate of the three older brothers was established; but not for long. There followed the attempt to preserve at least a federative unity by means of periodic meetings of the leading princes. Vladimir Monomach and after him his son Mstislav were the last of the Kievan princes to succeed in maintaining the unity of Kievan power. After them the Kievan realm broke down.

Following its dismemberment some of the local princes, and particularly those of Suzdal and Galicia, continued to extend their claims on a Pan-Russian suzerainty but actually in that period any attempt at the establishment of suzerain-vassal relations between the princes could affect princely relations only within single branches of the Rurikide family, or within single principalities. The tendency now was to use the terms of family relationship to cover the political notions of seniority between the princes. Thus Prince Iziaslav II said to his uncle Viacheslav when offering him the Kievan throne: "Thou art my father; take Kiev and all the land; keep for thyself whatever pleases thee and give me the rest" (1150).

In northeastern Russia—in Suzdalia, to be more exact—the principle of suzerainty developed more fully. In 1171 Andrei Bogoliubsky, Prince of Vladimir in Suzdalia, installed in Kiev and near-by towns the three brothers Rostislavichi with the understanding that they would follow his political lead. In 1174, not being satisfied with their loyalty, he commanded them thus: "Since you do not obey my will, thou, Roman, get out of Kiev; thou, David, out of Vyshgorod; and thou, Mstislav, out of Belgorod; go all of you to Smolensk and divide that land as you wish." In this case the Rostislavichi protested vigorously, complaining that Andrei addressed them not as independent princes but as if they were his vassals (*podruchniki*). Significantly enough, Andrei's brother and successor on the throne of Vladimir-in-Suzdalia, Vsevolod III, accepted the title of grand duke. It is at this juncture that to genealogical terms of seniority we find the political added: "Thou art our lord (*gospodin*) and father"— in such words the princes of Riazan addressed Vsevolod III in 1180. And even Prince Vladimir II of Galicia wrote to him: "My father and lord, help me to keep Galicia, and I shall be God's and thine with all Galicia, always obedient to thy will." It may be recalled in this connection that Vladimir II's grandfather Vladimirko recognized the authority of the Byzantine emperor as his suzerain. In a sense, this not only meant an introduction of the principle of vassalage into Russian political life but separated the Galician principality from the Russian confederation, legally at least.

Altogether, it is obvious that from the middle of the twelfth century the principles of suzerainty and political vassalage are in ascendancy in both Suzdalia and Galicia. Here we have to admit that interprincely relations in both eastern and western Russia were developing in the direction of a feudal scale of rulers. There is no evidence, however, of the existence of any reciprocal contracts between the suzerain and the vassal princes. Moreover, the federative idea of the equality of all the ruling princes did not entirely disappear. All the princes continued to think of themselves as "brothers." The idea of princely solidarity was too strong to be superseded at once by the new notions of suzerainty and vassalage. None of them could forget that they were all "grandchildren of the same grandfather."

What is even more important, because of the peculiarities of the Russian system of government in the Kievan period princely authority was but one of the elements of power and no change in the interprincely relations could affect the basic principles of the city-state or entirely eliminate the authority of the veche. Not only in Novgorod but in Kiev as well, people never forgot in this period that they were endowed with certain basic political rights.

"We do not like to be disposed of as if we were part of the deceased prince's estate," protested the Kievans when they rose against Prince Igor Olgovich (1146).

"Thou art our prince," said the Kievans to Prince Iziaslav II, "we do not want any princes of the Olgovichi branch."

In Chapter VI (sec. 12) I have discussed the question of the characteristics of the social and economic formation to which Kievan Russia belongs, attempting to answer the question by pointing out certain similarities between Kievan Russia and the Byzantine as well as the Roman Empire. We may now raise one more question, namely: to what political category should Kievan Russia be referred? And here again our answer will be that there is a noticeably greater similarity between Kievan Russia and Byzantine and classical antiquity than between Russia and feudal Europe. Only, in this connection one would think—in addition to the Byzantine Empire—not of the Roman Empire but of republican Rome and the Greek democracies. There, as in Russia of the Kievan period, the city-state was the basic pattern politically. In Italy, Rome rose to exclusive predominance and eventually became the nucleus of a world empire. In Russia, the city of Kiev did not succeed, even in the period of political unification, in occupying such an exclusive position.

In a sense each of the Russian lands of the Kievan period was a city-state in itself and may thus be likened to the Greek *polis*. And at least one of those Russian city-states, "Lord Novgorod the Great," was able to build up a colonial empire of its own, in some ways not unlike the Roman.

What are the sociological implications of the parallels I have tried to establish between Kievan Russia and classical antiquity? It may be argued that modern capitalism and democracy have continued the tradition—logically, at any rate—of the capitalism and democracy of classical times. In a sense we consider our own civilization as a heritage of classical antiquity. Chronologically, however, in western and central Europe the feudal age was wedged in between. It is only in Byzantium that we can see a kind of historical bridge from the Roman Empire to modern states—admitting, of course, that the bridge was gradually shattered by feudal pressure even long before it collapsed: first under the weight of the Crusaders and then, after brief repairs, under the might of the Ottomans.

In my opinion Kievan Russia may be considered, both economically and politically, together with Byzantium as another extension of the capitalistic regime of antiquity projected against the feudal age— with the difference that, unlike Byzantium, Russia also followed the Greek democratic traditions of the classical age politically. But when all is said, as there are no "pure" races, so there are no "pure" economic or political formations, either. Like Byzantium, Kievan Russia was open to feudalizing influences even prior to its eventual collapse before the onslaught of the Eastern hordes.

As to the peculiarity of the socio-economic and political evolution of Kievan Russia—as compared with western and central Europe— shall we call it a sign of "progressiveness" or "backwardness"? Was there a "retardation" or a premature "acceleration" of the historical process in Russia? The answer will depend on each reader's own point of view. From the author's view, it is enough to emphasize the fact that in this period, there was a basic difference in economic and political development between Russia and Europe.

# Chapter VIII

# THE RUSSIAN FEDERATION, 1139–1237

## 1. Introductory Remarks

THE unity of the Kievan realm, sustained with strenuous effort but only moderate success by that great ruler Vladimir Monomach and his first two successors, broke up definitely with the death of Iaropolk II in 1139. Each princely branch of the house of Riurik now tried to secure the leadership for itself but none was strong or popular enough on a national scale to achieve its object. Each succeeded in controlling only its own principality, the resources of which were never sufficient to serve as a basis for restoring national unity. From time to time the princes formed temporary alliances, one group against another; less often, attempts were made to create a national coalition to meet an emergency such as invasion by the steppe peoples. Such coalitions never lasted long, however, and few of them gained the ends for which they were formed. From a realistic point of view, Russia at this period consisted of several different states.[1]

And yet, in spite of all the interprincely rivalry and constant internecine wars, there remained a faint sense of the basic unity of Russia as such. While constantly on the alert against each other, the princes never completely lost the tradition of their dynastic unity and from time to time would remember that they were "neither Magyars nor Poles but grandsons of a common grandfather." And similarly, the author of that great epic poem, the *Lay of Igor's Campaign*, would invoke the unity of the Russian people—the "Rusichi," the "descendants of the Dazhbog." Moreover, the role of the Church as a unifying element must not be overlooked. Even when the princely throne of Kiev lost its former prestige, the metropolitan of Kiev remained the primate of the Russian bishops. It is likewise significant that according to medieval Russian law the citizens of the various principalities, when in a Russian land not their own, were placed in a special cate-

---

1. See Baron M. A. Taube, "Études sur le développement historique du droit international dans l'Europe Orientale," Académie de Droit International, *Recueil des Cours,* 1926, Pt. 1, p. 404.

gory, differentiated from that of foreign nationals. They were known in each of the lands as "outsiders" (*inogorodnie* or *inozemtsy*); the non-Russian foreigners as "aliens" (*chuzhezemtsy*).[2]

Psychologically, then, even in this period of visible disunity Russia remained a kind of federation—a very loose federation, indeed; yet not a mere mechanical agglomeration of wholly independent states, either. In spite of this it is apparent that, while under Iaroslav the Wise and even under Vladimir Monomach the centripetal forces outweighed the centrifugal, the relationship between the two was now reversed. What were the causes of this change?

If we examine the political history of the period only, we may be tempted to see the primary cause of disintegration in the interprincely struggle. Such an approach would be superficial, however. As we know, the prince at this time was not an absolute monarch. His authority was limited both by the council of his boyars and by the city veche. What is even more to the point, he derived his actual strength from the druzhina and the cities themselves. Without the support of his druzhina and the financial backing of the merchants he was powerless; which means, that if the citizens granted their support to the prince they were interested in his enterprises. Thus the prince was not alone responsible for any of his wars against any other prince. Behind the princes stood other, more powerful forces. The interprincely rivalry, more often than not, was but an outward expression of the much deeper rivalry between cities and principalities.

The motives of this rivalry were many and various. First of all, ethnic divergencies must not be neglected. This was the embryonic period of the formation of the Ukrainian and Belorussian nationalities. To be sure, differences in the language between various groups were still slight but the tendency was to divergency rather than unity. And in this case, as in many others, language was but a symbol of cultural customs and habits. The opposition of the Kievan population to the Suzdalian boyars brought into Kiev by Prince Iuri Dolgoruky in 1154 may be considered one of the first expressions of the Russo-Ukrainian rivalry.

Economically the growth of regional commerce was an important factor among those which undermined the unity of the Kievan realm. In the tenth century Kiev played a leading role in the Byzantine commerce. However, to maintain its leadership in the west Eurasian foreign trade it had to control the Azov area as well. With the loss of

2. Vladimirsky-Budanov, *Obzor*, p. 383.

Tmutorokan in the late eleventh century, Kiev was all but cut off from Oriental trade. Simultaneously the Cumans threatened to sever the Dnieper riverway to Byzantium. Still more important, Byzantium itself now became less interested in the Kievan trade. Following the treaty of 1082 between Byzantium and Venice, the Venetians took over the larger part of the Byzantine maritime trade and eventually established their "factories" in the Black Sea area.

The sack of Constantinople by the knights of the Fourth Crusade and the establishment of the Latin Empire (1204–61) signalized the end of normal trade relations between Byzantium and Kiev. The overland trade with Bohemia and central Germany, through Galich, partly replaced the Byzantine trade in Kievan economy of the twelfth and early thirteenth centuries. Other regional centers and routes of commerce now became prominent: Smolensk and Novgorod thrived on the Baltic trade; Riazan and Suzdal tried to expand their trade with the Orient through the intermediary of the Volga Bulgars and the Cumans.

Another important factor in the disintegration of the Kievan realm was the growth of the boyar group—the landowning class—in each of the principalities. B. D. Grekov, with some other Soviet historians, is even ready to lay chief emphasis on this process on what they call the growth of feudalism in Russia.[3] In the separatist tendencies of the feudal grandees they see the main cause of the downfall of Kiev. Exception may be taken here, as on many occasions, to the abuse of the term "feudal." The boyars in this period were almost as closely interested in commercial development as were the merchants and the foundations of agricultural economy were still capitalistic rather than feudal.

On the other hand, one has indeed to recognize that the social and economic growth of the single principalities was an important factor in the new political set-up. The provincial society was rapidly developing its material and spiritual culture and each city and principality now considered itself self-sufficient, both economically and culturally. Thus, paradoxically enough, the political weakness of Russia in this period was partly the result of her economic and cultural growth. If there was a sickness it was concomitant to the growth of a rising democracy. It is possible that eventually some kind of new political and economic unity might have been achieved in Russia

3. Grekov, *Kievskaia Rus'*, p. 296.

along democratic lines but the Mongol invasion put an end to any possibilities of such a solution of the crisis.

## 2. The Struggle for Kiev (1139–69)

The thirty-year period following the death of Iaropolk II was rich in dramatic events of both a political and a personal nature. Less conspicuous, but not less important, were the economic and cultural changes behind the political scene.

Economically, the core of the struggle was the maintenance of commercial highways. One group of princes was interested in controlling the central overland route from west to east—from Galicia to Suzdal. Another group tried frantically to restore the old riverway to Byzantium—from Novgorod via Smolensk and Kiev to the Black Sea.

Culturally, the main problem was that of the national autonomy of the Russian Church as against its subjugation to Constantinople.

Politically, the interprincely strife was aggravated by the interference of Byzantine diplomacy and by close relations between the princes of each group and certain foreign powers, such as the Cumans, Hungary, and the Byzantine and Holy Roman Empires.

The Russian wars of the late eleven-forties and the eleven-fifties enter into the picture of the general diplomatic and military conflict in Europe of this period and their significance cannot be properly understood outside it. This was the period of the so-called "League of the Two Empires," an alliance between the Byzantine emperor Manuel Komnenus and the German king Konrad Hohenstaufen. The league was directed primarily against Hungary and the Sicilian Normans. The immediate point at issue between Byzantium and Hungary was control of Serbian affairs, while the Normans, establishing themselves in Sicily, were threatening to undermine Byzantine strategic and commercial interests in the central Mediterranean. As to the conflict between Konrad of Germany and Roger of Sicily, this was the result of Roger's intervention in the struggle between the Guelfs and the Ghibellines in Italy on the side of the former; Konrad, as a Hohenstaufen, was the patron of the Ghibellines and was opposed in Germany by the house of Welf (from which the Italian name "Guelf" was derived). Both sides were eager to secure as many allies as they could. King Vladislav of Bohemia as well as the Russian princes Vladimirko of Galicia and Iuri of Suzdal sided with the

League of the Two Empires; Vladimirko even acknowledged himself vassal (*hypospondos*) of the Byzantine emperor. On the other hand, Louis VII of France supported Roger of Sicily and Prince Iziaslav II of Kiev concluded an alliance with King Géza of Hungary. Thus in this period Kiev was diplomatically connected with both Paris and Palermo, albeit indirectly.[4]

As to the Russian background of these intricate events, the old rivalry between the house of Monomach (the Monomashichi) and the house of Oleg (the Olgovichi) was now aggravated by a split between the Monomashichi themselves, due to which the Olgovich prince Vsevolod succeeded in seizing Kiev soon after Iaropolk II's death. Vsevolod II (1139–46) was a skillful and daring politician; his position was handicapped, however, by the fact that he was considered an intruder by the Kievan population. They tolerated him on certain conditions, always ready to limit his authority. In church politics he aimed at a greater autonomy of the Russian Church and whenever a vacancy occurred tried to arrange that a native Russian instead of a Greek should be appointed bishop. Finally the metropolitan of Kiev, Michael—a Greek—left for Constantinople, forbidding any Russian bishop to conduct services (1145).

Following Vsevolod's death, the Kievan veche refused to accept any more princes of the house of Oleg, giving its preference again to the Monomashichi. But there was no unity among the latter and several contended for the Kievan throne. The main conflict was between Iziaslav II (son of Mstislav I) and his uncle Iuri of Suzdal.

Iuri based his claims on his genealogical seniority; Iziaslav; on his popularity among the Kievan population as well as on the support of Kiev's Turkish auxiliaries, the Chernye Klobuki. Of the two princes, Iziaslav was certainly a greater man and the better ruler. Had he come to power under different circumstances he might have won for himself a position similar to that of his father Mstislav I or his grandfather Vladimir Monomach. He was born too late, however, for the task of restoring the predominance of Kiev. Iziaslav II reigned from 1146 to 1154 with few intermissions but most of his energies were consumed in forestalling the attacks of Iuri and his ally Vladimirko of Galicia. Twice Iuri succeeded in seizing the city with the help of the Cumans (1149 and 1151), only to be ousted each time by Izia-

4. See Hrushevsky, II, 152–153; V. G. Vasilievsky, "Iz istorii Vizantii XII veka," *Trudy*, IV (Leningrad, 1930), 43–84; G. Vernadsky, "Relations byzantino-russes au XII-e siècle," *Byzantion*, 4 (1929), 269–276.

slav, supported by the Hungarians. It was only after Iziaslav's death that Iuri finally entered Kiev, where he reigned for three years (1155-57) until his own demise.

Iziaslav had inherited from his predecessor the ecclesiastical conflict with Constantinople. Since he opposed Constantinople politically, he had no intention of going to Canossa. Instead, he made a bold move, summoning all the Russian bishops to Kiev for the election of a new metropolitan. There were ten bishops in the Russian Church at this time: six natives and four Greeks. The latter boycotted the council, which met in spite of their opposition. Kliment of Smolensk, one of the best educated church leaders of medieval Russia, was elected metropolitan (1147). He was not, however, recognized by the Patriarch of Constantinople and was eventually removed when Iuri—an ally of the Byzantine emperor—succeeded Iziaslav on the throne of Kiev. Full authority of the Patriarch in Russian Church affairs was restored and it was not until the middle of the fifteenth century that the Russian Church emancipated itself from the tutelage of Constantinople.

Iuri and his Suzdalian boyars were not popular among the Kievan citizens, who used the occasion of his death to loot his palace as well as those of his boyars. A descendant of David of Chernigov now established himself in the city for a brief period but the Kievans again gave their preference to the house of Monomach, and in 1159 Rostislav of Smolensk (brother of Iziaslav II) was invited to occupy the throne. In his policies Rostislav I (1159-67) followed Iuri rather than his brother, attempting to secure a close understanding with Byzantium in both ecclesiastical and political matters. A relative of the Byzantine emperor visited Kiev in 1164-65 as envoy extraordinary and it appears that among the matters discussed was that of clearing the Dnieper riverway of Cuman bands and the resumption of trade flotillas from Kiev to Constantinople. In 1166 the prince, at the head of several associated princes, convoyed the merchant caravan down the Dnieper River and the expedition was repeated in 1168 under his successor Mstislav II.

Rostislav must have become interested in the Dnieper River trade even prior to his rule in Kiev, at the time when he was prince of Smolensk. Smolensk was an important commercial and cultural center and the Smolensk merchants were also interested in the codification of commercial law. When Rostislav became prince of Kiev he was in a position to bring about a full coöperation between Smolensk and

Kievan business interests. Presumably it was during his reign in
Kiev that the revision of the Expanded Version of the *Pravda Russkaia*, in which so much attention is paid to commercial law, was completed.

The period of prosperity for Kiev did not last long and the political balance was soon upset by the aggressive policies of Prince Andrei
of Suzdal (Iuri's son). Economically, Suzdal was in a position to
serve as a link between Oriental and Baltic commerce; hence the
interest of Suzdalian princes in controlling Novgorod. But the city
was at the same time the starting point of the north-south riverway
from the Baltic to the Black Sea and Kievan princes were as much
interested in controlling it as were the Suzdalians. Unfortunately for
Kiev, the unity in the princely family there was broken after Rostislav's death in 1167, the latter's sons objecting to the rule of their
cousin Mstislav II. Andrei of Suzdal now saw his chance and offered
his support to the Rostislavichi. On March 8, 1169, his strong army
took "the mother of Russian cities," as Kiev was known, and sacked
it mercilessly.

### 3. Keeping the Balance between East Russia and West Russia (1169–1222)

Following his conquest of Kiev, Andrei became the most powerful
of the Russian princes. He was a haughty man obsessed by the monarchical idea. He attempted to introduce the principle of Byzantine
absolutism into Russian political life by undermining the institution
of the veche on the one hand and subordinating all other princes to
his suzerainty on the other. As to the boyars, he treated them as his
servitors rather than councilors. In order to dispose of the interfering
veche of the city of Suzdal, he moved the capital of the principality to
the new and smaller city of Vladimir; then, not wanting to depend on
it, either, built himself a sumptuous palace in a near-by village, Bogoliubovo, from which he became known as Bogoliubsky. Andrei was
an able and forceful ruler but he was born two centuries too soon
and, while he was to be admired by the Muscovite chroniclers, his contemporaries were not prepared to share his ideas. He was assassinated
in 1174.[5]

5. In Soviet historical scholarship Andrei is highly praised as a constructive leader
and a predecessor of Ivan the Terrible and Peter the Great. See N. Voronin, "Kultura
Vladimiro-Suzdalskoi zemli XI–XII vekov," *Istoricheskii Zhurnal*, 1944, No. 4, p.
37.

It was characteristic of Andrei that he did not go to Kiev after the seizure of the city by his troops but had the Kievan throne occupied by minor princes whom he treated as his vassals. This also was clear evidence of the end of Kiev's political prominence. From the point of view of Suzdalian interests, to control Novgorod was even more important than to possess Kiev. In 1170 Andrei sent an army against the northern metropolis but it was repulsed by the Novgorodians. A legend ascribed their success to the miraculous intercession of Our Lady. Novgorod, however, depended for its food on the import of grain from the south and since Andrei was in possession of both Suzdal and Kiev he applied, as we would say now, "economic sanctions" against the proud city, which had to sue for peace.

Novgorod may be considered the northern outlet for Suzdalian trade; the southern route down the Volga River to the Caspian was controlled by the Bulgars, who served as middlemen in the trade with the Caucasus. Occasionally the Suzdalian princes must have dreamed of piercing the Bulgarian barrier. The Persian poet Khaqani (d. 1194) tells the story of a daring Russian raid on Shirvan in the Caucasus, around 1174.[6] It seems probable that these Russians may have descended the Volga from Suzdalia, breaking through the section of the river held by the Volga Bulgars. It may be mentioned in this connection that the author of the *Lay of Igor's Campaign* says, around the year 1185, that Prince Vsevolod III of Suzdalia is in a position "to spray the water out of the Volga River by the oars [of his boats]." This is obviously an allusion to naval campaigns undertaken by the Suzdalian princes, one of which may have been the Shirvan expedition of 1174.

In spite of his control of Novgorod and Kiev, Andrei was not able to extend his authority over all Russia. The Chernigov principality remained independent, as did Volynia and Galicia. After Andrei was removed from the political stage a kind of balance of power was established in the country as a whole. In the center an agreement was reached between the Olgovichi and the Rostislavichi, by which Sviatoslav of Chernigov occupied the Kievan throne (as Sviatoslav III) with the Rostislavichi as his associates. In the west that powerful prince Iaroslav Osmomysl (son of Vladimirko), admired so much by the author of the *Lay of Igor's Campaign*, reigned in Galicia until 1187. In Volynia the descendants of Iziaslav II were firmly established

6. V. Minorsky, "Khaqani and Andronicus Comnenus," *BSOAS*, 1945, *11*, 557–559; see also Dorn, pp. 388–390, 524–530.

and in 1199 his grandson Roman seized the throne of Galicia as well, after which he became master of all of western Russia.

In Suzdalia, after a period of troubles, Andrei's brother Vsevolod III succeeded in gradually restoring political unity as grand duke of Vladimir.

The attention of the Kievan and Chernigovan princes in this period was concentrated mostly on the struggle with the Cumans. In 1184 Sviatoslav III and the Rostislavich Riurik successfully frustrated the Cuman attempt to attack Kiev. In the next year one of the lesser Chernigovan princes, Igor of Novgorod-Seversk, with some other junior princes undertook a daring raid against the nomads with the object of reaching the lower Don area. The raid ended in catastrophe. This episode became the subject of the famous epic poem, the *Lay of Igor's Campaign*. In the following years the struggle against the Cumans continued with intermittent success. Meanwhile, Roman of Volynia and Vsevolod of Suzdal vied for control of the Kievan throne, each trying to disseminate rivalry and distrust among the lesser princes of the Kievan region. In 1200, however, Roman—by this time ruler of both Volynia and Galicia—turned his attention to the Cumans, who were threatening Byzantine interests in the Balkans. The prince agreed to come to the assistance of the Byzantine emperor and a severe blow was administered to the nomads.

The effect of Roman's victory was, however, undermined by new dissensions among the Russian princes. Presumably instigated by Vsevolod of Suzdalia, several Kievan and Chernigovan princes, with Riurik playing a leading role, revolted against Roman's suzerainty. Allying himself with the Cumans, of whom a decade earlier he had been the most bitter foe, Riurik attacked Kiev, which his allies then plundered mercilessly (1203). According to the chronicles, "no such woe ever had befallen Kiev during the whole time since the conversion to Christianity." Roman retaliated by a successful campaign against the Cumans (1204–5). He had, however, to compromise with Vsevolod of Suzdalia and a new prince was set up in Kiev under their joint tutelage. Roman's death in a battle with the Poles (1205) left Vsevolod as the most powerful of the Russian princes. Absorbed in strengthening his own principality of Suzdalia, Vsevolod interfered little in Kievan affairs, letting his namesake of the house of Oleg rule as Vsevolod IV from 1206. The two Vsevolods died in the same year (1212).

After that a Rostislavich, Mstislav III, established himself in Kiev and the Kievan people enjoyed a brief spell of peace. For both Suzdalia and Galicia this was a period of trouble, caused in Suzdalia by dissensions between Vsevolod III's sons and in Galicia by the opposition of the boyars to the princes and the intervention of the Hungarians and the Poles. On the other hand, the relations between the Russians and the Cumans improved somewhat and the Cumans even helped Prince Mstislav the Daring (grandson of Rostislav I) to oust both the Poles and the Hungarians from Galicia (1221).

## 4. Defense of the Frontier

For the period following the dismemberment of the Kievan realm it would not be proper, in a strictly juridical sense, to speak of the boundaries of Russia as a whole, since each principality was practically independent. However, as has already been said, from a broader historical point of view it is possible to think of the combination of Russian states as of an ethnic and cultural community, even if not a well-defined political body. From such a point of view the boundary line between each of the single Russian principalities and a foreign nation may be considered merely a section of the Pan-Russian boundary. It is from this angle that I wish to discuss here the story of the defense of Russia's frontiers by the Russian people in the second half of the twelfth and first third of the thirteenth centuries.[7]

In the north the Novgorodian expansion early reached both the White Sea and the Arctic Ocean and, except for some local clashes between Russian and Norwegian fishermen, there was no problem of defense in that quarter. In the northeast, Novgorodian commercial expansion toward the Ural Mountain range progressed without meeting much opposition from the local Finnish tribes. In the middle Volga region the Russians of Suzdalia faced the comparatively strong and well-organized state of the Volga Bulgars, with whom they maintained close commercial relations. Militarily and politically, the situation was stabilized until the early thirteenth century, when the Suzdalian princes assumed an aggressive attitude toward the Bulgars. Before long, however, the Mongols solved the problem in their own way.

Thus it was not in the north or northeast but in the southeast and in the west that the Russians of the Kievan period were in real danger

---

7. There is no comprehensive monograph on this subject. For the earlier background (tenth and eleventh centuries), see B. D. Grekov, *Bor'ba Rusi za sozdanie svoego gosudarstva.*

of devastating raids and at times had to struggle for their very existence.

## a. The Southeast

From the middle of the eleventh century down to the Mongol invasion the south Russian steppes were dominated by the Cumans. Like their predecessors the Patzinaks, they made no attempt to create a centralized empire which would control both steppe and forest zones, apparently satisfied by their pastoral way of life.[8] Horse and cattle breeding constituted the mainstay of their national economy but their khans were not averse to supplementing their income by both commerce and war. In commerce the Cumans' role was rather passive; they derived their profit chiefly from customs duties on transit trade. The Khoresmian merchants in this period played a predominant role in the overland caravan trade and the Byzantine and Venetian merchants exploited the maritime trade through the Crimean ports. Presumably a considerable part of the foreign goods brought into the Cuman steppe area, both from the Orient and via the Black Sea, were meant for Russia.

War rather than commerce was the element proper to the Cumans themselves. However, they hardly had any definite program of far-reaching military expansion. One important objective in their struggle with the Russians was to round out their control of the steppes by occupying the northern fringe of the prairies—that is, the forest-steppe zone—in order to prevent the Russians from building ramparts there, thus keeping the gates to Russia open for themselves.

The main motive of their constant raids on Russia was to obtain as much booty as possible. They were primarily interested in the live goods obtained—captives whom they converted into slaves and subsequently sold to the Oriental and Venetian merchants. While their raids did not amount to a real danger to Russian independence, taken together they constituted a constant drain on Russia's resources and on the Russian people.

As we know, the Russian princes themselves by their internecine strife made it easier for the Cumans to exploit Russia. In the early

8. On the Patzinaks and the Cumans, see Moravcsik, *Byzantinoturcica*, I, 46–48 (ample bibliography); on the Patzinaks, see also Rasovsky, "Pechenegi, Torki i Berendei na Rusi i v Ugrii," *SK, 6* (1933), 1–66; Menges, "Etymological Notes on Some Päčänäg Names," *Byzantion, 17* (1945), 256–280. On the Cumans, see D. A. Rasovsky, "Polovtsy," *SK, 7* (1935), 245–262; *8* (1936), 161–182; *9* (1937), 71–85; *10* (1938), 155–178; *11* (1939), 95–128. P.V., "Polovtsy i Rus'," *Slavia, 16* (1939), 598–601.

twelfth century, due chiefly to the policies of Vladimir Monomach, they succeeded in defeating the main Cuman forces and, temporarily at least, localized the danger. However, in the second half of the twelfth century the Cumans regained their strength and profiting by Russian interprincely disputes succeeded in reëstablishing their position. In 1203, as we know, they raided the city of Kiev. In the following year Prince Roman of Volynia organized a strong campaign against them which was highly successful but Roman's death (1205) prevented the Russians from duly enforcing their victory. In 1210 the nomads again raided the Pereiaslav land.

On the whole, however, after 1203 the attitude of the Cumans appears to have become less hostile and their leading khans were inclined to enter into agreements with the Russians. On the Russian side, Prince Mstislav the Daring supported a policy of friendship with the Cumans and took advantage of it by using them as his allies against the Poles and the Hungarians. When all is said, the Russians in the early thirteenth century, in fact, were well on their way to stabilize their relations with the Cumans. For this, as for many other things, the Mongol invasion completely changed the whole picture.

## b. The West

Three nations lived on Russia's western frontier in the Kievan period: the Hungarians, the Poles, and the Lithuanians. In the late twelfth century the Germans made their appearance in the Lithuanian area and before long succeeded in pushing out or conquering a part of the Lithuanians as well as the latter's neighbors to the north, the Letts and Estonians. Let us examine briefly the development of political and military events on Russia's western frontier as regards each of the three countries first mentioned.

As we know, Hungary took an active part in the struggle between the Russian princes in the middle of the twelfth century.[9] She was then an ally of Kiev and an enemy of Galicia. Since of all Russian principalities Galicia was closest to her geographically, it was but natural that the core of Russo-Hungarian rivalry should be the problem of control over Galicia. During the reign of Iaroslav Osmomysl (1152–87) the principality was sufficiently strong to ward off any attempt at offensive action on the part of Hungary but following his death trouble began, due to the strife between his two sons—one of

9. For general information on the Russo-Hungarian relations, see Soloviev and Hrushevsky; for a bibliography of the history of Hungary, see Chap. XI, n. 27.

whom was illegitimate—and to the interference of Prince Roman of Volynia. Iaroslav's legitimate son Vladimir, a profligate by nature, escaped to Hungary, where King Béla promised him every assistance. The Hungarians then seized Galicia but, instead of returning it to Vladimir, Béla proclaimed his own son Andrew king of the principality. Vladimir was brought back to Hungary and imprisoned.

At first King Andrew tried to win the loyalty of his new subjects by an orderly and just rule. However, after the attempt of a second cousin of Vladimir to enter Galich the tenor of Hungarian rule changed for the worse. According to the chroniclers a reign of terror followed in Galich; Russian women were raped and horses stabled in the boyars' houses and in churches. Meanwhile Prince Vladimir succeeded in escaping from his dungeon and fled to Germany, asking Emperor Frederick Barbarossa for protection. He promised Frederick to pay him an annual tribute of two thousand grivna if he were reinstated by the latter's help on the Galician throne. Being engaged in a bitter struggle for Palestine, Frederick could give no active help but recommended Vladimir to Prince Kazimierz of Krakow, who sent Polish troops to Galich to support the exile's claims. At the approach of the expedition the Galich men rose against the Hungarians and expelled King Andrew (1190). Vladimir once more occupied the throne of Galicia but Andrew did not abandon his claims. From this time on the name of that land was included in the title of the kings of Hungary.

After Vladimir's death Prince Roman of Volynia seized Galicia with the help of the Poles (1199). Roman died in 1205; his sons Daniel and Vasilko were mere infants and the government of the principality was taken over by their mother, Roman's widow, and the council of the boyars. At this juncture Prince Riurik of Kiev in alliance with the Olgovichi of Chernigov made an attempt to establish his authority in the area. Roman's widow appealed to Andrew, now king of Hungary, for protection. With the help of Hungarian troops the Galician boyars repelled the Kievan and Chernigovan forces.

The Olgovichi, however, did not consider the matter closed and concluded an alliance with the Poles. Again King Andrew interfered in Galician affairs and the Poles agreed to withdraw. Finally, however, the Olgovich Vladimir, son of Prince Igor of Novgorod-Seversk (of *Lay* fame), was invited by the Galician boyars to take the throne. Roman's widow with her two sons meanwhile sought refuge in Roman's patrimony, Vladimir-in-Volynia. The new prince's first act was to send a messenger to the elders of the city of Vladimir with the demand that all members of Roman's family be extradited to him. The unhappy family had to flee to Poland, whence Daniel was sent to Hungary and placed under the guardianship of King Andrew.

But the trouble in Galicia was not over, owing to continued strife between the Russian princes as well as the conflicting interests of the Poles and the Hungarians. Each of these two neighbors coveted the land and, neither being strong enough to ward off the other's claims, both were satisfied with a policy of dividing Galicia from Volynia and keeping each of these two Russian countries as weak as possible.

The Igorevichi (sons of Igor of Novgorod-Seversk), Vladimir and his brothers, now seemed more dangerous to the Hungarians than the Romanovichi (the sons of Roman) and the Hungarians helped the leading Galician boyar Vladislav to occupy Galich in the name of the Romanovich Daniel. The Igorevichi, except for Vladimir, were captured and executed.

Around 1212 the boyar Vladislav was proclaimed prince of Galicia —the only known case in the Kievan period of princely title in one of the Russian lands held by a man not of the Riurik dynasty. Daniel and his mother now sought the protection of Duke Leszek the White of Poland, who was worried by Vladislav's coming to power, since he considered him a Hungarian agent. Leszek finally decided to come to terms with the Hungarians over the head of Vladislav. It was agreed that King Andrew's son Koloman should marry Leszek's daughter Salome and be recognized prince of Galich. The city of Peremyshl was ceded to the Poles; Vladimir-in-Volynia given to the Romanovichi; Liubachev granted to a Pole, the voevoda of Sandomir (Sandomierz). The boyar-prince Vladislav was deported to Hungary and imprisoned there (1214).

Peace in Galicia was reëstablished, but not for long. As a result of King Andrew's petition to the Pope, the latter crowned Koloman King of Galicia on condition that the people should be converted to Roman Catholicism. This resulted in the rise of local opposition to Hungarian rule. Andrew further offended Leszek by taking Peremyshl back from him; the duke was enraged and asked Prince Mstislav the Daring of Novgorod—then one of the leading Russian princes—to intervene in Galician affairs.

As soon as Mstislav approached Galich the local populace greeted him as their savior. The Hungarians had no alternative but to flee. Mstislav was proclaimed prince of Galicia and in order to legalize his power gave his daughter Anna in marriage to Daniel. The new ruler was ready to treat Leszek as his friend; Daniel, however, undertook to recover all the Volynian and Galician cities occupied by the Poles. Leszek's answer was to resume his alliance with Andrew of Hungary against the two Russian princes. The latter had to retreat and Galich was once more occupied by the Poles and Hungarians.

Knowing Mstislav's fighting spirit, the allies feverishly prepared for further struggle. King Andrew sent strong reënforcement to Galich, consisting of both Hungarian and Czech troops under the command of the Hungarian general Fyle, whom the Galician chronicle characterizes as "the haughty one." Fyle foresaw an easy victory over the Russians. According to the chronicles he used to say, "Lots of pots can be broken by one stone," and "A sharp sword and a gallant steed—this is enough to defeat Russia." [10] Meanwhile Mstislav concluded an agreement with the Cumans and reënforced his retinue by their troops.

The opponents met near the banks of the Dniester River. The battle was fierce and at first the Hungarians and the Poles seemed to have the upper hand but at the critical moment Mstislav with his picked retainers and the Cumans attacked the enemy from the rear. The encircled Hungarians and Poles fought bravely to the end; Fyle lost most of his army and the Cumans scattered over the battlefield robbing the corpses and catching horses.

The triumphant Mstislav proved to be a cautious politician and agreed to a compromise with King Andrew. The latter's youngest son, likewise Andrew by name, was engaged to Mstislav's daughter, to whom the prince appointed Galicia as her future dowry. It appears that in making this deal Mstislav took into consideration the advice of the Galician boyars (1222). In the next year the Mongols administered a severe defeat to the Russian princes at Kalka (see sec. 5, below). Mstislav's prestige was seriously undermined by the defeat and his self-assurance considerably shaken. He decided to appease the Hungarians and let young Andrew take actual possession of Galich, reserving for himself the control of Ponizie, the lower Prut region of Galicia. Following his death, however (in 1228), the original prince of Galicia—Daniel, son of Roman—presented his claims to the principality. After a protracted struggle with the Hungarians and Poles for the control of both Volynia and Galicia, Daniel was

10. *PSRL*, II (1843), 162.

able fully to restore his father's patrimony. He crowned his efforts by finally establishing his rule in Galich in 1237.

The story of Russo-Hungarian relations, as may be seen from the above outline, is closely interwoven with Polish policies. While several episodes of Russo-Polish relations have thus been mentioned in connection with the Hungarian events, we have now to examine relations with Poland as a separate problem.[11]

The story of these relations in the Kievan era may be divided into two periods: the first from the late tenth century to the middle of the twelfth, and the second from the middle of the twelfth century to the Mongol invasion. In the first period both Russia and Poland were unified states; in the second each was a loose federation with no central government of any authority. As a result, in the first period the struggle between the Kievan princes and the Polish kings was a strife between two nations; in the second it assumed a more local character and of the Russian principalities only Volynia and Galicia were immediately affected.

In regard to the first period, as we know, twice in the course of the eleventh century Polish kings attempted to conquer Kiev, profiting by the internecine strife between the Russian princes. King Boleslaw I entered the city in 1019 as the ally of Prince Sviatopolk I, and Boleslaw II seized it in 1069 as Prince Iziaslav I's protector. In neither case were the Poles able to establish their authority in Kiev permanently; in both cases the occupation was of short duration.

The unity of the Polish state came to an end in 1138, when King Boleslaw III, before dying, divided Poland into appanages between his sons. His testament is similar to that of Iaroslav the Wise. During the subsequent struggle between the brothers, the throne of Krakow played the same role in Polish politics as the throne of Kiev in the Russian, being endowed with a national prestige. Mieszko the Old, of all the late king's sons, proved the strongest ruler in his own principality. He attempted to curb the aristocracy and promote the interests of the princely treasury. Both his social and financial policies resulted in constant clashes with the nobility. His younger brother Kazimierz the Just, on the contrary, attempted to appease the lords and was more popular among them, as a result of which he succeeded in extending his control over more cities and provinces than any of his brothers. But in each case his control was weak.

11. I. A. Linnichenko, *Rus' i' Polsha do kontsa XII veka*. For a bibliography of the history of Poland, see Chap. XI, n. 12.

Both Mieszko and Kazimierz established, through the marriages of their sons and daughters, close family ties with a number of Russian princes. Because of the friendly relations in this period between the Polish and west Russian princely families, the west Russian boyars did not always consider the Polish princes outsiders and in some cases were even ready to give them preference over Russian princes. When in 1199 Roman finally seized Galich with Polish help, the boyars sent a deputation to Kazimierz's son Leszek the White, offering him the throne of Galicia. It is obvious in this case that they were more interested in their social privileges than in the national aspects of government. Roman was dreaded because of his ruthless curbing of the privileges of the Volynian boyars.

The relations between Roman and Leszek, friendly at first, later deteriorated for both religious and personal reasons. Leszek was a devout Roman Catholic and it was probably at his suggestion that the Pope sent his envoys to Roman in 1204, urging him to accept Roman Catholicism and promising to place him under the protection of St. Peter's sword. Roman's answer, as recorded in the chronicles, was characteristic enough: pointing to his own sword he asked the envoys, "Is the Pope's sword similar to mine? So long as I carry mine, I need no other." [12] His arrogance must have greatly offended Leszek. Besides this there was also a personal misunderstanding between the two. Having helped Roman to establish himself in Galicia, Leszek was prepared to consider him his vassal. In this he miscalculated, however; Roman, who was one of the leading Russian princes of the period, was not disposed to recognize any ruler as his suzerain. Finally Leszek, supported by his brother Konrad of Mazovia, undertook a sudden campaign against Roman. The latter was caught unaware and killed in the first battle (1205).

As I have recounted just above, following Roman's death the Hungarians seized Galicia once more. Not sufficiently strong to oust them, Leszek again turned to the Russians, inviting Mstislav the Daring to come to Galich. When he became too strong the Poles again, in turn, sided with the Hungarians against him but, as we saw, without success. Nor were the Poles able to prevent Prince Daniel from recovering the throne of Galich in the twelve-thirties.

12. Karamzin, III, 115–116; Hrushevsky, III, 11–12. It must be noted that we have no authentic text of the parleys between the Pope's envoys and Prince Roman. The only evidence is a gloss in the so-called "Radziwill" chronicle. Roman's answer, therefore, must be considered legendary; the legend itself, however, must have been based on the actual fact—the Pope's embassy to Roman and its failure.

On the whole, it may be said that in this period the Poles had little. chance of establishing permanent control over western Russia, both because of the strength of the Russians and by reason of the constant intervention of Hungary. In this political triangle the Russians were able to keep their ground in spite of a number of temporary reverses.

International rivalry in the Lithuanian and east Baltic areas was no less complex than in Galicia. The Poles were as much interested in Lithuanian affairs as the Russians and before long the Germans extended their *Drang nach Osten* to the east Baltic area; simultaneously both the Danes and the Swedes attempted to penetrate in Estonia.

In contrast to both the Russians and the Poles, the Lithuanians did not succeed in establishing any political unity among themselves in the Kievan period. Each tribe was led by its own chieftains and, while at times two or more tribes united against a foreign enemy, such alliances were only temporary. In the twelfth century the bulk of the Lithuanians were still pagans.

Examining Russo-Lithuanian relations in the Kievan era we have again to differentiate Russian policies during the supremacy of Kiev from those at the time of the federation. In the first period Russian campaigns against the Lithuanians—as, for example, under Vladimir I—had objectives of national scope; in the second the struggle was localized and only west Russian lands, such as Volynia, Polotsk, Pskov, and Novgorod, were immediately interested in Lithuanian and east Baltic affairs.

On the whole the Russians were at first more aggressive than the Lithuanians, the Letts, and the Estonians. The princes of Novgorod were able to keep their authority firmly over the eastern part of Estonia and the northern part of Livonia (now known as Latvia), where, as we know, the Russian city of Iuriev was founded in the eleventh century. The princes of Polotsk gradually extended their control down the Western Dvina River to its very mouth. The Volynian princes were no less active in subduing the neighboring Lithuanian tribes. Prince Roman, whose grim determination toward the Poles and Hungarians we have seen, was remembered in the chronicles for his harsh treatment of Lithuanian captives, whom according to the legend he harnessed instead of oxen to drag the plows on his estates.[13]

13. Soloviev, II, 314, suggests that the legend should not be accepted literally; in his opinion, Roman simply attempted to make agriculturists out of the Lithuanians, to which they objected. See, however, Hrushevsky, III, 16.

However, when the Germans appeared in the east Baltic area the Lithuanians and Letts became more dangerous to the Russians. In some cases they acted as auxiliary troops for the Germans. In other instances, not willing to submit to the Germans, they began to move eastward and in this way eventually collided with the Russians.

The Germans were first attracted to the east Baltic area by commercial interests (from 1158). Soon, however, missionaries followed and then came the soldiers to protect both German commerce and the German faith. It should be noted that the missionaries' primary objective was to convert pagan Letts and Lithuanians; later, however, the German crusade was directed against both the pagans and the Greek Orthodox. Around 1186 the German missionary Meinhardt accompanied a group of merchants to Livonia and asked the permission of the prince of Polotsk to convert pagan Letts to Christianity. Permission was granted and Meinhardt built a church—and incidentally a fort around it—at Yxkuell in the lower region of the Western Dvina.[14]

This first outpost of Germanism in Livonia was originally under the ecclesiastical authority of the Bremen chapter. By the close of the twelfth century a number of German pilgrims were already settled in the area. In order to promote the speedy conquest of Livonia its third bishop, Albert von Buxhoewden, visited the rulers of Sweden and Denmark as well as various German potentates, asking their help. Supported by the Danish fleet he founded the city of Riga in 1201. In the next year he created the Order of Sword Bearers, known also as the Livonian Order. Cross and sword were its symbols, and indeed, those of the whole German offensive in Livonia. In 1207 the German emperor granted Bishop Albert all Livonia as his fief. The bishop, in turn, gave one third of the country in possession to the Sword Bearers.

As the princes of Polotsk claimed the whole basin of the Western Dvina River as their territory, Bishop Albert at first acted cautiously, insisting that he was interested only in proselytizing the natives and not in territorial conquest. The Russians held two strongholds on the river: Kukenois, about twenty-five miles upstream from Yxkuell, and Gertzike, approximately halfway between Riga and Polotsk. The Russian control over the neighboring Lett and Lithuanian tribes was weak, however. The natives were supposed to pay tribute but were

14. On the German expansion in Livonia, see L. A. Arbuzov, *Ocherk istorii Lifliandii, Estliandii i Kurliandii* (St. Petersburg, 1912), pp. 8–41. See also Baron M. A. Taube, "Russische und litauische Fürsten an der Düna," *JKGS, 11* (1935), 367–502.

otherwise not interfered with. Now both the Russians and the Germans demanded their loyalty and the natives' plight was one to be pitied. According to the chronicles, in some cases they decided by lot which faith to accept—the German or the Russian.

Occasionally the local Russian princes under the authority of the prince of Polotsk were themselves ready to compromise with the Germans. In 1207 Viachko, Prince of Kukenois, appeared in Riga and offered Bishop Albert half his town for protection against the natives. The bishop gladly accepted the offer but was not able to protect Viachko against his own (the bishop's) followers, the German knights, one of whom raided Kukenois and arrested the prince. Although at the insistence of the bishop he was soon freed, he had lost confidence in the Germans and killed those sent by Albert to Kukenois. At the approach of the German army Viachko burned his town and hid in the forest, whence for some time he harassed the Germans with guerilla warfare. Meanwhile the prince of Gertzike, Vsevolod, based his policy on an agreement with the neighboring Lithuanian tribesmen. He married a Lithuanian princess and helped the Lithuanians to raid the German settlements. In 1209 Bishop Albert led an expedition against him, storming and burning Gertzike. Vsevolod then decided to recognize the bishop as his suzerain and was reinstated in the stronghold as Albert's lieutenant.

In 1212 the bishop scored a major diplomatic victory by concluding an agreement with the prince of Polotsk by which the latter abandoned his claims to tribute from the Lett and Lithuanian tribes in the lower Western Dvina basin. In addition, the bishop and the prince concluded an alliance against the Ests. In the same year the prince of Pskov gave his daughter in marriage to Albert's brother. This, however, cost him his throne, since the Pskov people, more farsighted than their prince, disapproved of the appeasement policy.

The Novgorodians were as aware of the German danger as the Pskovians. In 1212 Prince Mstislav the Daring besieged the Lett stronghold of Odennpäh, south of Iuriev, and imposed tribute on the neighboring tribes. In 1221 a Novgorodian army raided German settlements on the Aa River northeast of Riga. According to the German chronicles the Russians destroyed a number of German churches, burned the grain in the fields, and took men, women, and children into captivity.[15] They were not able, however, to seize the fortress of Kes (Wenden). The war continued for several years, each side doing as

15. Karamzin, III, 192-193; Karamzin, Notes, III, No. 200.

much harm to the other as it could. In 1224 the Germans conquered the city of Iuriev, which they renamed Dorpat. Characteristically enough, both sides used natives as auxiliary troops: in this period the Letts supported the Germans and the Lithuanians the Russians.

Simultaneously the Swedes and Danes showed their interest in Estonia. In 1219 the King of Denmark built the fortress of Reval and, although four years later he was defeated by the Ests, subsequently Estonia became a Danish possession (1237).

While the Sword Bearers and the Danes were conducting their crusade in Livonia, a new center of German aggression was created in Prussia: the Teutonic Order.[16] The Prussians, one of the fiercest Lithuanian tribes, opposed any attempts on the part of the Poles either to Christianize or to conquer them. Almost yearly they undertook devastating raids on adjacent Polish lands, especially on Mazovia. Finally Prince Konrad of Mazovia, brother of Leszek the White, decided to call to his assistance the knights of the Teutonic Order, which had been first organized in Palestine but later lost its ground there. Its headquarters had shifted to Venice, whence the grand master of the Order began negotiations, first with the king of Hungary and then with the prince of Mazovia, offering his help against the enemies of either. Konrad granted to the Order the Chelm district as a base of future operations against the Prussians.

The first group of Teutonic knights arrived in Mazovia in 1229. More followed and before long the Teutonic Order was ready to start a ruthless offensive against the Prussians. The organization of the Order proved highly efficient and the spirit of the knights extremely militant. A systematic plan of campaign was prepared in advance. For each year a small district of Prussia was marked for conquest. As soon as it was occupied by the Crusaders, natives in it were either slain or driven out, castles and churches were built, and German colonists settled. The schedule of districts to be conquered was made in accordance with general strategic considerations. The conquest of the whole of Prussia required more than thirty years but when it was completed—around 1285—the country was thoroughly Germanized. The first Prussian district to be conquered by the Crusaders was that of Thorn (Toruń), in 1231.

16. On the Teutonic Order, see C. Krollmann, *Politische Geschichte des Deutschen Ordens in Preussen* (Königsberg, 1932); E. Maschke, *Poland und die Berufung des Deutschen Ordens nach Preussen* (Danzig, 1934); L. Koczy, *The Baltic Policy of the Teutonic Order* (Toruń, 1936).

In 1234 the Pope granted the Teutonic Order the districts of Kulm (Chelm) and Thorn in permanent possession. This action made the knights legally independent of the authority of the prince of Mazovia. In 1237 a union between the Teutonic and Livonian orders was accomplished, with supreme authority vested in the former. This agreement made the Teutonic Order the major military power in the east Baltic area for almost two centuries. As the conquest of Prussia was nearing its close, the knights turned their aggression against other neighbors: Russia, Lithuania, and Poland. Indeed, Prince Konrad's move of inviting the Teutonic knights to Prussia proved to be the worst political mistake ever made by a Polish ruler.

### 5. The First Appearance of the Mongols: the Battle of the Kalka (1223)

As we know (see sec. 4 a, above), relations between the Cumans and the Russians improved markedly in the early thirteenth century. Before long, however, the khanate of the Cumans had to face new international troubles, being exposed to dangers from both south and east.

The danger from the south was represented by the Seljuqs, who appeared in the eastern part of Asia Minor in the late eleventh century.[17] In the second half of the twelfth century they ousted the Byzantines from central Anatolia. Their position became especially favorable after the Fourth Crusade and the establishment of the Latin Empire in Constantinople (1204), after which two Greek states of local importance survived on the fringe of Asia Minor: the "Empire" of Nicaea and the "Empire" of Trapezunt (Trebizond). Neither could serve as a check to the ambitions of the Seljuq sultans. The "emperor" of Trapezunt acknowledged himself a vassal of the Seljuq sultan and agreed to pay a yearly tribute. Dominating the Byzantines politically, the Seljuqs were also ready to exploit the benefits of Greek commerce and even to expand them. In 1214 they seized the port of Sinop and rerouted through it the Anatolian commerce with the Crimea, for which previously Trapezunt had served as the main base.

Before long the sultan, presumably advised by Byzantine and Ossetian merchants, decided to extend his control over the Black Sea to the Crimean ports. Complaints by some merchants arrested in the Crimea served as a pretext and in 1221 a fleet carrying Seljuq soldiers was sent to Sudak (Sugdea). According to the chronicler Ibn-al-Bibi,

17. For a bibliography of the Seljuqs, see Chap. XI, n. 121.

the inhabitants of the city pledged their loyalty to the sultan without opposition and expressed their readiness to coöperate with the Seljuqs against the Cumans and the Russians. A Cuman-Russian army ten thousand strong attacked Sudak but was defeated by the Seljuqs. The Russian prince then sent an envoy to the headquarters of the Seljuq commander and a friendly agreement was concluded between the Russians and the Seljuqs. According to Iakubovsky's plausible conjecture, the Russian prince in question may have been one of the Riazan princes.[18]

The painful impression made on the Cumans by the seizure of Sudak was soon superseded by a new fear caused by the appearance of a much more formidable enemy: the Mongols. These were not immediate neighbors of the Cumans in the east; in order to penetrate to the Cuman steppes the Mongols had first to pierce the Khoresmian Empire. In the twelfth century relations between Khoresm and the Cumans were peaceful. The role of the Khoresmian merchants in Cuman commerce has already been mentioned. In the early thirteenth century Khoresm became the center of a powerful empire headed by the shah Muhammad (1200–1220). By the end of his reign his authority was recognized in most of Turkestan as well as in northern Persia and in Azerbaijan. It might have been expected that he would eventually try to extend it to the Black Sea as well. However, before he was able to do so he clashed with the Mongols, which caused the downfall of both himself and his realm.

The origins of the Mongol Empire and the cause of Mongol expansion will be discussed in the next volume of this work. Suffice it to say here that the Mongol union was first consolidated by the general assembly of Mongol clans (Kurultai) in 1206. It was then that one of the Mongol clan leaders, Temuchin, was proclaimed Supreme Emperor (Chingis Khan). His first drive was directed against China; Peking surrendered in 1215. In 1218 Chingis Khan offered a treaty of friendship and free trade to Muhammad, the Khoresm shah. The latter's answer was to order the Mongol envoys murdered. In the next year Chingis Khan personally led his armies to Turkestan and the Khoresmian Empire crumbled to pieces.

At this juncture Chingis Khan did not contemplate any permanent conquests in the territories west of Turkestan. He sent, however, a strong cavalry corps under the command of two of his ablest generals,

18. A. I. Iakubovsky, "Rasskaz Ibn-al-Bibi o pokhode maloaziiskikh Turok na Sudak," *VV,* *25* (1927), 53–76.

Jebe and Subutai, to reconnoitre the "western lands." They went around the southern shore of the Caspian Sea, penetrated into Transcaucasia, crushed the Georgian army, and then, advancing northward along the eastern shore of the Caspian, defeated the Ossetians in the northern Caucasus and entered the land of the Cumans, after which they raided the Crimea. In the Don area the Brodniki pledged their allegiance to the Mongols.

The Cumans looked to the Russians for assistance. Several khans, among them Kotian, father-in-law of Mstislav the Daring, came in person to plead for help. "Today the Tartars [Mongols] have seized our land," Kotian argued. "Tomorrow they will take yours." [19] Under Mstislav's influence several of the Russian princes agreed to cooperate with the Cumans against the Mongols. At the war council of Russian princes it was decided not to wait for the coming of the Tartars but to attack them deep in the Cuman steppes. Besides Mstislav the Daring, the following major Russian princes agreed to take part in the campaign: Mstislav III of Kiev, Mstislav of Chernigov, and young Daniel of Volynia. The powerful grand duke of Suzdal, Iuri, declined to come personally to the assistance of the south Russian princes but somewhat belatedly sent his nephew, the prince of Rostov, with a division of troops.

The united forces of the south Russian princes went down the Dnieper River to Khortitsa Island, which was to serve as the base of the steppe campaign; here the Cumans joined the Russians. At this first stage of the expedition the Russians were met by Mongol envoys who offered to the princes a Mongol-Russian alliance against the Cumans. The Russians were by that time definitely committed to cooperation with the Cumans and could not accept the Mongol offer. Disregarding all traditions of warfare, the princes ordered the envoys executed, in spite even of the fact that (in my opinion) they were Christians, of the Nestorian denomination. [20]

The first skirmish took place on the banks of the Dnieper River. In this vanguard battle Mstislav the Daring succeeded in defeating a detachment of Mongol troops. The effect of this victory was rather unfortunate, since it gave the Russians an exaggerated idea of their strength. Crossing the Dnieper, their armies marched through the steppes for eight days before they met the main Mongol force at the

19. *PSRL*, VII (1856), 129; X (1885), 89.
20. G. Vernadsky, "Were the Mongol Envoys of 1223 Christians?" *SK, 3* (1929), 145–148.

banks of the Kalka River. There was no unity of command in the Russo-Cuman army or in the Russian army proper. Without consultation with the princes of Kiev and Chernigov and not waiting for their troops to be ready, Mstislav the Daring and the Cumans attacked the Mongols. The results were disastrous. According to the chronicles, the Cumans were the first to be smashed by the Mongols and in their panicky flight spread confusion in the Russian ranks. At any rate, the forces of Mstislav the Daring and the princes associated with him, including Daniel of Volynia, were completely disorganized; Daniel was wounded in the battle. Mstislav and Daniel galloped back to the Dnieper River with only a few retainers. A number of other princes, including Mstislav of Chernigov, perished during the flight. Meanwhile the third Mstislav—the prince of Kiev—decided to stay in his hastily fortified camp. For three days the Mongols attacked the camp but could not take it. They then offered to let Mstislav and his army go back to Kiev unharmed for a ransom. The chieftain of the Brodniki, Ploskinia, who had joined the Mongols, swore on their behalf that the provisions of the agreement would be duly honored. Instead, as soon as the Russians were off guard the Mongols rushed upon them and slew all they could catch. Mstislav and two other princes were seized alive, laid on the ground, and covered with boards, on which the Mongol officers sat for their victory banquet. The unhappy princes were suffocated. It may be remembered that according to the Mongol tradition the blood of royalty is sacred and should not be shed. Ironically, then, due honors were granted to the Russian princes in this case.

Learning of the disaster, the approaching Rostov troops turned back northward, only too glad to escape the slaughter. Following their victory, the Mongols pursued the remnants of the Russian armies westward to the Dnieper River, destroying towns and villages and killing or capturing the inhabitants. However, the Mongol generals were not ordered to stay in Russia but were soon called back by Chingis Khan, who considered the task of reconnoitering the west successfully completed. The Mongol force returned eastward through the land of the Volga Bulgars. The latter refused to recognize the authority of Chingis Khan and even administered a serious defeat to the troops of Jebe and Subutai on their march. This the Mongols could not forget and thirteen years later before attacking Russia they conquered the Bulgars.

The sudden arrival of the Mongols in 1223 and their no less sudden disappearance added a mysterious touch to the bitterness of the Russian defeat. As the chronicler recorded: "We do not know where these evil Tartars came from and whither they went; only God knows." [21]

## 6. Time Runs Short (1223-37)

As we look back on that span of fourteen years between the battle of the Kalka and Batu's invasion, being ourselves nine hundred years the wiser, we cannot suppress the feeling that Russia lived then on borrowed time without being sufficiently aware of it. If any attempt was made by the Russian princes to reconnoitre behind the Volga and the Caspian, we do not know of it. We do know that some Russians were interested in Asiatic affairs and tried to procure information about Asia from books. It was in this period that the story of "Prester John" was translated into Russian.[22] The book deals with the alleged Christian realm in central Asia, from which Europe expected help against the Moslems in the Levant. The legend was based upon the actual fact of the conversion to Nestorianism of a number of Mongol and Turkish tribal rulers in the twelfth century. None was, of course, strong enough to control the tide of Mongol invasion. If the Russians believed in the legend, they were to be bitterly disappointed before long.

The news of the defeat administered to the Mongols by the Volga Bulgars must have heartened the Russians by showing them that the newcomers from the Far East were not invincible. Actually, the Volga Bulgars and the Cumans constituted but a thin screen, hardly adequate to protect Russia from the recent newcomers, but the Russians did not even seem to think they needed that screen, at least in the case of the Volga Bulgars, against whom the Suzdalian princes led a stubborn struggle in just this period. Relations with the Cumans continued friendly, however.

As the princes of both Kiev and Chernigov had perished in the battle of Kalka, there was a change on their thrones. The new princes, Vladimir III of Kiev and Mikhail of Chernigov, followed the lead of the prince of Galicia, Mstislav the Daring. Thus the union of Kiev, Chernigov, and Galicia was established, though as a loose alliance, and it also had the backing of the Cumans under Khan Kotian.

Northeastern Russia formed a political body of its own, especially since the Suzdalian princes succeeded in keeping Novgorod under

21. *Novgorodskaia Letopis' po Sinodalnomu Spisku* (St. Petersburg, 1888), p. 220.
22. N. K. Gudzii, *Istoriia drevnei Russkoi literatury*, pp. 172-173.

their control as well. Two sons of Vsevolod III coöperated closely with each other: Iuri II was grand duke of Vladimir (from 1217) and Iaroslav, prince of Novgorod (from 1222). Combining their efforts they attempted to fulfill a common plan of economic policy, with the aim of securing the use of the commercial highway from the Baltic Sea to the middle Volga. Iuri took charge of the southeastern end of this highway, trying to break the barrier presented by the state of the Volga Bulgars. As a preliminary measure he attempted to detach from the Bulgars and conquer the Finnish tribe of Mordva. He built an important fortress at the confluence of the rivers Volga and Oka, which he named "Lower Novgorod" (Nizhni Novgorod, now Gorky), characteristically enough. Simultaneously the prince of "Upper" Novgorod, Iaroslav, concentrated his attention on strengthening his control of the Baltic. He raided the land of Iam (that is, the northern shore of the Gulf of Finland) and in 1227 extended his authority over Karelia, converting the population to Christianity. He had also to be on the alert against German encroachments.

Meanwhile the political equilibrium in western Russia was temporarily upset by the death of Mstislav the Daring (1228). Eventually however, as we know, the young prince Daniel (son of Roman) succeeded in restoring order in Volynia and later in extending his authority to Galicia (1237). Thus on the eve of the Mongol invasion the political situation in Russia was pretty well stabilized. While there was no complete unity among the princes, there existed two regional alliances, the northeastern and the southwestern. Also, the danger of Cuman raids was apparently eliminated, at least for the moment, through a friendly agreement with the Cuman khans.

The ground seems thus to have been sufficiently cleared for the eventual reëstablishment of a Pan-Russian union—in any case, the political situation looked considerably better than at the close of the twelfth century. But the writing was on the wall, although the Russians did not see it. Before long the Mongol invasion was to smash to pieces the whole political and economic structure of Kievan Russia.

# CHAPTER IX

# RUSSIAN CIVILIZATION IN THE KIEVAN PERIOD

## 1. Introductory Remarks

IN THE history of any nation there are periods during which the national culture embodies a certain unity and homogeneity, the foundations of its spiritual life being identical for all classes of society. These may be called organic or monistic stages of cultural history.

The organic stages are alternated with periods of change when old foundations of culture are being replaced by new, as a result of which inner contradictions come to the fore and a certain dualism, or even pluralism, evolves. More often than not this is aggravated by a social cleavage, the cultural life of the upper and lower classes of the nation following divergent trends. These periods may be called dualistic or pluralistic stages of cultural history. They are dynamic rather than static.

In the history of Russian civilization the alternating sequence of monistic and pluralistic epochs is as clear as in that of any other nation, if not even more so. The Muscovite period, prior to the schism of the Russian church in the middle of the seventeenth century due to the Old Believers' movement, is obviously that of cultural monism. Orthodox Christianity in its peculiar Muscovite form was then accepted as the guiding principle of all classes of society. The church schism of the seventeenth century and the ensuing Europeanization of Russia so vigorously sponsored by Peter the Great upset the old cultural stability and introduced an era of pluralism. At the base of it, throughout the whole Imperial period, lay the dualism of the Europeanized culture of the upper classes and the Muscovite cultural traditions in which, spiritually, the lower classes continued to live. The present Soviet period is again that of cultural monism, the spiritual life of the nation being shaped by Marxian dialectics.

If we approach the Russian civilization of the Kievan period from the same angle, we may define it without any hesitation as an age of cultural dualism. This was caused by Russia's conversion to Christianity. Sociologically there are striking parallels between the impact on Russian culture and society of Christianization in the Kievan period and of Europeanization in the Imperial. Both were protracted processes; both affected first the upper classes of society and accentuated the cultural cleavage between the elite and the masses.

It would be a mistake to speak of the Russian people of the Kievan period as a primitive and barbarous nation, without making due distinction between the learned upper crust of the nation and the *hoi polloi*. In fact, already in the middle of the eleventh century Russian intellectuals—such, for instance, as Metropolitan Ilarion—were highly cultured persons, on the level of their Byzantine and western European contemporaries.

While the upper cultural stratum was thin, it was large enough to serve as a medium for the cultivation of such outstanding personalities as this same Ilarion. He himself felt encouraged by the existence of such a medium and explicitly addressed his sermons not to the average people but to those who were "saturated with the sweetness of book-learning."

Thus Russia's conversion to Christianity resulted not only in a religious dualism, until the new faith was absorbed by the whole nation, but in a cultural dualism in general. Accordingly, in speaking of the Kievan civilization we are obliged to discriminate between the literature and art of the learned on one hand and folklore and folk art on the other. Of course the two cultural worlds were not isolated from each other, especially as Christianity gradually enveloped more and more of the various social strata.

The new church art as expressed in both architecture and painting appealed by its sumptuousness even to the pagan masses; on the other hand, the motifs of pre-Christian folk art, represented in embroideries and woodcarving, were cherished by the learned. Similarly, in the field of literature Byzantine didactic tales, especially the apocrypha, early affected the Russian folklore, while the Russian folk poems were equally appreciated among the lower and upper classes, preparing the ground for the development of the epic poetry of the learned, of which the *Lay of Igor's Campaign* is the highest expression.

## 2. Language and Script

Not long before his death, the novelist Ivan Turgenev (1818–83) found solace in meditating upon the beauty of the Russian tongue—"the great, mighty, veracious and free Russian language. . . . Is it possible to believe that such a language has not been given to a great people?"

A century before Turgenev, the illustrious scientist Mikhail Lomonosov (1711–65) praised the Russian language in even more elaborate manner.

The Holy Roman Emperor, Charles V, used to say that Spanish was the proper language in which to converse with God; the French to converse with friends; German with enemies; and Italian, with women. Had he known Russian, he would certainly have added that this was the proper language to converse with all of the parties mentioned, since it has the magnificence of the Spanish, the vivacity of the French, the force of the German, and the tenderness of the Italian. The Russian has, besides, the wealth and conciseness of both Greek and Latin.

This Russian language, so highly praised by Turgenev and Lomonosov—what was it like in the early Middle Ages? Every modern language is a product of a long evolution; in a sense, every generation speaks its own language. The difference by centuries is, of course, even more marked. Lomonosov's language seemed antiquated to Turgenev's contemporaries and there is much in Turgenev's language which seems oldfashioned to us.

The difference between the Russian language of Lomonosov's age —the eighteenth century—and that of Metropolitan Ilarion, of the eleventh century, is naturally even more substantial than between Lomonosov and Turgenev. Yet Ilarion's style was already elaborate and well balanced, and so we may safely assume that the Slavonic Russian language of his age had been in its turn the product of a long evolution.

Ilarion was a learned monk and his address on "Law and Grace" is a sample of the literary Russian style of his day. For a more vivid language—the racy Russian of the laymen of the Kievan period— we must turn to the epic poems and first of all to the beautiful *Lay of Igor's Campaign* of the late twelfth century. Taken together, these two documents of Old Russia—Ilarion's sermon and the *Lay*—constitute solid evidence of the maturity achieved by the language already seven centuries before Lomonosov.

From the time of Russia's conversion to Christianity, the Russian language was subjected to the drastic influence of so-called "Church Slavonic"—the language of the church services and religious books. The church books were first translated into Slavic by Ss. Cyril and

Methodius during their Moravian mission (863–85). While the phi-
lologists still argue as to the nature of the Slavic language which the
"Slavic Apostles" spoke and wrote, it may be safely assumed that the
Macedonian (Salonike) dialect served them as a base. During their
stay in Moravia their language must have been influenced by the
west Slavic dialect and after their disciples migrated to Bulgaria the
Bulgarian language entered the picture as one more element in the old
Church Slavonic.[1]

Altogether, the Church Slavonic played in the growth of the Russian literary language a role similar to that of the Latin in the formation of French and of French in that of English. The difference is that
the Bulgarian language is of the same family as the Russian and the
similarities between single Slavic languages must have been in the
ninth century much more marked than they are now. The connection
between the two was therefore much more organic than that between
the Latin and the Keltic, or between French and Anglo-Saxon. Without fear of exaggeration, one may say that the Church Slavonic has
constituted through the ages, and still constitutes, the backbone of
literary Russian.[2]

In spite of the close relations between Church Slavonic and Old
Russian, there were also some points of difference between the two.
For the former, nasal sounds similar to the French *on* and *en* are
characteristic. In Old Russian, at least from the tenth century on,
there were no nasal vowels. Another phonetic difference was the
tendency of the Russian toward sonority: thus instead of Church
Slavonic combinations of *ra, la,* and the like, we find in the Russian
*oro, olo,* etc. Consequently the Church Slavonic *brada* ("beard") becomes *boroda* in Russian, and to the Church Slavonic *glava* ("head")
the Russian *golova* corresponds.[3]

Modern Russian is one of the three languages of the east Slavic
group, the other two being Belorussian (White Russian) and Ukrain-

1. On Ss. Cyril and Methodius, see *Ancient Russia,* pp. 353–359. By "Bulgarian language" the Slavic language of the Bulgarians is meant here and not the original
language of their Turkish conquerors, the Bulgars.

2. On the Church Slavonic language, see W. Vondrak, *Altkirchenslavische Grammatik*
(2d ed. Berlin, 1912); Prince N. S. Trubetskoy, "Altkirchenslavische Sprache" (mimeographed, Vienna, 1934); N. van Wijk, *Geschichte der altkirchenslavische Sprache* (Berlin and Leipzig, 1931).

3. See A. S. Nikulin, *Istoricheskaia grammatika russkogo iazyka* (Leningrad, 1941),
pp. 23–26; L. A. Bulakhovsky, *Istoricheskii kommentarii k russkomu literaturnomu
iazyku* (Kharkov and Kiev, 1937), pp. 50–52. (I am indebted to Roman Jakobson for
this reference.)

ian. The division of the east Slavic group into these three languages was the result of a protracted process in which political and cultural differences were a factor—differences which came to the fore during the Mongolian period (thirteenth to fifteenth centuries). Prior to that, there were two main phonological regions in Russia: the south Russian and north Russian groups of dialects. Within the first there developed the Ukrainian and the Belorussian languages and the south Great Russian dialect; within the second, the north Great Russian dialect. The latter two combined to form the foundations of the Great Russian language, now known simply as Russian.[4]

As we know, the Russians lived from time immemorial in close contact with various Iranian and Turkish tribes. It is therefore only natural that a number of Iranian and Turkish words should be found in the Russian vocabulary. The borrowing of Turkish as well as Mongol terms increased markedly after the Mongol invasion of the thirteenth century but some had already penetrated into the Russian during the Kievan period and even much earlier.[5]

In addition to the influence of the Oriental languages on medieval Russian, the Russian vocabulary of the period contained also words borrowed from various European languages: from the Greek, Latin, Norse, and German. These borrowings represent various stages in the commercial and cultural interrelations between Russia and her neighbors.

The Russians received from Bulgaria the so-called "Cyrillic" alphabet,[6] which has been used in Russia from that time, though with some modifications. As the nasal sounds disappeared early in the Russian language, the characters representing them became superfluous and were gradually neglected.

In the beginning of the eighteenth century, under Peter the Great, the Russian characters were given a somewhat romanized form, which became known as the "lay alphabet"; the old Church Slavonic alpha-

4. R. Jakobson, "Remarques sur l'évolution phonologique du russe," *Travaux du Cercle Linguistique de Prague*, *2* (1929), 66–76; Prince N. S. Trubetskoy, "Einiges über die russische Lautentwicklung und die Auflösung der gemeinrussischen Spracheinheit," *ZSP*, *1* (1925), 287–319; see also S. P. Obnorsky, *Ocherki po istorii Russkogo literaturnogo iazyka starshego perioda.*

5. F. Miklosich, "Die türkischen Elemente in den südost—und osteuropäischen Sprachen," *AWV 34, 35, 37, 38* (Vienna, 1884–90); P. Melioransky, "Turetskie elementy v Slove o Polku Igoreve," *ANORI*, *7*, Pt. 2 (1903) pp. 273–302; L. Wanstrat, *Beiträge zur Charakteristik des russischen Wortschatzes* (Leipzig, 1933). See also R. Jakobson, *K kharakteristike evraziiskogo iazykovogo soiuza* (Prague, 1931).

6. See *Ancient Russia*, pp. 355–357.

bet continued to be used for ecclesiastical books, however. Following the Revolution of 1917, the "lay" alphabet was even more simplified by the elimination of several antiquated characters.

Printing was introduced in Russia a century after Gutenberg; in the Kievan period, of course, it had not been in use anywhere in Europe. All books were in manuscript. Until the fourteenth century the script in Russia was uncial (*ustav*) but in that century a simplified form known as "semi-uncial" (*poluustav*) came into use. In the less formal writing this soon gave place to cursive (*skoropis'*). For secret communications various forms of cryptogram (*tainopis'*) were applied. Until the Mongol period all books were written on parchment but in the fourteenth century rag paper began to compete with parchment and gradually prevailed.

Parchment was costly and uncial writing slow. Producing a book, even a few copies, or preparing a single copy of it entailed great expense. In a sense, books were a luxury. And yet they must have been available in great quantities in old Russia. In spite of frequent fires and the wholesale destruction of books during wars, especially during the Mongol invasion, more than five hundred books and one hundred charters and deeds written in the period from the eleventh to the fourteenth centuries have been preserved, mostly in monastery libraries. In addition, many books of the Kievan period are known through later copies. The number of manuscript books written or copied in Russia in the period from the eleventh to the seventeenth centuries, and still extant, is around fifty thousand.[7]

### 3. Folklore

Language is primarily a means of conversing between people. It is a link between the individual and the social group, whether a primary social unit like the family or the zadruga, or a wider social group—a clan, a tribe, a nation. In its social capacity language performs various official functions, serving the church, the state, the courts. In the stage of a "literary language" it is the vehicle of education, science, literature.

Before this final cultural stage is reached, language goes through a long process of organic growth as the self-expression of individuals and groups in their work and leisure. The products of this self-

7. N. K. Nikolsky gives an even higher figure—75,000—but he includes South Slavic manuscripts found in Russian libraries. N. K. Nikolsky, "Russkaia knizhnost' drevnerusskikh bibliotek (XI–XVII vekov)," *OLDP*, CXXXII (n. d.; *ca.* 1907).

expression are what we usually call "folklore." The remnants of this old poetical tradition have survived chiefly among the peasants, at least in Russia, and therefore the term "folklore" has become almost synonymous with "people's literature," meaning by that the literary production of the lower classes. In the ancient period the situation was different, since the rise of creative power in the field of literature was based on the coöperation of all social groups. In the Kievan period, following Russia's conversion to Christianity and the appearance of written texts, a peculiar dualism developed in the literary art. As Roman Jakobson aptly puts it:

> For many centuries Russian written literature remained almost entirely subject to the church: with all its wealth and high artistry, the old Russian literary heritage is almost wholly concerned with the lives of saints and pious men, with devotional legends, prayers, sermons, ecclesiastical discourses, and chronicles in a monastic vein. The old Russian laity, however, possessed a copious, original, manifold, and highly artistic fiction, but the only medium for its diffusion was oral transmission. The idea of using letters for secular poetry was thoroughly alien to the Russian tradition, and the expressive means of this poetry were inseparable from the oral legacy and oral traditions.[8]

The basic element of Russian folklore is the song—in it language and rhythm, word and melody, are closely interwoven. A Russian proverb says, characteristically enough, "Not a word can be omitted from a song." And it has been said that "the song is the living chronicle of the Russian people." From time immemorial Russians have marked in song the whole course of their lives: work and play, joy and sorrow, small things and great historical events.

Russian folklore has accompanied the Russian people through its whole history and it is only recently that its springs have begun to dry up under the impact of industrialized and mechanized civilization. Among the villagers, especially in north Russia, the reciters of old sagas (*bylina*) are still held in great esteem.[9]

Leaving aside the *Lay of Igor's Campaign*—which obviously was created not by "the people" but by an individual artist belonging to the aristocracy at that—the first written text of a Russian folk poem, a "spiritual song" (*dukhovnyi stikh*) in this case, is dated in the fifteenth century.[10] The oldest known manuscript of Russian folk bal-

8. *Russian Fairy Tales* (New York, Pantheon, 1945), pp. 632–633.
9. See M. S. Kriukova, *Noviny* (Moscow, 1939), and *Stariny* (Moscow, 1943); M. R. Golubkova, *Dva veka v polveka* (Moscow, 1946).
10. M. Speransky, *Russkaia ustnaia slovesnost'*, p. 363.

lads proper is that written in 1619 for Richard James, an Oxford graduate who served as chaplain to the English merchants in Russia.[11] To an Englishman, therefore, the credit must go for pioneering in the province of Russian folklore studies. The James manuscript contains only six songs.

Most of specimens of Russian folklore we know of—including prose folklore such as fairy tales—were written down or, in more recent times, recorded phonographically, in the course of the eighteenth, nineteenth, and twentieth centuries.[12] There is thus no formal evidence for dating these materials except the date of their recording, which in most cases is comparatively recent.

For some of the epic songs the *terminus post quem* may be established from their contents. Thus the song on the death of the general (voevoda) Skopin-Shuisky, one of those set down for James, obviously could not have been written before 1610, the date of his death. In most cases, however, such an approach is not feasible. Some of the epic songs glorifying Prince Vladimir the Saint may have been composed in his time but we cannot be sure that the text we have is the original.

It is thus a very hard task indeed to try to select, out of the general fund of old Russian folklore, that part which may definitely be referred to the Kievan period. We may feel sure that a particular folk song is very old but we can hardly prove it in each particular case; yet it is obvious that the roots of this folklore, as also of the Russian folk art, go deep into history—in many cases farther back even than the Kievan period. Therefore any picture of the civilization of that period will be incomplete if the folklore is ignored and even a tentative dating of some songs is better than abandoning the point altogether.

It is almost certain that some of the so-called "ritual songs" (*obriadovaia pesnia*)—originally meant to accompany or symbolize the various stages of the agricultural cycle—are very old.[13] Traces of

---

11. P. K. Simoni, "Velikorusskie pesni zapisannye v 1619–1620 godakh dlia Richarda Dzhemsa," *ANORS, 82*, No. 7 (1907). See also S. Konovalov, *Oxford and Russia* (Oxford, Clarendon Press, 1947), pp. 9–10. E. J. Simmons, *English Literature and Culture in Russia (1553–1840)* (Cambridge, Harvard University Press, 1935), p. 35.

12. For an outline of the history of Russian folklore stories, see Speransky, *op. cit.*, pp. 5–178. On the folklore of the Kievan period, see *Istoriia Russkoi literatury*, I, A. S. Orlov, V. P. Adrianova-Peretts, and N. K. Gudzii, eds. (Moscow and Leningrad, 1941) pp. 216–256 (subsequently quoted as *Istoriia Russkoi literatury*).

13. On the Russian folk song, see S. Rybakov, "Russkaia pesnia," *ES,* Half-Volume LIII (St. Petersburg, 1899), pp. 310–321; and T. V. Popova, "Russkaia narodnaia

pagan religion, of worship of the sun and the earth, are discernible in many of them. To this group belong the songs adapted to the festivities of the winter solstice (*koliady*), the vernal equinox (*maslenitsa*), the summer solstice (*semik* or *rusalia*), and the autumnal equinox. Following Russia's conversion to Christianity the former pagan festivals were adjusted to Christian holidays and the texts of some of the songs changed accordingly, the old koliady songs now playing the role of carols.

In many cases evidence of the archaic origin of a song, in addition to its contents, may be found in the antiquity of its form of melody. On the whole there is enough indirect evidence to indicate that a number of Russian ritual songs originated in the Kievan period, if not much earlier. An important branch of the ritual songs is the cycle of wedding songs, which corresponds to elaborate ceremonies accompanying the old Russian wedding ritual, still observed in recent times among the peasants. To each move in the cycle a special song corresponds. Some are very gay; others melancholy and even sad.

Epic songs (*stariny, byliny*) which by their contents may be referred to the Kievan period are many.[14] These poems usually deal with the glorious deeds of valiant knights (*bogatyri*) defending the Russian land from the steppe nomads. In some cases the opponent of the Russian knight is a Jew (*Zhidovin*). This is an obvious reference to the Russian struggle with the Khazars. In most cases, however, the enemy in the reading of the extant text is a Tartar, which of course for the Kievan period would be an anachronism, since the Tartars—as the Mongols were known in Russia—appeared only in the thirteenth century.

The knights glorified in the epic songs of the Kievan time are mostly members of the druzhina of Prince Vladimir the Saint. While they are always ready to defend him and his realm, there is no servility about them and they speak frankly to the prince, even on some occasions abusing him and his wife. They are not disciplined soldiers but

pesnia," *Istoriia russkoi muzyki*, M. S. Pekelis, ed., I (Moscow and Leningrad, 1940), 7–65.

14. The literature of the Russian epic song (*bylina*) is very extensive. For a brief survey of the *byliny* (which is the plural form), see Speransky, *op. cit.*, pp. 178–328. Among important monographs on the subject, see especially I. Zhdanov, *Russkii bylevoi epos;* V. F. Miller, *Ocherki Russkoi narodnoi slovesnosti;* A. P. Skaftymov, *Poetika i genezis bylin.* See also Bibliography, XI. On the meter of the Russian epic poetry, see Prince N. Trubetskoy, "W sprawie wiersza byliny rosyjskiej," *Z Zagadnień poetiki, 6* (Wilno. 1937), 100–110; R. Jakobson (forthcoming).

rugged individualists and indeed each of them is portrayed with his own character and personality. Their senior is Ilya of Murom, a heavy, bulky man of peasant origin, straightforward and brave but without much subtleness or urbanity. His chief adjutant is Alësha Popovich, the priest's son, who relies on his cunning. Dobrynia Nikitich—a boyar—is represented as a man of noble character and generous disposition. Another popular personage in the gallery of bogatyr' portraits is the dandy Churilo Plenkovich, whose charms no girl can withstand.

To the Vladimirian bylina cycle other epic poems were later added, among them the tale of Volkh Vseslavich, describing the adventures of Prince Vseslav of Polotsk, and that of Diuk Stepanovich, which originated in Galicia in the twelfth century and reflects that country's close relations with the Byzantine Empire. The famous poem, "Sadko, the Rich Merchant," an early version of which must likewise have been composed in the twelfth century, is a typical Novgorodian story. Its hero is not a steppe bogatyr' but a merchant adventurer; wealth, and not military valor, gives color to the story.

Another Novgorodian bylina—on Vasili Buslaev—is in quite a different vein. Vaska (diminutive for Vasili) is one of the restless youth leaders of the great city-republic; he is always looking for trouble and recognizes no authority. He is a freethinker, has no veneration for the church, and nurtures no superstitions—"he believes neither in dreams nor in sneezes," as the poet puts it.

To return to the "steppe byliny," it should be pointed out that some of them have close parallels in both Iranian and Turkish folklore.[15] Thus, for example, some episodes in the story of Ilya of Murom remind us of the great Persian epic, the *Shah-nama*. Presumably the Ossetians were the middlemen between Russian and Persian poetry and the Ossetian influence as such may also be seen in some of the Russian epic songs. Characteristically, the hero of one of the old Russian byliny is called Sviatogor ("Knight of the Holy Mountains"). By these mountains presumably the Caucasian range is meant.[16]

---

15. See especially V. V. Stasov, "Proiskhozhdenie Russkikh bylin," *Sobranie Sochinenii*, III (St. Petersburg, 1894), 948–1259. In 1924-25 and 1925-26, Nicholas N. Martinovitch delivered at Columbia University courses on "Oriental Origins and Influence in the Old Russian Epic Poetry" and "Oriental Elements in the Old Russian Epic Poetry" (not yet published).

16. V. F. Miller, *Ekskursy v oblasti russkogo narodnogo eposa;* see especially Appendix I, "Kavkazsko-russkie paralleli." G. Dumézil questions the validity of some of

In conclusion a few words should be said about the Russian fairy tale.[17] It has been extremely popular with the Russian people throughout the whole history of the country. As a branch of Russian folklore it is rich and varied. There are two main types of the fairy tales: the magic and the satirical. Tales of the magic type, with their "self-flying rugs" (*kovër-samolët*), "self-serving tablecloths" (*skatert'-samobranka*), and so on, probably have their roots in pagan sorcery. Their popularity is explained by the people's longing for devices which would make life easier.

The satirical fairy tales gave bent to people's irritation against political and social injustice. It is interesting that some fairy-tale personages, such as the Baba-Iaga, are mentioned in the chronicle— evidence of the popularity of fairy tales in the Kievan period.[18]

## 4. Music

The study of old Russian folklore is as important for an understanding of the historical background of Russian music as for the proper approach to Russian poetry.[19]

The Russian song has its own melodic, harmonic, and rhythmic peculiarities. A number of old Russian songs are composed in the so-called pentatonic scale in which the shortest step adopted is a "tone" or "whole step." As the late Prince N. S. Trubetskoy pointed out, this scale is to be found in the folk music of the Turkish tribes in the basins of the Volga and Kama rivers, among the Bashkirs, the Siberian Tartars, and the Turks of Central Asia, as well as among the natives of Siam, Burma, and Indo-China.[20]

In this sense the music of at least a group of the old Russian folk songs may be called Eurasian rather than European. In Ukraine the pentatonic scale is to be found only in a few very ancient songs, while among other Slavs its use is even more rare. On the other hand, it is interesting to note that the pentatonic scale has been preserved also

Miller's parallels between the heroes of the Ossetian legends and those of the Russian byliny; even he recognizes, however, the close similarity between the Ossetian Mukara and the Russian Sviatogor; see G. Dumézil, *Légendes sur les Nartes* (Paris, 1930). Note V, "Entre la Perse et la Russie," pp. 200–209.

17. Speransky, *op. cit.*, pp. 392–432.

18. *Istoriia Russkoi literatury*, I, 235.

19. On old Russian music, see N. Findeizen, *Ocherki po istorii muzyki v Rossii*, I; M. S. Pekelis, ed., *Istoriia Russkoi muzyki*, I, chaps. i–ii.

20. Prince N. S. Trubetskoy, *K probleme Russkogo samopoznaniia* (Prague, 1927), p. 29.

in the Keltic folk song, among the Scotch, the Irish, and in Brittany. Other Russian songs seem to follow the traditions of ancient Greek music.

It may be added that the Russian folk song is predominantly diatonic; elements of chromaticism are very rare. Most of the Russian songs are polyphonic. All the parts are independent and each has a beauty of its own but all go to make up the whole. The song is begun by the leader, who carries the main theme. The other singers modulate and embellish it to create an original contrapuntal effect. In this respect the Russian folk song differs markedly from the folk songs of the Oriental peoples, most of whom sing in unison.

The rhythm of the Russian song is partly determined by the nature of the living tongue but depends also to a great degree on the artistic intuition of the creator and performer. Measures in 5/4 and 7/4 time are typical.[21]

In addition to choral singing, solo singing was also practiced in Kievan Russia, especially at princely banquets where heroic ballads, like the *Lay of Igor's Campaign,* were recited. In most cases the rhapsodist accompanied himself on a psaltery (gusli). There is a poetic description of such a performance in the *Lay:* "It is not ten falcons that Baian launched against a flock of swans; it is his inspired fingers that he laid on the living strings [of his psaltery]. And those strings rang, as by themselves, glory to the princes."

Professional rhapsodists must have been numerous. They traveled from one public festival to another, performing not only in princely palaces but in the town market places and at village fairs as well. They were generally known as *skomorokhi*. The skomorokhi worked in companies and as a class must receive the credit for preserving through ages the traditions of ancient folk art in Russia.

In addition to the psaltery, various other musical instruments were used in old Russia, such as the *sopel* (a wooden pipe) and *bubny* ("tambourine"). The latter was also an indispensable part of military bands, as were bugles and horns of various kinds. Undoubtedly some Oriental instruments, such as the harp and the bandore, were well known. Besides military bands, the princes had special orchestras for palace banquets and festivals.

As to religious music, little is known concerning the pagan ritual. Mas'udi mentions musical melodies which may be heard by the trav-

21. Nina Vernadsky, "The Russian Folk-Song," *Russian Review,* 3 (1944), 94–99; Rybakov, *loc. cit.;* Popova, *loc. cit.*

eler approaching a certain pagan temple in the land of the Slavs. It is known that horns were used by the pagan priests of the Baltic Slavs.[22] Presumably some kind of singing and music constituted a feature of pagan ritual in Kiev as well.

Following Russia's conversion to Christianity, church singing became an essential element of Russian musical culture. In accordance with the Byzantine tradition the Russian Church avoided instrumental music, unless the church bells are to be counted as such.[23] On the other hand, vocal music—choral singing, to be more exact— early achieved a high degree of perfection.

It was the Byzantine system of modes ("echoes") that served as the basis for the Orthodox Church singing. The system comprises eight "echoes" (glas), of which four are considered the main ones ("authentic") and four supplementary ("plagal"). The system was derived from the old Greek harmony and was adapted to church music by St. John of Damascus (d. 760).

At first, Russian church singing was unisonal. Its notation has been preserved in a number of manuscripts, of which the oldest is a Novgorodian church book of the eleventh century. It is in so-called "sign" (znamennaia) notation. However, there existed in Russia in the period from the eleventh to the fourteenth century another system of notation known as kondakarnaia, from kondak (Κοντάκιον), collect-hymn. Unfortunately it has not as yet been deciphered in full but from what is so far known it is apparent that it corresponded to polyphonic singing.[24]

## 5. Theater

Theater is one of the major branches of modern Russian art and it has even been suggested that the Russians have innate abilities for the stage. However, theater in the modern sense has developed in Russia only since the late seventeenth century. In the Muscovite period—the age of Shakespeare—Russia had no theater as such.

The situation in regard to the Kievan period is not quite clear. We have, first of all, to consider the folklore background. The ritual

22. Findeizen, op. cit., I, 30.

23. Church bells were introduced in Russia around the middle of the eleventh century under western influence. Their average size in the Kievan period was small. See Golubinsky, Istoriia, I, Pt. 2 (2d ed. Moscow, 1904), pp. 151, 152.

24. On the old Russian Church singing, consult Findeizen, op. cit., I, 80–103. M. Brazhnikov's works are inaccessible to me (see on them Igor Boelza, "Istoki russkoi muzyki," Sovetskoe Iskusstvo, August 3, 1945).

of folk festivals, with its dancing, rhythmic dialogue, and so on, contained many an element of theatrical art. So did the ritual of weddings and of funerals.[25]

The elaborate cycle of the old Russian wedding ceremonies amounted to a play in which not only the bridegroom and the fiancée but their relatives and friends as well each had a part of his or her own. The cycle consisted of several acts, beginning with the coming of the kinsmen of the bridegroom to the house of the father of the bride, usually at night, as the old ritual required. The performance lasted for several days in the homes of the relatives of each side in turn. As has been already mentioned, a variety of songs was an essential feature of the ceremonies, a special song for each day and each stage of the occasion.

Characteristically, Russian peasants even in recent years, in referring to a wedding, say, "to play a wedding" (*igrat' svad'bu*). Funerals likewise had their established ritual, in the performance of which the professional woman lamenter (*plakalshchitsa*) played an important role. In the *Lay of Igor's Campaign* the Lamenter (*Karna*) bewails the fate of the whole Russian land devastated by the steppe nomads.

It is against this folklore background that the activities of the traveling actors (*skomorokhi*) should be examined.[26] Most of the skomorokhi are supposed to have been low-grade actors and musicians, a kind of jongleurs or buffoons. However, one must bear in mind that our information about them derives chiefly from ecclesiastical sources.

The Russian clergy considered the skomorokhi shows an evidence of paganism and tried unsuccessfully to suppress them altogether. The clergy were guided by the decisions of the so-called Quinisexta Church Council, held in Constantinople in 692, which condemned all kinds of theatricals. But the Byzantine Church itself abandoned its rigorism in the period of iconoclasm (eighth century) and even more so in the period of the Macedonian dynasty (ninth to eleventh centuries). The Byzantine theater, which was an outgrowth of the Roman mime, survived until the last day of the Empire.[27] Incidentally,

25. P. N. Sakulin, *Russkaia literatura*, I, pp. 181–182.

26. On the *skomorokhi*, see Findeizen, *op. cit.*, I, pp. 145–170.

27. On the Byzantine theater, see G. La Piana, *Le rappresentazioni sacre nella litteratura bizantina* (Grotta Ferrata, 1912); V. Cottas, *Le Théâtre à Byzance* (Paris, 1931). On the theater in Russia, see B. Malnick, "The Origin and Early History of the Theatre in Russia," *SEER*, 19, 203–227.

the Byzantine mime was the origin of the Turkish popular theater, the *Orta oiunu, Karagöz,* and *Meddah.*[28]

In view of the close cultural relations between Kievan Russia and Byzantium, we may surmise that Byzantine actors visited Russia on many occasions, initiating the native skomorokhi into the essentials of theatrical art. As we shall see, in the murals of St. Sophia of Kiev Byzantine jongleurs were represented against the background of the Hippodrome but the mime was of diverse nature and in addition to low-grade shows more serious plays were also produced in Constantinople. Whether some of these found their way to Kiev is not known.

The Byzantine actors, on some occasions at least, wore masks [29] and so did the skomorokhi. It is with the skomorokhi shows that the development of the puppet theater in medieval Russia must be connected. The first known reference to it is found in a fifteenth-century manuscript.[30]

In addition to the secular theater, a religious (mystery) drama developed in Byzantium, as likewise in western Europe during the Middle Ages. In a sense the Byzantine Mass is in itself a sacred drama and the elaborate ritual of the Church of St. Sophia was permeated with theatrical effects. It was precisely this dramatic element in the Byzantine ritual which attracted Vladimir's envoys to Christianity more than anything else. According to the chronicle, as we saw earlier, the envoys after attending Mass in St. Sophia Cathedral in Constantinople wondered whether they were on earth or in heaven. Later on, visitors from the Russian country districts must have had the same sensation as they attended the services in St. Sophia of Kiev and other major churches in Russian cities. Wall paintings, mosaics, and icons placed all around the church provided the necessary setting for the sacred drama of the mass, the deep symbolism of which would otherwise be missed by the congregation.

In Byzantium, from the earliest period of its history, special solemn services with an elaborate ritual had been developed for the commemoration of the main church festivals, especially for Palm Sunday, Holy Week, and Easter, as well as for Our Lady days. Gradually

28. Nicholas N. Martinovitch, *The Turkish Theatre* (New York, Theatre Arts, Inc., 1933), and "The Turkish Theatre: the Missing Link," *Moslem World, 34* (1944), 54–55.

29. Cottas, *op. cit.,* p. 45.

30. Findeizen, *op. cit.,* I, 147. On the development of the Russian puppet theater since 1636, in which year the German traveler Adam Olearius attended a "Petrushka" show in Moscow, see V. Peretts, "Kukolnyi Teatr na Rusi," *Ezhegodnik Imperatorskikh Teatrov,* 1894–95, Supplement 1, pp. 85–185.

around each of these services religious processions and mysteries were built and out of them the Byzantine religious drama finally came into being. It is significant that on the reception in the Imperial Palace of Princess Olga of Russia (A.D. 957) a religious play was produced.[31]

We can thus be sure that Russians, even before Russia's official conversion to Christianity, were acquainted with the dramatic expansion of the Byzantine Church service. There is no evidence that religious drama, as such, was introduced in Russia prior to the sixteenth and seventeenth centuries but special services for commemoration days and Holy Week were held already in the Kievan period, although probably not then as elaborate as in the later time.[32]

## 6. Fine Arts

Most of the monuments we know of the old Russian architecture and painting represent church art. Since the Russian church was but a branch of the Byzantine, Russian church art obviously had to follow Byzantine patterns, at least in the initial period of the spread of Christianity over Russia. For this reason it is often said that, from the point of view of the history of art, Kievan Russia was but a province of Byzantium.

It cannot be denied that the Byzantine influence in early Russian architecture and painting was very strong. And yet the actual process of Russian artistic development was much more involved than might be inferred from the theory of the "Byzantinization" of Russia or any rigid doctrine of the kind. First of all, our knowledge of the old Russian art is incomplete. While a number of church buildings have been preserved, monuments of lay architecture have not, since most of the private houses were of wood and thus more perishable than the church buildings. Furthermore, no buildings of the pre-Christian era have been preserved except for a few foundations and we are thus not in a position to examine the relation between the pagan and the Christian architecture. Also, the term "Byzantine art" itself needs some elucidation. There were several schools of it and distinctions must be made—for example, between the architectural style of Con-

31. Constantine Porphyrogenitus, *De Cerimoniis Aulae Byzantinae*, pt. II, chap. xv in *PG*, CXII, col. 1112.

32. Venetia Cottas is mistaken when she assumes that a Slavic version of the *Triod'* appeared in Russia only in the late fourteenth century (Cottas, *op. cit.*, p. 144). There exist in Russian libraries copies of the *Triod'*, dated in the eleventh and twelfth centuries. See Makarii, II (3d ed., 1889), 240; III (3d ed., 1888), 116–117.

stantinople and that of the Byzantine provinces, such as Thrace and Macedonia on the one hand and Anatolia on the other.

To start with the problem of pre-Christian architecture in Russia, an oval foundation of a building was excavated in Kiev around 1908 which is considered the remains of a pagan temple, although of this there is no positive proof. On this ground it has been suggested that pagan temples in Russia must have had an oval shape.[33] There is no definite evidence for such a general conclusion. If we look for parallels in other Slavic countries, the Temple of Svantovit on the island of Rugen—one of the major Slavic pagan sanctuaries—was square.

The first Christian churches must have been built for the Russians, if not yet by them, soon after their first conversion in 866. Presumably one of them was at Tmutorokan. In 1022 Prince Mstislav of that city built another church there which was to serve as a model for the cathedral at Chernigov, founded by the same prince. At the time of his death in 1036 it was not yet completed but was finished later.[34]

Although the Chernigov cathedral was restored several times, its original architectural features were preserved. It is arranged on the Byzantine quincuncial or "five-spot" plan; some influence on it of the architectural style of Transcaucasian churches is likewise evident.[35]

The first of the sumptuous Kievan churches was the so-called Church of the Tithe (Desiatinnaia), founded by Vladimir the Saint in 991 and finally completed in 1039. According to Kenneth J. Conant it was begun on the plan of a Byzantine three-naved basilica but later adapted to have twenty-five individual compartments planned for vaulting, though not the twenty-five cupolas suggested by some.[36]

Even prior to this Vladimir had ordered a cathedral to be built in Novgorod, around 989. We learn from the chronicles that the first St. Sophia of Novgorod, which was of wood, had thirteen "tops" (*verkhi*). Some archaeologists have been ready to see cupolas in this

33. A. I. Nekrasov, *Ocherki po istorii drevnerusskogo zodchestva XI–XVII vekov*, p. 18.

34. On the Russian churches of the Kievan period, besides the general histories of Russian art listed in the Bibliography, see S. H. Cross, H. V. Morgilevski, and K. J. Conant, "The Earliest Medieval Churches of Kiev," *Speculum*, 11 (1936), 477–499; K. J. Conant, "Novgorod, Constantinople, and Kiev in Old Russian Church Architecture," *SEER*, 22 (1944), 75–92; and Nekrasov, *loc. cit.* A. I. Nekrasov, *Drevnerusskoe izobrazitelnoe iskusstvo*, quoted by Conant, *op. cit.*, p. 90, is inaccessible to me.

35. Conant, *op. cit.*, p. 82. Cross, Morgilevsky, and Conant, *op. cit.*, p. 488.

36. Conant, *op. cit.*, p. 87.

term but it seems more plausible that the "tops" may be explained simply as so many elements of roofing.[37]

According to Conant, one of the architects of this cathedral may have been an Ossetian (Iasian). The type of design must have affected that of some other early Russian churches, both in Novgorod and Kiev.

The two most spectacular monuments of Russian architecture of the eleventh century are the St. Sophia Cathedral, built in 1037–1100 in Kiev, and the second Novgorodian cathedral, of the same name, founded in 1045. The Kievan cathedral survived in poor shape, being mutilated by fires and restorations. The Novgorodian fared a little better until the German invasion but was severely damaged by the Germans before their retreat in 1944.

St. Sophia of Kiev in its original shape must have been a magnificent cathedral. It was square, the inside being divided into sections by columns. It had five apses—all on the eastern side—and thirteen cupolas; a huge one in the center and twelve lesser ones around it. The cathedral was beautifully decorated inside with wall paintings, mosaics, and icons.

Taken as a whole, St. Sophia of Kiev was an outstanding specimen of the Byzantine style but was not a mere copy of any of the then-existing Byzantine churches. It is thought that the so-called "New Church" (Nea Ecclesia) in Constantinople, completed in 881, served as a basic pattern for the edifice, as well as for some other Kievan churches built during Iaroslav's reign. The Kievan St. Sophia was, however, much more complex architecturally than its prototype. Motifs of Byzantine provincial art (Anatolian, in this case) are also noticeable in it. Besides, the possibility of some influence of the Novgorodian wooden architecture is not excluded, especially in regard to the number of cupolas, as corresponding to that of the Novgorodian "tops."

The second St. Sophia of Novgorod was built of stone on the ground of the first wooden one, consumed by fire in 1045. The Novgorodian St. Sophia is a more austere and less sumptuous temple than the Kievan but has a charm of its own. Its proportions are decidedly different, the apses being more extended and, while the main body of the church is of a rectangular shape, it is not a square. The church has six cupolas.

According to A. I. Nekrasov, some of the architectural features of

37. See the conjectural restoration by Conant, *idem*, p. 78.

St. Sophia of Novgorod belong to the Romanesque type.[38] With the rise of local cultural centers in the course of the twelfth century, most of the capitals of the rival Russian principalities were adorned by churches which, if less spacious than the Kievan St. Sophia, had each a peculiar style of its own.[39]

It is significant that the churches of both western Ukraine (Galicia and Volynia) and eastern Russia (Suzdalia and Riazan) show in their style a combination of both Romanesque and Transcaucasian (Georgian and Armenian) stylistic influences. As shown by recent excavations, the Riazan church of the early twelfth century had the form of the so-called "Armenian Cross."[40]

The second half of the twelfth and the early thirteenth century were the period of blossoming of Suzdalian architecture.[41] As we know, the principality of Vladimir-in-Suzdalia came to prominence in that period under the guidance of such able rulers as Andrei Bogoliubsky and Vsevolod III. Both were enthusiastic builders. It is known from the chronicles that Andrei invited to Suzdalia architects from various countries. The historian V. N. Tatishchev states that on one occasion Emperor Frederick Barbarossa sent to Andrei master builders from Germany.[42] Tatishchev does not indicate his authority for the report but his statements are usually reliable. We know that the Suzdalian princes were in friendly relations with both the Byzantine and the Holy Roman Empire. Presumably, also, Andrei employed some Georgian and Armenian architects, as well as west Russian builders from Galicia.

The presence of so many foreign architects in the eleven-fifties and the eleven-sixties must have stimulated the artistic activities of the native Suzdalian architects as well and in 1194 the chronicler observes that Vsevolod used Russian master builders alone in renovating the cathedrals of Suzdal and Vladimir.[43]

The two outstanding monuments of Andrei's reign are the Cathedral of the Dormition of Our Lady (Uspenie) in Vladimir (built in

38. Nekrasov, *Ocherki po istorii drevnerusskogo zodchestra XI–XVII vekov*, p. 38.

39. For a survey of all the churches built in the Kievan period, see Golubinsky, *Istoriia*, I, Pt. 2 (2d ed. Moscow, 1904), pp. 1–161.

40. Nekrasov, *op. cit.*, pp. 76–77.

41. On the Suzdalian churches, besides the general works on the history of Russian architecture, see I. I. Tolstoy and N. P. Kondakov, *Russkie drevnosti*, VI (St. Petersburg, 1899); Fannina W. Halle, *Die Bauplastik von Wladimir Ssusdal;* Nekrasov, *op. cit.*, pp. 99–140.

42. See *idem*, p. 112.

43. *PSRL*, I, Fasc. 2 (2d ed. Leningrad, 1926).

1158–61, restored in 1185–89; renovated in 1194) and the charming miniature Church of Intercession of Our Lady (Pokrov) on the banks of the river Nerl near Bogoliubovo (1165). In Vsevolod's reign the St. Dimitri Cathedral in Vladimir was built (1194–97), famous for the plastic decoration of its outside walls. No less remarkable is St. George's Cathedral in Iuriev-Polsky, built by Vsevolod's son Sviatoslav (1230–34). Its walls are also decorated in bas-reliefs which are even more spectacular than those of the St. Dimitri.

Although each of these churches is individually different, all may be said to belong to the same general architectural type, the "Suzdalian" type, characterized by harmonious composition and graciousness of lines and decoration. In architectural and plastic details there are striking parallels between the Suzdalian and the Armenian and Georgian churches, as well as between the Suzdalian and the western Romanesque. However, it would hardly be proper to call the Suzdalian style and churches western Romanesque, as is often done, without reservations. As the late N. P. Kondakov rightly pointed out, Romanesque art itself evolved under the Byzantine influence and there are many "Romanesque" elements in the Byzantine art of the eleventh and twelfth centuries. The art of some east European countries, such as western Ukraine, Serbia, and Hungary, belongs to that Byzantine-Romanesque type and in Kondakov's opinion it is to western Ukraine (Galicia and Volynia) that we must look in any attempt to locate the sources of Suzdalian art.[44]

In any case, if there are Romanesque elements in Suzdalian churches, the churches themselves look quite different from the Romanesque churches of Bohemia, Germany, and France. Altogether, it hardly can be denied that by blending various elements of the Byzantine, Transcaucasian, and western Romanesque art, the architects— both foreign and Russian—employed by the Suzdalian princes succeeded in creating a new and highly consummate style in Russian art. Kenneth Conant calls it "authentically classic" and "worthy of the hellenistic spirit, together with a sense of serenity and assurance which is never absent from the greatest works of art." [45] Later on, the Suzdalian churches in their turn served as models for the Muscovite churches of the fifteenth century, built by Italian architects.

In addition to churches, both Andrei and Vsevolod built sumptuous palaces for themselves. According to the chronicler, both foreigners

44. Tolstoy and Kondakov, *op. cit.*, VI, 6–11, 48–58.
45. Conant, *op. cit.*, p. 90.

and Russians flocked to Bogoliubovo to admire Andrei's residence there. Nothing remains of this palace above the surface of the earth but its foundations have recently been excavated, from whose evidence we may obtain some idea of the grandiose architectural ensemble which included the palace itself, several towers, and a cathedral, all connected by arcades.[46]

While both the church and the princes sponsored the development of architecture, the church objected to sculpture, which was identified with pagan art. So strong was the prejudice in old Russia against statues that not only in church art but even in the lay art statuary had no place. As a result, sculpture in Kievan Russia had only a subordinate development and even bas-reliefs were mostly used for decorative purposes.[47] Among the few specimens of Russian sculpture of the period, marble sarcophagi in the St. Sophia Cathedral at Kiev may be mentioned, one of them—that of Iaroslav the Wise—elaborately ornamented. Among the stone bas-reliefs of saints, that of St. George and St. Dimitri of the twelfth century, in the wall of the St. Michael Monastery, is of rough workmanship but not devoid of a certain force of expression. The carved stone and plastic ornamentation of the walls of the St. Dimitri Cathedral in Vladimir and the Church of St. George in Iuriev-Polski is extremely varied and picturesque. Besides various representations of Christ and the saints there are there figures of real and fantastic animals and birds, including centaurs and gryphons.

Painting, like architecture, enjoyed the sponsorship of the church and its development was not artificially checked like that of sculpture. On the other hand, not as many examples of Russian painting of the Kievan period have been preserved as of the architecture and our knowledge of it is therefore necessarily incomplete.[48]

The first painters employed in Russia were "Greeks," that is, Byzantines. Most of them seem to have come from Anatolia. It is fortunate that at least some of the wall paintings in St. Sophia's Cathedral at Kiev have been preserved. These murals illustrate the life

46. *Istoriia Russkoi literatury*, I, 37.

47. On the Russian sculpture of the Kievan period, see Baron N. N. Vrangel, "Istoriia Skulptury," in I. Grabar, ed., *Istoriia Russkogo iskusstva*, V, 9–14; Tolstoy and Kondakov, *op. cit.*, VI; *Istoriia Russkoi literatury*, I, 27, 29, 30, 37, 38.

48. On the Russian painting of the Kievan period, besides the general histories of Russian art, see N. P. Kondakov, *Russkaia ikona*, there is an abridged edition of this work in English: N. P. Kondakov, *The Russian Icon*. For further references, see Bibliography, XII.

of Our Lady, Christ, and St. George, patron saint of Iaroslav the Wise.

On the walls of the staircase leading to the choir balcony scenes of life in Constantinople were portrayed. Of these, a representation of drivers and chariots of the Hippodrome races is still extant. Fragments of circus scenes with acrobats, hunters, musicians, and jugglers have also been preserved. In the execution of the murals of the twelfth century, such as those in the churches of two Kievan monasteries—St. Michael and St. Cyril—as well as in the so-called Nereditsa Church near Novgorod, Russian painters must have collaborated with the Greek. At Nereditsa, Armenian painters were probably engaged as well. The Nereditsa Church has become one of the painful casualties of the German invasion.

As to icon painting, its story is similar to that of the wall painting. At first icons were either brought ready made from Byzantium or painted by Greek masters in Russia. Later, native painters were trained, the first to attain fame among his contemporaries being a certain Alimpi mentioned in the *Paterik* of the Monastery of the Caves. Byzantine icons of exceptional beauty were occasionally imported throughout the twelfth century. Presumably it was Iuri Dolgoruky who brought from Constantinople the famous icon of Our Lady which his son Andrei deposited in the Cathedral of the Dormition at Vladimir and which, under the name of the icon of Our Lady of Vladimir, became one of the sacred symbols of old Russia.

The art of mosaic was applied to the decoration of St. Sophia and several other churches in Kiev as well as in Chernigov.[48a] The art of enameling became very popular—Russian artists of the Kievan period reached a very high level of technique in cloisonné. In the treasure hoards, such as that found at Riazan in 1822 and at Kiev in 1889, there are some extremely fine specimens of gold and enamel jewelry dating from the twelfth century. The blossoming of this branch of applied arts is evidence of the artistic maturity of the Kievan civilization.[49]

There is also no doubt that the art of embroidery was highly developed in Kievan Russia but few items of it have been preserved. Both in convents and in princely palaces skilled embroiderers were

48a. See S. H. Cross, "The Mosaic Eucharist of St. Michael's (Kiev)," *ASEER, 6,* Nos. 16/17 (1947), 56–61.

49. Tolstoy and Kondakov, *op. cit.,* V (St. Petersburg, 1897), 101–145; Kondakov, *Russkie klady,* I, 83–144.

trained and princesses especially patronized the art, exercise of which, however, was by no means limited to the palaces. Almost every house-wife, both in the towns and in rural districts, must have been familiar with at least the rudiments of this accomplishment, which may thus be considered a branch of folk art in the wider sense of the term. The roots of this art go far back into the past. It is significant that the basic motifs of Russian peasant embroidery date from the Scythian and Sarmatian eras.[50]

A few words should be said in this connection on the role of orna-mentation in Russian art. Both the "vegetal" and the "animal" styles were popular. The former seems to have penetrated into Russia from Byzantium. The latter, as we know, was characteristic of Scythian and Sarmatian art. In the early Middle Ages it spread all over Eu-rope. It appears that the expansion of the animal style in medieval Russian art was the result of both the traditions of the Sarmatian era and the influence of the western patterns which in themselves repre-sented but a variant of the same traditions. Considerable influence of the decorative art of the Islamic Near East on Russian art may also be assumed. The variety of forms of ornamentation is characteristic of all the manifestations of the Russian artistic spirit, especially in the applied arts. It is revealed in the illumination of manuscripts, in embroidery, in enamels, in wood carving, and so on. It affects not only the art of the upper classes but the folk art as well; the same traditions have been carried on and preserved in the Russian peasant art of more recent periods.

## 7. Religion

Russian paganism has already been discussed (see Chap. II). While the pagan cult was forbidden from the close of the tenth century, pagan beliefs could not be so easily eradicated. At first only the city people took Christianity more or less seriously; in remote rural dis-tricts paganism held its ground for a long time under the thin veneer of Christian rites. The result was the so-called "double-faith," *dvoc-verie*. People may have worn crosses and attended church services but they did not abandon the celebration of the pagan festivals, too.

Gradually the two rituals merged, with victory on the Christian side, at least in outward appearance. Christian saints replaced the old deities in the people's mind. Elija the prophet was identified with Thunder, substituting for Perun; the old God Veles was transformed

50. See *Ancient Russia,* p. 100.

into St. Vlas (Blasius); St. Trifon, through a series of iconographic accidents, became associated with falconry, and so on.[51] Similarly, old pagan festivals were adapted to Christian holy days; thus the traditional *Semik* (summer equinox rites) merged with *Troitsa* ("Pentecost").

At first the adaptation was somewhat mechanical. Gradually, however, the old beliefs waned and the new struck firmer roots. As a matter of fact, paganism had no chance of withstanding Christianity, not only because the latter was the higher religion but also because it represented a higher civilization in general. Being accepted by the elite of Russian society as early as the eleventh century, it produced a number of truly enlightened leaders.

It is the "cult"—that is, the totality of church services and prayers —that best reveals the core of Greek Orthodoxy and it is the celebration of the Mass that constitutes the core of the Orthodox cult. Indeed, historically speaking it was mainly through the Mass—or, perhaps better, through the church ritual in general—that people were trained to become Christians in Kievan Russia. To be sure, the symbolism of the church ritual could at first be appreciated by only a few. There were, however, many elements in the church service which to a greater or lesser degree appealed to the bulk of the congregations. Such were, for example: readings from both the New and the Old Testament, which were a regular part of the services; hymns arranged in the so-called "canon," devoted to the glorification of Christ and the Virgin Mary and to prayer to them for intercession and protection; collect-hymns of a special kind (known as *kondak*), the object of which was to explain the meaning of the church holy days, and so on. All this was offered not in Latin or Greek but in Slavonic and was thus accessible to the audience. Icons and murals representing biblical scenes were meant to illustrate the contents of the readings and the hymns and were undoubtedly of great help to the congregation. Finally, further explanation was offered in sermons. The latter, especially when delivered by outstanding church leaders, were usually written down and circulated in many copies for the literate, the number of whom had increased considerably by the end of the eleventh century. Besides the sermons, excerpts from the works of the Byzantine church fathers and lives of saints were also at the disposal of readers, helping them to master the new faith.

51. N. V. Malitsky, "Drevnerusskie kulty selskokhoziaistvennykh sviatykh," *GA*, XI, No. 10 (1932).

What was the cumulative effect of the Orthodox "cult" and didactic literature on the minds of the first generations of church-goers in Russia? Perhaps the most important result was the new sense of moral responsibility of every man or woman for his or her deeds, and even thoughts, to which the idea of the future life and the Last Judgment supplied a sanction. While the notion of a future life was known to Slavic paganism, there was hardly any connotation attached to it of responsibility for life on earth. Far as the Russian neophyte may have been from the Christian ideal in his actual living, that ideal became an important factor in his mind. If he sinned, he also repented, and a new element of inner struggle for perfection enriched his spiritual life and religious experience. Thus an important psychological change came about for the Russian people.

The change affected not only the individual but likewise the society as a whole. The new attitude made it possible for the legislator to abolish altogether the old custom of class feud and bloody revenge. Broadly speaking, the notion of social responsibility accompanied that of individual responsibility. Church leaders were expected to show the way to the nation and some of them duly contributed their share; among other things, by objecting to the institution of slavery. Monasteries became so many centers of what may be called social work, by organizing hospitals and homes for the aged as well as promoting charities. Some of the princes followed suit. Education was likewise sponsored by both the church and the princes and it was also the church which first assumed the task of recording the history of the nation.

In the old Russian historical annals the basic idea of the responsibility of both rulers and people for their deeds was emphasized and misfortunes such as famines and wars were explained as so many cases of God's visitation to punish men for their sins.

Let us now examine some of the literary documents of the Kievan period—hymns, prayers, lives of saints, and so on [52]—which may illuminate for us the religious mentality of Russians in that age. It is significant that, not content with the traditional hymns received from Byzantium, a number of educated Russians tried their own hand at writing new hymns and prayers. Bishop Kirill of Turov is the author of a penitence canon (not preserved) and several hymns and

---

52. In addition to the general histories of the Russian church, as well as those of Russian literature, listed in the Bibliography, see George P. Fedotov, *The Russian Religious Mind: Kievan Christianity*.

prayers, all permeated with the notion peculiar to him of a stern God-head and helpless mankind.[53] The metropolitan Ilarion wrote a "prayer for Russia" which is another sample of his forceful literary style and greatness of mind.[54]

A prayer attributed to a layman, Prince Vladimir Monomach, in a sense continues Ilarion's tradition but is more personal in its scope. It is addressed to Christ and the Virgin Mary. As a ruler Vladimir implores the Holy Virgin to preserve the city over which he reigns as her city. As a man he is concerned with his own soul: "Incline, O my soul, and consider my deeds that thou has done; bring them before thine eyes, shed tears from mine eyes and confess openly all thine actions and thoughts to Christ, and be purified." [55]

From the ecclesiastical point of view, the appearance of saints is a barometer of the level of religion in a nation and the newly converted Russia needed saints to convince herself as well as the outside Christian world of her religious maturity. While most of the Byzantine saints are bishops and monks, Russia's first two canonized saints were, characteristically enough, laymen and not members of the clergy: they were the princes Boris and Gleb already mentioned, both sons of Vladimir "the Saint," who was himself canonized much later. The third Russian saint was Feodosi, abbot of the Monastery of the Caves. In all, in the Kievan period, eleven Russians were canonized.[56]

Canonization calls for the writing of lives of the saints, and hagiography constituted an important branch of Byzantine literature. Among the innumerable Byzantine vitae some are purely legendary, while others are based upon real biographical traits; which, however, were often shaded by the later editors and compilers. Gradually a conventional standard was established for writing a *"life."* In spite of the fact that authors of the early Russian vitae tried to follow the Byzantine pattern, their work is less conventional and closer to life than that of their masters.

The life of Feodosi was written by Nestor, a learned monk of the Monastery of the Caves.[57] His object was to collect materials essential for the canonization of the late abbot, which the elders of the

53. For Kirill's sermons, see Ponomarev, I (St. Petersburg, 1894), 126–198.

54. Ponomarev, I, 76–78.

55. Cross, pp. 312, 313.

56. On the canonization of Russian saints, see E. E. Golubinsky, *Istoriia kanonizatsii sviatykh v Russkoi tserkvi.*

57. The text of the "Life of Feodosi" has been edited by A. A. Shakhmatov and P. A. Lavrov in *Chteniia,* 1899, Pt. 2.

monastery were then striving to have officially approved. In spite of this, Nestor's work is not an official panegyric but an honest biographical record, although adapted to the rules of Byzantine hagiography. The monk had not known Feodosi personally, for he entered the monastery shortly after the great abbot's death, but he lived in the atmosphere of fresh memories of the departed leader and had ample opportunity of conversing with Feodosi's disciples. Thus, for Nestor, Feodosi is in a sense a living man and not a mere ideal, which makes his work personal rather than abstract. On Ss. Boris and Gleb two works exist: their "Life," written by the same Nestor, and the anonymous "Tale" (*Skazanie*). Both were written at the close of the eleventh or in the initial years of the twelfth century.[58]

Saints Boris and Gleb, as we have seen, were murdered in 1015 immediately after the death of their father Vladimir by order of their brother Sviatopolk I, who wanted to eliminate any potential rivals for the Kievan throne (see Chap. IV, sec. 2).

The assassination of the two brothers was a shock to the Russian people at large. While not exactly martyrs for the faith, they were considered innocent "sufferers" who sacrificed themselves for the ideal of brotherly love. It is noteworthy that the first Czech saint, Václav, was also a murdered prince; and incidentally Nestor was acquainted with his "Life."

Boris' attitude is that of nonresistance to evil, the result of a literal acceptance of Christ's words. It was for their innocent suffering that Boris and Gleb were considered saints by the larger masses of the Russian people.

Sympathy for suffering was one of the basic expressions of Christian feeling in old Russia—one may say, indeed, one of the pillars of popular religion as opposed to official theology, especially as interpreted by monks of the type of Kirill of Turov. Were a man even a criminal or a heretic, from the point of view of the popular religion suffering purified him.

Knowing this, we may well understand the reasons for the popularity in old Russia of one of the Byzantine apocrypha, the so-called "Virgin Mary's Journey through the Inferno." [59] Its theme is that used by Dante for his *Divina Comedia* but there are no classical

58. D. I. Abramovich, ed., "Zhitiia sv. Borisa i Gleba; sluzhby im," *Pamiatniki drevnerusskoi literatury*, II (Petrograd, 1916). On Boris and Gleb see Fedotov (as in note 52), pp. 94–110.

59. "Khozhdenie Bogoroditsy po mukam," in N. Tikhonravov, *Pamiatniki otrechennoi russkoi literatury*, (Moscow, 1863), II, 23–30.

paraphernalia in the Byzantine legend. Here the Holy Virgin herself travels through the nether regions, with the Archangel Michael as her guide. The legend is permeated with deep religious feeling and sympathy for the suffering. Impressed by the tortures of sinners, the Virgin implores God to pardon them. At first He is implacable but finally agrees to send Christ to talk with the damned, and the Saviour promises them a period of rest once a year from Maundy Thursday to Pentecost. It is characteristic that according to the tale not only laymen but clergy as well, including bishops and monks, are found in the Inferno by the Holy Virgin.

It is obvious that the legend did not originate in official church circles and reflects rather the spirit of the humble layman. This is also seen in the attitude of the Virgin toward heretics, whom she blames, but moderately; the only ones whom, as a mòther, she cannot forgive are those responsible for Christ's passion and death.

The greatest representative of early Russian monasticism, St. Feodosi, was—judging from his "Life"—closer in spirit to popular Christianity than to the learned theologians.

The foundations of monasticism, as Feodosi preached [60] and practiced them, were prayer, humility, work, and charity. Even as abbot he wore shabby clothes and did not shun any manual work. He was against ascetic excesses, for which he was blamed by the disciples of Antoni, the founder of the monastery—a recluse whose followers insisted on living in subterranean cells. It was Feodosi who succeeded in moving the monastery from underground up the hill. Although he attempted to introduce the Byzantine monastic statutes, Feodosi was not a strong disciplinarian, preferring to lead by setting an example to the brethren in his own behavior. The results were often unsatisfactory and some of his opponents complained of laxity of monastic discipline during his priorship. He himself was aware of failures but continued to believe in advice and moral self-improvement rather than disciplinary measures.

That the true spirit of Christianity revealed itself in Kievan Russia, not only through its monks but through laymen as well, may best be seen from Vladimir Monomach's "Testament."

So far, for the sake of simplification, I have dealt with Greek Orthodox Christianity only, which became Russia's official religion in 988 and to which the majority of converted Russians belonged.

60. For the text of Feodosi's sermons, see Ponomarev, I, 33–43. On Feodosi see Fedotov, *op. cit.*, 110–131.

However, in addition to the established church the Russian people in the Kievan period were influenced by diverse other currents of religious thought.

First of all, the so-called "Bogomil heresy" must be mentioned here.[61] This was a branch of Manichaeism, a dualistic religion which originated in Persia in the third century A.D. In the tenth and eleventh centuries a section of the Bulgarian clergy and a considerable number of laymen in Bulgaria fell under its influence. According to Manichaeism, two forces rule the world: the evil principle and the good, or, as the Bogomils put it, God and Satan. God represents the spiritual element and Satan the material. This dualism is reflected in man, since his flesh is created by Satan and only his soul by God.

Prominent among the Bulgarian heretics of the tenth century was the priest Jeremiah, to whom a compendium of apocrypha is attributed; and indeed, in some of the apocrypha—as for example that on Adam and Eve—traits of Manichaeism may be observed. The Bogomil doctrine became popular among the poor and the oppressed, since it offered an explanation of the origin of social inequality.

Considering everything material to be evil, the Bogomils abhorred wealth and denounced the rich as Satan's retainers. They also opposed the established church, with its riches. In the twelfth and the thirteenth centuries the "heresy" spread westward to northern Italy and southern France, where its adherents became known as the Cathari and Albigenses, respectively. In view of the close connection between Bulgaria and Russia, the Bogomil movement may easily have penetrated into Russia as well and there is in fact some evidence of the acquaintance of the Russians with Manichaeism.[62]

The apocrypha presented a convenient channel for the spread of the Bogomil ideas to Russia but it may also be supposed that outright expositions of the Manichaean doctrine were likewise available. A prominent Russian monk, St. Avraami of Smolensk, was accused by his opponents of reading a heretical work known as *Glubinnaia Kniga, The Book of Depth,* which may have been a Manichaean treatise.

---

61. On the Bogomils, see F. Rački, "Bogomili i Patareni," *Rad Jugoslavenske Akademije,* 7 (1869), 48–179; *8* (1869), 121–187; *10* (1870), 160–263; Zlatarski, *Istoriia na Bulgarskata Drzhava prez Srednite Vekove,* I, Pt. 2, pp. 551–559; II (Sofia, 1934), 352–366; V. N. Sharenkoff, *A Study of Manichaeism in Bulgaria* (New York, Columbia University Press, 1927); D. Obolensky, *The Bogomils* (Cambridge, Cambridge University Press, 1948).

62. *Istoriia Russkoi literatury,* I, 83–86.

That Bogomil ideas were preached in Russia may be seen from the story of the boyar Ian, son of Vyshata, recorded in the *Book of Annals*. In 1071 Ian came to the Beloozero district in northern Russia to collect tribute and there had a dispute with certain magicians who declared that "the devil made man, and God set a soul in him." [63]

It should be noted that Bulgaria was not the only possible source of Manichaeism for Kievan Russia. In view of the lively commercial intercourse with Oriental countries, a contact with Manichaeans in central Asia may easily have been established.

Of other religions and denominations, Roman Catholicism and Judaism had a number of followers in Kievan Russia. The influence of Judaism has already been mentioned in another connection (Chap. VI, sec. 11).

As to Roman Catholicism, its adherents were chiefly German merchants staying in Russia. There was a Roman Catholic church in Smolensk and two in Novgorod. A Dominican monastery in Kiev is mentioned in western sources. [64] In spite of the fact that the break between the Greek and the Roman churches was made final in 1054, the attitude of the Russians toward Roman Catholicism was not belligerent in this period and individual Russians did not shun contact with Roman Catholics; in any case, certainly neither the princes nor the merchants.

It is significant that all the anti-Catholic polemic treatises which circulated in Russia in the Kievan period were either translations from the Greek or written by Greeks in Russia. [65]

## 8. Literature

Belles-lettres, especially fiction, were not fully emancipated in the Middle Ages. The medieval reader was attracted to books not so much by their literary value, if any, as by the moral education or instruction of some kind to be extracted from the narrative. The church in its turn encouraged the moralistic tendency in order to use it for Chris-

63. Cross, pp. 239–244.

64. On the Church of Rome and Roman Catholicism in Kievan Russia, see W. Abraham, *Powstanje organizacji kościoła lacinskiego na Rusi* (Lvov, 1904); Hrushevsky, III, 298–301; M. Shaitan, "Germaniia i Kiev v XI veke," *LZ, 34* (1927), 23–26.

65. On the relations between the Russian church of the Kievan period and Roman Catholicism, see Golubinsky, *Istoriia*, I, Pt. 1 (2d ed. Moscow, 1904), pp. 588–603; N. Baumgarten, "Chronologie ecclésiastique des terres russes du X au XIII siècle," *OC*, No. 58 (1930); B. Leib, *Rome, Kiev et Byzance à la fin du XI-e siècle*.

tian indoctrination and therefore sponsored every kind of didactic poetry or prose along this line.

Owing to these circumstances, in speaking of Russian literature of the Kievan period we have to deal not only with fiction and belles-lettres proper but with intermediate types such as didactic or instructive literature, and even with religious literature in so far as it had artistic value.

The Bible, in Kievan Russia as in the medieval west, was the main source not only of religious inspiration but of creative literature as well. The influence of the Bible was even much more direct in Russia than in the west, since the Russians could read and enjoy it in a language close to the vernacular.

From the point of view of literary development the influence of the Old Testament was more important than that of the New. The Russians of this period used the Old Testament chiefly in the condensed form of the so-called *Paleia,* whose compiler did not discriminate between canonical books and the apocrypha.[66] This, however, made the compendium even more attractive to the Russian reader. Besides the Bible he had at his disposal translations of various other works of religious literature and Byzantine literature in general. From the point of view of literary history, the church hymns, lives of saints, and instructive legends of various kinds were the most important among the specimens of Byzantine religious and semi-religious literature made available to the Russians.

It must be noted that no work of Greek belles-lettres, either classic or Byzantine, except for one Byzantine epic poem written in "vulgar" Greek, was translated into Russian in the Middle Ages. Presumably this was due to the guiding hand of the church, if not directly to church censorship.

Whether the average Russian of the Kievan period would have appreciated Sophocles or Euripides is another question. He would probably have enjoyed Homer, as the metropolitan Kliment, who is said to have read Homer in Greek, apparently did. The erotic novel of the late Hellenistic and early Byzantine periods might have had a strong appeal to some of the Russian literati at least and we may well imagine the author of *Daniil Zatochnik* reading *Daphnis*

66. The so-called "historical" *Paleia* was published in *Chteniia* 1881, Pt. 1, under the editorship of A. N. Popov; the *Paleia* with commentaries (*tolkovaia*), in *OLDP,* No. 93 (1892).

*and Chloe* with considerable delight, even if he thundered against the "evil women."

Turning now to the apocrypha it must be pointed out that some of them originated in the Orient—in Syria, Egypt, and even India. Byzantium served as their depository, from which they were subsequently borrowed by Russia and western Europe. It is only with reservations that Christian and pseudo-Christian legends of the apocryphal type may be called Byzantine, except for a few.

Among the Christian apocrypha the "Virgin Mary's Journey through the Inferno" became especially popular in Russia, as I have noted. Of the non-Christian apocrypha the "Story of Solomon and Kitovras" is representative. It is one of the legends of the building of the temple by Solomon. Stones for the purpose had to be hewn without the use of iron tools and to perform this work Solomon tamed, by ruse, a magician by the name of Kitovras ("Centaur"). The latter is portrayed as a seer of the future and interpreter of riddles and dreams. In the west the same theme appears in the legends of Merlin as well as those of Solomon and Morolphe.[67]

In the field of didactic biographical legend the "Story of Varlaam and Iosaf" (Barlaam and Josaphat) met with great response on the part of the Russian reader. Originating in India, it represents a variation of the life of Buddha. In the eighth century it was adapted to the Christian mentality and rewritten in Greek by John of Damascus, according to a tradition which is not very reliable.[68] Its central theme is the vanity of all earthly life, its hero a prince who abandons his throne to become a hermit.

To the same genre of didactic literature the "Story of Akir the Wise" (Ahikar) belongs, likewise a favorite with the Russians.[69] The story seems to have originated in Babylonia in the seventh century B.C. and must have been adapted to Byzantine tastes at about the same period as the "Story of Varlaam and Iosaf." The hero, Akir,

67. A. N. Veselovsky, *Slavianskie skazaniia o Solomone i Kitovrase i zapadnye legendy o Morolfe i Merline* (St. Petersburg, 1872; 2d ed. in Veselovsky's collected works, *Sobranie Sochinenii*, VIII [Petrograd, 1921]); Tikhonravov, *op. cit.*, I, 254–258.

68. For the Greek text of "Barlaam and Josaphat," see *PG*, XCVI. The earliest Russian manuscript extant is dated in the sixteenth century but its style shows that the translation had been made long before. The Russian text was first published in Moscow in 1680.

69. "The Story of Akir the Wise" was translated into Slavic in the eleventh century. The earliest extant manuscript dates from the fifteenth century. See A. D. Grigoriev, "Povest ob Akire Premudrom," *UW*, 1913, Pt. 4; Sakulin, *op. cit.*, I, 118.

is represented as a grandee falsely accused of treason, the calumniator being his nephew. The king orders Akir executed, from which fate he is saved by an old friend. Subsequently the kingdom is threatened by enemies and it is Akir who saves it by his wisdom; he does not hold any grudge against the king but punishes his nephew. The moral: "Whoever digs a pit for another to fall in, falls there himself."

Of quite a different nature is the legendary biography of Alexander the Great, one of the most popular fantastic novels of the late hellenistic and early medieval period. A Russian translation of "Alexandria" appeared in probably the eleventh or twelfth century; no full manuscript of it has been preserved but parts of the novel were included in the old Russian compilation of world history known as *The Greek and Roman Annals* (see sec. 10, below).[70]

Quite apart from the learned Byzantine tradition stood the Greek folk poem, *Digenis Akritas*, an epic of Byzantine frontiersmen in Anatolia defending Christianity against Islam. The poem appeared in the tenth century and the Russian translation of it in the twelfth, under the title *Devgenievo Deianie* (*The Deeds of Digenis*). The translation is in excellent style, reminding one of the *Lay of Igor's Campaign;* indeed, it may be surmised that the author of the *Lay* was well acquainted with *Digenis*.[71]

The original Russian literature of the Kievan period followed to a considerable extent the Byzantine pattern as revealed in Slavic translations. It would be a mistake, however, to deduce from this that the Russian authors showed no creative power of their own. On the contrary, some of them reached the very heights of literary art.

In the field of didactic church literature and hymnography, Bishop Kirill of Turov was one of the most popular authors. In both his hymns and his sermons he showed a considerable literary skill in spite of his abuse of conventional rhetoric. Of the lives of saints, the anonymous story of the passion of Ss. Boris and Gleb is perhaps the best from the point of view of literary technique.

But it is the metropolitan Ilarion who towers above all others, not only by the contents of his writings but also by their form. In his "Discourse on Law and Grace" (see Chap. III, sec. 5), he shows himself one of the truly great masters of the art of rhetoric. The "Discourse" is excellently planned and every detail in it is a jewel of high

70. V. M. Istrin, *Aleksandriia Russkikh khronografov* (Moscow, 1893).

71. Henri Grégoire, *Digenis Akritas* (New York, The National Herald, 1942) (in Modern Greek) ; M. N. Speransky, "Devgenievo Deianie," *ANORS, 99*, No. 7 (1922).

order. Ilarion uses various devices of literary ornament, such as symbolic parallelism, metaphors, antitheses, rhetorical questions, and so on, all with a perfect sense of proportion.

In lay literature, historical narrative was the field for which the Russians showed predilection. The *Book of Annals* (see sec. 10, below) is not only a historical treatise but likewise a compendium of historical novels and short stories. Each of these stories purports to be an accurate record of the event described, and most of them certainly are. But at the same time many a story has high artistic value and in some fiction obviously prevails over fact. Among the historical and pseudohistorical accounts included in the *Book* are, for example, that of Oleg's campaign to Byzantium; of Olga's revenge upon the Drevlianians for the murder of her husband; the so-called "Korsun Legend" of Vladimir's conversion; the story of the blinding of Prince Vasilko; that of Prince Igor of Novgorod-Seversk's disastrous campaign against the Cumans; and many others.

Some of these stories must have been borrowed from various epic poems which originated among the members of the princely druzhina; others represent honest narratives of fact, like the Vasilko story— this was apparently written by the priest who consoled the unfortunate prince after the cruel mutilation to which he was subjected. Some of the other stories must have been written down by the chronicler on the basis of what he heard from eyewitnesses of the events; still others must have circulated separately. In some cases, while one version of the story was included in the chronicle, variants existed independently outside the chronicler's ken. Such was the case with Prince Igor's campaign, of which two records were included in two versions of the chronicle, while simultaneously a heroic poem was written on the subject, the famous *Lay*.[72]

As Ilarion's discourse is the superlative embodiment of the old Russian learned literature, so is the *Lay* the peak of old Russian poetry. As a matter of fact, scholars still argue as to whether the *Lay* is written in verse or in rhythmic prose; in either case, it is poetry at its height and its language is racy and powerful.

The *Lay* is essentially dynamic; at its core it is a record of military valor. Some episodes are lyric, however, like that of the infatuation of a captive Russian youth for a Cuman princess—only casually hinted at—or the laments of Igor's wife.

72. H. Grégoire, R. Jakobson, *et al.,* "La Geste d'Igor," *Annuaire, 8* (1948); A. S. Orlov, *Slovo o Polku Igoreve;* V. Peretts, *Slovo o Polku Igorevim* (Kiev, 1926).

Behind the personal drama of the defeated Igor emerges the national tragedy of Russia, torn as she was at the time by interprincely discords and harassed by the constant inroads of the steppe nomads. Portraits of the Russian princes mentioned in the story are vivid and forceful. The steppe through which the Russians move to their defeat, the animal life around the marching warriors, the armor and vestments, both Russian and Cuman, all are described not only with the true spirit of poetry but with a remarkable factual accuracy.

The *Lay* is permeated with pagan spirit. Whether to the author the names of the Slavic gods he mentions meant something in religious sense or whether he invokes them by way of poetic license only is hard to say. In any case the spirit of the poem is not Christian in the ecclesiastical sense and if the author was a member of the Church he must have been a poor one. He apparently belonged to the druzhina of the prince of Chernigov and was well acquainted with Russian folklore and well read in historical and epic literature, including the *Judaic War* by Josephus Flavius and the *Digenis Akritas*.

In the opening stanzas the author invokes a bard of older times, Baian, as his ideal, although he will not follow Baian's style and asserts his freedom to write in his own way. This Baian must have been a contemporary of Prince Mstislav of Tmutorokan, also mentioned in the *Lay;* none of his works has been preserved.

The only known manuscript of the *Lay of Igor's Campaign* was a copy made in Pskov in the fifteenth century. It was discovered by Musin-Pushkin in 1795 and a transcript was then made for Empress Catherine II. The *Lay* was published in 1800 and in 1812 Musin-Pushkin's manuscript perished in the Moscow fire of Napoleon's invasion. Catherine's transcript and the first edition (for which Musin-Pushkin's manuscript was used) are all that remain as documentary evidence. Since both are full of copyist's mistakes and typographical errors, the exegesis of the *Lay* is an extremely difficult task.

However, in spite of the fact that only one manuscript survived until 1812—or at least, only one was ever discovered—we know that the *Lay* was read and admired in the thirteenth and fourteenth centuries. A passage from it was quoted in the early thirteenth century in a version of the book called the *Petition of Daniil Zatochnik,* while in the late fourteenth century it served as a model for *Zadonschina,* a historical poem glorifying the Russian victory over the Mongols in 1380.

The *Petition of Daniil Zatochnik* is another remarkable work of the old Russian literature.[73] As in the case of the *Lay*, the author remained anonymous. Judging from the contents of the work, he must have been a minor retainer (*dvorianin*)—possibly a former slave— of one of the Suzdalian princes. *Zatochnik* in old Russian means a prison inmate and it has therefore been suggested that the *Petition* must have been written by a disgraced courtier whom his prince imprisoned. Such an explanation of the circumstances in which the work was written is hardly tenable. The *Petition* is not a biographical document but a satire. In an elaborate rhetorical style the author implores the prince to make use of his (the author's) talents. He represents himself as a persecuted pauper and confesses his aversion to military service but vaunts his intellect and education and offers himself for the position of the prince's adviser. As evidence of his wisdom he intersperses his petition with ample quotations from the Bible, the Physiologus, "Pchela," the "Story of Akir the Wise," and so on. His tone is now humble to the point of servility, now arrogant or even revolutionary. At times he craves wealth, then ridicules those who are tempted by splendid vestments and rich food. He abhors the possibility of the prince's suggestion that he marry a wealthy girl and on that subject outdoes himself in strong invective against women. But, while representing himself as a misogynist, he also refuses to become a monk and finds expressive enough words to explain his aversion to monasticism; in fact, in one of the versions of the *Petition* the author's fiery opposition to the "black clergy" and the boyars assumes political significance.

In a way the *Petition* as a whole is a document of protest against human stupidity and social inequality, and an apology of wit. The author was apparently a well-educated man with a keen mind.

A no less remarkable human document, although of entirely different scope and tone, is Vladimir Monomach's autobiography, which constitutes a major part of his "Testament."[74] While the author of Daniil's *Petition* is one of the few Russian literati of the period, Vladimir is a soldier and statesman who merely records his deeds and ex-

73. P. P. Mindalev, *Molenie Daniila Zatochnika* (Kazan, 1914); N. N. Zarubin, ed., "Slovo Daniila Zatochnika," *Pamiatniki drevnerusskoi literatury*, III (Leningrad, 1932).

74. Cross, pp. 301–309; N. N. Shliakov, "O pouchenii Vladimira Monomakha," *ZMNP, 329* (1900), 96–138, 209–258; I. M. Ivakin, *Kniaz' Vladimir Monomakh i ego pouchenie*, I (Moscow, 1901); M. P. Alekseev, "Anglo-saksonskaia parallel' k poucheniiu Vladimira Monomakha," *ODRL*, II (1935) 39–80; A. S. Orlov, *Vladimir Monomakh* (Moscow and Leningrad, 1946).

periences. However, in doing so he exhibits a considerable gift for writing, which he must have cultivated by intense reading. His autobiography is not only permeated with lofty ideas but likewise displays his taste for a healthy life with its simple pleasures, as well as his admiration for the beauty of nature.

It must be said in conclusion of this section that our knowledge of the Russian literature of the Kievan period is but fragmentary. So many manuscripts of this time perished both during the Mongol invasion and after that we shall probably never know what we have lost with them. Furthermore, most of what was preserved has been found in church archives and the clergy had little reason to care to preserve specimens of the lay literature—especially with a pagan "deviation" like Igor's *Lay*, which explains the fact that only one copy of that work survived as long as it did.

Presumably not only the number of works but also the variety of style in the literature of the Kievan period was much greater than we are ordinarily prepared to admit.

### 9. Education

Like art, education in Kievan Russia was sponsored by both the church and the princes. The church needed a trained clergy; the princes, clerks for their administration. But there was more to it than mere practical considerations. Following Russia's conversion to Christianity both Prince Vladimir and the church leaders were faced with the immense task of spreading Christian culture in Russia, a task which they approached in a true missionary spirit. It is to the credit of Vladimir and his advisers that they built not only churches but schools as well. Thus compulsory baptism was followed by compulsory education.

So far as we can judge, not only from the chronicles but from casual reference in other sources as well, schools were thus founded not only in Kiev but also in provincial cities. From the "Life of St. Feodosi" we know that a school existed in Kursk around the year 1023. By the time of Iaroslav's reign (1019–54), education had struck roots and its benefits were apparent.

Around 1030 Iaroslav founded a divinity school in Novgorod for three hundred children of both laymen and clergy to be instructed "in book-learning." [75] As a general measure, he bade parish priests "teach the people." Presumably theological seminaries were planned

75. *PSRL*, IX, 79 (*A. D.* 1029).

in each eparchy under the supervision of the respective bishops.

Not content with establishing schools, Iaroslav conceived an ambitious plan for advancement of learning in Russia on broad foundations (see Chap. IV, sec. 3). It is not known how long Iaroslav's academy functioned; it can hardly have survived the sack of Kiev by Andrei Bogoliubsky's armies in 1169.

The example of Vladimir and Iaroslav in educational leadership must have inspired other Russian princes of the eleventh and twelfth centuries. Unfortunately the information available in the chronicles and other sources on education becomes very scanty for the period following Iaroslav's death (1054). Such data as we possess we owe mostly to that eminent Russian historian of the eighteenth century, V. N. Tatishchev, who had at his disposal some versions of chronicles since lost, as a result of which Tatishchev's *Russian History* contains much information on various subjects not otherwise available to us. Such is precisely the case with education in the late Kievan period. Many a supercritical modern historian has refused to accept Tatishchev's information as valid; in particular, Golubinsky has criticized his data on education in Kievan Russia in the late eleventh and the twelfth centuries as spurious.[76] Such summary rejection is certainly unjust; besides, in almost each case the validity of Tatishchev's information may be supported by consideration of the indirect evidence available.

Let us first take the case of Princess Anna (Ianka), daughter of Vsevolod I of Kiev. It is known that in 1086 Vsevolod founded a convent, in which Ianka took the veil. According to Tatishchev she organized there a school for girls, who were taught reading and writing as well as handicrafts and singing. Golubinsky derides the possibility of a woman's initiative in education in Russia at that period.[77] Yet it is known that other Russian princesses received good educations and were interested in learning. Ianka's aunt, Queen Anne of France, was, in any case able to sign her name (see Chap. XI, sec. 4). Princess Evfrosinia of Polotsk (1001-73), who like Ianka became a nun, was renowned not only for her beauty but also for her learning. As both Ianka and Evfrosinia seem to have been permeated by the same missionary spirit as Vladimir the Saint and Iaroslav the Wise,

---

76. Golubinsky, *Istoriia*, I, Pt. 1, pp. 871-880. See also A. Wanczura, *Szkolnictwo w starej Rusi*. It should be noted that later on, in his article on "schedography," Golubinsky had to admit that he had underestimated the level of Russian education in the Kievan period. See Sec. 10 (d) and n. 115, below.

77. Tatishchev, II, 138. Cf. Golubinsky, *Istoriia*, I, Pt. 1, p. 873.

Ianka's alleged attempt to sponsor the education of girls certainly should not seem to us extravagant.

An outstanding leader in education, according to Tatishchev, was Prince Roman of Smolensk (son of Rostislav I of Smolensk and Kiev). He is said to have founded in Smolensk several schools in which, among other subjects, Greek and Latin were taught. For the endowment of these schools Roman used all his fortune, so that when he died (in 1180) the people of Smolensk had to make a collection for his funeral.[78]

In Suzdalia Prince Konstantin, son of Vsevolod III, is credited by Tatishchev with collecting a Greek and Slavic library, organizing a translation project (from Greek to Russian), and bequeathing—in 1218—his house in Vladimir as well as part of the income from his estate to a school where Greek was to be taught.[79]

The authenticity of Tatishchev's information in both of these cases has been questioned. And yet, according to other sources available, both Smolensk and Suzdalia were important intellectual and artistic centers in the late twelfth and early thirteenth centuries and it would be hard to explain their cultural blossoming without the assumption that good schools existed at this period in both places, so that Tatishchev's data fit well into the general historical picture.

While we may surmise that there were both elementary and higher schools in Kievan Russia, we know little of the curriculum of either. A prayer book known as the *Book of the Hours* (*Chasoslov*) was used as the first reader, with the Psalter to follow. The school discipline must have been stern. From the "Life of St. Avraami of Smolensk" (thirteenth century) it may be seen that the students at times fell into despair [80] and in the so-called *Pchela,* a collection of aphorisms translated from the Greek, grammar school is mentioned as one of the "three woes," the other two being poverty and a vicious wife.[81] It appears that some children of princely and boyar families were sent to Constantinople for education. The author of *Daniil Zatochnik* remarks, among his other witticisms of a humble man: "I did not go overseas to take lessons from the philosophers"—which implies that some others did.

While no educational statistics for the period are available, it may

78. Tatishchev, iii, 238, 239.
79. *Idem*, III, 416.
80. Sobolevsky, *op. cit.,* p. 5.
81. *Ibid.*

safely be assumed that Russia at this time had a fair number of schools, at least in the cities, and that the percentage of literacy, at least among people of the upper classes, was high. In any case, the princes and the clergy were all' literate. Also, it must be assumed that there was formed in the Kievan society a real elite; not numerous, perhaps, but one which reached a high cultural level.

## 10. The Humanities

### a. Theology and Philosophy

Theology was the cornerstone of medieval spiritual culture in both western and eastern Europe—philosophy being considered the mere "handmaid of theology." In this respect the development of speculative thought followed in Kievan Russia the same general course as in Byzantium and the west.

Judging from the writings of some of the Russian clergy of the Kievan period, such as the metropolitans Ilarion and Kliment and Bishop Kirill, the Russian elite was then on the same intellectual level as in Byzantium and the west. However, the Russian learned men of the period left no systematic works in either theology or philosophy. Their writings—at least those which have been preserved— consist of sermons and brief essays. With due reservations, one must agree with the Reverend George Florovsky that the old Russian theological culture seems to have remained "mute" for several centuries; although, as the same author emphasizes, one should not deduce from the lack of philosophical self-expression in writing of the Kievan Russian that his mind was not cultivated enough for philosophical speculation.[82] An indication as to what people think may be given by what they read and consequently a brief survey of the works of Greek theological literature available to the Russians of the period in Slavic translation will not be out of place here.[83] It should be noted that old Russian translations from Latin are also known.[84]

82. G. Florovsky, *Puti Russkogo bogosloviia*, p. 1.

83. A. S. Arkhangelsky, *K izycheniiu drevnerusskoi literatury* (St. Petersburg, 1888), and *Tvoreniia otsov tserkvi v drevnerusskoi pismennosti*, I–IV (Kazan, 1889–90) (inaccessible to me); Golubinsky, *Istoriia*, I, Pt. 1, pp. 880–924.

84. See A. I. Sobolevsky, "Dva slova o drevnikh tserkovno-slavianskikh perevodakh s latinskogo," *ANORI, 2* (1904), Pt. 4, pp. 401–403, and *Zhitiia sviatykh v drevnem perevode na tserkovno-slavianskii s latinskogo iazyka* (St. Petersburg, 1904). See also A. V. Florovsky, *Chekhi i Vostochnye Slaviane,* I (Prague, 1935), 111.

At the time of Russia's conversion the New Testament was fully translated into Slavic. The Gospel was available in two forms. Some manuscripts contained the continued text of the four Gospels. This was known as the "Tetra-Evangel." In others, selections from the Gospels were arranged in the order in which they were read in church, according to the yearly cycle of services. This was called the "Aprakos." The Acts of the Apostles and the Epistles were available in a separate book, called *Apostol* (*The Apostle*). The books of the Old Testament each circulated separately and, when in the late fifteenth century Bishop Gennadi of Novgorod ordered them all collected in order to prepare a complete code of them, some were found missing, so that they had to be translated anew. The first printed Slavic edition of the whole Bible appeared in 1581.

Among the Old Testament books the Psalter was the favorite of the Russian reader. It was widely read among all classes of the people and often quoted. The prophets were likewise popular. Of the historical books there was an abridged collection known as *Paleia* (from the Greek *Palaia Diatheke*, "Old Testament") (see sec. 8, above). In it was included material not only from the canonical books but also from the apocrypha.

It should be noted that the term "apocrypha" is used in this discussion not in its Protestant connotation but in the sense it has in the Greek and Roman churches: thus the so-called deuterocanonical books (found in the Septuagint Version but not a part of the Hebrew Bible) are not considered apocrypha. Indices of books prohibited by the church existed in Byzantium and one of them appeared in Slavic translation in 1073 but, since there were several such indices the contents of which were not identical, some confusion was unavoidable, especially in a newly converted nation like Russia. Not only laymen but even bishops at times were unable firmly to discriminate between the "true" and the "false" books.

Among the apocrypha were the so-called "Gospels" of Jacob, Nicodemus, and Thomas; also variants of the story of Adam and Eve, of the twelve biblical patriarchs, of David and Solomon, and so on. One of the popular eschatological apocrypha, "Virgin Mary's Journey through the Inferno," has already been mentioned above. Incidentally, there is an interesting gloss in the Russian translation of the "Journey." Worship of the sun and moon and earth is given in the story as the reason for which some inmates of the Inferno have been confined there; at this juncture the Russian text adds, "also those who worshipped Troian, Khors, Veles, and Perun"—that is, the gods of Slavic paganism.[85]

Two basic manuals of Orthodox Christian doctrine were available in Slavic translation: *The Catechetic Sermons* by St. Cyril of Jerusalem and the *Exact Exposition of the Orthodox Faith* by John of Damascus. The latter was translated by Exarch John of Bulgaria in the tenth century, in abridged form.[86] Among other works of the pre-Byzantine and Byzantine fathers, some of the treatises of Athanasius of Alexandria, Basil the Great, and Gregory Nazianzen are represented by Slavic manuscripts of Bulgarian and early Russian origin. A fragment of the *Logos Katecheticos* of Gregory of Nyssa and two excerpts from Maxim the Confessor's works are included in Sviatoslav's *Collection* (*Izbornik*) of 1073.[87]

There is little evidence in this period of independent Russian work in dogmatics. While Metropolitan Ilarion thoroughly mastered the principles of Christian philosophy and theology, his approach—at least judging from his "Discourse on Law and Grace"—is from the angle of philosophy of history rather than from that of scholasticism.

Kirill of Turov's sermons came closer to dogmatic speculation but, while they show the constructive abilities of his mind, they hardly add anything important to the Byzantine store of theological knowledge. Kirill emphasizes the gulf between God and man and makes little effort to bridge it. His Christ is an implacable judge rather than the "Son of Man." Repentance and obedience are man's chief virtues but even if he excels in them he has little hope for salvation.

Kliment of Smolensk (Smoliatich), Metropolitan of Kiev from 1147 to 1155, was considered by his contemporaries the main luminary of Russian theology. Says the chronicler: "Never before in Russia has there been such a philosopher as Kliment." This prelate appears to have read Homer, Plato, and Aristotle. In any case, he was criticized for quoting from them by narrow-minded Christian rigorists such as the priest Foma of Smolensk. Incidentally, it may be pointed out here that in the Byzantine schools of the eleventh and twelfth centuries the reading of Homer was obligatory and Byzantine theo-

85. Tikhonravov, *op. cit.*, II, 23.
86. Published in *Chteniia*, 1877, Pt. 4.
87. The *Izbornik* of 1073 is published phototypically by the *OLDP*, 1880; see also *Chteniia*, 1883, Pt. 4.

logians of this period were fond of looking to Homer for allegorical parallels for the interpretation of Scripture.[88] Unfortunately the manuscript of only one epistle of Kliment has been preserved and even that is not the original text but a revision by a pupil, one Afanasi. It is addressed to the above-mentioned Foma, against whose criticism Kliment defends his method of allegorical and symbolic exegesis.[89]

Turning now to the philosophical literature as distinct from the theological (in so far as the two can be dissociated for the period), the *Dialectics* (*Philosophical Chapters*) by John of Damascus is based upon Aristotle but the earliest known manuscript of this important work in Slavic translation dates from the fifteenth century; a short excerpt from the "Dialectics" was, however, included in Sviatoslav's *Izbornik* of 1073. On Plato, the Russian reader of the Kievan period could, if he knew no Greek, obtain some general information—as well as misinformation—from Georgius Monachus' *Chronicon* and from John Malalas' *Chronographia*.[90]

Neoplatonism is best represented in Byzantine Christian literature by the treatise of Pseudo-Dionysius the Areopagite on the "Celestial Hierarchy." There is no evidence of any Slavic translation of this work prior to the fifteenth century. It seems then that the average Russian reader of the Kievan period could become acquainted with the thought of classical and hellenistic philosophers only through the meager excerpts from their works included in various collections of aphorisms which were extremely popular both in Byzantium and Russia. One of the best known of these collections is the so-called *Melissa* (*Bee*), which was compiled in Greek in the eleventh century and translated into Slavic probably in the twelfth century, under the name of *Pchela*.[91] It contains quotations from the works of Democritus, Plato, Aristotle, Philo, Epictetus, and others. To be sure, neither these quotations nor the summary of classical and hellenistic phi-

88. N. Skabalanovich, "Vizantiiskaia nauka i shkoly v XI veke," *Khristianskoe Chtenie*, 1884, Pt. 1, pp. 344–369, 730–770; M. Speransky, *Perevodnye sborniki izrechenii v Slaviano-Russkoi pismennosti* (Moscow, 1904), p. 64.

89. Kh. M. Loparev, ed., "Poslanie Mitropolita Klimenta," *Pamiatniki Drevnei Pismennosti*, XC (St. Petersburg, 1892); N. K. Nikolsky, *O literaturnykh trudakh Klimenta Smoliaticha*.

90. See M. V. Shakhmatov and D. Chizhevsky, "Platon v drevnei Rusi," *RIOP, 2* (Prague, 1930), 49–81.

91. V. Semenov, ed., "Drevniaia russkaia Pchela," *ANORS, 54,* No. 4 (1893); Speransky, *Perevodnye sborniki izrechenii v Slaviano-Russkoi pismennosti*, pp. 155–328.

losophy in the patristic works could replace the originals but we should not forget that the medieval reader was able to extract from his sources much more than we might expect. That reader—at least the typical one—did not skim his book. His was what may be called a static method of reading: he read a paragraph at a time and pondered over each sentence. Given a few basic ideas of any philosopher, he was able to reconstruct at least part of the argument, if not always along the philosopher's original line.

The above considerations bear on the reader familiar with the Slavic language only. But, as I have pointed out on several occasions, there was also in Kievan Russia a small elite to whom the Greek originals were accessible as well. Besides, many of the Russian bishops and abbots of the Kievan period were Greeks by origin and education, and these likewise served as intermediaries between Byzantine and Russian scholarship.

## b. History

In their historical writings the Russian scholars of this period showed much more maturity, and achieved more independence, than in the fields of theology and philosophy. It was, of course, to Byzantine historical literature that the Russians first looked for a pattern to follow but once started they were soon able to proceed on their own.

The initiative in recording historical events belonged to the clergy, more particularly to the monks. The first Russian chronicle appears to have been written in Novgorod in the early eleventh century and the first comprehensive history of Russia appeared in Kiev a century later. It was called the *Book of Annals* (*Povest' Vremennykh Let*).

In some of the later copies of the *Book* its authorship is ascribed to the monk Nestor of the Monastery of the Caves at Kiev. As we know (see sec. 7, above), Nestor is the author of two biographical essays, the "Discourse" ("Chtenie") on the two prince-martyrs, Boris and Gleb, and the "Life of Feodosi," abbot of the monastery. Nestor was born around 1056 and died some time after 1112. That he was also the author of the *Book of Annals* is denied by many outstanding scholars. The problem of the authorship of the *Book* is a moot one, especially since it must be connected with that of the nature of the work as a whole. Until the late nineteenth century it was considered a monolithic piece of work, written by one man at one time. Further studies, especially those by A. A. Shakhmatov, have shown that in its final form it is a compilation based upon a number of earlier chronicles.[92]

The first Kievan chronicle seems to have been started in 1039 and its origin should apparently be connected with the organization of the Kievan diocese about that year, as well as with Iaroslav's educational reforms. Presumably the writing of the chronicle was sponsored by the metropolitan of Kiev. Later on, a copy of it was sent to the Monastery of the Caves, whose monks undertook the recording of further events.

Around 1073 a revision of both the original chronicle and the supplementary notes was undertaken by the then leading monk of the monastery, Nikon the Great.

It is supposed that in 1095, following the death of Prince Vsevolod, the Kievan chronicle was revised once more with the addition of some new materials. Then, around 1110, presumably at the initiative of Prince Sviatopolk II, a more ambitious project was started by the monks of the Monastery of the Caves—that of writing, on the basis of the earlier chronicles, a comprehensive history of Russia. This was the first version of the *Book of Annals*.

According to Priselkov, Nestor was the chief editor of this work.[93] However, S. A. Bugoslavsky has shown that the literary style, as well as the interpretation of some events, in the *Book of Annals* differs from that of the two "Lives" written by Nestor.[94] In any case the first version of the *Book* was not "published," in the sense in which the phrase may be applied to manuscripts.

With the death of Sviatopolk II and the accession to the throne of Vladimir II, the position of the Monastery of the Caves was somewhat undermined. By order of the new government the copy of the *Book of Annals* was taken from the monastery and sent to another one more favored by Vladimir—the St. Michael Monastery at Vydubichi. There the manuscript was revised by Sylvester, the abbot there (1114–16). In 1118 a new edition of the *Book* was prepared by an anonymous writer. Traces of all these various versions are still discernible in the extant codices, of which the Laurentian of the late

92. A. A. Shakhmatov, *Razyskaniia o sostave drevneishikh letopisnykh svodov* (St. Petersburg, 1908), also *Povest' Vremennykh Let*, I, and "Povest' Vremennykh Let i ee istochniki," *ODRL*, 4 (1940), 11–150. See also M. D. Priselkov, *Istoriia Russkogo letopisaniia XI–XV vekov* (Leningrad, 1940).

93. M. D. Priselkov, *Nestor Letopisets* (Petrograd, 1923).

94. S. A. Bugoslavsky, "K voprosu o kharaktere i ob'eme literaturnoi deiatelnosti Nestora," *ANORI* 1914, Pts. 1, 3.

fourteenth century and the Hypatian of the early fifteenth century are the two outstanding. The main difference between the first ("Nestor's") edition of the *Book* and the two following (Sylvester's and the anonymous one) is in the attitude of the respective editors toward princely policies. While "Nestor" is critical of Vsevolod I and sympathetic to Sviatopolk II, both Sylvester and the anonymous editor are unfriendly to Sviatopolk II and admirers of Vsevolod's son Vladimir Monomach. In a sense we have here a case of the debate between the "Byzantinophiles" (Vsevolod and his son Vladimir) and the "Westernizers" (Sviatopolk II).

Except for the varying editorial touches, basically the *Book of Annals* is the fruit of the labors of the first editor ("Nestor"). It is not a mere record of events but a comprehensive treatise on the origins and development of the Kievan realm; a combination of what Hegel calls "original history" and "reflective history." The *Book* starts with a geographical and ethnographical survey of the Slavic world, against which the formation of the Kievan state and the main events of Russian history down to 1110 are then described.

The Christianization of Russia and her struggle against the steppe nomads constitute the two main themes. The compiler's philosophy of history is akin to that of the Byzantine historians and western annalists of the period. He has a keen feeling of Providence and is therefore apt to moralize on history and politics. In his view, the misfortunes which afflict mankind are God's punishment for men's sins. The compiler or compilers used manifold materials in the preparation of the *Book*—such as the works of some of the Byzantine histories available in Slavic translation; archive documents, such as the Russo-Byzantine treaties; earlier Russian chronicles and records, etc. Statements by eye witnesses of events described, as for example by the Chiliarch Ian or the priest Vasili, have also been used. In many cases, however, the chronicler's narrative is based upon some less reliable source—a folk poem or a legend. These are easily discernible and can hardly mislead the modern reader.

In addition to the *Book of Annals* several other chronicles were written in the Kievan period. Among them the Novgorodian chronicle, the Kievan chronicle of the mid-twelfth century, the Volynian and Galician chronicles of the late twelfth and early thirteenth centuries, and the Suzdalian chronicle of the same period may be mentioned here.[95] Besides works of native scholarship the Russian reader had

95. See Sources, III, 1.

at his disposal Slavic translations of a number of works of the Byzantine historians, such as John Malalas (*The Greek and Roman Annals,* of the sixth century), Georgius Synkellus (late eighth and early ninth centuries), and Georgius Monachus (ninth century). In addition, the *History of the Judaic War* by Josephus Flavius (first century) was translated into Slavic in the eleventh century and enjoyed considerable popularity in medieval Russia.[96]

### c. Political Thought

Following Russian conversion to Christianity, the political thought of educated Russians—what we may call the Russian intelligentsia of the Kievan period—was conditioned by Christian ideals. As in western Europe, the Bible was for the Russian of this age the fountainhead not only of religious wisdom and literary inspiration but of political and social philosophy as well. Byzantine philosophical and political treatises constituted another source of development for Russian political thought. But neither the political philosophy of the Bible nor that of the Byzantine writers is monolithic. In various parts of both the Old and New Testament, as well as in the works of the Byzantine writers, different ideas were expounded. Thus, for example, in the Old Testament quotations both for the support of monarchical government (Deuteronomy 17.14–20) and against it (I Samuel 8.10–18) may be found. In the Byzantine political writings likewise there exists a considerable variety of opinion on the nature of monarchical authority. There were in Byzantium, for example, two schools of thought concerning the relations between the emperor and the church, each emphasizing the prerogative of one of them.[97] It is obvious, then, that while the Russians had much material at their disposal in the Biblical and Byzantine political literature—as well as in classical philosophy—they had to make their own selection of

96. John Malalas, *Chronographia,* Slavic Version, V. M. Istrin, ed., *ANZI,* Ser. 8, Vol. I, No. 3 (1897), *NUIF, 10* (1902), *13* (1905), and *17* (1913); *ANORS, 89,* No. 3 (1911), and No. 7 (1912); *90,* No. 2 (1913); *91,* No. 2 (1914). On the Slavic version of Georgius Synkellus' *Chronographia,* see V. M. Istrin, ed., *Khronika Georgiia Amartola* (Leningrad, 1920–30. 3 vols.), II, 286–289, and M. Weingart, *Byzantské kroniky v literature cirkevneslovanské,* I, 52–54. The Slavic version of Georgius Monachus' "Chronicle" has been edited by Istrin, *Khronika Georgiia Amartola.* For the Slavic version of Flavius Josephus, see V. M. Istrin and A. Vaillant, ed., *La Prise de Jerusalème de Josèphe le Juif* (Paris, 1934–1938. 2 vols.).

97. See G. Vernadsky. "Vizantiiskie ucheniia o vlasti tsaria i patriarkha," *Recueil N. P. Kondakov* (Prague, 1926), pp. 143–154. G. Ostrogorsky, "Otnoshenie tserkvi i gosudarstva v Vizantii," *SK, 4* (1931), 121–134.

it and to ponder over it seriously in building up a system of political ideas of their own, best adapted to reality.[98]

While no comprehensive treatise on government appeared in Kievan Russia, many interesting observations and remarks on the topic may be found in the various sermons and epistles of Russian bishops and monks of the period, as well as in the *Book of Annals*. An examination of these excerpts may provide us with a pretty clear idea of the main trends of political thought among the Russian intelligentsia of the time. All the Russian writers of the period accept the institution of monarchy; none, however, is in sympathy with absolutism. It is significant that nowhere in the Russian writings of the period can any reference be found to the principle of Roman imperial law: "the ruler is not bound by the laws" (*princeps legibus solutus est*). On the contrary, in almost every Russian discourse on government it is emphasized that the ruler is bound by the law. Thus the monk Iakov in his epistle to Prince Dimitri (which was the Christian name of Iziaslav I), written around 1072, insists that the ruler should not "abandon his guiding principles," even under threat of force, and should not tolerate any arbitrariness in his administration.[99] By "law" and "guiding principles," the Russian writers understood chiefly the Christian moral law but also the established practices of just government. They do not advocate any definite legal limitations of the princely power. It may be noticed in this connection that it was only toward the close of the period that the first European constitutional charters were granted: the Magna Carta in 1215 and the Golden Bull of Hungary in 1222. On the other hand, the city of Novgorod even in the Kievan period had limited princely authority by special charters and these charters may be considered as so many elements of a general constitutional law. Unfortunately none of the Novgorodian charters of the pre-Mongolian period has been preserved (see Chap. VII, sec. 6). Nor were the customs of Novgorod recommended in any of the learned Russian political discourses of the period. In this respect Russian political theory lagged behind the political realities. This being so and constitutional guarantees being nowhere advocated in Russian political writing, the crux of the problem for the writers lay in the moral and intellectual character of the prince. In

---

98. On Russian political thought of the Kievan period, see V. Valdenberg, *Drevnerusskie ucheniia o predelakh tsarskoi vlasti* (Petrograd, 1916); also M. V. Shakhmatov, *Ucheniia Russkikh letopisei domongolskogo perioda o gosudarstvennoi vlasti*, I–II.

99. Iakov's epistle is published in Makarii, II, 324–327.

this sense the Russians followed Plato's idea of the king-philosopher. "He who accepts great authority should have a great mind," reads a quotation from Plato in *Pchela*.[100]

Accordingly, the *Book of Annals* praises good princes and fulminates against the bad ones. The good prince reveres law and justice and establishes his administration along these lines. The bad prince— personally he need not be a bad man—neglects the administration and lets his agents plunder the people. To prevent misrule the prince must rely on the advice of experienced "councilors"—that is, on the council, or Duma, of the boyars (see Chap. VII, sec. 3 b). If he breaks the tradition and surrounds himself with young and inexperienced councilors whom he himself selects—as, according to the *Book of Annals*, Prince Vsevolod I did toward the end of his life—the result is a mismanagement of affairs and ruin of the people.

This amounts to a mild approval of the aristocratic element in government. As to the democratic element, the veche, no attention is paid to it in the political discourses which have been preserved. However, traces of democratic tendencies in Russian political thought may be seen in the chronicles. Thus we find in the Laurentian chronicle the following statement: "From aboriginal times, the Novgorodians, as well as the Smolensk, and the Kiev, and the Polotsk men, and the people of other lands, used to assemble for the veche for the deliberation of their affairs." [101] This is not so much a statement of fact as it is a presentation of the political claims of Novgorodian democrats.

While no such specific claims are preferred in the learned political discourses known to us, we find in several of them an expression of the general idea of a moral compact between the prince and the people. A bad prince, who breaks this compact, invokes the wrath of God. Calamities such as famines and wars are God's punishment for men's sins. The prince and the people are bound by a common historical link and either is responsible for the sins of others. On this, the Russian of the period could read in *Pchela:* "The state perishes either through men's faults or from God's visitation." The first phrase is based on Plato; [102] the second has been added by the Christian editor. The attitude of the intelligent Russian toward the problem was anything but passive. If the people were perverted, the prince had to re-

100. Semenov, *op. cit.*, p. 104, based upon Plato, *Republic*, V, 18 (473); cf. *Republic*, VII, 5 (520).

101. *PSRL*, I, Pt. 2 (2d ed. 1927), cols. 377, 378.

102. Plato, *Leges*, p. 683 E.

educate them. If the prince was bad, the people had to replace him by another. In this spirit of active resistance to evil, the Russian might find guidance in another aphorism ascribed to Plato which he could likewise read in *Pchela:* "He who abstains from injustice is to be honored; but he who prevents others from doing injustice deserves even more credit; if the first is worthy of a crown, the second deserves several crowns." [103]

## d. Philology

The great work of Ss. Cyril and Methodius, which had at first a specific object only—the adaptation of Slavic to the needs of the church—resulted in giving impetus to Slavic culture and civilization at large. Indeed, the Slavic apostles themselves were filled with enthusiasm for their cultural mission.

To his translation of the Gospel Constantine the philosopher (St. Cyril) wrote a remarkable poetic foreword.[104] It started with the following inspired lines:

> Now hear with your understanding!
> Thus hear, Slavic people!
> Hear the Word which feeds human souls,
> The Word which strengthens the heart and the mind,
> This Word ready for the cognition of God!

Constantine then emphasized the importance for the Slavic people —for any people—of hearing the Gospel and having books in their own language. "And, therefore, Saint Paul has taught: I had rather speak five words with my understanding that I might teach others also, than ten thousand words in an unknown tongue." Constantine's ideas were further developed by Metropolitan Ilarion of Kiev, who says that the new faith demands new tongues just as new wine requires new skins.[105] Because of the enthusiasm of Slavic intellectual leaders of the period for their language and literature, we must suppose that some of them at least were interested in what we now call Slavic philology.

Evidence of the existence of such an interest may be seen in the essay, "On the [Slavic] Characters," written by Khrabr, a Bulgarian

103. Semenov, *op. cit.,* pp. 49–50; cf. Shakhmatov, *RIOP 2* (Prague, 1930), pp. 66–67.
104. P. A. Lavrov, "Materially po istorii vozniknoveniia drevneishei Slavianskoi pismennosti," *Trudy Slavianskoi Komissii,* I (Leningrad, 1930), 196–198. For the English translation and interpretation, see R. Jakobson, "The Beginnings of National Self-Determination in Europe," *Review of Politics,* January, 1945.
105. Ponomarev, I, 67; Jakobson, *op. cit.,* p. 39.

monk of the tenth century.[106] It is a remarkable inquiry into the origins of the Slavic alphabet. The earliest known manuscript copy of it is that of the former Synodal Library at Moscow, dated 1348. There is no doubt, however, that the work was known in Russia already in our period.

While the new Slavic literature had been born, so to say, the umbilical cord connecting it with the Byzantine mother-literature was not at once cut. The work of translation from the Greek to Slavic, started by Ss. Cyril and Methodius in Moravia in the ninth century and continued by their disciples in Bulgaria in the tenth, was resumed with much success by Iaroslav the Wise in Kiev in the eleventh century. The dependence of Slavic scholarship on Byzantine literature presupposes the existence in this period of a considerable number of trained translators, learned men who knew both languages. Some were Greeks, others Bulgarians; still others Russian.

It is obvious that they must have used some early grammars and dictionaries to help them in their work. And, indeed, there is some evidence showing that Russian learned men of the period were acquainted with so-called "schedography"—the art of the right use of words. Byzantine schedographic manuals usually contained both the basic rules of grammar and comments on word meanings. These materials were arranged alphabetically. In his polemic letter to the priest Foma the metropolitan Kliment concedes that Foma's teacher, a certain Grigori, knows "the alpha and the beta and the grammar of all the twenty-four letters [of the Greek alphabet]" but adds (not mentioning himself) that there are men under his guidance who likewise know their alpha and beta thoroughly. The reference is undoubtedly to the study of schedographic manuals.[107]

Some of the translators employed by Iaroslav I may have taught Greek in the Kievan schools. In the Smolensk schools of the second half of the twelfth century both Greek and Latin may have been taught. That teachers of still other languages were available in Kiev in the eleventh century may be seen from Vladimir Monomach's "Testament," mentioned earlier, in which he says that his father Vsevolod I while residing in Kiev had learned five languages (Russian, of course, not included).

---

106. S. G. Vilinsky, *Skazanie Chernoriztsa Khrabra* (Odessa, 1901) ; Lavrov, *op. cit.*, pp. 162–164. J. Vašic, *Mnicha Chrabra Obrana Slovanského Pisma* (Brno, 1941).

107. E. E. Golubinsky, "Vopros o zaimstvovanii domongolskimi Russkimi ot Grekov tak nazyvaemoi skhedografii," *ANORI, 9*, Pt. 2 (1904), pp. 49–59.

Since Vsevolod's first wife was a Byzantine princess and his second a Cuman princess, we may be sure that he knew both Greek and the Cuman tongue. What three other languages he studied is open to conjecture. Most likely they were the Latin, the Norse, and the Ossetian.

### e. Jurisprudence

In western Europe in the Middle Ages two systems of law vied one with the other: the Teutonic and the Roman. As the Teutonic peoples occupied the former provinces of the Roman Empire one after another they brought with them their own customs and traditions, which had for them a binding force. Gradually this Teutonic law prevailed over the Roman almost everywhere in the west. In southern Europe, however, the Roman law was not completely extinguished and from the late eleventh century a revival of interest in it became noticeable, through the work of the so-called "glossators" or commentators upon Justinian's *Digest*. The law school at Bologna was the main center of these studies in the twelfth century. This movement in juridical thought resulted eventually in the so-called "reception of the Roman law" in most countries of continental Europe. It was a protracted process; in Germany for example the "reception" took place only in the late fifteenth century.

The progress of jurisprudence in Russia followed a different course. Russia, except for Transcaucasia, the Crimea, and Bessarabia, was never a part of the Roman Empire. Therefore the Slavic traditional law, in many respects akin to the Teutonic, constituted the original foundation of Russian law, historically speaking. However, since Russia was connected geographically and commercially with the Byzantine Empire, she was open to the influence of Byzantine jurisprudence even prior to her conversion to Christianity. The Russo-Byzantine treaties of the tenth century are very important in this respect.

Now, the Byzantine law, except of course for the canon law, was a direct historical extension of Roman law. It was in the early Byzantine period, under Justinian, that the Roman law was finally codified. Thus through Byzantium the Russians early became acquainted with Roman law. Assimilation of Byzantine law became inevitable for Russia after her conversion to Christianity, especially when it came to canon law. Byzantine collections of church canons and of the imperial decrees concerning the church are known as "nomocanons." There were several versions of them. From Vladimir the Saint's Church Statute (*Tserkovnyi Ustav*), we know that he consulted one of these collections. The Russian term for Nomocanon is *Kormchaia* ("The Rudder Book," which corresponds to the Greek Πηδάλιον).[108]

As to Byzantine lay law, the most popular legal manuals, such as the *Ecloga,* the *Procheiron,* and the *Nomos Georgicos* (agrarian law), were well known in medieval Russia. Excerpts from both the *Ecloga* and the *Procheiron*—if not yet the full text of each—were available in Slavic translation already during the Kievan period. The *Nomos Georgicos* was probably translated in the late twelfth or early thirteenth century.[109] In the tenth century a Slavic law manual known as the *Court Law for People* (*Zakon sudnyi liudem*) was compiled in Bulgaria.[110] It was based on the *Ecloga* chiefly and was very popular in Russia.

As a result of the translation of the above-mentioned law codes and manuals, the Russian jurist of the eleventh and twelfth centuries, even if he knew no other language than Slavic, had at his disposal a fairly well-stocked shelf of juridical books. To those who knew Greek, all the original codes were of course available. It should be noted, however, that in spite of the acquaintance of the Russian jurists with Byzantine law the first version of the *Pravda Russkaia* (*Lex Russia, Russian Law*), set down in the early eleventh century and known under the name of Iaroslav's *Pravda,* is based on Slavic traditional law, akin to the Anglo-Saxon laws, the *Lex Salica,* and other so-called *Leges Barbarorum.*

The second Russian code, known as the *Pravda* of Iaroslav's sons and dating around 1072, is devoted chiefly to the protection of the prince's servitors and the princely estates. Its sources are various princely decrees; however, its contents enable us to surmise a certain influence by both the German princely law and the Byzantine law. The so-called Expanded Version of the *Pravda Russkaia,* presumably codified in the eleven-sixties, is a much more elaborate code than the first two and shows the hand of a jurist well versed in Byzantine law.[111]

Though familiar with the Byzantine law, the Russian jurists of

108. See N. Suvorov, *Uchebnik tserkovnogo prava* (4th ed., Moscow, 1912), pp. 139–152, 170–177. See Sources, II, 2, C.

109. A. Albertoni, *Per una esposizione del diritto Bizantino* (Imola, 1927), pp. 50–52. See Sources, II, 2, A.

110. T. Saturnik, *Příspěvky k šíření Byzantského práva u Slovanů,* pp. 143–164.

111. On the *Pravda Russkaia,* see M. N. Tikhomirov, *Issledovanie o Russkoi Pravde;* of the earlier literature, L. K. Goetz, *Das russische Recht.* The best edition of the texts is by B. D. Grekov, ed., *Pravda Russkaia,* I. English translation, *Medieval Russian Laws,* pp. 26–56.

the twelfth century did not accept all its norms without reservations. On the contrary, they showed a remarkably independent attitude toward their Byzantine teachers, which is in itself an evidence of the high level of juridical thought in Kievan Russia. The Russians accepted what seemed to them useful for Russian law and rejected, or modified, everything they considered incompatible with Russian ways. Thus they followed the principles of the Byzantine law—or rather, in this case, Roman law—in legalizing interest on loans. As is well known, the western law of this period, under the influence of the church, did not recognize the legality of interest on loans, which was considered "usury." While following the Byzantine lead in the matter of loans, the Russian jurists did not accept either capital or corporal punishment from the Byzantine tradition. In each case, when the Byzantine manuals prescribed flogging or other forms of corporal punishment, the *Pravda* replaces it with money fines: so many grivna instead of so many lashes.

A comparison of various versions of the *Pravda* may help to characterize the methods of codification applied by the Russian jurists. Starting with a specific case, they gradually built up general norms of law. Thus when the people of Dorogobuzh killed the master of the stable (*koniukh staryi*) of Prince Iziaslav I, the latter decreed that the murderers should pay eighty grivna as bloodwite. This was duly recorded and in the *Pravda* of Iaroslav's sons a bloodwite of eighty grivna was enacted for the murder of any princely master of the stable, with a reference to the Dorogobuzh case; however, in the revised edition of the *Pravda* (the so-called "Expanded Version") even that reference was omitted.

To take another case, the *Pravda* of Iaroslav's sons contains an article in which a fine is prescribed for killing a prince's *khop* or herdsman—so known, as we saw earlier, because in the tenth and early eleventh centuries many herdsmen were of Patzinak origin, belonging probably to the Khop tribe (see Chap. VI, sec. 11). A prince's herdsmen were more often than not his slaves. And in the corresponding section of the Expanded Version of the *Pravda*, "herdsman" has been replaced by "slave" (kholop), the scope of the article being thus made general instead of specific.

Another interesting example of the editing methods of Russian jurists of the period is the amalgamation of the *Pravda* with the tenth-century *Zakon sudnyi liudem* or "Court Law for People" mentioned above, the combined version of which appeared in the late twelfth or early thirteenth century.[112]

## 11. Sciences and Technology

The development of modern science is identified in our thought with western Europe. Such an identification if applied to the early Middle Ages would be wrong. The scientific traditions of Greek scientists of the Hellenistic period were absorbed, from the eighth century on, by Arabic scholars and for several centuries the Arabic-speaking countries took the lead in science and medicine. Byzantium served to a certain extent as an intermediary between East and West. It was, however, through a direct contact with the Arabic-speaking scientists of Spain, Sicily, and southern Italy that science and medicine began to make real progress in the West, beginning in the twelfth century. The Salerno school of medicine became, in the late twelfth and the thirteenth centuries, one of the important factors in the assimilation of Arabic learning by the West but generally speaking it was only in the fourteenth and fifteenth centuries that scientific progress in the West assumed larger proportions and a more rapid tempo.

Since Russia had received her Christian civilization from Byzantium and was in contact with some Oriental countries, one would think that she was not unfavorably placed for the promotion of scientific development. Actually, however, the emphasis in Russian medieval civilization was on the humanities and the arts and not on science. There is no evidence, for the Kievan period, that scientific studies were pursued in Russia in any systematic way and there was no teaching of science in old Russian schools except for elementary mathematics. Some antiquated Byzantine compendiums on cosmography and natural history, such as the *Christian Topography* by Kosmas Indicopleustes and the *Physiologus*, were available in Slavic translations[113] but except for one mathematical essay no original Russian treatise on science appeared, or at least none has been preserved. And yet the Russians were keen observers of nature and at

112. S. V. Iushkov, ed., *Rus'ka Pravda*, pp. 137–168.
113. The Slavic versions of both the "Christian Topography" and "Physiologus" have been published by the Society of Connoisseurs of Old Literature; see "Kniga glagolemaia Kozmy Indikoplova," *OLDP*, No. 86 (1886), and "Fiziolog," A. Karneev, ed., *OLDP*, No. 92 (1890). See also A. I. Sobolevsky, "Materialy i issledovaniia," *ANORS*, 88, No. 3 (1910), pp. 168, 169, 173.

least some of them were endowed with highly inquisitive minds, as we may judge from scattered notes of a scientific nature in various Russian works of the period, as well as from a number of technical devices. It may be added that our knowledge of the progress of applied science in old Russia is incomplete, since no systematic record of technical invention has ever been made.

To start with mathematics, by the time of the conversion to Christianity Russians were already familiar with the use of decimal numeration within the limits from 1 to 10,000. Fractions with the denominator of two and multiples of two were used, as well as some other simple fractions such as $\frac{1}{3}$, $\frac{1}{5}$, $\frac{1}{7}$, and their respective subdivisions following the dual system.[114] Presumably before the invention of the Slavic alphabet Greek characters and signs were used for notation. These were later replaced by Slavic characters. By the twelfth century the numeration had been extended to 10,000,000.

The church was interested in promoting mathematical studies for paschal calculations bearing on the table of dates of Easter, which had to be established well in advance. Chronological studies likewise depended on some knowledge of mathematics. In his work on chronological and paschal calculation, "The Science of Knowing the Numbers of All Years" (1134), the Novgorodian monk Kirik used fractions with denominators of five and multiples of five, extending them to units of the seventh order—that is, to the type: $\frac{1}{78125}$. In V. V. Bobynin's opinion, Kirik's work is early evidence of a typically Russian trend in mathematical research, which he calls "arithmoalgebraic."[115]

Knowledge of mathematics, and especially of some rudiments of geometry, was also essential for architects but no Russian work of this nature is known for the period. While no Russian astronomical treatises of the time have come down to us, the astronomical data of the Russian chronicles are very exact.[116]

The information on zoölogy to be drawn from the *Physiologus* was utterly unscientific; however, practical acquaintance with the animal world was widespread in Kievan Russia because of the fact that hunting was at this period not only a sport but the means of subsistence of a considerable section of the Russian people. That the

114. V. V. Bobynin, "Sostoianie matematicheskikh znanii v Rossii do XVI veka," *ZMNP, 232* (1884), 183–209.

115. *ES,* Half-Volume LV, 724.

116. D. O. Sviatsky, "Astronomicheskie iavleniia v Russkikh letopisiakh s nauchno-kriticheskoi tochki zreniia," *ANORI, 20* (1915), Pt. 1, pp. 87–208, and Pt. 2, pp. 197–288.

Russians knew well the habits of animals and birds is demonstrated by pertinent remarks on animals in Vladimir Monomach's "Testament" as well as in the *Lay of Igor's Campaign*.

Botanical studies were confined, one may assume, to the knowledge of medicinal herbs, used both by trained physicians and by "medical men" of the people. This brings us to the problem of the old Russian medicine. Medical knowledge appears to have been on a somewhat higher level in Kievan Russia than information on natural science. First, we know from the chronicles that both Syrian and Armenian doctors practiced in Russia; [117] Syria was within the Arabic scientific sphere and Armenian medicine was likewise well developed.[118] Secondly, it may be assumed that each prominent doctor, whether foreign or native, spread medical knowledge by training assistants. From the *Russian Law* we know that in the case of a brawl resulting in injuries the offender had not only to make a compensation payment to the injured man but also to pay the physician's fee.[119] Apparently the practice of seeking a doctor's help was widespread and a sufficient number of doctors must have been available. Hospitals sponsored by the church are mentioned in some of the princely charters and church statutes of the period. Little is known of the medical knowledge of the "magi" (*volkhvy*) and "medicine men" of the period. Presumably many of their devices and recipes served as the foundation of the so-called "people's medicine" (*narodnaia meditsina*) of the later periods.[120] It should be noted that the magic of the volkhvy was not based on superstitions alone. There were also, in their medical practice, elements of real intuition and sound judgment, especially in regard to the curative use of herbs, massage, poultices, and so on.

The Russian contribution to geographical knowledge was more definite than in other scientific fields. Among Russians of this period there seems to have been more interest in, and more disposition to study, history and geography than any other branches of either humanities or science. The first history of Russia—the *Book of Annals* —is in a sense a geographical treatise and not only a historical one.

117. Soloviev, III (Moscow, 1854), 43–44.

118. On Arabic medicine in the early middle ages, see G. Sarton, *Introduction to the History of Science* (Baltimore, Carnegie Institution of Washington, 1931, 2 vols.); on Armenian medicine during the twelfth century, see Vol. II, Pt. 1, pp. 136, 306, 441, 442.

119. *Medieval Russian Laws*, pp. 27, 39.

120. On the Russian "people's medicine," see G. Popov, *Russkaia narodnobytovaia meditsina* (St. Perersburg, 1903); N. Vysotsky, "Ocherki nashei narodnoi meditsiny," *MAIZ, 17* (1911), 1–168; Zelenin, *Russische (ostslavische) Volkskunde,* pp. 256–258.

While the general geographical introduction to the *Book* is based upon conventional Biblical and Christian notions, the concrete information given on the regions occupied by Slavic tribes is very precise and shows the compiler's skill in handling geographical problems.[121]

It is significant that we find very accurate geographical data even in Russian poetical works of the period, especially in the famous *Lay*.[122] That some Russians understood the importance of precise data in geographic exploration is shown by Prince Gleb's measurement, in 1068, of the width of Kerch Strait.[123]

Of Russian travel reports of the period two have been preserved, both pilgrimages to the Holy Land. The first is the itinerary of Abbot Daniil of Kiev, who visited Jerusalem in 1106–7; [124] the second, that of Dobrynia of Novgorod, whose journey was made in 1200–1201.[125] Daniil begins his narrative with Constantinople and not with Kiev, which is unfortunate from the point of view of the student of Russian history and geography. He traveled through the Sea of Marmora and the Dardanelles to Rhodes, then coasted along Lycia to Cyprus and Jaffa, whence he reached Jerusalem. On his homeward journey he was attacked by pirates near Lycia but succeeded in saving his life and returning to Constantinople and then to Russia.

While Daniil's attitude is on many occasions typical of the wonder-seeking type of pilgrim, his record is on the whole both accurate and conscientious. When he repeats the words of others, he says so. Says he, "If I have written without learning, there is here at least no lie; for I have described nothing that I did not see with my very eyes." Comparing Daniil's narrative with that of the Englishman Saewulf, a native of Worcester (*itinerabat* 1102–3), C. Raymond Beazley finds that Daniil's account "is in general fuller, as well as more accurate and more observant." [126] Daniil's intercourse with King Baldwin of Jerusalem is of particular interest. It is significant that the traveler is devoid of any animosity against the "Latins"—i.e., the Roman

121. See N. P. Barsov, *Ocherki Russkoi istoricheskoi geografii*.

122. P. N. Savitsky, "Literatura fakta v Slove o Polku Igoreve," *Sveslavenski Zbornik* (Zagreb, 1930), pp. 344–354.

123. See A. Spitsyn, "Tmutarakanskii Kamen'," *ORSAT*, XI (Petrograd, 1915); see Orlov, *Bibliografia*, No. 1, pp. 1–2.

124. M. A. Venevitinov, ed., "Zhitie i Khozhdenie Daniila," *Pravoslavnyi Palestinskii Sbornik*, Nos. 3, 9 (St. Petersburg, 1883–5). Cf. C. R. Beazley, *The Dawn of Modern Geography*, II (London, 1901), 155–174.

125. Kh. M. Loparev, ed., "Kniga Palomnik Antoniia Novgorodskogo," *Pravoslavnyi Palestinskii Sbornik*, No. 51, (St. Petersburg, 1899). Cf. Beazley, *op. cit.*, II, 214, 215.

126. *Idem*, II, 162.

Catholics. On the other hand, his warm Russian patriotism is noticeable; he asks, and receives, King Baldwin's permission to place his lamp on the Holy Sepulchre "in the name of the whole Russian land."

Dobrynia of Novgorod is better known under his monastic name, Antoni. What we have of his account is, properly speaking, merely a brief description of the churches of Constantinople, as well as of the relics kept in them. It is, however, priceless for the archaeologist, since Dobrynia visited the Imperial City four years before its capture by the Crusaders and was thus one of the last travelers to see St. Sophia and other Byzantine churches in all their splendor.[127]

We have now to turn to the old Russian technology, an examination of which shows a considerable amount of information of a practical nature in the domain of applied chemistry and physics. Thus the Novgorodian assayers of silver may be considered skilled experts highly qualified for their job.[128] It is likewise noteworthy that Russian enamelers of the period succeeded in producing for their work temperatures as high as from 1,000 to 1,200 degrees (Celsius).[129] In the salt industry Novgorodian technicians were apparently familiar with the principle of concentrated solutions; they also knew how to regulate the precipitation of salt by changing temperature.[130] The interest of Russian architects in applied physics is shown by their use of resonators or sound amplifiers (*golosniki*) in Novgorodian and Suzdalian churches. The golosniki were earthenware pots embedded in the walls, their mouths open to the interior of the church. The principle was, of course, already known to Vitruvius.[131]

It may not be amiss to mention here that the Russians were also acquainted, although in a negative way (as the object of their enemies' devices) with the chemical warfare of the period. Thus, as we know, Igor's fleet was destroyed by the "Greek fire" in 941. In the twelfth century, Khoresmian technicians hired by the Cumans used flame-throwers against the Russians.[132] In this case Azerbaijan naptha must have served as the chief ingredient for producing the flame. It was likewise through the Khoresmians that the Russians became familiar

---

127. See N. P. Kondakov, *Vizantiiskie tserkvi i pamiatniki Konstantinopolia* (Odessa, 1887), pp. 73–74; cf. D. V. Ainalov, "Primechaniia k tekstu knigi Palomnik Antoniia Novgorodskogo," *ZMNP*, New Series, *3* (1906), 233–276, and *18* (1908), 81–106.

128. T. Rainov, *Nauka v Rossii XI–XVII vekov*, p. 29.

129. *Idem*, p. 30.

130. *Idem*, p. 31.

131. *Idem*, p. 32.

132. *PSRL*, II, 129 (A.D. 1184).

with the gigantic mechanical arrow-throwers known in Persian as *chir-i-chakhr* and in Russian as *shereshir*.[133] The author of the *Lay of Igor's Campaign*, alluding to Vsevolod III's authority over the princes of Riazan, says that he uses them as so many live shereshir arrows. In naval warfare Prince Iziaslav II of Kiev is credited with the invention of a new type of warship, used by him on the Dnieper River. The appearance of the vessel is described, in the Kievan chronicle, in the following words: "Iziaslav built boats in an ingenious way: the oarsmen were invisible, only the oars could be seen, and the men were not, since the boat was decked. And the soldiers stood on the deck in armor and shot arrows. And there were two helmsmen, one in the bow and one in the stern; and they could steer the boat where they wanted without turning it." [134] There is a rather crude picture of such a boat in the Radziwill Chronicle.[135] Although the chronicle was written in the fifteenth century, it has been suggested that at least some of its illustrations were copied from earlier originals. In the present case, however, the artist seems simply to have tried to follow the description in the text, with the result that the picture may hardly be considered an accurate representation of Iziaslav's boat.

As to industrial technology, a sawmill at Korsun (in the Kievan land) is mentioned in the chronicles under the year 1195. It was driven by the water power of the rapids of the Ros River and was certainly not the only one of its kind in existence.[136] The dredging of certain rivers in order to improve the channel I have also mentioned.

We must not forget that these data are only fragmentary and do not give us an adequate picture of the actual development of Russian technology in the period. Such a picture cannot be obtained because of the lack of material, especially as the chroniclers were mostly monks and not interested in technology.

133. See Melioransky, *op. cit.*, pp. 296–301.
134. *PSRL*, II, 59 (A.D. 1151).
135. Radziwill Chronicle, *OLDP*, CXVIII (1902), folio 189 b.
136. *PSRL*, II, 146; M. V. Dovnar-Zapolsky, *Istoriia russkogo narodnogo khoziaistva*, I, 264.

# Chapter X

# THE WAYS OF LIFE

## 1. City and Country Life

IN PREREVOLUTIONARY Russia, in the late nineteenth and early twentieth centuries, life in the cities differed greatly from that in the country. While the Europeanized urban centers represented the modern age with all its amenities, technical inventions, and intellectual facilities, the peasants still lived, psychologically and culturally, in an extension of the Muscovite period, as it were. True, the mansions of the gentry, built mostly in the Russian "Empire style," with their libraries, collections of paintings, and so on, were like so many oases of European culture but their potential and actual civilizing influence was more than counterbalanced by the intellectual and social gulf between the squires and the villagers. The village itself, however, did not remain immutable. Rapid growth of educational facilities and a less rapid infiltration of technology into the rural districts was gradually changing the peasant life, especially after the abortive revolution of 1905, when petty credit institutions and coöperative societies added much to material progress.

Sociologically there are many similarities between Kievan Russia and the late imperial Russia, the contrast between the urban and rural life presenting one of the important parallels between the two ages. In old as in modern Russia the cities were the first to be affected by new cultural tendencies, while the villages lagged far behind. The gulf between Ilarion's audience—men "saturated with the sweetness of book-learning"—and the inhabitants of remote rural districts who were still illiterate pagans was as great as that between the city elite and the "dark people" of the villages in the late nineteenth century. Economically, Russian cities of the Kievan period lived in an age of commercial capitalism and of highly developed civic law, while the villagers in outlying districts knew no intricate economic or financial transactions except to pay the tribute imposed on them. The cities were resplendent with gorgeous cathedrals and princely palaces; the villages had nothing to show but their log cabins. Churches were few in the rural districts and, while the number of princely and boyar country mansions increased, their owners spent only part of their time there, being more closely connected with the cities than with their estates; as a result of which the latter could hardly, at that period, become centers of culture except for their economic importance in some cases.

Thus in speaking of the manner of life of the Russians of the Kievan period we have carefully to differentiate between cities and rural districts. The urban life we know better because it left more traces in our sources of information. Of the rural life little is known except what can be extracted from the folklore. Incidentally, folklore was one of the links between the cities and the villages as well as between the upper and lower classes. Epic poems and fairy tales (*byliny* and *skazki*) were as much appreciated in the princely and boyar mansions as in the village and, as we know, the minstrel (*skomorokh*) was a welcome guest at both city banquets and village feasts.

## 2. Dwellings and Furniture

The severity of the Russian winter, especially in the north, compelled the Russians to pay more attention to the solidity of their houses than was necessary for the inhabitants of southern or western Europe. The purpose of a house in Russia was to keep man warm in winter rather than anything else. And yet in the Kievan period no stone or brick buildings were built except for churches and princely palaces. The two basic types of Russian dwelling are the log cabin in the north and the frame house (of timbers filled with clay) in the south—the *izba* and *khata*, respectively.[1] Wood being more perishable than stone, no example of the wooden houses of old Russia has been preserved but we may obtain some idea of them from the log houses of north Russian peasants built in the eighteenth and nineteenth centuries. In contrast to the miserable huts of Belorussia and central Russia, the north Russian izba is usually a spacious home, well built and warm and more often than not decorated on the outside with wood carvings. Of such a type the old Novgorodian house must have been, while in central Russia and Belorussia even then the log cabins must have been smaller. Even a small izba usually consisted of three parts: the main room with an oven, the hall, and an unheated room across the hall, used either as an extra room in summer or as a storeroom

1. *Ancient Russia*, p. 110.

(*klet'*).[2] A house of several rooms was known as a *khoromy*. Around the house, barns and stables were built, also a bathhouse (*bania*); the yard was then fenced with pales. The homestead of a boyar must have differed from that of a liudin only in its dimensions. The princely palace was, of course, much more spacious and elaborate. Its two characteristic features were the hall (*gridnitsa*) and the tower (*terem*). In the Kievan palace these two buildings were made of stone from the tenth century on. The hall served as the headquarters of the princely retinue. In the terem the female part of the princely family had their abode. The word *terem* seems to derive from the Greek (room," "chamber"); consider, however, the Persian *tarem* ("pavilion," "portico").[3]

Stepping down the social ladder now, the smerdy lived in smaller log cabins or, in the south, in khaty. Stoves were originally made of baked clay but later they were built of bricks. The stove was often rather spacious; it served the house for heating, for boiling water, for cooking and other purposes. In central Russia peasants occasionally used it for bathing as if it were a miniature bathhouse.

For window panes mica was used instead of glass. In the evening clay lamps, burning fat or vegetable oil of some kind, supplied the light; copper candlesticks with wax candles were also used. In the poorer houses a *luchina* ("wood splinter") must have been the popular lighting device, as it was in many a peasant hut in the days of the empire prior to the introduction of kerosene oil. The furniture consisted of beds, tables, benches, and chairs, all of wood. In the boyar and merchant houses some of the furniture, especially armchairs, was adorned with elaborate carving. Tables were covered with homespun cloth or lace. Washstands were supplied with ewers and bowls made of copper. It was in such a ewer that the Novgorodian bishop Ioann once caught a demon, if we are to credit his "Life." [4]

## 3. Dress

Masculine dress in summer consisted of a linen shirt and linen trousers. It was in such attire that Grand Prince Sviatoslav appeared

2. On the Old Russian dwelling, see Aristov, pp. 84–85; S. K. Shambinago, "Drevne-russkoe zhilishche po bylinam," *Iubileinyi Sbornik v chest' V. F. Millera* (Moscow, 1900), pp. 129–149.

3. On *terem,* see Aristov, p. 85; K. A. Inostrantsev, "O tereme v drevne-russkom i musulmanskom zodchestve," *ORSAT,* IX, (1913), 35–38; V. F. Rzhiga, "Ocherki iz istorii byta do-Mongolskoi Rusi," *IMT,* V (1929), 9 ff.; Chadwick, pp. 29, 36, 77, 81, 90.

4. Aristov, p. 119.

before Emperor John Tzimiskes in 971 (see Chap. II, sec. 5). Sviato-slav was a rigorist; even in his time, and more so in the eleventh and twelfth centuries, princes and boyars preferred costly garments made of imported silk or brocade fabrics (*pavoloka* and *aksamit*). In the cold seasons linen and silk articles served as underwear, over which woolen garments were worn. To denote the latter several terms were used, such as *svita, miatelia, koch,* and so on. The svita seems to have been the most commonly used type, worn by princes and peasants alike—a kind of caftan. The miatelia, a mantle or cloak, is mentioned in west Ukrainian and Novgorodian sources. The koch probably served as an overcoat. The prince's dress mantle was known as a *korzno*.[5] In winter, especially when traveling, sheepskins and fur coats were donned. These were of two kinds: the sleeved coat, tight in the waist (*kozhukh*), and the loose cloak, more often than not also sleeved (*shuba*). A kozhukh of the common type was made of sheep-skin. For cloaks, bear, wolf, and marten skins were widely used.

The princely type of dress is illustrated in the famous miniature of Sviatoslav's *Collection* (*Izbornik*) of 1073, in which Prince Sviato-slav II, his wife, and his five sons are portrayed.[6] According to N. P. Kondakov, the attire, except for headgear and collars is typically Byzantine.[7] The prince wears a caftan of dark purple-blue color with tight sleeves ending in cuffs of golden brocade; the hem at the bottom is red. Over it he has a dark blue robe with wide gold hems, fastened with a ruby clasp. His boots are of green morocco. The princess wears a light red dress with wide loose sleeves, a kind of dalmatic, belted with a wide golden band. On her head she wears a large kerchief, or rather shawl, of which one end rests on her right shoulder. Sviatoslav's headgear consists of a sable cap with a low crown of golden fabric. His sons wear high fur caps. An inter-

5. *Idem*, pp. 138–142. See also P. Savvaitov, *Opisanie starinnykh russkikh utvarei, odezhd, oruzhiia, ratnykh dospekhov i konskogo pribora* (St. Petersburg, 1896), *s.v. Korzno* and *Kots'*.

6. Sviatoslav's "Izbornik" of 1073 was published, phototypically, by the Society of the Connoisseurs of Russian Literature, *OLDP*, LV (1880). It is to be noted that, while four sons of Sviatoslav are distinctly represented in the miniature, only the fur cap of the fifth can be seen above the representation of Sviatoslav's wife. Some scholars, including N. P. Kondakov, considered this fur cap a part of the princess' headgear. However, since there is a caption containing the names of all five princes, they must all have been represented and thus the fur cap in question must be considered as belonging to one of the princes and not to his mother.

7. N. P. Kondakov, *Izobrazheniia Russkoi kniazheskoi sem'i* (St. Petersburg, 1906), p. 40. A. V. Artsikhovsky's book (see Bibliography, XII) is inaccessible to me.

esting detail of the young princes' attire is the low collar each of them wears, presumably a variation of neck ring (*torques, grivna*).

Another illustration of the princely attire of the eleventh century may be found in the miniatures inserted in the so-called "Gertrud Codex," a Psaltery copied by order of Archbishop Egbert of Trier (977–93). The miniatures date from the late eleventh century and contain figures of Prince Iaropolk (son of Iziaslav I) and his wife and mother. The costumes they wear are in conventional Byzantine style.[8] In Kondakov's opinion, the miniatures were painted by a Polish or west Ukrainian (Galician) icon-painter.

We turn now to the Russian ladies' garments.[9] In summer they consisted of a linen shirt and a woolen skirt (*ponëva*). In northern Russia instead of the skirt a sleeveless dress, a kind of pinafore, was worn. This is the so-called *sarafan* but it must be noted that in old Russia the term was also applied to men's garments; the masculine sarafan was a light summer overcoat.[10] The word is of Iranian origin. Wealthy women, especially of the cities, dressed in silk and brocade even more eagerly than the men. In wintertime rustic women wore sheepskins but the proper attire for a respectable lady was a fur coat. Women of wealthy families wore sable and beaver. In the *Lay of Igor's Campaign* Iaroslavna, the wife of the unfortunate Prince Igor, in bewailing her husband's fate expresses her wish to dip the sleeve of her beaver coat in the waters of the Danube River, to wipe with it Igor's wounds. The less pretentious women were satisfied with coats of marten or even squirrel. Fur also served for winter caps for both men and women; sable and beaver were considered the proper thing. In summer the men wore felt hats with high crowns, known as the "Greek hats." The women's headgear—a headband in the shape of an open crown—was known as a *kika* or, if high in front, as a *kokoshnik*. A wealthy lady would have her kokoshnik ornamented with precious stones.

For footgear the men wore high boots (*cherevi* or *sapogi*); those of the wealthy people were of fine leather—green, yellow, or red. Dandies such as the legendary Churilo Plenkovich of the byliny ordered their

---

8. See Count A. A. Bobrinskoy, "Kievskie miniatiury XI veka," *RAO, 12* (1901), 351–371; Kondakov, *loc cit.;* V. N. Shchepkin, "Miniatiura v Russkom iskusstve dotatarskogo perioda," *Slavia, 6* (1928), 742–757.

9. Aristov, p. 141. See also I. I. Sreznevsky, *Materialy dlia slovaria drevnerusskogo iazyka*, III, cols. 262, 263, *s.v.* "Sarafan."

10. Aristov, pp. 141, 142, 148.

boots made with long curved toes. Low leather shoes (likewise known as *cherevi*) were also used, especially by the women. In the forest zone the villagers wore bast shoes made of fiber or bark of willow, birch, or oak trees.

Full formal attire was not complete without jewels and ornaments of various kinds, of which of course women were especially fond.[11] Men, however, did not shun gold and silver ornaments either. Sviatoslav I wore a golden earring. Princes' retainers frequently wore golden neck rings (*torques*) and neck chains. These, however, were symbols of office rather than mere ornaments. Certain accessories of the dress of the wealthy, such as clasps and buttons, were also made of gold and silver and more often than not ornamented with precious stones or pearls. The belt was considered a man's finest ornament. Gold and silver belts were articles of the princely wardrobe par excellence. Silk and leather belts were usually adorned with silver plaques and clasps, artistically ornamented.[12] The repertory of rich women's jewels and ornaments included a variety of elaborate articles, such as gold and silver earrings, temple pendants, necklaces made either of pearls or of gold and silver coins (known as *monisto*), enameled golden crowns, bracelets, and rings of various kinds.

## 4. Food

Bread and meat were the two main items in the diet of Russians of the Kievan period.[13] In south Russia the bread was made of wheat flour, in the north rye bread was more common. In years of famine dried goosefoot leaves were sometimes added to the flour. In wealthy houses, as well as in the monasteries on feast days, in addition to the ordinary bread, a rich kind baked with honey and poppy seed was served. As to meats, beef, mutton, and pork were the most familiar, as well as that of geese, fowl, duck, pigeons, and cranes. Horse meat was occasionally used by soldiers during a campaign and by civilians during a famine. The flesh of any kind of wild animals and birds was eaten; as is shown by the contemporary sources, deer, wild boar, hare, even bear, were on the fare, together with grouse, hazel-grouse, and other game birds. After the conversion to Christianity, the new church, mindful of the ancient canons, objected to the eating of meat

---

11. See N. P. Kondakov, *Russkie klady*, I Iu. V. Gotie, *Zheleznyi vek v Vostochnoi Evrope*, pp. 235–239.

12. Aristov, p. 160.

13. For food and beverages of the old Russians, see Aristov, pp. 73–80; Rzhiga, *op. cit.*, chap. iii.

of wild animals such as bear and even hare, considering them "unclean." Moreover, following the Old Testament with its strictures against the use of meat with blood, it objected to the eating of birds strangled in snares.[14] It appears, however, that in this regard the clergy's admonitions were mostly wasted on their parishioners, whose age-long habits prevailed over the new ritualism; in the Muscovite period more attention was paid to these church regulations.

The church encouraged the eating of fish. Wednesdays and Fridays were proclaimed meatless days and three periods of fasting, including Lent, were established besides. Fish of course had been on the Russian diet even before Vladimir's baptism, and caviar must have been also, although the first mention of it occurs in a source of the twelfth century.[15] Eggs, dairy products, and vegetables supplemented the fare. In addition to butter, vegetable oils made from hemp or flax seeds were sometimes used, chiefly during the fast periods. Olive oil was imported.

Little is known of the Russian cuisine of this time. Meat was either boiled or grilled, vegetables either boiled or eaten raw. Corned meat and cured ham are also mentioned in the sources. Pies, which later became the favorite Russian culinary creation, are mentioned in sources of this period only twice.[16] Both millet gruel and oatmeal porridge must have been common dishes. In the princely households a chef or head cook (*stareishina povarom*) presided over a large kitchen establishment and the cooks were probably well trained and skillful. Since some were of foreign origin (Turkish and Hungarian cooks are mentioned), their cuisine may have included foreign recipes. The assortment of kitchen utensils included copper kettles, trivets, and frying pans; also knives of various kinds.

Let us now turn to the matter of beverages. In those times, as in ours, the Russians did not shun drink. According to the *Book of Annals*, Vladimir's main reason for rejecting Islam was the teetotalism prescribed by that religion. "Drinking," said he, "is the joy of the *Rus'*. We cannot exist without that pleasure." [17] Russian drinking,

---

14. The so-called "Kirik's Queries" (*Voproshanie Kirikovo*) addressed to Bishop Nifont of Novgorod contain interesting material for the study of the clergymen's dilemmas concerning the proper attitude toward food. This valuable document is published in *RIB*, VI (1880), cols. 21–62. Kirik, as we know, was also a student of mathematics (see Chap. IX, sec. 11).

15. "Kirik's Queries," *RIB*, VI, 32.

16. Aristov, p. 77; Sreznevsky, *op. cit.*, II, col. 933, *s.v.* "pirog."

17. Cross, p. 184.

for the modern reader, is invariably associated with vodka but in the Kievan period no distilled liquor was prepared. Three kinds of drinks were consumed. *Kvas,* a nonalcoholic or only mildly alcoholic brew was made chiefly from rye bread—a kind of near beer. It must have been a traditional beverage of the Slavs since it is already mentioned in the record of the journey of the Byzantine envoy to the Hunnic khan Attila in the early fifth century, together with mead.[18] The latter (*med*) was extremely popular in Kievan Russia, being brewed and consumed by both laymen and monks. According to the chronicles, Prince Vladimir the Saint, on the occasion of the opening of a church at Vasilev, ordered 300 kettles of mead prepared.[19] In 1146 Prince Iziaslav II found in the cellars of his rival Sviatoslav 500 casks of mead, as well as eighty casks of wine.[20] Several kinds of mead were known, such as sweet, dry, peppered, and so on. Beer (*pivo*) was likewise generally consumed. Wines were imported from Greece and, besides the princes, the churches and monasteries imported wine regularly for liturgical use.

As to the table service, gold and silver dishes were available in the princely households, especially on state occasions; also gold and silver spoons. The *Book of Annals* contains a characteristic story about Vladimir the Saint's retainers, who complained that the prince let them eat with wooden spoons instead of silver ones. Vladimir immediately ordered silver spoons to be supplied to them.[21] There were no forks and everybody was supposed to use his own knife to cut meat or bread. For drink, gold and silver beakers and bowls were the proper thing. Commoners had to be satisfied with pewter or wooden dishes, wooden spoons, and pewter beakers and bowls.

## 5. Health and Hygiene

In the Kievan period the Russians were better housed and better fed than in later times. Undoubtedly the average Russian then consumed more meat than the peasants of the Imperial period. As a result, the Russian people seem then to have been healthier and more robust than their descendants of the nineteenth century. Also, in spite of the growth of cities, the latter were less crowded than in modern times. On the other hand, medical knowledge of the period—not in Russia

18. See *Ancient Russia,* p. 143.
19. Cross, p. 209.
20. *PSRL,* II (1843), 27.
21. Cross, p. 210.

alone—was unable to cope with epidemics and, when they struck, people were helpless and considered them tokens of God's wrath. In
ordinary illness people expected assistance either from the learned
physicians or—especially in rural districts—from magicians and
medicine men. Rudiments of hygiene were supplied, however, more
by sound judgment and popular tradition than by either magic or
science. As to one important point, elementary bodily cleanliness
was secured by the regular use of steam baths, in any case in northern Russia, where a bathhouse was an indispensable appurtenance
of every homestead. In the south the steam bath was less popular.
There is a characteristic story in the *Book of Annals* about the
legendary journey of the Apostle Andrew to Novgorod. "Wondrous
to relate," says he, "I saw the land of the Slovene, and while I was
among them, I noticed their wooden bathhouses. They warm them
to extreme heat, then undress, and after anointing themselves with
tannic acid, they take young reeds and lash their bodies. They actually
lash themselves so violently that they barely escape alive. Then they
drench themselves with cold water, and thus are revived. They think
nothing of doing this every day, and actually inflict such voluntary
torture upon themselves." [22] This humorous but fairly accurate description of the north Russian steam bath is one of the early tokens
of the Kievans' mocking attitude toward the Novgorodians—an episode, as it were, in the war of jokes between the two tribes, of which
the ridiculing of the Great Russian (Moskal or Katsap) on the part
of the Ukrainian and the former's mockery of the latter (Khokhol)
is but a historical extension.

In 1090 one of the Russian bishops of Greek origin, Efrem of
Pereiaslav, who was a great builder, embellished the city with many
structures and among other things "constructed a stone bathhouse
such as had never heretofore existed in Russia." [23] This was apparently a Roman bath.

Besides the use of bathhouses, another sound tradition was the
Russian care for keeping food, in particular bread and water (for
drinking), in meticulous cleanliness, putting it out of the reach of
animals, especially dogs. There is something religious in the old-
time Russian's reverent attitude toward bread and water and indeed
its origins may be sought in certain trends of Slavic paganism; in the
harvest festivals in respect to bread and the *rusalia* for water. Chris-

22. *Idem,* p. 139 (wording of translation slightly changed).
23. *Idem,* p. 260.

tianity added its blessing to the old religious reverence, offering special services on the day of Transfiguration ("Saviour's Day," August 6), which coincided with the old harvest festival, and on that of Epiphany (January 6), when water was blessed. The church introduced besides, or rather tried to introduce, the notion of the uncleanness of certain kinds of animal food, as noted above; which, however, hardly had any hygienic significance. Fasts prescribed by the church might have changed the diet of the Russian people—and eventually did (let the physicians decide whether it was helpful to health or not) —but in the Kievan period were not strictly observed. In its ordinances as to food as well as sex behavior the church, of course, was concerned with the observance of old canons and not with hygiene. Sexual licentiousness was considered sin; therefore the clergy denounced it. They did more than this, however, in trying to regulate the sexual aspects of marriage as well. Thus it was forbidden to cohabit on Saturdays and Sundays, and those who did were not supposed to enter church on those days.

## 6. The Cycle of Life

The cycle of human life is eternal, in the sense in which it is determined by nature. Man is born, grows up, marries, begets children, and dies. It is but natural that he should desire properly to observe the main landmarks of the cycle. In our days of urbanized and mechanized civilization the ceremonies bearing on each link of the chain of life are reduced to a minimum. Not so in the old times, especially in the age of the clan organization of society, when the landmarks of the life of the individual were considered a part of the clan life. Among the ancient Slavs as among other primitive peoples the observance of the cycle of life was marked by elaborate ceremonies reflected in the folklore. Following the conversion to Christianity, the church assumed the sponsorship of some of the old ceremonies and introduced new rites of her own; as, for example, for baptism and the celebration of the name day, in honor of the patron saint of each man or woman.

Simultaneously the medieval church, permeated as it was with Biblical notions, degraded woman at the very threshold of the cycle. The mother was considered unclean, for physiological reasons, for forty days following the birth of a child and was not allowed to enter the church during this period.[24] She might not attend the baptism of her children.

24. *RIB*, VI, 34.

In the Russian princely families it was usual, in the Kievan period, to give the child two personal names: first a Slavic one (or Slavicized Norse); and secondly a Christian name. The first was known as the "princely name" par excellence. As we know, Vladimir at his baptism received the Christian name of Vasili (Basil); his son Iaroslav, the name of Iuri (George). Both these princes were baptized as adults but the habit of giving two names was preserved among their descendants, whose children were baptized within a few days after birth. Eventually some of the princes—as for example Vladimir— were canonized under their Slavic names and in this way old Slavic names were included in the roster of Christian personal names.

At an age between two and four the young princeling was tonsured as a mark of his rank and on that occasion received a special blessing of the church. It was usual to perform the rite on the boy's name day; following it, he was put on horseback in anticipation of his career as a warrior. Both events were celebrated by a sumptuous banquet in his father's palace.[25] The boy was then entrusted to the care of a governor (*kormilets*) and at about the age of seven he was taught to read and later to write. Princely children appear to have received instruction from private tutors. Such must likewise have been the case, usually, with the children of the boyars, although under Vladimir and Iaroslav they were ordered to send their children into the newly established public schools. The commoners' children were sent to schools, if educated at all. In rural districts most of the people must have remained illiterate.

Marriage customs in the pagan period varied with the various tribes. Among the Radimichians, the Viatichians, and the Severians, the bridegroom had to kidnap his bride. With some other tribes the proper thing was to pay the clan for her. This habit may have developed out of the redemption for kidnapping. Eventually the outright payment was replaced by a gift on the part of the bridegroom to his fiancée or to her parents (*veno*). Among the Polianians custom required that the fiancée be brought by her parents or their deputies to the house of the bridegroom, with her trousseau delivered next morning.[26] Traces of all these old customs may be seen distinctly in Russian folklore, particularly in the marriage ceremonies even of later times.

After Russia's conversion to Christianity, both engagement and

25. Soloviev, III (Moscow, 1853), 8.
26. Laur., col. 13.

wedding were sanctioned by the church. At first, however, only the princes and boyars cared for the church blessing. The bulk of the population, especially in the rural districts, were satisfied with recognition of the marriage by their respective clans or communities. Cases of avoidance of church wedding by common people were frequent even as late as the fifteenth century.

Under the Byzantine law, in accordance with the habits of people of the south, low age requirements were set for the prospective couple: the *Ecloga* of the eighth century allows marriage at the age of fifteen for men and thirteen for women. In the *Procheiron* of the ninth century the requirements are even lower: fourteen years for the bridegroom and twelve for the bride.[27] As we know, both *Ecloga* and *Procheiron* were available in Slavonic translation and the validity of both manuals was recognized by Russian jurists. In medieval Russia even the low age requirements of the *Procheiron* were not always observed, however, especially in the princely families where marriages were determined, more often than not, by considerations of diplomacy. At least one case is known when a prince's son was married at the age of eleven and Vsevolod III gave his daughter Verkhuslava in marriage to Prince Rostislav, when she was only eight. When the parents of the bride saw her off "they both wept because their dear daughter was so young." [28]

Divorce was allowed by Byzantine law on the ground of absence of the spouse from home for more than three years without communication or news of him (or her) being received; also for adultery and for certain other reasons. In medieval Russia divorce could also be obtained if one of the married couple, or both, desired to enter monastic life.[29] A monk or nun was considered dead to the world. Princes were sometimes compelled by their rivals to enter a monastery as an alternative to being slain. Gradually the habit developed among the reigning princes of assuming *skhima* (highest monastic orders) as soon as they felt the approach of death.

Funeral rites in pagan times included a memorial banquet celebrated at the place of burial. Over the tomb of a prince or any outstanding warrior a high barrow (*kurgan*) was made and professional lamenters were hired to deplore his death (see Chap. IX, sec. 5). These continued to perform their duties even at Christian funerals,

27. *Ecloga*, Title II, Art. 1. *Procheiron*, Title IV, Art. 3.
28. Soloviev, *loc. cit.*
29. Vladimirsky-Budanov, *Obzor*, pp. 436–438.

the wording of some of the laments being changed to fit Christian·
notions. Christian funeral rites, like other church services, were of
course borrowed from Byzantium. John of Damascus is the author
of the Orthodox *panikhida* ("funeral service") and the Slavonic
translation is worthy of the original. For Christian burial cemeteries
were laid out, usually close to the churches. The bodies of outstanding princes were deposited in sarcophagi placed in the crypt of the
cathedral of the prince's capital.

Death terminates man's earthly life; but for a Christian the earthly
life is only a preparation for life beyond the tomb. And the existence
of a soul in that future life had to be secured by prayers. In order to
guarantee the continuance of prayers, a wealthy man would bequeath
part of his property to a monastery. If for some reason he failed to
do so, his relatives had to take care of the matter. The deceased's
Christian name would then be inserted in the *synodik*—a list of names
to be mentioned, with prayers, at every Mass or at least on certain
days set by the church for the remembrance of the departed. A
princely family usually kept its own synodik in the monastery of
which the princes of that branch were traditional benefactors.

## 7. The Manner of Life

The schedule of everyday life of a Russian of the Kievan period
can be more easily reconstructed for princes than for commoners,
since in the sources more attention is paid to the former. Vladimir
Monomach advised his sons to get up before sunrise and to start the
day with prayers, in church whenever there was an early service, or
at home. After breakfast a reigning prince was supposed to attend
to state affairs—this meant mostly presiding either over the meeting
of the boyar council or over a session of the supreme court. Dinner
was at about eleven; the members of the council and other retainers
usually dined with the prince. Occasionally priests and monks were
also invited, in any case during Lent.[30]

At noon everybody went to bed. According to Vladimir Monomach,
"This is the time set for rest by God himself." [31] In the late afternoon
the princes must have occupied themselves with the management of
their palaces and stables and sundry affairs. Supper was served about
six o'clock. In the evening the ruler, if he was a lover of book learning, might do some reading. The prince's sons, if they were of age but

30. Soloviev, III, 10, 11.
31. Cross, p. 306.

had no appanages of their own, must have participated in their father's labors. His wife and daughters were expected to occupy themselves chiefly with handicrafts. Some were also fond of books, however.

The daily schedule of a boyar family must have been very similar to that of princely families. The merchants must have spent most of their time in the market and the artisans in their shops. In rural districts the daily routine varied, depending on the season and the kind of agricultural work proper to it. In winter, when there was no work on the land, the peasants must, as in later periods, have engaged in handicraft or looked for employment in the cities. Womenfolk in all social strata but the highest were expected to cook and to do all kinds of home chores in addition to sewing and knitting.

The everyday routine was often interrupted by festivals and other social events. Old festivals of pagan times were gradually replaced by church holidays but in the manner of celebrating these holidays pagan customs were noticeable for a long time in spite of the clergy's objections. Each of the great church festivals, as Christmas, Easter, Pentecost, and Transfiguration, was not only marked by special church services but also by social gatherings, songs and dances, and special food. On such occasions the prince was expected to open the doors of his palace to the city people for sumptuous banquets, at which musicians and jongleurs entertained the guests. In addition to the princely banquets there were private banquet associations, or fraternities, the members of which usually belonged to the same communal or professional group. Such fraternities played an important role in the social life of the large cities, especially Novgorod and Pskov.

The princely hunting expeditions may, in a sense, be likened to social festivals. In a big hunt not only the prince himself but his boyars and retainers, including the womenfolk, took part.[32] Occasionally two or more princes arranged a joint hunt; in such a case friendship in sport might be conducive to a family agreement or a political rapprochement. Horse races are mentioned in the sources of the period less frequently than hunting parties. Tournaments were practically unknown in Russia except through foreigners. An elaborate horse race which seems to have ended in a tournament was staged in Kiev by the Hungarians in 1150.[33]

32. Soloviev, III, 10.
33. *PSRL*, II, 46.

## 8. Public Calamities

Not only gay events but sad occurrences as well interfered at times with the everyday routine of the old Russian. Mankind was lashed, in the Middle Ages, by four scourges: epidemics, famines, fires, and wars; Kievan Russia was no exception to this intermittently calamitous state of things. Epidemics, nationwide and local, are mentioned in the chronicles on several occasions. In 1092 both the Polotsk and the Kievan lands were visited by some sort of plague. In Polotsk many persons struck by it fell in the streets; rumor had it that the dead invisibly flew along the streets and stabbed the living.[34] In 1158 severe epidemics and epizootics spread in Novgorod. According to the chronicle, so many men, horses, and cows died that the bodies could not be buried for a long time and one could not reach the market place for the stench. In 1187 the spread of some kind of epidemic disease was recorded in Suzdalia. Illness affected every house and in some houses all were stricken, so that there was no one even to give a drink of water to the suffering persons. In 1203 epizootics struck Novgorod once more.[35]

Famines are likewise mentioned in the chronicles.[36] A failure of crops in the land of Rostov is recorded in 1070. In 1127 untimely severe frosts ruined the harvest in the land of Novgorod. Scarcity of grain and prohibitive prices of bread resulted in famine and starvation: people ate linden leaves, birch bark, straw, and moss —mortality was high and corpses were strewn in the streets and the market place in the city of Novgorod. Parents sold their children to foreigners. Scarcity of grain and high prices of bread are also mentioned in the Novgorodian chronicle under the years 1137, 1161, 1188, 1215. In 1230 famine assumed such proportions in Novgorod that cases of cannibalism are recorded in the chronicle. Even in fertile Ukraine crops were poor occasionally, as for example in 1193.

Fires occurred even more frequently than either epidemics or famines. The fact that except for the churches all buildings in Russian cities of this period were wooden made them especially vulnerable.[37] In 1124 the city of Kiev was consumed by fire almost completely; if we are to believe the chronicler (which we don't in this case), six hundred churches were destroyed. In Novgorod eleven

34. Cross, p. 264.
35. Soloviev, III, 43.
36. *Idem*, III, 42, 43; Aristov, pp. 81–82.
37. Soloviev, III, 35, 36; Aristov, p. 245.

disastrous fires were recorded during the period from 1054 to 1228. In the fire of 1211 fifteen churches and 4,300 homes burned down. Between 1183 and 1198 Vladimir in Suzdalia was thrice burned. In 1194 Staraia Russa, Ladoga, and Gorodishche were partly destroyed by conflagration. In 1211 Rostov burned down and in 1221 Iaro-slavl.

While the spread of epidemics and famines and, partly even, the occurrence of fires were the result of natural causes—or rather of man's inability to control the forces of nature—wars, were caused by men themselves and of all of the four scourges war was perhaps the most terrible. In Kievan Russia it was certainly the most frequent. In addition to constant raids by the Turkish nomads on the southern Russian principalities, the Hungarians, the Poles, and the Lithuanians ravaged the western fringes of Russia and when the Germans appeared on the Russian borders in the late twelfth and early thirteenth centuries they introduced new methods of systematic pressure and methodical devastation. No less devastating, however, were the inter-necine wars between the princes themselves. Between 1055 and 1228 eighty interprincely wars are recorded, which means that there was a war almost every second year. Most of them, however, affected only part of Russia. Central Ukraine (the principalities of Chernigov, Kiev, and Volynia) served as the chief battleground for princely rivalry. In western Ukraine (Galicia) only six cases of domestic wars are registered for the period; in the land of Smolensk, likewise six; in the land of Riazan, seven; in Suzdalia, eleven.[38] Both the people at large and some of the best representatives of the ruling class under-stood well the folly of these wars in which the wealth of the nation—of the "descendants of Dazhbog," as the author of the *Lay of Igor's Campaign* puts it—was wasted. As we saw earlier (Chap. IV, sec. 5), some efforts were made to prevent them by interprincely agreement. However, so long as there were powerful social groups to which war could be profitable, either on an international or a local scale, there was little hope of stopping it altogether. The Mongol invasion put a curb, temporarily at least, on domestic wars but it was a bitter medicine indeed.

38. Soloviev, III, 40, 41.

# Chapter XI

# RUSSIA AND THE OUTSIDE WORLD IN THE KIEVAN PERIOD

## *1. Preliminary Remarks*

BASICALLY the feeling of Russians of the Kievan period toward foreigners was friendly. In peacetime the foreigner coming to Russia, especially the foreign merchant, was considered a "guest" (*gost'*); in the old Russian language the term *gost'* even acquired the connotation of "merchant" in addition to its original meaning.

In its attitude toward foreigners Russian law stood out in bold relief to the German law, which included such institutions as *Wildfang* and *Strandrecht* ("strand law"). According to the first, any foreigner (and any native "lordless" man) could be seized by local authorities and turned into a serf of the palgrave. Under the second, shipwrecked foreigners, together with their stranded goods, belonged to the lord of the land along the coast where the boat went aground—the duke or the king.[1] As we know (Chap. II, secs. 2 and 3), in their treaties with Byzantium of the tenth century the Russians pledged not to take advantage of the strand law when it came to Greek travelers. Whether they had gone by it prior to 907 we do not know. As to the *Wildfang*, it is nowhere mentioned in any Russian source of the period. Neither was the *droit d'aubain* (the right of the state to inherit the estate of a foreigner who happens to die within the boundaries of that state) known in Kievan Russia. It is noteworthy that in case of the bankruptcy of a Russian merchant his foreign creditors had priority over Russian creditors in the settlement of claims.

In studying the problem of the intercourse between Russia and foreign countries one has to take into consideration not only the field of organized political and economic relations but also that of reciprocal cultural influences, as well as the personal contact between the

1. Vladimirsky-Budanov, *Obzor*, p. 385. On *Wildfangrecht*, see R. Schröder, *Lehrbuch der deutschen Rechtsgeschichte* (4th ed. Leipzig, 1902), pp. 808, 844, n. 4. On the "strand law," see Schröder, pp. 533–534; G. Waitz, *Deutsche Verfassungsgeschichte*, VIII (Kiel, 1878, 275; E. Mayer, *Deutsche und französische Verfassungsgeschichte*, I (Leipzig, 1899), 102–103.

Russians and the foreigners. From this point of view we should be especially interested in collecting information about Russians traveling and sojourning abroad as well as about foreigners visiting Russia, whether on official missions, on business, or for any other reason.

Our survey of appropriate data may perhaps be made more intelligible by discussing each group of Russia's neighbors separately. Let us start with an examination of relations between the Russians and their next of kin: the non-Russian Slavs.

## 2. Russia and the Slavs

Prior to the beginning of the German "drive to the east" (*Drang nach Osten*) the Slavs occupied most of central and eastern Europe, including even some territories west of the Elbe River.[2] Around 800 A.D. the western boundary of the Slavic settlements followed approximately the line from the mouth of the Elbe River southward to the Gulf of Trieste—from Hamburg to Trieste, as it were.

During the next three centuries—the ninth, tenth, and eleventh—the Germans consolidated their hold on the Elbe River and attempted to extend their authority over the Slavic tribes east of it, with intermittent success and reverses. During the twelfth century they succeeded in firmly establishing their control of the region between the Elbe and the Oder. Meanwhile the Danes attacked the Slavs from the north and in 1168 Arkona, the Slavic stronghold on the island of Rugen, fell to them. In the early thirteenth century, as we know (see Chap. VIII, sec. 4), the Germans extended their drive to the Baltic area and crusading Prussia came into being, to become the bulwark of Germanism in eastern Europe. Combining various methods, such as extension of the political suzerainty of the Holy Roman Empire, as well as dynastic unions, colonization, infiltration, and so on, the Germans by the late nineteenth century had established their control in one way or another as far east as the Carpathian and Danubian areas, including also Bosnia and Herzegovina and the Dalmatian coast of the Adriatic.

During the first World War they made an effort to penetrate farther east and at one time succeeded in occupying Ukraine, the Crimea, and Transcaucasia. During the second World War their plans were even more ambitious and included a program of permanent political and economic enslavement of the Slavic peoples, as well as the sys-

2. On the history and civilization of the Slavs, see L. Niederle, *SS*, and *Život starých Slovanů* (Prague, 1911–34). 3 vols.

tematic destruction of Slavic civilization. Their failure to achieve this resulted not only in the restoration by the Slavs of their position as on the eve of the second World War but in the recovery of some territories farther to the west, long lost to them. The western frontier of the Slavic world is now back where it was around 1200 A.D.—along the line from Stettin to Trieste. Thus the clock of history has been set some seven-hundred-odd years back and the Slavs are now given a new chance in an entirely different international situation and entirely new cultural surroundings.

In that Slavic sea of central and eastern Europe, two islands of different ethnic stock have been preserved. These are Hungary and Romania. The Hungarians, or Magyars, represent a mixture of Finno-Ugrian and Turkish tribes; [3] the Hungarian language is still permeated with Turkic elements; besides, the Hungarian vocabulary contains many words borrowed from the Slavic. As we know (see Chap. II, sec. 2), they invaded the middle Danubian plains in the late ninth century and have held their ground there since. The Romanians belong by language to the Latin family. The Romanians speak a Romance language, the foundation of which, historically, is the vulgar Latin spoken by Roman soldiers and settlers in the lower Danube area. The Latin basis of the Romanian language has been affected to a considerable degree by other linguistic elements, Slavic in particular. [4] Modern Romania was formed in the middle of the nineteenth century by a union of two principalities, Moldavia and Wallachia. Neither of these existed in the Kievan age, however. In fact, the early Romanian tribes at that time had not established any organized political union nor did they populate the whole of the present Romanian territory. Most of them were pastoral people. A group of them, the so-called Kutso-Wallachians or Kutso-Vlachs, settled in Macedonia and Albania. Another group led a secluded life in the Transylvanian highlands until the late twelfth or early thirteenth century, when some of the tribes belonging to it were pushed

---

3. See G. Moravcsik, *Byzantinoturcica*, I, 58–64.

4. On Romanian language, see H. Tiktin, "Die Rumänische Sprache," *Grundriss der Romanischen Philogogie*, G. Gröber, ed., I (Strassburg, 1906), 564–607; J. A. Candrea-Hecht, *Les Éléments latines de la langue roumaine* (Paris, 1902); K. S. Jensen, "Die nichtlateinischen Bestandteile im Rumänischen," *Grundriss der Romanischen Philologie*, G. Gröber, ed., I, 524–534; A. Rosetti, *Istoria limbii Române* (Bucharest, 1938–40) 3 vols. (reviewed by G. Bonfante, *Language, 18* [1942], 287–292); S. Puşcariu, *Die rumänische Sprache*, I (Leipzig, 1943) (I am indebted to Professor Bonfante for this reference.) See also G. Bonfante, "L'Origine des langues romanes," *Renaissance, 1* (1943), 573–588.

southward and eastward by the Magyars and descended into the valleys of the Pruth and Danube rivers, where they founded the principalities of Moldavia and Wallachia.[5]

There was no unity, either political or cultural, among the Slavs during the Kievan period. In the Balkan peninsula the Bulgars, the Serbs, and the Croats formed each a state of its own. The tsardom of Bulgaria, as we know,[6] was founded by the Turkish tribe of Bulgars in the late seventh century; by the middle of the ninth it was partly Slavicized. Under Tsar Simeon (888–927) it became the leading Slavic state. Later, however, its strength was undermined by internal dissensions and Byzantine imperialism. The Russian invasion under Sviatoslav (see Chap. II, sec. 5) added to the troubles of the Bulgarian people. It must be noted, however, that Sviatoslav's aim was to establish a huge Russo-Slavic empire with Bulgaria as its cornerstone. In the early eleventh century the Byzantine emperor Basil II (called "Bulgarocton"—"Slayer of the Bulgars") crushed the Bulgarian army and made Bulgaria a Byzantine province. It was only in the late twelfth century that the Bulgars, aided by the Wallachians, succeeded in emancipating themselves from Byzantium and restoring their own tsardom.

In Serbia centrifugal forces were stronger than in Bulgaria and it was only in the second half of the twelfth century that most of the Serbian tribes recognized the authority of the "Great *Zhupan*," Stephen Nemanja (1159–95).[7] The kingdom of Croatia was formed in the course of the tenth and eleventh centuries.[8] In 1102 the Croats elected Koloman (Kálmán) of Hungary their king and a personal union was thus established between Croatia and Hungary, with the latter in a leading role. Even earlier than the Croats, the Slovaks in northern Hungary recognized the authority of the Magyars. Generally

5. On the history of the Romanians, see N. Boretsky-Bergfeld, *Istoriia Rumynii* (St. Petersburg; 1909); N. Jorga (Iorga), *Histoire des Roumains et de leur civilisation* (Paris, 1920); N. Banescu, *Historical Survey of the Rumanian People* (Bucharest, 1926); R. W. Seton-Watson, *A History of the Roumanians* (Cambridge, Cambridge University Press, 1934).

6. See *Ancient Russia*, chap. 6, sec. 6, 7; chap 7, sec. 7–9; and chap. 8, sec 7.

7. On the history of the Serbs, see K. Jireček, *Geschichte der Serben*, I (Gotha, 1911); S. Stanojević, *Istorija Srpskogo naroda* (3d ed. Beograd, 1926).

8. On the history of Croatia, see F. Šišić, *Pregled povijesti Hrvastskogo naroda* (Zagreb, 1916); N. Tomašić, *Fundamente des Staatrechtes des Königreichs Kroatien* (Zagreb, 1918); J. Horvat, *Politička povijest Hrvatska* (Zagreb, 1936). H. Grégoire, "L'Origine et le nom des Croates et des Serbes," *Byzantion, 17* (1945), 88–118.

speaking, medieval Hungary was not a centralistic state, and not exclusively nationalistic either. Being surrounded by Slavs it was influenced by Slavic culture in many ways.

As to the Czechs, their first state, formed around 623, was not of long duration.[9] The kingdom of Great Moravia was a second attempt at unity among the western Slavs [10] but was destroyed by the Hungarians in the early tenth century. The third Czech state was formed in the middle of the tenth century and played an important role in European politics throughout the Middle Ages, especially because of its association with the Holy Roman Empire; from the middle of the tenth century most of the rulers of Bohemia recognized the German emperor as their suzerain.[11]

The Polish tribes achieved a degree of political unity in the late tenth century under King Boleslaw I (Boleslaw the Brave, 992–1025). As we know (see Chap. VIII, sec. 4), following the death of Boleslaw III (1138) the Polish kingdom became a loose federation of local principalities, not unlike the Russian federation.[12] Prior to the dismemberment of Poland the Polish kings maintained an aggressive foreign policy, at times threatening the integrity of the Kievan realm and the Czech kingdom alike. An interesting trend of Polish expansion is the westward tendency. It was Boleslaw I who first formed the ambitious plan of uniting the Baltic and Polabian Slavs under his authority in order to check the German *Drang nach Osten*. Boleslaw III was the last of the Polish rulers to interest himself in the fate of the Baltic Slavs.

Let us now turn to the westernmost group of Slavs, settled as they

9. G. Vernadsky, "The Beginnings of the Czech State," *Byzantion, 17* (1945), 315–328.

10. *Ancient Russia,* chap. 8, sec. 6; see also G. Vernadsky, "Great Moravia and White Chorvatia," *JAOS, 65* (1945), 257–259; N. N. Martinovitch, "Zhupan, the Ruler in White Chorvatia," *JAOS, 67,* (1947), p. 61; G. Vernadsky, "Note on Zhupan," *JAOS, 67* (1947), p. 62.

11. On the history of the Czechs, see V. Novotný, *České Dějiny,* I, Pts. 1–3 (Prague, 1912–28); V. Novotný, ed., *Ceskoslovenská Vlastivěda,* IV (Prague, 1932); K. Krofta, *A Short History of Czechoslovakia* (London, Williams & Norgate, 1935); S. H. Thomson, *Czechoslovakia in European History* (Princeton, Princeton University Press, 1943); R. W. Seton-Watson, *A History of the Czechs and Slovaks,* (London and New York, Hutchinson & Co., 1943).

12. On the history of Poland, see V. Grabenski, *Istoriia Polskogo Naroda,* Russian translation, N. Iastrebov, ed. (St. Petersburg, 1910); A. Brückner, *Dzieje kultury Polskiej,* I; R. Grodecki, S. Zachorowski, and J. Dabrowski, *Dzieje Polski średniowiecznej* (Krakow 1926), I; Z. Wojciechowski, *Mieszko I and the Rise of the Polish State* (Toruń and Gdynia, 1936); O. Halecki, *A History of Poland* (2d ed. New York, Roy, 1943).

were in the territory now known as Germany. These may be divided into two branches, the Baltic Slavs and the Sorbs.[13] The latter are also referred to as Polabian Slavs—that is, Elbe River Slavs, since the Elbe is known among the Slavs as Laba (or Labe).

The Baltic Slavs are linguistically akin to the Poles. They were divided into a great number of tribes, forming at times loose unions or associations. In that sense we may speak of four main groups of Baltic Slavs. The westernmost is that of the Obodrichi. They were settled in Holstein, Luneburg, and western Mecklenburg. Next to them, in eastern Mecklenburg, western Pomerania, and western Brandenburg, lived the Liutichi. To the north of them, on the island of Rugen as well as on the two islands of the Oder estuary (Uznoim and Volyn), were the abodes of the daring seafaring tribes of the Ranians (Rani) and Volyni (Vulini, Vilini). The territory between the lower Oder River and the lower Vistula was occupied by the Pomorane (or Pomeranians), from *more*, "sea"—the "by-the-sea people". Of these four tribal groups the first three (the Obodrichi, the Liutichi, and the islanders) are completely extinct and only the eastern section of the Pomorane partly survived, due to the fact that they were included in the Polish state and thus saved from Germanization.

The region to the south of the Baltic Slavs, known in modern times as Thuringia and Saxony, was populated by the Sorbs. Of these only a small group survived, around Kottbus (Chotěbuz) and Bautzen (Budyšin), known as the Lusatians (Luzhichane).

There was even less political unity among the Baltic Slavs than among the Balkan Slavs. The Obodrichi even coöperated at times with the Germans against their Slavic neighbors. It was only in the late eleventh and early twelfth centuries that the Obodrichian princes attempted to unite the Slavic tribes of the Baltic area. Their state proved ephemeral, however, especially because political discord among the Slavs was at the time aggravated by religious dissension —the struggle between Christianity and paganism.

We are thus faced with the problem of the religious background

---

13. The Sorbs are also known as Serbs, although they are not identical with the Balkan (Yugoslav) Serbs. In order to avoid any possible misunderstanding, I shall use the name Sorbs, when speaking of Polabian Slavs and Serbs, for the Balkan people of that name. On the Baltic and Polabian Slavs, see A. Gilferding (Hilferding) *Sobranie Sochinenii*, IV (St. Petersburg, 1874); I. Pervolf, *Germanizatsiia Baltiiskikh Slavian* (St. Petersburg, 1876); D. N. Egorov, *Kolonizatsiia Meklenburga v XIII veke* (Moscow, 1915, 2 vols.); Niederle, *SS*, III (2d ed. Prague, 1927).

of medieval Slavdom. The first Slavic tribe to accept Christianity was the Dalmatians, in the early ninth century, but, as we know, it was in Moravia, through the labors of Ss. Cyril and Methodius, that Christianity scored its first important victory on Slavic soil, around the year 863.[14] Bulgaria followed, around 864.[15] The Serbs and the Croats were Christianized in the late ninth and early tenth centuries. A group of Russians were converted, as we know, about the same time as the Bulgarians [16] but it was only in the late tenth century that both Russia and Poland officially became Christian countries.

Paganism held its ground most stubbornly in the north, among the Baltic Slavs. We should not overemphasize the primitiveness of the Slavic religion. It must have been a rather complicated system of beliefs.[17] Slavic deities enjoyed a considerable prestige among the Teutonic neighbors of the Slavs and even the kings of Denmark used to send presents to the temple of Svantovit in Arkona.[18] However, following the Christianization of the Germans and the majority of the Slavs, the pantheon of the Baltic tribes became an isolated institution and their religion was doomed to provincialism. The reason the Baltic Slavs clung so long to their oldfashioned gods was that for them Christianity meant Germanization. In this connection it should be noted that the failure of the Slavic liturgy to hold its ground in Moravia and Bohemia was a tragic event not only for the Czechs but for the Baltic Slavs as well. Had the program of Cyril and Methodius won out in Bohemia, the Slavic liturgy might have spread northward to the Polabian Sorbs and Baltic Slavs and might have attracted them to Christianity, which they could then have considered a national religion. As things actually developed, the Baltic and Polabian Slavs had either to accept German priests and the Latin liturgy or to oppose Christian missions in general. Once they chose the second course, they sealed their own cultural and political isolation, since they thereby lost contact even with their kin, the Czechs and the Poles, who had already been converted to Christianity.

In view of the variety of the political and cultural background of the Slavs during the Kievan period it will be advisable, in discussing Russia's intercourse with her Slavic neighbors, to differentiate be-

14. *Ancient Russia,* pp. 357–359.

15. *Idem,* pp. 359–363.

16. *Idem,* pp. 345–353.

17. See G. Vernadsky, "Svantovit, Dieu des Slaves Baltiques," *Annuaire,* 7, (1944), 339–356.

18. Saxo Gramaticus, *Gesta Danorum,* A. Holder, ed., p. 567.

tween three regions: (1) the Balkan peninsula, (2) central and eastern Europe, and (3) the Baltic area.

(1) In the Balkan area, Bulgaria had the greatest significance for Russia.[19] In her pagan period Russia, as we know (Chap. II, sec. 5), came close to extending her control over the Balkan country. Following Russia's conversion to Christianity, Bulgaria became an important factor in developing Russian civilization by supplying that country with liturgical and theological books in Slavic translation as well as by sending priests and translators to Kiev. Certain Bulgarian authors, as for example John the Exarch, became quite popular in Russia. It would not be an exaggeration to say that Russian church literature of the early Kievan period rested on a Bulgarian foundation. Of course the Bulgar literature of this time consisted mostly of translations from the Greek, so that Bulgaria's role, from the Russian point of view, was essentially that of intermediary between Russia and Byzantium. This was also true in commerce; the Russian trade caravans passed Bulgaria on their way to Constantinople and there is little evidence of any direct dealing with the Bulgars.

While there is much paleographic and philological evidence on the influence of the Bulgarian literature on the Russian, information on personal intercourse between the Bulgarians and Russians, except for the period of Sviatoslav's invasion, is scant. One of the wives of Vladimir the Saint, presumably the mother of Boris, was a captive Bulgarian girl. Strangely enough, throughout the Kievan period there were no matrimonial ties between the Russian and Bulgarian ruling houses.

There is little evidence on the relations between the Russians and the Serbo-Croats in the chronicles of the Kievan period. In the *Book of Annals,* however, we find some brief but precise information on Serbia and Croatia. From other sources it is known that intellectual intercourse between the Russians and the Serbs was not inconsiderable.[20] Serbian manuscripts found their way to Russia; from the late eleventh century on Serbian influence on Russian literature was gradually replacing the Bulgarian. On the other hand, Russian manuscripts appeared in Serbia, as so many tokens of Russian cultural influence. It is noteworthy that Serbian scholars were acquainted

19. On the history of Bulgaria, see V. Zlatarski, *Istoriia na Bulgarskata Drzhava prez Srednite Vekove,* I–II (Sofia, 1918–1934) ; see also S. Runciman, *A History of the First Bulgarian Empire* (London, G. Bell, 1930).

20. See M. N. Speransky, "K istorii vzaimootnoshenii Russkoi i Iugo-Slavianskoi literatur," *ANORI, 26* (1923), 143–206.

both with the *Book of Annals* and with Ilarion's "Discourse on Law and Grace." The latter was used by the Serbian monk Domentian in his "Lives" of the Serbian saints Simeon and Savva, written around 1265; undoubtedly copies of Ilarion's works were available in Serbia much earlier than that. Mount Athos offered a meeting place for Russian and Serbian monks. Russian monks first settled there in the ten-seventies, in the Xylourgou Monastery; in 1089 they moved to the St. Panteleimon Monastery, while the Serbs took over the Xylourgou. From 1100 to 1169 the St. Panteleimon was in a state of decay and such Russian monks as remained on Mount Athos lived at Xylourgou among the Serbs. In 1169 the Serbs received the St. Panteleimon, which they shared with the Russians until 1197, when they moved to the Khilandar Monastery, thenceforth the main center of Serbian monasticism; the Russians now remained in possession of the St. Panteleimon, known since as Russikon.[21]

Of dynastic ties between the Russians and the Serbo-Croats only one case is known. In 1150 Prince Vladimir of Dorogobuzh (son of Mstislav I) met in Hungary, and married, a Yugoslav princess who was a relative of the Hungarian king. Presumably she was the daughter of Beloš, a Serb by origin; he was *ban* (governor) of Croatia, and his wife was a Croatian.[22]

(2) While Bulgaria was a Greek Orthodox country and Serbia, after some vacillations, likewise aligned herself with the Greek Church, the countries of central and eastern Europe—Czechia, Hungary, and Poland—became parts of the Roman Catholic world, as did Croatia also. It should be noted, however, that in each of these four countries the people showed much hesitation before their final acceptance of the Roman Catholic hierarchy and all were won to Roman Catholicism only after a period of intense inner struggle. The final schism between the Greek and the Roman Church took place in 1054. Prior to that the chief problem before the peoples of central and eastern Europe was not that of ecclesiastical allegiance—to Rome or Constantinople—but of the language of the church service, the choice being between the Latin and the Slavic. As we know, at one time the Pope was prepared to recognize, with some reservations, the use of the Slavic language for the Moravian church. Later on, under German influence, the recognition of Slavic was revoked and after the

21. *Idem*, pp. 176–178; see also Golubinsky, *Istoriia*, I, Pt. 2, pp. 741–745; G. A. Ilyinsky, "Znachenie Afona v istorii Slavianskoi pismennosti," *ZMNP, 18*, (1908), 1–41.
22. Baumgarten, "Généalogies," IX (1927), 23, 71.

death of St. Methodius (885) his disciples were driven from Moravia to Bulgaria.[23] Even after that, the Moravians and part of the Czechs clung for some time to the Slavic tradition and as late as in the eleventh century Mass was offered in Slavic in several Czech and Moravian churches, including the Sázava Monastery south of Prague.[24]

Czech missionaries were also active in Poland and there are indications that at first both Latin and Slavic were used in Polish churches but in 966 the Latin form of Christianity was preferred by Prince Mieszko out of political considerations as a concession to the German emperor. From then on the use of Slavic in church services gradually declined and finally came to an end.

Slavic influence was very strong in Hungary in the tenth and eleventh centuries since the Magyars were, at first, less numerous than the Slavs subjected to them. Originally the ancestors of the Magyars—the Ugrian and Turkish tribesmen—were pagans but during their stay in the north Caucasian area and the Pontic steppes they came in contact with Byzantine Christianity. In the second half of the ninth century, at the time when the Slavs in both Bulgaria and Moravia were already converted to Christianity, some of the Magyars visited the Danubian regions and became converted as well. It is significant that the Magyar word for "cross" is *kereszt*, obviously borrowed from the Slavic *krest*. When the Magyars occupied Hungary, opportunity for the work of both Byzantine and Slavic missions became ample.[25] In the late tenth century Duke Géza himself was baptized according to the Greek ritual through the influence of his first wife, who had been converted by a Byzantine missionary. However, Géza's second wife was a Roman Catholic and their son, Stephen the Saint, not only changed his religious allegiance from Byzantium to Rome but accepted the royal crown from the Pope (1000) and became a staunch protector of the Roman Catholic Church in Hungary. The struggle between the Byzantine-Slavic and the Latin Church continued in Hungary throughout the eleventh century, with the

23. *Ancient Russia,* p. 358.

24. On the role of the Sazava Monastery in the history of Slavic letters, see A. V. Florovský, *Chekhi i Vostochnye Slaviane,* I (Prague, 1935), 127–129, 142; V. Chaloupecký, *Prameny X Stoleti* (Prague, 1939), chap. 8; R. Jakobson, *Moudrost Starých Čechů* (New York, Československý Kulturný Kroužek, 1943), pp. 65–67.

25. Gy. Moravcsik, "Byzantine Christianity and the Magyars in the Period of their Migrations," *ASEER, 5,* Nos. 14, 15 (1946), pp. 29–45, and "The Role of the Byzantine Church in Medieval Hungary," forthcoming in *ASEER.*

Byzantinophiles and Slavophiles gradually losing ground. As has already been said, in 1102 King Koloman (Kálmán) by an agreement with the Croat nobility received the crown of Croatia in addition to that of Hungary, which resulted not only in a political union between Hungary and Croatia which was to last until 1918 but also in the gradual Latinization of the Croatian church.

On the other hand, in the wider cultural as well as political sense, the union with Croatia strengthened for some time the Slavic element in Hungary. Significantly, Koloman's code of laws was issued in Slavic, at least according to K. Grot.[26] During the reigns of Bela II (1131–41) and Géza II (1141–61) Bosnia was placed under the Hungarian protectorate and in this way close relations were established between Hungary and the Serbian lands, Bela II's wife Elena being a Serbian princess of the house of Nemanja. From the late twelfth century, however, the Slavic element in Hungary was on the wane.[27]

The victory of Roman Catholicism in central and eastern Europe meant the victory of the Latin language over the Slavic. Latin became the official language of the church service as well as of state chancelleries. It also became the foundation of the school curricula and of education at large, which accentuated the incipient cultural cleavage between Russia and her western neighbors.

In spite of the growing ecclesiastical and scholastic differences between Russia and central and eastern Europe, a lively intercourse was maintained in the Kievan period between the Russians on the one hand and the Czechs, Slovaks, Magyars, and Poles on the other. Culturally, the Czech nation was, in this period, the leading factor in that part of the Continent. Polish culture achieved maturity only later; in the sixteenth and seventeenth centuries Polish influence on the Ukrainian and Russian civilization was of paramount importance. Things were different in the Kievan period; as a matter of fact, Poland herself was at this time considerably under the influence of the Czech civilization. Nor was the Polish culture in this age superior to the Russian; in many fields—as for example literature and

26. K. Grot, "Istoriia Vengrii," *ES,* Half-Volume X (1892), p. 890.

27. On the history of Hungary, see Grot, *Moraviia i Madiary,* and *Iz istorii Ugrii i Slavianstva v XII veke* (Warsaw, 1889); N. Boretsky-Bergfeld, *Istoriia Vengrii* (St. Petersburg, 1908); E. Malyusz, *Geschichte des ungarischen Volkstums* (Budapest, 1940); B. Hóman, *Geschichte des ungarischen Mittelalters* (Berlin, 1940) (inaccessible to me); D. G. Kosary, *A History of Hungary* (Cleveland and New York, The Benjamin Franklin Bibliophile Society, 1941); Moravcsik, *Byzantinoturcica,* I, 58–64.

arts—the Russians were decidedly more mature than the Poles. Consider the epic poetry, for example. Even if we leave aside the *Lay of Igor's Campaign* as a unique work of genius, nothing comparable to the Russian byliny was created by medieval Polish folk poets. As to the literature of the learned, it was mostly in Latin, which was also, to a certain extent, the case with the Czechs.

As the knowledge of Latin was very restricted in medieval Russia, the Latin literature of the Czechs and Poles had little chance of directly influencing Russian thought. However, some translations from Latin into Slavic were made, presumably in Czechia, which then circulated in Russia. To this group of texts belong the comments on the Gospel by Pope Gregory the Great, as well as the apocryphal "Gospel According to Nicodemus." A number of lives of saints and prayers to saints were likewise translated from the Latin.[28]

The tenacity of the Slavic tradition in the Sazava Monastery also made possible direct contact between Russian and Czech literati. Czecho-Russian cultural intercourse was lively and of great significance. It is apparent that the Russian "Lives" of Ss. Boris and Gleb, of the eleventh century, present some parallels with the "Life of St. Václav" of Bohemia. Moreover, the latter, as well as that of St. Ludmila, also circulated in Russia. Another interesting evidence of the reciprocity in Czecho-Russian cultural relations is the fact that Ss. Boris and Gleb were commemorated in the Sazava Monastery as late as in 1095.[29]

An interesting aspect of the cultural intercourse between Russia and her western Slavic neighbors is that contained in the historiography of the time. According to N. K. Nikolsky's plausible argument, the compiler of the Russian *Book of Annals* used some Czecho-Moravian legends and narratives in describing the relations between the Russians, the Poles, and the Czechs.[30] Czech scholars seem to have participated in the translation of theological and historical books sponsored in Kiev by Iaroslav the Wise. It is likewise significant that some information on Russia and Russian affairs may be found in the works of Czech and Polish chroniclers of the twelfth and early thirteenth centuries—for example, that of the continuator of the

28. Florovsky, *op. cit.*, p. 111.

29. *Idem*, pp. 128, 151; Chaloupecký, *op. cit.*, 435–438; Jakobson, *op. cit.*, pp. 71, 72.

30. N. K. Nikolsky, "Povest' Vremennykh Let," *ANSR*, II, 1–106.

Chronicle of Kosmas of Prague, and of Vincent Kadlubek in Poland.[31]

The political and military relations between Russia and her western neighbors have already been discussed in preceding chapters (see Chaps. III, IV, and VIII, above). In regard to commerce, the trade route from Ratisbon to Kiev (see sec. 4, below) crossed both Poland and Bohemia. In addition to this transit trade both countries undoubtedly had direct commercial intercourse with Russia. Unfortunately only scraps of evidence of it can be found in the extant written sources of the period. It should be noted that the Jewish merchants of Ratisbon were in close contact with those of Prague. The Jews thus served as a link between the German and Czech commerce and the Russian.[32]

Personal contact through war and commerce between the Russians on one hand and the Poles, Hungarians, and Czechs on the other must have been ample. In some cases Polish prisoners of war were settled in Russian towns, while Polish merchants were frequent guests in south Russia, especially in Kiev. One of the Kievan city gates was known as the Polish Gate, an indication that in this section of the city there were numerous Polish settlers. As a result of Polish intervention in Kiev in the eleventh century (see Chap. IV, sec. 4), a number of prominent Kievans were taken to Poland as hostages. Most of them were later returned. As we know, the king of Poland at that time knighted a number of Volynian squires (see Chap. VII, sec. 3).

Personal intercourse between the Russians and Poles as well as between the Russians and the Hungarians was especially lively in the west Russian principalities, Volynia and Galicia. Not only princes but the noblemen of the respective countries had ample opportunity to meet.

As to princes, matrimonial ties between the members of the royal houses of Russia, Hungary, Poland, and Czechia were extensive.[33] As regards Hungary, four Hungarian kings of the Kievan period (Andrew I, Ladislas [László] the Saint, Koloman, and Andrew II)

31. Kosmas (Cosmas) Pragensis, *Chronica Boemorum*, B. Bretholz, ed.; V. Regel, "O khronike Kozmy Prazhskogo," *ZMNP*, *270* (1890), 221–261; *271* (1890), 108–148; Jakobson, *op. cit.*, p. 71; W. Kadlubek, *Chronica Polonorum*, A. Przezdiecki, ed., also in *MPH*, II, 193–447.

32. Florovsky, *op. cit.*, pp. 188, 189.

33. On the matrimonial ties between the members of the royal houses of Russia, Hungary, Poland, and Czechia, see Baumgarten, "Généalogies," *loc. cit.*, "Le Dernier Mariage de St. Vladimir," *OC*, XVIII (1930), 165–168, "Pribyslava de Russie," *OC*, XX (1930), 157–161, and "Cunegonde d'Orlamonde," *OC*, XX (1930), 162–168; D.

had Russian wives. Stephen III was engaged to a Russian princess but for some reason the marriage did not take place.[34] As to Hungarian wives of Russian princes, it is known that Rostislav of Tmutorokan married Lanka, daughter of Béla I; and Vladimirko of Galicia, a daughter of Koloman. Thus, speaking in crude commercial terms, Russia exported more brides to Hungary than she imported.

In Russo-Czech relations the contrary was true. Two of Vladimir the Saint's numerous wives were Czech princesses. In the twelfth century two Russian princes (Sviatopolk, son of Mstislav I; and Iaroslav, son of Iziaslav II) had Czech wives. Only one Russian princess—of Galicia—is known to have married a Czech prince (Vratislav of Brno).

In regard to Poland, the matrimonial turnover was more nearly equal. Eight Russian princes are known to have had Polish wives and eleven princesses were married to Poles in the Kievan period. Among the princes were three of Kiev (Sviatopolk I, Iziaslav I, and Mstislav II); among the Poles, three kings of Poland (Kazimierz I, Boleslaw II, Boleslaw III) and several princes of Krakow (Boleslaw the Curly-headed, Mieszko the Old, Kazimierz the Just, and Leszek the White).

The number of dynastic ties is in itself a significant indication of the close contact between the Russians and the western Slavs and Magyars. It is to be regretted that in most cases we know little of the life of Russian princesses abroad, or of the foreign brides in Russia. Presumably when the sources are silent it means that the marriage was a happy one. Of the unhappy alliances, that of Evfimia of Kiev to King Koloman of Hungary may be mentioned here.[35] A daughter of Prince Vladimir Monomach, Evfimia belonged to one of the best Russian families not only as to social position but culturally and morally as well. Her marriage to Koloman took place in 1112. Koloman, king of Hungary from 1095, was much older than his bride. His first wife had died in 1103, leaving him two sons. After the death of his elder son he appears to have worried about the succession to the throne, as a result of which he decided to marry again. He was an able ruler but personally a cruel and unattractive man; at least he is so de-

---

Rasovsky's review of Baumgarten's works in *SK, 2* (1928), 374, 375, and *SK, 4* (1931), 308, 309; see also B. Leib, *Rome, Kiev et Byzance à la fin du XI-e siècle*, pp. 152–158; Florovsky, *op. cit.*, pp. 58–72.

34. Karamzin, *Notes*, II, Note 40.

35. See S. P. Rozanov, "Evfimia Vladimirovna i Boris Kolomanovich," I, *OGN*, 1930, pp. 585–599.

scribed by the Hungarian chroniclers of the period. Being monks, they may have been prejudiced against him because of his coolness to the church and to monasticism. In any case, the atmosphere of Koloman's court in the eight years following the death of his first wife could hardly make him an ideal husband. Evfimia must have been shocked by the dissolute ways of the court, the constant intrigues, and most of all by the tactlessness of Koloman himself. Before long she felt that she could not endure her new life and returned to her father in Kiev. By this time she was already pregnant and in Kiev she gave birth to a son, Boris.

King Koloman died in 1114, being succeeded by the son of his first marriage, Stephen. At the latter's death, Béla the Blind, son of a cousin of Koloman, assumed the throne and at this juncture Boris presented his claims to the Hungarian crown, in which he was supported by the Poles. In order to undermine the validity of his pretensions his Hungarian opponents spread the story of his not being Koloman's son. According to this tale, Evfimia had been unfaithful to the king and Boris was the son of her lover. Since nobody had accused her of adultery at the time she left her husband and since the story was circulated for the first time at a moment of violent political conflict, it was presumably mere slander. It served its purpose, however, by undermining Boris' prestige and eventually preventing universal recognition of his rights on the throne.

Evfimia died in 1139. Her son Boris had an adventurous career. Following the death of his grandfather and protector, Vladimir Monomach (1125), he was sent to Constantinople to complete his education.[36] As the relations between Byzantium and Hungary were tense in this period, the emperor befriended him as a potential tool of Byzantine diplomacy and around 1130 gave him a cousin of his own in marriage. In 1131, by the order of King Béla's energetic wife Elena, sixty-eight Hungarian noblemen were killed as potential supporters of Boris while attending a meeting of the Hungarian diet. The next year Boris, supported by the Poles and also by the Russians and the Cumans, invaded Hungary but his army was defeated by the royal troops. Boris became a political exile, staying now in Poland, now in Austria, now in Bohemia, and trying in vain, whenever Hungary was in a difficult position, to seize his opportunity. In 1147 he succeeded in entering the country with the support of Austrian troops but was defeated again. Being threatened with capture, he hid in the baggage

36. *Idem*, II, *OGN*, 1930, pp. 649–671.

train of King Louis VII of France, whose troops were at the time crossing Hungary on their way to the Holy Land. While Hungarian spies discovered his whereabouts, King Louis refused to give him up and conducted him safely to Constantinople, where the vagrant prince was again taken under protection by the Byzantine emperor. He took part in the ensuing war between Byzantium and Hungary and was killed in a skirmish in 1154.

(3) Our information on the relations between the Russians and the Baltic Slavs in the Kievan period is scant. And yet commercial intercourse between Novgorod and the Baltic Slav cities must have been quite lively. Russian merchants were accustomed to visit Volyn in the eleventh century and in the twelfth there existed a corporation of Novgorodian merchants trading with Szczecin (Stettin).[37] In the *Lay of Igor's Campaign,* among the foreign minstrels at the court of Prince Sviatoslav III of Kiev the Veneditsi are mentioned.[38] It would be tempting to see in them the inhabitants of Vineta of the Volyn island but there seems to be more reason to identify them as Venetians. As to dynastic ties, at least two Russian princes had Pomeranian wives; and three Pomeranian princes, Russian wives.[39]

### 3. Russia and Scandinavia

Scandinavian nations are now regarded—and rightly so—as part of the Western world. From the modern point of view, then, it would be logical to discuss Norse-Russian interrelations under the heading "Russia and the West" (see next section). And yet it certainly is more convenient to treat Scandinavia separately, since historically and culturally it was in the early Middle Ages a world apart, a bridge between East and West, rather than a section of either. In fact, in the Viking age the Scandinavians not only harassed a great number of Eastern and Western lands by their constant raids but actually established their control over certain areas on both the Baltic and the North Sea, not to mention their expansion in the Mediterranean and Black Sea regions.

Culturally, the Scandinavian nations remained for a long period outside the pale of the Church of Rome. While the "Apostle of Scandi-

37. See N. Gratsiansky, "Krestovyi pokhod protiv Slavian 1147 goda," *Voprosy Istorii,* 1946, No. 2–3, p. 104. Cf. Aristov, pp. 198, 199.

38. *Slovo,* p. 22.

39. Baumgarten, *"Généalogies,"* pp. 72, 73.

navia," St. Ansgarius, started preaching Christianity in Denmark and Sweden in the ninth century, it was only in the late eleventh century that the new faith made real progress in Denmark and not until 1162 that the rights and privileges of the Church were formally approved there. In Sweden the old pagan sanctuary at Uppsala was destroyed in the late eleventh century; in 1248 the Church hierarchy was finally organized and celibacy of the clergy confirmed. In Norway the first king to attempt Christianization of the country was Haakon the Good (936–60), himself baptized in England. Neither he nor his immediate successors were able to complete the religious reform. In 1174 the privileges of the Church were finally confirmed in Norway.

From the social angle, in contrast to France and western Germany, serfdom has been unknown in Norway and Sweden; it was not introduced in Denmark until the sixteenth century. Thus the peasants in Scandinavia remained free during the Kievan period and throughout the Middle Ages. Politically, again in contrast to the West, the assembly of freemen (*thing*) was of paramount importance in both administrative and judicial matters in Scandinavian countries until at least the twelfth century.

The early period of Norse-Russian relations was examined in the preceding volume of this work.[40] As we know, the Norsemen were intimately connected with the establishment first of the Russian kaganate and then of the Kievan realm. We have, however, clearly to differentiate the various stages of Norse expansion in Russia and a brief review of this sequence will be in order here.

The Swedes, who apparently came first and penetrated to south Russia as early as in the eighth century, merged with the native Antian Slavic tribes, borrowing from the natives the very name of Rus'; the Danes and Norwegians, represented by Riurik and Oleg, coming as they did in the second half of the ninth century, lost no time in merging with the Swedish Rus'.[41] The participants in these two

40. *Ancient Russia,* chaps. 7 and 8. See also J. Bromberg (Ia. A. Bromberg), "Zametki po voprosam rannei istorii Rusi i Vostoka Evropy, II. K voprosu o proiskhozhdenii imeni Rus'," *Novoselye, 21* (1945), 96–98; S. H. Cross, "The Scandinavian Infiltration into Early Russia," *Speculum, 21* (1946), 505–519. For the Kievan period, see F. Braun, "Das historische Russland im nordischen Schrifttum des 10. biz 14. Jahrhunderts," *Eugen Mogk Festschrift* (Halle, 1924), pp. 150–196; S. H. Cross, "Yaroslav the Wise in Norse Tradition," *Speculum, 4* (1929), 177–197, 363; Chadwick.
41. See *Ancient Russia,* chaps. 7 and 8.

early currents of Norse expansion established themselves on Russian soil for good and firmly identified their interests with the native Slavs, especially in the Azov and Kiev areas.

The Norse immigration to Russia did not end with Riurik and Oleg, however. New bands of Scandinavian warriors were invited to Russia by the princes in the course of the late tenth and eleventh centuries. Some came on their own initiative. These newcomers were called Varangians by the Russian chroniclers to differentiate them from the old settlers identified as Rus'. It is clear that the old Norse settlers were considered a part of the Russian background already in the ninth century. The Varangians, however, were foreigners, not only from the point of view of the native Russians but also from that of the Russified Norsemen representing the earlier Norse penetration.

As we know, Prince Igor hired Varangians to reinforce his army in the Byzantine war (see Chap. II, sec. 3, above); Vladimir I used Varangians in his struggle against Iaropolk I and later lent some of them to the Byzantine emperor (see Chap. III, sec. 2); Iaroslav I depended upon Varangians in his campaigns against Sviatopolk I and Mstislav of Tmutorokan. Both from the Russian and the Norse sources we know that Varangians also used to come to Russia as individuals or in small groups to offer their services to the Russian princes or just in search of adventure.

Narratives of such adventures have been preserved in a number of Norse sagas. Of these, the saga of Olaf Tryggvason refers to the reign of Vladimir the Saint.[42] The Eymund saga describes the adventures of a group of Icelanders who came to Russia in the early eleventh century and took an active part in Iaroslav's struggle with the prince of Polotsk as well as with his other adversaries.[43] In the Kievan "Paterik" we find a story about a Varangian, Shimon, who offered his services to Prince Iaroslav the Wise.[44]

Scandinavians also visited Russia on their way to Constantinople and the Holy Land. Thus in 1102 King Erik Ejegod of Denmark appeared in Kiev and was warmly received by Prince Sviatopolk II. The latter sent a guard of honor of his best warriors to accompany Erik to the Holy Land. On his way from Kiev to the Russian frontier Erik was greeted with ovations. "Priests joined the procession carry-

42. See Sources, III, 4.

43. See A. I. Liashchenko, "Eymunder Saga i Russkie letopisi," *AN*, 1926, pp. 1061–1086; also Sources, III, 4.

44. V. Iakovlev, ed., *Pamiatniki russkoi literatury XII i XIII vekov*, pp. 61–64.

ing relics of saints, with the singing of hymns and pealing of the church bells."[45]

Besides the evidence of the literary sources, both Russian and Norse, on the voyages of Scandinavians to Russia, there is also some epigraphic evidence. One runic inscription of the first half of the eleventh century is concerned with a Norseman who fell in Russia as a warrior. In another a Norse merchant dealing with Russia is referred to. In two other inscriptions Novgorod is mentioned.[46] All the above inscriptions were found outside Russia. Within the country, a stone with an inscription which may be dated in the first half of the eleventh century was found on the island of Berezan, which as we know (see Chap. II, sec. 2) was an important station on the way from Kiev to Constantinople. It reads as follows: "Grani erected this monument to the memory of his comrade Karl."[47]

It must be noted that not all the Varangians who came to Russia were involved in military adventure. Some of them—perhaps I should say most of them—were attracted by commercial interests. As we know, the prosperity of Novgorod was founded on the exploitation of Baltic commerce and, while later on the German cities united in the Hanseatic League constituted the major factor in the trade of the West with Novgorod, in the eleventh and early twelfth centuries the Varangians were especially interested in it. Presumably the trade in slaves was the branch of commerce to which they paid particular attention. A special article of the *Russian Law* deals with the case of a fugitive slave escaping from his Varangian master.[48]

Since Varangian merchants were frequent guests in Novgorod and some of them resided there permanently, they eventually built a church there which is mentioned in the Russian chronicles as the "Varangian Church." In the twelfth century the Baltic, or Varangian, trade with Novgorod went chiefly through the island of Gotland. Hence the organization of the so-called Gotlander "factory" in Novgorod.[49] As the German cities extended their commercial transactions

45. Leib, *op. cit.*, p. 277.

46. Braun, *op. cit.*, pp. 164–165.

47. F. Braun, "Shvedskaia runicheskaia nadpis naidennaia na ostrove Berezani," *AK, 23* (1907), 66–75.

48. *Pravda Russkaia*, Short Version, Art. 11 (*Medieval Russian Laws*, p. 28). My interpretation of this article differs from the traditional one. According to the latter, the article deals not with a slave who escapes from his Varangian master but with a fugitive slave of another master whom the Varangian hides in his house. Either way, the Varangian is represented as dealing in slaves.

49. Aristov, p. 199.

to Novgorod, they likewise at first depended upon the intermediary service of Gotland. In 1195 a commercial treaty was signed between Novgorod on one hand and the Gotlanders and Germans on the other.[50]

It should be kept in mind that the Baltic trade provided a two-way passage and, while Scandinavian merchants used to travel in Russia, Novgorodian merchants likewise traveled abroad. They established their "factory" and built a church in Visby on Gotland; also visited Denmark, as well as Lübeck and Schleswig. It is recorded in the Novgorodian chronicles that in 1131 seven Russian ships perished with all their cargo on return voyages from Denmark. In 1157 King Sweyn III of Denmark seized a great number of Russian ships and divided the goods they carried among his soldiers. Incidentally, it may be noted here that in 1187 Emperor Frederick I granted equal rights for trading in Lübeck to the Gotlanders and the Russians.[51]

As in their social relations with other peoples, the personal contact of the Russians with the Norsemen may best be documented by a reference to dynastic ties.[52] Presumably four of Vladimir I's wives (prior to his conversion) were of Scandinavian extraction. Iaroslav I's consort was Ingigerda, daughter of King Olaf of Sweden. Vladimir II's son Mstislav I had a Swedish wife—Christina, daughter of King Inge. Inversely, two Norwegian kings (Harald Haardraad in the eleventh century and Sigurd in the twelfth) took Russian brides. It should be noted that after Harald's death his Russian widow Elizabeth (daughter of Iaroslav I) married King Sweyn II of Denmark; and after Sigurd's death his widow Malfrid (daughter of Mstislav I) married King Erik Emun of Denmark. Another Danish king, Waldemar I, likewise had a Russian wife. In view of the close connection between Scandinavia and England, the marriage of Gyda of England to Vladimir Monomach may also be mentioned here.[53] Gyda was the daughter of Harold II. After his defeat and death in the battle of Hastings (1066) his family sought refuge in Denmark and it was the king of Denmark who arranged the match between Gyda and Vladimir.

Because of the lively intercourse between the Scandinavians and Russians, the Scandinavian influence on the development of Russian

---

50. For the text of the treaty, see *Khristomatiia*, I (1908), 93–96; Goetz, *Deutsch-russische Handelsverträge des Mittelalters*, pp. 14–72.

51. Aristov, pp. 199, 200, 206, n. 643.

52. Baumgarten, "Généalogies," p. 68.

53. *Ibid.;* see also R. Hakluyt, ed., *Voyages* (Everyman's Library Edition), I (London, J. M. Dent & Sons; New York, E. P. Dutton & Co., 1932), p. 83.

civilization must have been of considerable importance. Indeed, there is even a tendency in modern historical scholarship to overestimate it and represent the Norse element as the leading factor in the formation of the Kievan state and culture. A new approach to the problem, from the point of view of the student of folklore, may be found in A. Stender-Petersen's book, *The Varangian Saga as the Source of the Old Russian Chronicle* (1934). According to this scholar the old Norse-Russian sagas originated in the Oriental and Byzantine milieu and only later spread from east to north.[54] Altogether it is obvious that the Norse influence in Russian folklore and historiography were the result of a complicated process. In any case one should not oversimplify the problem by assuming, without reservations, a wholesale importation to Russia of purely Norse ideas and habits directly from Scandinavia. To the Norse-Russian cultural intercourse either side, indeed, contributed its share and both were to some extent dependent on the Byzantine and Oriental background.

From the philological angle, the absence in the Russian vocabulary of any words of Norse origin bearing on intellectual and spiritual life should be noticed. Most of the Norse loan words in Russian (not numerous altogether) are terms of princely administration, as, for example, *grid'* ("bodyguard"), *tiun* ("steward"), and *iabetnik* ("agent"). Incidentally, "knout" (in Russian, *knut*) is also of Norse origin (*knutr*).[55]

## 4. Russia and the West

It is only with reservations that the term "west" is used here. The two pillars of the medieval "west" were the Roman Catholic Church and the Holy Roman Empire. From the religious point of view several nations of central and eastern Europe dealt with in the preceding section—Bohemia, Poland, Hungary, and Croatia—belonged to the "west" rather than to the "east," and Bohemia was actually a part of the Empire. On the other hand, there was not much unity at this time in western Europe as such. As we have just seen, Scandinavia remained aloof in many respects and was converted to Christianity much later than most of the other nations. England was for some time under Danish control and when she was brought into

54. A. Stender-Petersen, "Die Varägersage als Quelle der altrussischen Chronik," *Aarsskrift for Aarhus Universitet,* VI (Aarhus 1934), p. 246.

55. Thomsen, *Origin*, pp. 128–130. For a recent review of the whole problem of Norse influence on Russia—from the "Anti-Normanist" point of view—see V. A. Riasanovsky, *Obzor Russkoi kultury,* I, 161–289, 619–634.

closer relations with the Continent it was through the Normans—
that is, the Scandinavians, however Frenchified in this case.

In the south, Spain as well as Sicily for some time became an extension of the Arabic world. And commercially Italy was closer to
Byzantium than to the west. The Holy Roman Empire and the kingdom of France therefore constituted the backbone of western Europe
in the Kievan period.

Let us first turn to Russo-German relations.[56] Prior to the German
expansion in the east Baltic area in the late twelfth and early thirteenth centuries, the territory occupied by the Germans was not contiguous to that of the Russians. However, some contact between the
two peoples was maintained through trade and diplomacy as well as
through dynastic ties. The main German-Russian trade route in this
earlier period was through Bohemia and Poland. As early as in 906
the Raffelstätter customs statute mentions, among foreign merchants
coming to Germany, the Boemani and the Rugi.[57] Under the former
obviously the Czechs are meant; the latter may be identified as the
Russians.

The city of Ratisbon became the starting point for German trade
with Russia in the eleventh and twelfth centuries; German merchants
dealing with Russia formed a special corporation there, its members
being known as "Ruzarii." [58] As has been already mentioned (sec. 2,
above), the Jews likewise played an important role in the Ratisbon
trade with Bohemia and Russia. In the middle of the twelfth century
commercial connections between the Germans and Russians were likewise established in the east Baltic area, with Riga as the main German
commercial base, from the early thirteenth century. On the Russian
side both Novgorod and Pskov participated in the trade but its main
center in this period was Smolensk. As has been mentioned (see Chap.
V, sec. 8), an important commercial treaty was signed in 1229 between the city of Smolensk on one hand and Riga and a number of

56. On Russo-German relations in the Kievan period, see T. Ediger, *Russlands
älteste Beziehungen zu Deutschland, Frankreich und die römische Kurie* (Halle, 1911) ;
F. Braun, "Russland und die Deutschen in alter Zeit," *Germanica: Eduard Sievers zum
75, Gerburtstage* (Halle, 1925), pp. 678–727; M. E. Shaitan, "Germaniia i Kiev v XI
veke," *LZ, 34* (1927), 3–26. See also S. H. Cross, "Medieval Russian Contacts with the
West," *Speculum, 10* (1935), 137–144.

57. For the text of Raffelstädter customs statute, see *MGH, Capitularia*, II, 249,
250; cf. Florovsky, *op. cit.*, pp. 159–164.

58. On the German trade with Kiev, see V. G. Vasilievsky, "Drevniaia torgovlia
Kieva s Regensburgom," *ZMNP, 258* (1888), 121–150; L. K. Goetz, *Deutsch-russische
Handelsgeschichte*, pp. 540–543.

other German cities on the other. The following German and Frisian cities were represented: Riga, Lübeck, Söst, Münster, Groningen, Dortmund, and Bremen. German merchants visited Smolensk frequently; some of them resided there permanently. A German church of the Holy Virgin in Smolensk is mentioned in the treaty.[59]

With the development of active commercial relations between the Germans and the Russians and (as we shall see presently) with some diplomatic and matrimonial connections between the German and Russian ruling houses, the Germans must have collected a considerable amount of information on Russia. Indeed, reports of German travelers and records of the German chroniclers constituted an important source of knowledge of Russia not only to the Germans themselves but to the French and other west Europeans as well. In 1008 a German missionary, St. Bruno, visited Kiev on his way to the land of the Patzinaks to spread Christianity there. He was warmly received by Vladimir the Saint and given such assistance as could be offered. Vladimir personally accompanied the missionary to the Patzinak frontier. Bruno was favorably impressed by Russia and the Russians and in his report to Emperor Henry II represented the ruler of Russia as a great and wealthy king (*magnus regno et divitiis rerum*).[60]

The chronicler Thietmar of Merseburg (975–1018) likewise emphasized the wealth of Russia. He stated that Kiev had forty churches and eight markets.[61] The canon Adam of Bremen (d. 1074) in his book, *History of the Diocese of Hamburg*, called Kiev a rival of Constantinople and a bright ornament of the Greek Orthodox world.[62] The German reader of the period could also find interesting information on Russia in the *"Annals"* of Lambert Hersfeld (written around 1077).[63] Valuable information on Russia was also collected by the German Jew, Rabbi Moses Petachia of Ratisbon and Prague, who visited Kiev in the eleven-seventies on his way to Syria.[64]

As to diplomatic relations between Germany and Kiev, they began in the tenth century, as is shown by Otto I's effort to sponsor a

59. Aristov, p. 205.

60. G. Lozinskij, "La Russie dans la litterature française du Moyen Age," *RES, 9* (1929), 260.

61. Thietmar of Merseburg, *Chronicon*, F. Kurze, ed., pp. 257, 258.

62. Adam of Bremen, *Gesta Hammaburgensis Ecclesiae Pontificum*, B. Schmeidler, ed., p. 80.

63. Lambert (Lampert) Hersfeld, "Annales," *Opera*, O. Holder-Egger, ed., pp. 1–304.

64. E. N. Adler, ed., *Jewish Travelers* (London, G. Routledge & Sons, 1930), pp. 64–91 (no other edition of Rabbi Petachia's "Travels" is accessible to me); see Beazley, *The Dawn of Modern Geography*, II, 266–273.

Roman Catholic mission to Princess Olga (see Chap. II, sec. 4). In the second half of the eleventh century, in the struggle between the Russian princes, an attempt was made by Prince Iziaslav I to appeal to the German emperor for arbitration in Russian interprincely relations. Driven from Kiev by his brother Sviatoslav II (see Chap. IV, sec. 4), Iziaslav first turned to King Boleslaw II of Poland; receiving no help from that ruler he made for Mainz, where he asked Emperor Henry IV for assistance. To support his plea, Iziaslav brought rich presents: gold and silver vessels, precious fabrics, and so on. At that time Henry was involved in the Saxon war and could not send troops to Russia even had he been willing to do so. He sent an ambassador to Sviatoslav, however, to clarify the affair. The ambassador, Burchardt, was Sviatoslav's brother-in-law and thus naturally inclined to compromise. Burchardt returned from Kiev with rich gifts to support Sviatoslav's plea to Henry not to interfere in Kievan affairs, a plea in which Henry acquiesced.[65]

Turning now to German-Russian matrimonial ties,[66] at least six Russian princes had German wives, including two princes of Kiev—the above-mentioned Sviatoslav II and Iziaslav II. Sviatoslav's consort was Burchardt's sister Kilikia of Dithmarschen. The name of Iziaslav's German wife (his first wife) is not known. Two German marquises, one count, one landgrave, and one emperor had Russian wives. The emperor was the same Henry IV whose protection Iziaslav I asked in 1075. He married Evpraksia, daughter of Vsevolod I of Kiev, at that time a widow (her first husband was Henry the Long, Marquis of Nordmark). In her first marriage she seems to have been happy, at least reasonably so. Her second marriage, however, ended tragically; her dramatic story would need a Dostoevsky properly to describe and interpret it.[67]

Evpraksia's first husband died when she was hardly sixteen (1087). There were no children from this marriage and it appears that Evpraksia intended to take the veil in the Quedlinburg Convent. It so happened, however, that Emperor Henry IV, during one of his visits to the abbess of Quedlinburg met the young widow and was impressed by her beauty. In December, 1087, his first wife Berta died. In 1088 the engagement of Henry and Evpraksia was announced and in the

65. Hrushevsky, II, 62–64; Shaitan, *op. cit.*, pp. 9–11.

66. On the Russo-German matrimonial ties, see Leib, *op. cit.*, pp. 163–166; Braun, "Russland und die Deutschen in alter Zeit," *Germanica: Eduard Sievers zum 75, Geburtstage*, pp. 683–690; Baumgarten, "Généalogies," pp. 67, 68.

67. S. P. Rozanov, "Evpraxia-Adelgeida Vsevolodovna," *OGN*, 1929, 617–646.

summer of 1089 they were married in Cologne. Evpraksia was crowned empress under the name of Adelheid. Henry's infatuation with his bride did not last long and Adelheid's position at his court soon became precarious. Before long Henry's palace became the site of obscene orgies; according to at least two contemporary chroniclers, Henry joined the pervert sect of the so-called Nicolaitans.[68] Adelheid, who at first suspected nothing, was compelled to take part in some of the orgies. The chroniclers also relate that on one occasion the emperor offered Adelheid to his son Konrad. Konrad, who was of about the same age as the empress and was friendly disposed toward her, refused indignantly. Soon after, he revolted against his father.

While Henry kept abusing his wife in various ways, he at times had fits of jealousy. It should be noted that from 1090 he was engaged in a bitter struggle for the conquest of northern Italy as well as for control of the papal see. Adelheid was compelled to follow him to Italy and was kept in Verona under strict supervision. In 1093 she escaped and sought refuge at Canossa in the castle of Marchioness Matilda of Tuscany, one of Henry's most stubborn opponents. From there, advised by Matilda, Adelheid sent a complaint against her husband to the church council at Constanz (1094), which recognized Henry's guilt. Meanwhile Matilda introduced her protegée to Pope Urban II, who advised Adelheid to appear personally at the church council in Placentia (1095). She did so and publicly confessed before the council her participation in the orgies at Henry's orders. Her confession produced a great impression and she was absolved from any further penitential punishment.

Adelheid's confession meant for her moral torture and civic suicide; at the same time, although she did not think of it, it was a political action—a blow to Henry's prestige from which he never was able fully to recover. Two years after the fateful council Adelheid left Italy for Hungary, where she stayed until 1099, when she returned to Kiev. Her mother was still living and presumably took Adelheid—now again called Evpraksia—into her house. Henry IV died in 1106; late in the same year Evpraksia took the veil, presumably in the St. Andrew Convent at Kiev of which her eldest sister Ianka was in charge. She died in 1109 and was buried in the Monastery of the Caves.

Rumors of Evpraksia's participation in Henry's orgies and of her

68. C. Baronius, *Annales Ecclesiastici*, XII (Paris, 1887), 609 (as quoted by Rozanov, "Evpraxia-Adelgeida Vsevolodovna," pp. 629, 630). On the Nicolaitans, see P. J. Healy, "Nicolaites," *The Catholic Encyclopedia*, XI (1911), 67.

confession must have reached Kiev long before her return there. When she returned, in spite of the seclusion in which she tried to live, a new crop of rumors and slander must have run amuck in Kievan society. We find the repercussion of this gossip even in the Russian epic folklore, in the byliny. In a number of them the wife of Vladimir the Saint is represented as an unfaithful wench always falling in love with this or that one of his valiant knights. And in most of these byliny she is called Evpraksia. As S. P. Rozanov conjectures, the unhappy wife of Henry IV must have served as the prototype for her namesake in the byliny.[69] While the real Evpraksia was, of course, not Vladimir's wife but his great granddaughter, she was the sister of Vladimir Monomach and probably in this way her name became associated with that of Vladimir in the byliny.

While the position of Empress of Germany proved unbearable to the daughter of Vsevolod I, her aunt Anna (daughter of Iaroslav I) found the French throne quite agreeable.[70] The initiative in the case of Anna's marriage belonged to the French. In 1044 Matilda, first wife of Henry I of France, died childless and the king had to think of a second marriage. The fact that he eventually turned his attention to Kiev is evidence of the great prestige of the then prince of Kiev, Iaroslav the Wise. As a result, in 1049 a French embassy appeared in Kiev, in which two French bishops participated. Incidentally, it should be kept in mind that at this time there still was no official separation between the Roman and the Greek Church. Anna went to France, presumably in 1050. In 1051 her wedding with Henry was celebrated and she was crowned Queen of France. The following year their first son, Philip, was born. Eight years later Henry died (1060) and Philip became king. In view of his minority, a regent was appointed. Anna, as queen of France and mother of the king, likewise took part in governmental affairs. Her signature appears on several documents of the period; in one case she signed "Anna Regina" in Slavic characters.

Hardly a year had passed after the death of her royal spouse when

69. Rozanov, "Evpraxia-Adelgeida Vsevolodovna," pp. 643, 644.

70. Caix de Saint-Aymour, *Anne de Russie, reine de France et comtesse de Valois* (Paris, 1896) (inaccessible to me) ; S. Tr., "Anna Iaroslavna," *RBS*, II (1900), 193; M. Prou, *Recueil des Actes de Philippe I-er* (Paris, 1908), pp. xv, xvii–xxiii; A. Fleche, *Le Règne de Philippe I-er* (Paris, 1912) ; Leib, *op. cit.*, pp. 149–152; E. Gamillscheg and M. Vasmer, "Wiederum die Unterschrift der Anna Regina," *ZSP, 8* (1931), 124–128. M. Paléologue, "Anna Iaroslavna, Reine de France," *Illustration*, December 6, 1941.

Anna married again. Her second husband was Raoul de Crépy, Count of Valois, one of the most powerful and pugnacious French feudal lords of the period. She was his third wife and to marry her he had to repudiate his second wife on account, or under pretext, of the latter's infidelity. The clergy were indignant and Raoul was threatened with excommunication. The regent, in turn, was shocked by the queen's entering a second marriage after only a year of widowhood and no doubt the boy Philip suffered likewise. Gradually, however, peace was reëstablished in the royal family and Raoul was accepted as a member of the regency, in fact if not in law. When Philip came of age the influence not only of Raoul but of Anna as well rapidly faded away. Raoul died in 1074; the year of Anna's death is unknown. The last document she signed (as "Anna, mother of King Philip") is dated in 1075. In 1089 Philip granted a prebend to the Church of St. Quentin de Beauvais *pro remedio animae patris mei and matris meae.* Thus Anna died sometime between 1075 and 1089.

While Anna came to France and became queen before the division of the churches, she naturally sided with the Roman Church after the schism of 1054 and at this time received a second name, that of Agnes. As a matter of fact, the feeling of church unity was still strong and the difference between Rome and Constantinople for a rank and file member of either church was that of language and ritual rather than dogma. In that sense Anna entered the western church when she went to France and there was no need for her to think of her church allegiance in 1054. She was a devout worshipper and became known for her charities as well as for her land grants to various French churches and monasteries.

In spite of Anna's two successful French marriages, hers was the only case of a matrimonial tie between the Russian and French ruling houses in the Kievan period—in fact, in the whole course of Russian history. There is no evidence of any direct commercial relations between France and Russia in the Kievan period. However, the Belgians must have traded with Russia even if indirectly, through the Germans. It is known that Ypres cloth was highly appreciated in Novgorod.[71] Some personal contact between the Russians and the French became possible at the time of the Crusades, especially when French troops crossed Hungary. We have already seen above the adventure

71. Aristov, p. 204; H. Pirenne, "Draps d'Ypres a Novgorod," *RBPH, 9* (1930), 563–566;. A. Eck, "À propos des draps d'Ypres à Novgorod," *RBPH, 10* (1931), 591–594.

of Boris (a Russian on his maternal side) in the French baggage train. It is also likely that there were some Russian detachments in the Byzantine army at this period (see sec. 5, below) and the French were in contact with the Byzantines. Moreover, Russian pilgrims visited the Holy Land from time to time, which afforded another opportunity for Russians and French to meet. It is interesting to note that Russia and the Russians are mentioned frequently in medieval French poetry.[72]

Russian contact with Italy was conditioned by a number of factors, of which the Church of Rome was probably the most important. Relations between the Pope and Russia began in the late tenth century (see Chap. III, sec. 3) and continued, partly with Germany and Poland as intermediaries, even after the church schism of 1054. In 1075, as we saw, Iziaslav appealed for help to Henry IV. Simultaneously he sent his son Iaropolk to Rome to negotiate with the Pope. It must be noted that Iziaslav's wife was a Polish princess—Gertrude, daughter of Mieszko II; and Iaropolk's wife was a German princess, Kunegunde of Orlamünde. While both of these women must have become, officially, members of the Greek Orthodox Church at the time of their marriages, it seems that neither broke with Roman Catholicism in her heart. It was probably under their influence and at their advice that Iziaslav and his son turned to the Pope for assistance. We saw earlier that on behalf of his father and himself Iaropolk pledged loyalty to the pontiff and put the principality of Kiev under St. Peter's protection.[73] The Pope in turn, in a bull issued on May 17, 1075, granted the principality of Kiev to Iziaslav and Iaropolk as fief and confirmed their right to rule it. He then urged King Boleslaw of Poland to give full assistance to his new vassals. While Boleslaw procrastinated, Iziaslav's rival Sviatoslav died in Kiev (1076), which made his return there possible. As we know (see Chap. IV, sec. 4), he was killed in a battle with his nephews in 1078 and Iaropolk, who had no chance of keeping Kiev, was assigned by the senior princes the principality of Turov. He was killed by an assassin in 1087.[74]

Thus ended the dream of extending the authority of the Pope over

---

72. G. Lozinskij, *op. cit.*, pp. 71–88, 253–269; reviewed by D. Rasovsky in *SK, 9* (1931), 310, 311.

73. *Historica Russiae Monumenta*, A. Turgenev, ed., I (St. Petersburg, 1841), Nos. 1, 2, pp. 1–3; Hrushevsky, II, 65; Shaitan, *op. cit.*, pp. 11–26; M. A. Taube, "Rim i Rus" v do-mongolskii period," *Katolicheskii Vremennik, 2* (Paris, 1928) (inaccessible to me).

74. Hrushevsky, II, 76–77.

Kiev. However, the Catholic prelates watched closely further events in west Russia. In 1204, as we saw (Chap. VIII, sec. 4), the Pope's ambassadors visited Prince Roman of Galicia and Volynia to urge him to embrace Roman Catholicism but had no success.

Religious contact between Russia and Italy need not be connected exclusively with the activities of the Pope; it was in some cases a result of popular feeling. The most interesting instance of this elemental religious connection between Russia and Italy is the veneration of the relics of St. Nicholas at Bari.[75] In this case, of course, the object of veneration was a saint of preschism period, popular both in the west and the east. Still, the case is typical enough of the absence of denominational barriers in the Russian religious mentality of the time. While the Greeks celebrate the memory of St. Nicholas on December 6, the date of the saint's death, the Russians have a second St. Nicholas holiday on May 9. This was instituted in 1087 to commemorate the so-called "Translation of the Relics" of St. Nicholas from Myre, Lycia, to Bari, Italy. The relics were actually removed by a party of Bari merchants who traded with the Levant and visited Myre posing as pilgrims. They succeeded in snatching them away to their boat before the Greek guards realized what was going on, then made straight for Bari, where the clergy and officials received them enthusiastically. The whole operation was later explained as a desire to deposit the relics in a safer place than Myre, since that town was in potential danger of Seljuq raids.

From the point of view of the inhabitants of Myre it was plain robbery and it is understandable that the Greek Church refused to celebrate the event. The rejoicing of the Bari citizens, who were able to establish a new shrine in their town, and of the Roman Church which blessed it is likewise perfectly understandable. The speedy Russian acceptance of the holiday of Translation is more difficult to explain at first glance. However, if we take into consideration the historical background of southern Italy and Sicily, Russia's connection with it becomes clearer. This involves the old Byzantine interest in the region and the more recent Norman drive from the west. The Normans, whose original object was to fight the Arabs in Sicily, later established their control in the whole of southern Italy, a situation which resulted in a series of clashes with Byzantium. We have seen that there were Russo-Varangian auxiliary troops in the Byzantine army from at least the early tenth century. It is known that a strong

75. Leib, *op. cit.*, pp. 51–74.

Russo-Varangian corps participated in the Byzantine expedition to Sicily in 1038–42.[76] Among other Varangians, the Norwegian Harald, who later married Iaroslav's daughter Elizabeth and became king of Norway, participated in this expedition. In 1066 another group of Russo-Varangians in the Byzantine service was stationed in Bari.[77] This was before the "translation" of St. Nicholas' relics but it should be noted that some of the Russians liked the place so much that they settled there permanently and were eventually Italianized. Presumably it was through their medium that Russia became acquainted with Italian affairs and in particular took to her heart Bari's enthusiasm in her new shrine.

Since war was closely connected with commerce throughout this period, some commercial intercourse between the Russians and Italians must have resulted from all these military expeditions. In the late twelfth century, also, Italian merchants extended their operations to the Black Sea region. According to the provisions of the Byzantine-Genoese treaty of 1169, the Genoese were allowed to trade in all parts of the Byzantine Empire except "Rossia" and "Matracha." G. I. Bratianu explains these names as the Black Sea and the Sea of Azov.[78] Thus, in his opinion, the Bosporus remained closed to the Genoese. The explanation is not convincing; much more plausible is Kulakovsky's interpretation. He suggests that the two names refer not to the two seas but to specific localities. "Matracha" is certainly another name for Tmutorokan. "Rossia," in Kulakovsky's view should be identified as Kerch. Thus according to this scholar only the Sea of Azov was closed to the Genoese and not the Black Sea.[79]

In the period of the Latin Empire (1204–61) the Black Sea was also opened to the Venetians. Both the Genoese and the Venetians eventually established a number of commercial bases ("factories") in the Crimea and Azov areas. While there is no evidence of the existence of such factories in the pre-Mongol period, both Genoese and Venetian merchants must have visited the Crimean ports long before 1237. As the Russian merchants likewise· visited them, there was obviously the possibility of some contact between Russians and Ital-

76. V. G. Vasilievsky, *Trudy,* I (St. Petersburg, 1908), 288–303.

77. *Idem,* I, 332, 333.

78. G. I. Bratianu, *Recherches sur le commerce génois dans la Mer Noire au XIII-e siècle* (Paris, 1929), p. 50.

79. I. Kulakovsky, *Proshloe Tavridy* (2d ed. Kiev, 1914), p. 73; see also D. Rasovsky's review of Bratianu's book in *SK,* III (1929), 322–324. Rasovsky is inclined to identify "Rossia" as a port in the Sea of Azov.

ians in the Black Sea and Azov areas even in the pre-Mongol period.

Incidentally, it may be remarked that a considerable number of Russians must have come to Venice and other Italian cities unwillingly, in another connection with the Black Sea trade. These were not traders but just so many objects of trade—that is, slaves bought by the Italian merchants from the Cumans. Speaking of Venice we may recall the "Veneditsi" singers mentioned in the *Lay of Igor's Campaign*. As we have seen (sec. 2, above), these may be considered either Baltic Slavs or Venetians but most likely they were Venetians.

With Spain, or rather with the Spanish Jews, the Khazars were in correspondence in the tenth century.[79a] If any Russians came to Spain in the Kievan period, they must likewise have been slaves. It should be noted that in the tenth and eleventh centuries Mohammedan rulers of Spain used slaves as bodyguards or mercenaries. Such troops were known as "Slavic," although only a part of them were actually Slavs. Many an Arab ruler in Spain depended on this Slavic corps, several thousand strong,[80] to reinforce his power. Knowledge of Spain, if any, must have been hazy in Russia. In Spain, however, due to the research and travel of Moslem scholars residing there, as well as to the reports of Jewish merchants, a certain amount of information on Russia—old or contemporary—was gradually accumulated. Al-Bakri's treatise, written in the eleventh century, contained precious data on the pre-Kievan and early Kievan periods. Among other sources, Al-Bakri used the narrative of the Jewish merchant Ben-Yakub.[81] There was another important Arabic work containing information on Russia, by Idrisi, likewise a resident of Spain, who completed his treatise in 1154.[82] The Spanish Jew, Benjamin of Tudela, left a valuable record of his travels in the near East in 1160–73, during which he met a number of Russian merchants.[83]

79a. See P. K. Kokovtsov, *Evreisko-Khazarskaia perepiska v X vcke*, pp. 51–112.
80. R. Dozy, *Histoire des musulmans d'Espagne*, E. Levi-Provencal, ed., II (Leyde, 1932), 153–155; see also F. Grenard, *Grandeur et décadence de l'Asie* (Paris, 1939), pp. 30, 31.
81. A. A. Kunik and Baron V. Rosen, "Izvestiia Al-Bekri i drugikh avtorov o Rusi i Slavianakh," *ANZ, 32* (1879), Supplement 2, pp. 11–16, 65–117; Markwart, pp. 145, 146, 472. On Al-Bakri, see A. Cour, "Al-Bakri," *EL*, I (1913), 606–607. For a new edition of Ibrahim b. Yakub's report, by T. Kowalski, see *MPH*, New Ser., Vol. I (1946).
82. C. F. Seybold, "Idrisi," *EI*, II (1927), 451, 452.
83. Benjamin of Tudela, *The Itinerary of Rabbi Benjamin of Tudela*, A. Asher, tr. & ed. Cf. Beazley, *op. cit.*, II, 224–264.

## 5. Russia and Byzantium

The Byzantine Empire was both politically and culturally the major power of the medieval world, at least until the era of the Crusades.[84] Even after the First Crusade the Empire still occupied a place of paramount importance in the Near East and it was only the fourth expedition which signalized the decline of Byzantinism. Thus for most of the Kievan period Byzantium represented a higher level of civilization not only for Russia but in relation to western Europe as well. Characteristically enough, from the Byzantine point of view the knights of the Fourth Crusade were mere crude barbarians and it must be said that they certainly behaved as such.

For Russia the impact of Byzantine civilization meant more than for any other European country, except perhaps Italy and of course the Balkans. Together with the latter, Russia became part of the Greek Orthodox world; that is, in terms of the period, of the Byzantine world. The Russian church was but a branch of the Byzantine church; Russian art was permeated by Byzantine influences.

It must be taken into consideration that according to Byzantine doctrine the Greek Orthodox world was to be led by two heads, the Patriarch and the Emperor—the "symphony" between church and state was to constitute the foundation of Greek Orthodox society.[85] The theory did not always correspond to fact. In the first place, the Patriarch of Constantinople was not the head of the whole Greek Orthodox Church, since there were four other patriarchs, to wit: the bishop of Rome (i.e., the Pope, recognized as one of the ecumenical patriarchs prior to the schism of 1054) and the three Oriental patriarchs (of Alexandria, Antioch, and Jerusalem). In the case of Russia, however, this did not matter much, since in the Kievan period

---

84. Out of the extensive and ever-growing literature of Byzantine history, suffice it here to mention only a few important recent works: A. A. Vasiliev, *History of the Byzantine Empire* (Madison, Wis., 1928–29, 2 vols.) (new edition forthcoming); G. Ostrogorsky, *Geschichte des byzantinischen Staates;* M. V. Levchenko, *Istoriia Vizantii.* For a general outline of the Byzantine civilization, see C. Diehl, *Byzance: Grandeur et décadence* (Paris, 1920), and *Manuel d'art byzantin,* (Paris, 1925–26, 2 vols.); S. Runciman, *Byzantine Civilization* (London, E. Arnold, 1933). There is a special study on the influence of Byzantium on Russian civilization: V. S. Ikonnikov, *Opyt izsledovaniia o kulturnom znachenii Vizantii v Russkoi istorii* (Kiev, 1869). See also A. A. Vasiliev, "Economic Relations between Byzantium and Old Russia," *Journal of Economic and Business History, 4* (1931–32), 314–334; S. H. Cross, "The Results of the Conversion of the Slavs from Byzantium," *Annuaire, 7* (1944), 71–82.

85. V. V. Sokolsky, "O kharaktere i znachenii Epanagogi," *VV,* 1 (1894), 17–54; G. Vernadsky, "Vizantiiskie ucheniia o vlasti tsaria i patriarkha," *Recueil Kondakov* (Prague, 1926), pp. 143–154.

the Russian church was but a diocese of the Patriarchate of Constantinople and the authority of that patriarch was paramount.

But the nature of the relations between the emperor and the Patriarch of Constantinople could, and did at times, affect Russia. While theoretically the Patriarch was not subordinate to the emperor, actually on many occasions the election of a new patriarch depended on the emperor's attitude and the latter was in a position to interfere in church affairs. Eventually some of the Byzantine students of canon law were obliged to recognize the privileges of the emperor in church administration.[86]

Because of this, for a foreign nation to recognize the authority of the Patriarch of Constantinople meant also belonging to the political sphere of influence of the Byzantine emperor. As we know (see Chap. II, sec. 4), the Russian princes, as well as the rulers of other countries about to be converted to Christianity, realized the danger and took pains to avoid the political implications of conversion. Nevertheless, once a nation was converted, not only the Patriarch but the emperor as well claimed suzerainty over it and Russia was no exception to the rule. The desire of Vladimir I to preserve his independence resulted in both military conflict with Byzantium and an attempt to organize the Russian church as an autonomous body outside the Patriarchate of Constantinople (see Chap. III, sec. 3). Iaroslav the Wise, however, came to terms with Byzantium and accepted a metropolitan from the Imperial City (1037). Following this the emperor apparently considered Iaroslav his vassal and, when in 1043 a war started between Russia and the Empire, the Byzantine historian Psellus referred to it as to a "revolt of the Russians." [87]

While the Byzantine doctrine of the suzerainty of the emperor over other Christian rulers was never accepted by Iaroslav's successors in Kiev, a Galician prince formally acknowledged himself the emperor's vassal (hypospondos) in the middle of the twelfth century.[88] Gener-

86. So especially Balsamon who even says that the emperor is subject neither to the lay law nor the canon law; *PG,* CXXXVIII, col. 93.

87. M. Psellus, *Chronographia,* C. Sathas, ed., p. 129; *Michel Psellos: Chronographie,* E. Renauld, ed., II, 8. In his article, "Was Old Russia a Vassal State of Byzantium?" *Speculum,* 7 (1932), 350–460, A. A. Vasiliev sees in Psellus' words an evidence of the alleged fact that Russia should have been under the Byzantine protectorate since the time of Vladimir. Psellus, however, only says that during the reign of Basil II (Vladimir's contemporary) the empire was so strong that the Russians did not dare then to attack Constantinople.

88. G. Vernadsky, "Relations byzantino-russes au XII-e siècle," *Byzantion,* 4 (1928), 269–276.

ally speaking, however, Kievan Russia cannot be considered a vassal state of Byzantium. Kiev's subordination was along ecclesiastic lines and even in this field the Russians twice made an attempt to emancipate themselves: in the case of the metropolitan Ilarion in the eleventh century and that of Kliment in the twelfth.

Even though the Russian princes asserted their political independence from Constantinople, the prestige of both the imperial power and the patriarchal authority was great enough to influence their policies on many occasions. Constantinople, "the Imperial City" (Tsargrad) as the Russians used to call it, was regarded as the intellectual and social capital of the world. Because of all these various factors, in the relations between Russia and her neighbors the Byzantine Empire held a unique position: while her cultural intercourse with other nations was on an equal footing, with Byzantium Russia was essentially the debtor in a cultural sense.

Yet it would be a mistake to represent Kievan Russia as being entirely dominated by Byzantium, even culturally. While accepting the principles of the Byzantine civilization, the Russians adapted them to their own conditions. Neither in religion nor in art did they slavishly imitate the Greeks but rather developed an approach of their own. In regard to religion, the use of the Slavic language in the church services was, of course, of paramount importance for the naturalization of the church and the growth of a native religious mentality somewhat different from the Byzantine spirit.

Since ecclesiastical ties were the strongest element in cementing Russo-Byzantine relations, any survey of the latter and of the personal contact between the Russians and the Byzantines must start with the church and religion. The political and canonical aspects of the problem have already been briefly dealt with (see Chap. III, sec. 4; and Chap. VIII, sec. 2). Here we have to appraise rather the personal aspects of ecclesiastical relations. In the first place, all but two of the metropolitans of Kiev of the pre-Mongol period were Greeks; so also were about half the bishops. Those church dignitaries were undoubtedly accompanied by deacons and secretaries; thus there must have been at least a small circle of Byzantine intellectuals in every Russian bishopric. On the other hand, the Russian clergy and monks were accustomed to visit the main centers of Byzantine learning and monasticism, Mount Athos being their favorite place of pilgrimage. It was to Mount Athos that the future founder of the Kievan Monastery of the Caves, St. Antoni, went to prepare himself for his task.[89] Later, some Russian monks settled permanently there (see sec. 2, above).

The growth of the church in Russia was accompanied by a rapid development of church art and here again the role of imported Greek architects and painters was of paramount importance, especially in the eleventh century. Later on, some of the Russian students of art went to Byzantium for training, Mount Athos being an especially convenient place for them to start their icon-painting careers.

The relations between the Russian princes and the members of Byzantine royalty were likewise very extensive. In regard to dynastic ties,[90] the most important event was of course the marriage of Vladimir the Saint and Princess Anna of Byzantium, sister of Emperor Basil II (see Chap. III, sec. 3). Incidentally, one of Vladimir's wives during his heathen period was likewise a Greek, formerly the spouse of his brother Iaropolk (see Chap. III, sec. 2). Vladimir's grandson Vsevolod I (son of Iaroslav the Wise) also married a Greek princess. Of the grandsons of Iaroslav the Wise, two had Greek wives: Oleg of Chernigov and Sviatopolk II. The former married Theophano Musalonissa (before 1083); the latter, Barbara Komnena (around 1103)—she was Sviatopolk's third wife. The second wife of Vladimir Monomach's son Iuri was presumably of Byzantine origin. In 1200 Prince Roman of Galicia married a Byzantine princess, a relative of Emperor Isaak II, of the Angeli family.

The Greeks, on their part, proved to be interested in Russian fiancées. In 1074 Constantine Dukas was engaged to Princess Anna (Ianka) of Kiev, daughter of Vsevolod I. For reasons unknown to us the marriage did not take place and, as we know (see sec. 2, above, and Chap. IX, sec. 9), Ianka took the veil. In 1104 Isaak Komnenus married Princess Irina of Peremyshl, daughter of Volodar. About ten years later Vladimir Monomach gave his daughter Maria in marriage to the refugee Byzantine prince Leo Diogenes, allegedly son of Emperor Romanus Diogenes.[91] In 1116 Leo invaded the Byzantine province of Bulgaria; he met at first with some success, but was later

---

89. "Antonii Pecherskii," *RBS*, II (1900), 212.

90. On the Russo-Byzantine dynastic ties, see Baumgarten, "Généalogies," p. 69; Leib, *op. cit.*, pp. 169, 170.

91. There is much confusion in our information about this marriage. First of all, there is no definite evidence to show that Leo was Romanus' son. Secondly, according to Vasilievsky, *Trudy*, II (St. Petersburg, 1912), 37–49, Maria was not Vladimir II's daughter but a sister of his. In my opinion, Vasilievsky has not proved his case. See Hrushevsky, II, 115, 116.

killed. Their son Vasili was killed in a clash between the Monomashichi and the Olgovichi in 1136. The grief-stricken Maria died ten
years later.[92]

Vladimir Monomach's granddaughter Irina (Dobrodeia), daughter
of Mstislav I, was more fortunate in her marriage; her wedding with
Andronicus Komnenus took place in 1122. In 1194 a member of the
Byzantine house of the Angeli married Princess Evfimia of Chernigov, daughter of Sviatoslav III's son Gleb.

Because of these dynastic intermarriages many a Russian prince
felt himself at home in Constantinople and in fact many of the members of the house of Riurik visited the Imperial City, Princess Olga
of the tenth century being the first to do so. It is interesting to note
that in certain cases Russian princes were deported to Constantinople
by their relatives. Thus in 1079 Prince Oleg of Tmutorokan and
Chernigov was exiled "overseas to Tsargrad." [93] In 1130 the princes
of Polotsk, with their wives and children, were exiled by Mstislav I
"to Greece because they had violated the oath." [94] According to
Vasiliev, "this may be explained by the fact that the petty princes who
revolted against their ruler were held to account not only by the Russian prince, but by the suzerain of Russia, the Byzantine Emperor.
They were exiled as dangerous and undesirable not only to the Russian prince but also to the Emperor." [95] The explanation seems un-
convincing to me. First of all, as has been said, there is no evidence
that the Russian princes, except one Galician prince, recognized the
Byzantine emperor as their suzerain. Secondly, there is no evidence
that the princes exiled to Byzantium were tried there by the emperor;
they were merely given refuge. It was traditional for the Byzantine
emperors to open their hospitality to the exiled rulers of other countries. Not only did their presence enhance the prestige of the emperor
but some of them might eventually be used as tools of Byzantine
diplomacy, as was Boris, son of Koloman (see sec. 2, above).

Moreover, the Russian princes in their turn offered shelter to the
exiled members of Byzantine royalty, as to Leo Diogenes mentioned
above and to the future emperor Andronicus Komnenus. The latter, a
bold adventurer by nature, was imprisoned by his cousin Emperor
Manuel I but succeeded in escaping and made for Galicia, where he

92. *PSRL*, II, Pt. 1 (3d ed. Petrograd, 1923), col. 294.
93. *Idem*, col. 193. Oleg was arrested in Tmutorokan by the Khazars, presumably
at Vsevolod I's suggestion; see Hrushevsky, II, 72, 73.
94. *PSRL*, II, Pt. 1, col. 290.
95. Vasiliev, "Was Old Russia a Vassal State of Byzantium?" p. 356.

was well received by Prince Iaroslav Osmomysl (1165). Andronicus resided in Iaroslav's palace, ate and hunted with him, and even took part in the meetings of the boyar duma. Eventually he was pardoned by Manuel.[96] While Andronicus fled to Galicia, another member of the Komneni house, Manuel (whose exact relation to Emperor Manuel I is unknown) visited Kiev as envoy extraordinary of the emperor (1164–65).[97] It was as a result of this embassy that the Kievan princes took energetic measures to protect the Russo-Byzantine trade from the interference of the Cumans (see Chap. VIII, sec. 2).

Not only the princes but the members of their retinues likewise must have had ample opportunities of contact with the Byzantines. We have seen above that Russian troops participated in Byzantine campaigns in south Italy and Sicily in the eleventh century. Some Russians must have served in the Byzantine army operating in the Levant at the time of the First and Second Crusades. From the *Lay of Igor's Campaign* we may infer that Galician archers helped the Byzantines in the latter's war against the Seljuqs.[98]

Besides the church, the princes, and the army, one more social group in Kievan Russia was in constant intercourse with the Byzantines: the merchants. We know (see Chap. II, secs. 2, 3) that Russian merchants came to Constantinople in great numbers from the early tenth century on and were assigned permanent headquarters in one of the suburbs of the Imperial City. There is less direct evidence on Russian commerce with Byzantium in the eleventh and twelfth centuries but in the chronicles of the period Russian merchants "dealing with Greece" (*grechniki*) are mentioned on several occasions.[99]

## 6. Russia and the Caucasus

Geographically the Caucasus is a huge isthmus between the Black Sea and the Caspian. Ethnographically it has always been, and still is, an agglomeration of diverse racial elements, some of them forming comparatively large peoples but the majority consisting of small and even minute tribes. Historically, from time immemorial the Caucasus has lain at the crossroads of invaders and merchants converging from almost all possible directions. And finally, culturally—as may be expected—it has been the meeting place of East and West, of Chris-

96. Hrushevsky, II, 441, 442.

97. G. Vernadsky, "Relations byzantino-russes au XII-e siècle," *Byzantion*, 4 (1928), 270, 271.

98. *Slovo*, p. 30.

99. Hyp., col. 194; *PSRL*, II (1843), 93.

tianity and Islam, of Byzantinism and Orientalism, of the Iranian and Turkish civilizations and ways of life. Because of this complicated historical background it would not be proper to study the relation between Russia and the peoples of the Caucasus in the framework of either Russo-Byzantine or Russo-Turkish relations. The intercourse between Russia and the Caucasus must be approached as a separate problem.

The Caucasian range divides this general area into two main parts: Transcaucasia and the northern Caucasus or north Caucasian area. The latter consists of two different landscape zones: the mountainous region of the northern slopes of the main range and the steppes north of it. The steppe area is easily accessible from both the Don and Volga basins and has been controlled more often than not by the same nomadic peoples who dominated the Russian steppes. In the pre-Kievan and early Kievan periods it was under the control of the Khazars. Later, the Cumans used at least part of the area for grazing their cattle and horses.

Of the native tribes of the north Caucasus two seem especially important for the student of Russian history because of their early and intimate ties with the Russians. These are the Ossetians and the Kosogians. The Kosogians (Adyge), also known as Circassians, belong to the so-called Japhetide group of peoples; their abodes were in the basin of the Kuban River. They were conquered by Sviatoslav I around 963 (see Chap. II, sec. 5) and were later in close relations with the Russian princes of Tmutorokan (see Chap. IV, sec. 2).[100] The Ossetians represent a mixture of Japhetide and Iranian tribes; their language is Iranian. Historically they derive from the Alans and they are still called "Alans" in the Byzantine sources of the Kievan period. In Russian chronicles they are referred to as Iasians (Ias) or Asians (As).[101]

Originally, as we know,[102] the Alans occupied a considerable part of the south Russian steppes as well as the Azov and north Caucasian areas. In the Kievan period the Iasians filled a much more limited territory, being divided into smaller groups. One section of them lived in the central part of the Caucasian range, on both slopes of

---

100. On the Kosogian (Circassians), see A. Dirr, "Čerkesses," *EL*, I (1913), 834–836; Mirza Bala, "Çerkesler," *Islam Ansiklopedisi*, III (1945), 375–386.

101. On the Iasians (Ossetians, Alans), see V. Miller, "Osetinskie etiudy," III, *MU*, 8 (1887); I. Kulakovsky, *Alany* (Kiev, 1899); Minorsky, *Hudud al-Alam*, pp. 445–446; A. Zeki-Validi Togan, "Alan," *Islam Ansiklopedisi*, I (1944) (inaccessible to me).

102. See *Ancient Russia*, chaps. 3 and 4.

it, in the region of the present-day North Ossetian and South Ossetian autonomous areas. Another group lived in the lower Don area. In addition, smaller groups must have been scattered through the region along the eastern shore of the Sea of Azov, from the mouth of the Don to Tmutorokan. They also occupied part of the Crimea.

The Alans, especially that branch of them known as the Roxolani (Rukhs-As), played a role of paramount importance in the formation and consolidation of the Antes and other south Russian tribes.[103] Presumably the ruling class of the Antes was of Alanic origin. By the tenth century, however, the south Russian tribes, now led by princes of Scandinavian extraction, had severed their ties with the Alans and instead of the mixed Alano-Slavic tribes we have now to deal with two independent groups of peoples—the Russians and the Ossetians.

As a historical parallel to this division of two formerly united ethnic groups, the case of the French and the Germans may be considered. The Franks were a German tribe at the time of their conquest of Gaul. For about four centuries following the conquest the destinies of the French and German peoples were closely connected. Later, the Frankish Empire broke into its characteristic French and German parts but it was the French who kept the name of the original German conquerors, the Franks. Precisely in the same way it was the Slavs and not the Iranians who became known as the Russians, though originally Rukhs was the name of a branch of the Alans.

In regard to religion, the bulk of both the Ossetians and Kosogians were still pagans in the ninth century. However, from the time of the coming of the Arabs to Transcaucasia in the seventh century, Islam must have made some progress—very slow at first—among the Caucasian mountaineers. Christian missionaries—Armenian, Georgian, Byzantine—likewise visited the north Caucasian area and by the tenth century a considerable number of the Ossetians were converted to Christianity.[104] After the conversion of Russia another path was open to Christian missions among the Ossetians and Kosogians, through Tmutorokan.

Turning now to Transcaucasia, we find there two peoples with great cultural traditions: the Armenians and the Georgians, both converted to Christianity in the fourth century. In the seventh century a considerable part of Transcaucasia was conquered by the Arabs.

103. *Idem*, pp. 155–160 and *passim*.
104. I. Kulakovsky, "Khristianstvo u Alan," *VV*, 5 (1898), 1–18.

Before long, however, the latter met stubborn opposition on the part of both the Khazars and the Byzantines. Profiting by the struggle between the great powers, the Georgians as well as the Armenians succeeded in gradually emancipating themselves from Arab control. In the course of the ninth and tenth centuries several native principalities of feudal type established themselves in Georgia. That of Tao-Klarjeti, in the southwestern part of the country, eventually proved the strongest and later on, in the eleventh and twelfth centuries, its rulers succeeded in uniting most of Georgia. In order to withstand the attacks of the Arabs, and later those of the Seljuqs, the Georgian rulers had to appease Byzantium. King David Bagrationi of Tao (d. 1001) acknowledged himself a vassal of the Byzantine emperor, for which he was rewarded by the title of "Kuropalates." [105]

In Armenia the kingdom of Ani, centered in the northern part of the country, achieved actual independence and prosperity in the late tenth century. In the first half of the eleventh, however, it was conquered by the Byzantines. The latter did not profit much by their victory because of the subsequent invasion of the Seljuqs, who defeated both the Byzantines and the Armenians: in 1064 Ani was seized and seven years later the Seljuqs crushed the Byzantine army in the battle of Mantzikert (1071), after which Anatolia was open to them. The Seljuq conquest resulted in a terrible devastation of Armenia, one of the major catastrophes in Armenian history.[106]

Georgia was more fortunate, due partly to her more remote geographic position and partly to the abilities of her rulers. Instead of invading Georgia immediately after the Armenian campaign, Sultan Alp-Arslan accepted the rich presents sent to him by King Bagrat IV and spared the country. In the late eleventh century the Seljuqs threatened Georgia once more but the First Crusade changed the entire political and military set-up in the Near East and the attention

---

105. *Kuropalates*, "Guardian of the Palace," originally the title of one of the officers of the imperial guard; later on the term acquired the connotation of an honorary court title.

On the history of Georgia, see M. F. Brosset, *Histoire de la Géorgie* (St. Petersburg, 1849–58, 4 vols.); W. E. D. Allen, *A History of the Georgian People* (London, Kegan Paul, Trench, Trubner & Co., 1932). Cf. Prince C. Toumanoff, "On the Relationship between the Founder of the Empire of Trebizond and the Georgian Queen Thamar," *Speculum, 15* (1940), 299–312.

106. On the history of Armenia, see H. F. B. Lynch, *Armenia* (London and New York, Longmans, Green and Co., 1901, 2 vols.); H. F. Tournebize, *Histoire politique et religieuse de l'Armenie* (Paris, 1910); J. Laurent, *L'Arménie entre Byzance et l'Islam* (Paris, 1919).

of the Seljuqs was diverted from Georgian affairs.[107] King David II, surnamed "the Restorer," was quick to take advantage of the situation and administered a series of severe blows to the Seljuqs. During the reigns of David II (1089–1125) and Queen Tamara (1184–1213) Georgia achieved great prosperity. This was also the period of blossoming of Georgian arts and letters. The greatest Georgian epic poet, Shota Rustaveli, author of *The Man in the Panther's Skin,* was a contemporary of the queen. Both Byzantine and Persian influences may be felt in the Georgian literature and art of the period but the Georgian civilization itself was already quite mature.

The political and social regime of medieval Georgia was decidedly feudal. The feudal society was headed by the suzerain—"King of Kings"—but each of the feudal aristocrats was a *patroni* ("protector," "lord") to his own vassals and subjects. The holding of land was connected with the personal obligations of each holder to his superior. The peasants were subject to serfdom. The administration was likewise of feudal type, the holding of office being connected with the holding of lands and provinces. The governors of districts were known as *eristavi;* of larger provinces, *eristavt eristavi* ("governors of governors").[108]

In order both to strengthen the defense of the country and to curb the power of aristocracy, David II decided to create an armed force under immediate royal authority and to achieve this end invited a considerable number of Cumans to settle in Georgia. As we know (see Chap. IV, sec. 5), the Russians administered a series of severe defeats to the Cumans in the early twelfth century. Following this, the bulk of them retreated to the north Caucasian steppes and many of them welcomed David's offer. Those who accepted—forty thousand of them according to the Georgian chronicles—received land holdings in Georgia and constituted the backbone of David's army. As the ruler had expected, this measure resulted in considerable strengthening of the royal authority.[109]

The variety of cultural background of the peoples of the Caucasus was reflected in the nature of Russia's relations with them. The Russian princes were interested in the Ossetians and Kosogians chiefly from a military point of view. As we know (see Chap. IV, sec. 2), in the eleventh century Prince Mstislav of Tmutorokan used Kosogian

---

107. Allen, *op. cit.,* p. 96.
108. *Idem,* pp. 250–256.
109. Allen, *op. cit.,* p. 99.

auxiliary troops and many Kosogians and Ossetians joined his personal retinue. Presumably after the prince's death these guards went over to Iaroslav. Ossetians are also known to have held office in princely households. The chief steward (*kliuchnik*) in Prince Andrei Bogoliubsky's palace was an Ossetian. Incidentally, he later betrayed his master by joining the latter's assassins (1074).[110] The Ossetians, as well as some other mountain tribesmen in the Caucasus, had the reputation of being skillful armorers and it is probable that from them the Russians obtained a part of their armor. "Avar helmets" are mentioned in the *Lay of Igor's Campaign*.[111] The reference is not to the ancient Avars who passed through south Russia and eventually established themselves in Hungary [112] but to a tribe of the same name whose abodes were in Daghestan.

In the Cuman period the Russians were eager to maintain their relations with the Ossetians because of strategic and diplomatic considerations, since the latter were potential allies against the Cumans. As we know, a group of Ossetians (Ias) were settled in the lower Don region—that is, within the boundaries of the Cuman khanate. When the Russians entered this region in the year 1111 they were welcomed by the local population, presumably the Ias among others.[113] In 1116 Prince Vladimir Monomach sent his son Iaropolk to the Don once more. From this expedition Iaropolk brought to Kiev a number of Iasian retainers and a Iasian princess, whom he married.[114] Subsequently other Russian princes also had Ossetian wives, as for example two Suzdalian princes—Andrei Bogoliubsky and his brother Vsevolod III—and one Chernigovan, Mstislav, killed in the battle of Kalka in 1223.[115]

Less is known of the dynastic ties between the Russians and the Kosogians. It is recorded in the chronicles, however, that Prince Mstislav of Tmutorokan took to wife a Circassian princess whose first husband he killed in a duel.[116]

As the princely court and the druzhina constituted a milieu favorable to the development of epic poetry, comradeship in arms and dynastic ties between the Russians and the people of these two tribes

110. *PSRL*, I, Pt. 2, col. 369; see also Miller, *op. cit.*, III, 68.
111. *Slovo*, p. 13.
112. *Ancient Russia*, chap. v.
113. *Book of Annals*, Hyp., col. 263.
114. *Book of Annals*, col. 280; see also Miller, *op. cit.*, III, 66–68.
115. Baumgarten, "Généalogies," p. 70.
116. *Book of Annals*, Hyp. col. 133.

or tribal groups resulted in the familiarity of the Russians with Ossetian and Kosogian folklore. The influence of Ossetian epic poetry on the Russian byliny is undeniable (see Chap. IX, sec. 3).

The Ossetians served also as intermediaries in Russia's relations with Georgia and Armenia. The influence of Georgian and Armenian art, and especially architecture, on Russian art was of great importance. In the early Kievan period it was felt chiefly in Tmutorokan and Chernigov; in the late Kievan period, in Riazan and Suzdalia (see Chap. IX, sec. 6). But information on the personal contact between the Russians and the Georgians and Armenians is scant. It is known that Armenian doctors used to practice in Russia and it is supposed that Georgian and Armenian painters and architects were occasionally engaged. Armenian merchants must also have visited Russia frequently. As to dynastic ties,[117] the second wife of Prince Iziaslav II of Kiev was a Georgian princess, daughter of King Dimitri I. The marriage took place in 1154. Thirty years later Queen Tamara of Georgia chose a Russian prince as her husband—Iuri, the youngest son of Andrei Bogoliubsky.[118]

Following Andrei's death the latter's brothers had seized the power in Suzdalia, refusing to grant the young Iuri (born around 1160) recognition of his rights. Iuri then went to the Cumans (1176); as his grandmother, the first wife of Iuri I of Suzdalia and Kiev, was a Cuman princess, he must have had relatives among the Cuman khans. Nothing is known of his life in Cumania but in any case the ways of life in the Cuman horde, far from traditional civilization, could hardly be favorable to the development of Iuri's character. An embittered young refugee, he later became a bold and unscrupulous adventurer. He spent nine years among the Cumans before his chance came to return to a Christian country. In 1184 King George III of Georgia died leaving his throne to his young and able daughter Tamara. The Georgian nobles, resenting a woman on the throne, now saw their opportunity to curb the royal authority and expand their own privileges. Tamara's advisers, in turn, recommended a speedy marriage as the best means of strengthening her position and selected Iuri as the most suitable candidate.

In order to understand the motives behind their choice we must

---

117. Baumgarten, "Généalogies," p. 70.

118. On Prince Iuri, son of Andrei Bogoliubsky, see "Georgi (Iuri) Andreevich," *RBS*, IV (1914), 441, 442; Baumgarten, "Généalogies," p. 27; Allen, *op. cit.*, pp. 104–106.

remember that the main body of the royal army in Georgia consisted of Cumans, who must have kept close ties with their kin in Cumania and in that way may have heard of Iuri and may have wanted to support him. Queen Tamara's mother, moreover, was an Ossetian and so was Iuri's; thus Tamara and Iuri might be considered compatriots in a sense.

The marriage took place in 1185. At first Iuri produced an excellent impression on both his bride and the Georgian nobles. He also proved to be an able military leader, achieving great successes in the struggle against the Moslems. Gradually, however, the negative features in his character became obvious. He is described in the Georgian chronicles (perhaps with some exaggeration) as a vicious drunkard and a cruel despot. He was also charged with sodomy and, as two years after her marriage Tamara was still childless, she easily obtained the consent of the clergy to her divorce. Iuri was exiled to Byzantium (1188). In the following year Tamara married an Ossetian prince, on his maternal side a descendant of Georgian royalty.

Iuri was not, however, ready to accept his defeat as final. He played on the feelings of the aristocratic opposition to the queen and soon reëntered Georgia as the leader of a powerful revolt. At first he was quite successful and was even proclaimed king by his followers. Finally, however, Tamara was victorious and he was taken prisoner and again exiled to Byzantium (1191). Two years later the aristocratic party staged another revolt, even less successful than the first. In 1200 Iuri was banished from Byzantium and appeared at the court of the atabeg of Azerbaijan. He succeeded in gathering a band of Turks with whom he invaded Georgia once more, but was again defeated. The date of his death is not known.

## 7. Russia and the East

"The east" is as vague and conventional a notion as "the west." Russia's eastern neighbors were each on a different cultural level from the next and each endowed with its own peculiar characteristics.

Ethnographically most of the eastern peoples in the vicinity of Russia were Turks. In the Caucasus, as we know, the Ossetians represented the Iranian element. With the Iranians in Persia the Russians also had some intercourse, at least from time to time. Russian knowledge of the Arabic world was confined chiefly to the Christian elements there, as in Syria. With the peoples of the Far East—the Mongols, the Manchus, and the Chinese—they had acquaintance only in so far as those peoples intervened in the affairs of Turkestan. Likewise in Turkestan the Russians were in a position to meet Indians, at least occasionally.

From the religious and cultural point of view a distinction should be made between the area of paganism and that of Islam. The nomadic Turkish tribes in south Russia—the Patzinaks, the Cumans, and others—were pagans. In Kazakhstan and northern Turkestan most of the Turks had originally been pagan but as they extended their raids to the south and came in contact with the Mohammedans, they were rapidly converted to Islam. The Volga Bulgars represented the northernmost outpost of Islam in this period. In spite of the fact that they were separated from the main body of the Islamic world by pagan Turkish tribes, they succeeded in keeping close contact, in both commerce and religion, with the Mohammedans of Khoresm and southern Turkestan.[119]

It should be noted that politically the Iranian element in central Asia was on the decline from the late tenth century. The Iranian state under the Samanid dynasty, which flourished in the late ninth and the tenth century in southwestern Turkestan and northern Iran, was overthrown by the Turks around the year 1000.[120]

One of the former vassals of the Samanids now created a new state in Afghanistan and Iran. His dynasty is known as the Gaznevids. The Gaznevids also controlled the northwestern part of India. Their state did not last long, however, being destroyed by the new Turkish horde of the Seljuqs (1040).[121] Under the sultan Alp-Arslan (1063–72), the latter presently penetrated Transcaucasia (see sec. 6, above) and then started their drive westward against the Byzantine Empire. In

119. On the Volga Bulgars, see *Ancient Russia,* pp. 222–228; P. Golubovsky, "Bolgary i Khazary," *Kievskaia Starina, 22* (1888), 25–56 (inaccessible to me); W. Barthold (V. Bartold), "Bulgar," *EI,* I (1913), 786–791; V. Smolin, "Bolgarskii gorod Briakhimov," *KUO 33* (1925), 131–145; Akdes Nimet Kurat, "Bulgar," *Islam Ansiklopedisi,* II (1944), 781–796; A. P. Smirnov, "Volzhskie Bulgary," *IIM, 13* (1946), 158–159.

120. W. Barthold, *Istoriia kulturnoi zhizni Turkestana* (Leningrad, 1927), and *Id., Turkestan down to the Mongolian Invasion* (London, 1928).

121. On the Seljuqs, see J. Laurent, "Byzance et les Turcs Seldjoucides," *Annales de l'Est* (Université de Nancy), *27* (1913) and *28* (1914) (inaccessible to me); A. Krymskyi, *Istoriia Turechchyny* (Kiev, 1924), pp. 3–7, 9; F. Uspensky, "Vostochnaia politika Manuila Komnina," *Soobshcheniia Rossiiskogo Palestinskogo Obshchestva, 29* (1926), 111–138; "Seldjuks," *EI,* IV (1934), 208–213; A. I. Iakubovsky, "Seldzhukskoe dvizhenie i Turkmeny v XI veke," *OON,* 1937, pp. 921–946; G. Moravcsik, *Byzantinoturcica,* I, 64–66; B. N. Zakhoder, *Istoriia Vostochnogo Srednevekovia* (Moscow, 1944), pp. 88–96; V. Gordlevsky, *Gosudarstvo Seldzhukov v Maloi Azii* (Moscow and Leningrad, 1941).

the twelfth century they already controlled most of Anatolia and also spread southward, overrunning Syria and Iraq. They recognized the spiritual authority of the Caliphate of Bagdad, however. In Egypt, at that time, a separate caliphate—that of Cairo—established itself, the ruling dynasty being known as that of the Fatimites. In the late twelfth century Syria and Egypt were politically united by Saladin, known for his successes against the Crusaders.[122]

On the whole, it may be said that the Islamic zone east and southeast of Russia formed, in the Kievan period, the limit of the extent of Russia's acquaintance with the Orient. However, beyond it powerful peoples of Turkish, Mongol, and Manchu extraction were constantly on the move, struggling with each other. The dynamics of Far Eastern history resulted in the eventual penetration of some of the Far Eastern tribes into the Middle East and Russian ken. Thus, around 1137 a section of the people of Kitan, being expelled from north China by the Churchens, invaded Turkestan and established their rule there, which existed for about half a century until the growth of the Khoresmian empire.[123] It is from the name Kitan (also known as Kara-Kitai) that the Russian name for China, Kitai, derives. The next Far Eastern eruption directed westward was that of the Mongols.

It would seem that the Russians might have profited more by their intercourse with the Islamic peoples than with the pagan Turks. The Turkish tribes in the south Russian steppes were typical nomads and, while relations with them greatly enriched Russian folklore and folk art, no serious contribution to Russian science and education could be expected from this quarter. Unfortunately the intransigent attitude of the Russian clergy toward Islam and vice versa prevented any serious intellectual contact between Russians and Mohammedans, though this would have been so easy to establish in the area of the Volga Bulgars as well as in Turkestan. It was only with the Christians in Syria and Egypt that they had some intellectual connections. It is said that one of the Russian prelates in the early Kievan period was a Syrian.[124] It is also known that Syrian doctors practiced in Russia in the Kievan age. And of course, through Byzantium, the Russians were acquainted with the Syriac religious literature and Syrian monasticism.

122. On Saladin, see Sobernheim, "Saladin," *EI*, IV (1934), 84–89; P. K. Hitti, *History of the Arabs*, (3d ed. London, Macmillan and Co., 1946), pp. 645–653; Zakhoder, *op. cit.*, pp. 103–105.

123. Barthold, *Turkestan down to the Mongolian Invasion*, pp. 323–363.

124. *PSRL*, IX (1862), 57.

It may be added that in addition to the Greek Orthodox Christian Church, there also existed in the Middle East and central Asia two other Christian churches—the Monophysite and the Nestorian— but the Russians apparently avoided any intercourse with them.[125] On the other hand, some of the Nestorians as well as some of the Monophysites were interested in Russia, at least judging from the Syriac chronicle of Ab-ul-Faraj, alias Bar Hebraeus, which contains a certain amount of information on Russian affairs.[126] It was written in the thirteenth century but was partly based on the work of Michael, the Jacobite Patriarch of Antioch, of the twelfth century,[127] as well as on other Syriac materials.

Commercial relations between Russia and the Orient were lively and profitable for both. We know that in the late ninth and tenth centuries Russian merchants visited Persia and even Bagdad.[128] There is no direct evidence to show that they continued to travel there in the eleventh and twelfth centuries but they must in any case have visited Khoresm in this later period. The name of the Khoresmian capital, Gurganj (or Urganj), is familiar to the Russian chroniclers, who called it Ornach.[129] Here the Russians must have met travelers and merchants from almost every Oriental land, including the Indian. Unfortunately, no record of Russian travels to Khoresm has been preserved for this period. Speaking of India, the Russians of the Kievan period had at least a vague notion of Hinduism. "Brahmans—the pious men" are mentioned in the Book of Annals.[130]

---

125. On the Nestorians and Monophysites, see W. Barthold (V. Bartold), *Zur Geschichte des Christentums in Mittel-Asien bis zur mongolischen Eroberung* (Tübingen and Leipzig, 1901); B. J. Kidd, *The Churches of Eastern Christendom* (London, The Faith Press, 1927); W. F. Adeney, *The Greek and Eastern Churches* (New York, C. Scribner's Sons, 1932); D. Attwater, *The Dissident Eastern Churches* (Milwaukee, The Bruce Publishing Co., 1937); P. Y. Saeki, *The Nestorian Documents and Relics in China* (Tokyo, 1937).

126. On Bar Hebraeus (Gregory Ab-ul-Faraj), see W. Wright, *A Short History of Syriac Literature* (London, A. C. Black, 1894), pp. 265–281; R. Duval, *La Littérature syriaque* (Paris, 1907), pp. 408–410; A. Baumstark, *Geschichte der syrischen Literatur* (Bonn, 1922), pp. 312–320.

127. The Syrian Monophysites are known under the name of Jacobites. On Michael Syrus, see Wright, *op. cit.*, pp. 250–253; Duval, *op. cit.*, p. 401; Baumstark, *op. cit.*, pp. 298–300.

128. Ibn-Khurdadhbih, "Kitab al-Masalik wa'l Mamalik," *BGA*, VI (1889), 115 (French translation) and 154 (Arabic text); Firdausi, *Shahnama*, A. G. Warner and E. Warner, trs., VIII, 406; IX, 110.

129. W. Barthold, *Istoriia izucheniia Vostoka v Evrope i Rossii* (2d ed. Leningrad, 1925), p. 170.

130. In the *Book of Annals* Brahman is spelt *Rakhman*, Laur., cols. 14–15. See

Concerning Egypt, Soloviev states that Russian merchants visited Alexandria but the validity of his source of evidence is questionable.[131]

While personal contacts, through trade, between the Russians and the Volga Bulgars and Khoresmians must have been lively, the difference in religion presented an almost insurmountable barrier to any close social intercourse between the nationals of the two religious groups. No marriage ties between the Greek Orthodox and the Mohammedans were possible, unless of course one of the parties was ready to renounce his or her religion. Cases of conversion to Islam on the part of the Russians are practically unknown for this period, except for the Russian slaves shipped by Italian and Oriental merchants to various eastern countries. In this respect, contact with the Cumans was much easier for the Russians, since the pagans were less attached to their religion than the Mohammedans and did not hesitate to accept Christianity whenever the need arose, especially the womenfolk. Because of this, cases of intermarriage between Russian princes and Cuman princesses are frequent.[132] Among the princes to contract these alliances were such outstanding rulers as Sviatopolk II and Vladimir II of Kiev, Oleg of Chernigov, Iuri I of Suzdalia and Kiev, Iaroslav of Suzdalia, and Mstislav the Daring.

While, as we have just seen, religious exclusiveness precluded the possibility of direct intellectual contact between the Russians and the Moslems, in the field of arts the situation was different. In Russian decorative art the influence of Oriental patterns—such as the arabesque, for example—is clearly felt but of course some of these patterns may have reached Russia indirectly through the medium of either Byzantine or Transcaucasian contacts. In the case of folklore, however, we must acknowledge a direct influence of Oriental folklore on the Russian. As to the influence of Iranian epic poetry on the Russian, its main channel, apparently, was that of the Ossetian folklore. Turkish patterns are likewise clearly noticeable in Russian folklore, both in the byliny and the fairy tales. The striking similarity in the scale structure of the Russian folk song to that of the songs of some Turkish tribes has already been mentioned (see Chap. IX, sec. 4).

G. N. Roerich, "Indology in Russia," *Journal of the Greater India Society, 12* (1945), 69.

131. Soloviev, III, 48, refers to Benjamin of Tudela quoting the French edition of 1830; however, Asher reads "Roussillon" instead of "Russia" (*Itinerary*, I, 157); see also Beazley, *op. cit.*, II, 262, n. 2.

132. Baumgarten, "Généalogies," pp. 69, 70; Golubovsky, "Pechenegi, Torki i Polovtsy," *KU*, 1883, pp. 556–559.

Since a number of these tribes were under the control of, or in touch with, the Cumans, the role of the latter in the evolution of Russian folk music must have been of great importance.

To sum up, the Russian people were, throughout the Kievan period, in close and manifold contact with their neighbors—both eastern and western. There is no doubt that Russian civilization of the period profited much by this contact; basically, however, it represented the growth of the creative power of the Russian people themselves.

# ABBREVIATIONS

*AIK*   *Annales de l'Institut Kondakov.*
*AK*   Arkheologicheskaia Komissiia, *Izvestiia.*
*AN*   Akademiia Nauk, *Izvestiia.*
*Ancient Russia*   Vernadsky, G., *Ancient Russia* (New Haven, Yale University Press, 1943).
*Annuaire*   *Annuaire de l'Institut de Philologie et d'Histoire Orientales et Slaves.*
*ANORI*   Akademiia Nauk, Otdelenie Russkogo Iazyka i Slovesnosti, *Izvestiia.*
*ANORS*   Akademiia Nauk, Otdelenie Russkogo Iazyka i Slovesnosti, *Sbornik.*
*ANSR*   Akademiia Nauk, *Sbornik po Russkomu Iazyku i Slovesnosti.*
*ANZ*   Akademiia Nauk, *Zapiski.*
*ANZI*   Akademiia Nauk, *Zapiski po istoriko-filologicheskomu otdeleniiu.*
Aristov   Aristov, N. Ia., *Promyshlennost' drevnei Rusi* (St. Petersburg, 1866).
*ASEER*   *American Slavic and East European Review.*
*ASP*   *Archiv für slavische Philologie.*
*AWV*   Akademie der Wissenschaften, Vienna, *Denkschriften* (Phil.-Hist. Klasse).
Baumgarten, "Généalogies"   Baumgarten, N., "Généalogies et mariages occidentaux des Rurikides russes," *OC,* IX (1927).
*BGA*   *Bibliotheca Geographorum Arabicorum,* De Goje, M. J., ed. (Leyden).
*BID*   Bulgarsko Istorichesko Drushtvo, *Izvestiia.*
*Book of Annals*   *Povest' vremennykh Let.* See Sources, III, 1.
*BS*   *Byzantinoslavica.*
*BSOAS*   London University, School of Oriental and African Studies, *Bulletin.*
*BZ*   *Byzantinische Zeitschrift.*
Chadwick   Chadwick, N. K., *The Beginnings of Russian History: An Inquiry into Sources* (Cambridge, Cambridge University Press, 1930).
*Chteniia*   Moscow, Universitet, Obshchestvo Istorii i Drevnostei, *Chteniia.*
Cross   Cross, S. H., tr. *The Russian Primary Chronicle* (Cambridge, Mass., Harvard University Press, 1930).
*De Adm.*   Constantine Porphyrogenitus, *De Administrando Imperio, PG,* CXIII.
Diakonov, *Ocherki*   Diakonov, M. A., *Ocherki obshchestvennogo i gosudarstvennogo stroia drevnei Rusi* (4th ed. St. Petersburg, 1912).
Dorn   Dorn, B. A., "Kaspii," *ANZ, 26* (1875).
*EI*   *Encyclopaedia of Islam.*
*EK*   *Evraziiskaia Khronika.*
*ES*   Brockhaus-Efron, *Entsiklopedicheskii Slovar'.*
*GA*   Gosudarstvennaia Akademiia Istorii Materialnoi Kultury, *Izvestiia.*
Golubinsky, *Istoriia*   Golubinsky, E. E., *Istoriia Russkoi tserkvi.* See Bibliography, IX.
Hrushevsky   Hrushevsky, M. S., (Grushevsky), *Istoriia Ukrainy-Rusi.* See Bibliography, III.
Hyp.   Hypatian version of the *Book of Annals.*

*IIM* Akademiia Nauk, Institut Istorii Materialnoi Kultury, *Kratkie Soobshcheniia.*

Ikonnikov, *Opyt* Ikonnikov, V. S., *Opyt Russkoi istoriografii.* See Bibliography, I.

*IMT* Istoricheskii Muzei, *Trudy.*

Iushkov, *Narysy* Iushkov, S. V., *Narysy z istorii vynyknennia i pochatkovogo rozvytku feodalizmu v Kyivs'kii Rusi.* See Bibliography, VI.

*JAOS Journal of the American Oriental Society.*

*JKGS Jahrbücher für Kultur und Geschichte der Slaven.*

Karamzin Karamzin, N. M., *Istoriia Gosudarstva Rossiiskogo.* See Bibliography, III.

Karamzin, *Notes Primechaniia k Istorii Gosudarstva Rossiiskogo.* See Bibliography, III.

*Khristomatiia* Vladimirsky-Budanov, M. F., *Khristomatiia po istorii Russkogo prava,* I (6th ed. St. Petersburg and Kiev, 1908).

*KU* Kiev, Universitet, *Izvestiia.*

*KUO* Kazan, Universitet, Obshchestvo Arkheologii, Istorii i Etnografii, *Izvestiia.*

Laur. Laurentian version of the *Book of Annals.*

*LZ* Arkheograficheskaia Komissiia, *Letopis' Zaniatii.*

*MAIZ* Moscow, Arkheologicheskii Institut, *Zapiski.*

Makarii Makarii, Metropolitan, *Istoriia Russkoi tserkvi.* See Bibliography, IX.

Markwart Marquart, J., *Osteuropäische und ostasiatische Streifzüge* (Leipzig, 1903).

Marvazi Minorsky, V., *Marvazi on China, the Turks and India.* See Sources, III, 5.

*Medieval Russian Laws.* See Sources, II, 2D.

*MGH Monumenta Germaniae Historica.*

*MIAS* Akademiia Nauk, Institut Istorii Materialnoi Kultury, *Materialy i issledovaniia po arkheologii S.S.S.R.*

Miller Miller, V. F., "Osetinskie etiudy," Pt. III, *MU, 8* (1887).

Miller, *Slovar'* Miller, V. F., *Osetinsko-Russko-Nemetskii Slovar'* (Leningrad, 1927–34), 3 vols.

*MPH Monumenta Poloniae Historica* (*Pomniki Dziejowe Polski*), [First Series], 1864–93, 6 vols.; New Series, I (1946).

*MU* Moscow, Universitet, *Uchenye Zapiski,* Otdel istorikofilologicheskii.

Niederle Niederle, L., *Slovanské Starožitnosti,* Vol. I (2d ed. 1925–26); Vol. II (1906–10); Vol. III (2d ed. 1927); Vol. IV (1924) (Prague).

*NUIF* Odessa, Novorossiiskii Universitet, Istoriko-Filologicheskoe Obshchestvo, *Letopisi.*

*OC Orientalia Christiana.*

*ODRL* Akademiia Nauk, Otdel Drevne-Russkoi Literatury, *Trudy.*

*OGN* Akademiia Nauk, Otdel Gumanitarnykh Nauk, *Izvestiia.*

*OLDP* Obshchestvo Liubitelei Drevne-Russkoi Pismennosti, *Pamiatniki.*

*OON* Akademiia Nauk, Otdel Obshchestvennykh Nauk, *Izvestiia.*

Orlov, *Bibliografiia* Orlóv, A. S., *Bibliografiia Russkikh nadpisei XI–XV vekov.* See Sources, I, 1.

Orlov, *Istoriia* Orlov, A. S., Adrianova-Peretts, V. P., and Gudzii, N. K., eds., *Istoriia Russkoi literatury,* I. See Bibliography, XI.

*ORSAT* Russkoe Arkheologicheskoe Obshchestvo, Otdelenie Slavianskoi i Russkoi Arkheologii, *Trudy.*

*PG* Migne, J. P., *Patrologiae Cursus Completus.* Series Graeca.

Ponomarev Ponomarev, A. I., *Pamiatniki drevnerusskoi tserkovno-uchitelnoi literatury,* I–III (St. Petersburg, 1894–97).

Preobrazhensky Preobrazhensky, A. V., *Etimologicheskii slovar' Russkogo iazyka,* I–II (Moscow, 1910–16).

Presniakov, *Kniazhoe pravo* Presniakov, A. E., *Kniazhoe pravo v drevnei Rusi.* See Bibliography, V.

Priselkov Priselkov, M. D., *Ocherki po tserkovno-politicheskoi istorii Kievskoi Rusi.* See Bibliography, IX.

Procopius Procopius, *History of the Wars,* Dewing, H. B., ed. and tr. 5 vols. "Loeb Classical Library."

*PSRL Polnoe Sobranie Russkikh Letopisei.*

*RAO* Russkoe Arkheologicheskoe Obshchestvo, *Zapiski.*

*RAOKZ* Russkoe Arkheologicheskoe Obshchestvo, Klassicheskoe Otdelenie, *Zapiski.*

*RBPH Revue Belge de Philologie et d'Histoire.*

*RBS* Russkoe Istoricheskoe Obshchestvo, *Russkii Biograficheskii Slovar'.*

*RES Revue des Études Slaves.*

*RFV Russkii Filologicheskii Vestnik.*

*RIB Russkaia Istoricheskaia Biblioteka.*

*RIOP* Russkoe Istoricheskoe Obshchestvo v Prage, *Zapiski.*

*SEER Slavonic and East European Review.*

Sergeevich, *Drevnosti* Sergeevich, V. I., *Drevnosti Russkogo prava.* See Bibliography, VII.

*SIF* Akademiia Nauk, *Izvestiia,* Seriia Istorii i Filosofii.

*SK Seminarium Kondakovianum.*

*Slovo Slovo o polku Igoreve* (*Lay of Igor's Campaign*), phototypical reproduction of the first edition, Speransky, M. N., ed. (Moscow, 1920).

Soloviev Soloviev, S. M., *Istoriia Rossii s drevneishikh vremen.* See Bibliography, III.

*SVB Sbornik statei po istorii prava posviashchennyi M. F. Vladimirskomu-Budanovu* (Kiev, 1904).

*SZM* Sarajevo, Zemaljski Muzej, *Glasnik.*

Tatishchev Tatishchev, V. N., *Istoriia Rossiiskaia.* See Bibliography, III.

Thomsen, *Origin* Thomsen, V., *The Relations between Ancient Russia and Scandinavia and the Origin of the Russian State* (Oxford and London, 1877).

*UW* University of Warsaw, *Izvestiia.*

Vladimirsky-Budanov, *Obzor* Vladimirsky-Budanov, M. F., *Obzor istorii Russkogo prava* (7th ed. Petrograd and Kiev, 1915).

*VOZ* Russkoe Arkheologicheskoe Obshchestvo, Vostochnoe Otdelenie, *Zapiski.*

*VV Vizantiiskii Vremennik.*

*ZMNP Zhurnal Ministerstva Narodnogo Prosveshcheniia.*

*ZSP Zeitschrift für slavische Philologie.*

# SOURCES

For the archeological evidence, see Bibliography, XII.

## I. Epigraphics, Numismatics, and Sigillographics

### 1. Epigraphics

ARNE, T. J., *La Suède et l'Orient* (Upsala, 1914), pp. 7–14.

BRAUN, F., *"Shvedskaia runicheskaia nadpis' naidennaia na ostrove Berezani,"* *AK, 23* (1907).

ORLOV, A. S., *Bibliografiia Russkikh nadpisei XI–XV vekov* (Moscow and Leningrad, 1936).

SPITSYN, A. A., "Tmutarakanskii Kamen'," *ORSAT*, XI (Petrograd, 1915).

### 2. Numismatics and Sigillographics

ILVIN, (IL'IN) A. A., *Klassifikatsiia Russkikh udelnykh monet*, I (Leningrad, 1940).

—— *Topografiia kladov drevnikh Russkikh monet* (Leningrad, 1924).

LIKHACHEV, N. P., "Materialy dlia istorii Vizantiiskoi i Russkoi sfragistiki," Akademiia Nauk, Muzei Paleografii, *Trudy*, I (1928).

MARKOV, A., *Russkaia numizmatika* (Petrograd, 1915).

—— *Topografiia kladov vostochnykh monet* (St. Petersburg, 1910).

ORESHNIKOV, A., *Russkie monety* (Moscow, 1896).

PROZOROVSKY, D. I., *Moneta i ves v Rossii* (St. Petersburg, 1865).

SAVELIEV, P. S., *Mukhammedanskaia numizmatika* (St. Petersburg, 1846).

TOLSTOY, COUNT I. I., "Drevneishie Russkie monety," *RAO, 6* (1893), 310–382.

—— *Drevneishie Russkie monety velikogo kniazhestva Kievskogo* (St. Petersburg, 1882).

—— *Vizantiiskie monety* (St. Petersburg, 1912–14). 9 vols.

VASMER, R., "Über die Münzen der Wolga-Bulgaren," *Wiener Numismatische Zeitschrift, 57* (1924), 63–84.

## II. Legal Sources

### 1. International Treaties

#### A. Russo-Byzantine Treaties

A.D. 907. No full text available. Résumé in Laur., cols. 31–32. English translation, Cross, pp. 150–151.

A.D. 911. Laur., cols. 32–37. Reprinted in *Khristomatiia*, I, 1–7. English translation, Cross, pp. 151–154.

A.D. 945. Laur., cols. 46–53. Reprinted in *Khristomatiia*, I, 8–16. English translation, Cross, pp. 159–163.

A.D. 971. Laur., cols. 72–73. Reprinted in *Khristomatiia*, I, 17. English translation, Cross, pp. 176–177.

## B. Russo-German Treaties

A.D. 1189–95. Treaty between Novgorod and the Germans and the Gotlanders. *Khristomatiia*, I, 93–96.

GOETZ, L. K., *Deutsch-russische Handelsverträge*, pp. 14–72.

A.D. 1229. Treaty between Smolensk and Riga and other German cities. *Khristomatiia*, I, 97–108.

GOETZ, L. K., *Deutsch-russische Handelsverträge*, pp. 231–304.

## 2. Codes of Laws and Law Manuals

### A. Byzantine Law

*Agricultural Law (Nomos Georgikos)*. Ferrini, C., ed., *BZ 7* (1898), 558–571; Ashburner, W., ed., *Journal of Hellenic Studies, 30* (1910), 85–108; *32* (1912), 68–95. Pavlov, A. S., ed., *ANORS, 38* (1885), No. 3. With the old Slavic translation.

*Ecloga*, Zachariä von Lingenthal, ed., *Collectio Librorum Juris Graeco-Romani Ineditorum* (Leipzig, 1852), pp. 9–52. French translation, Spulber, C. A., ed., *L'Eclogue des Isauriens* (Cernautzi, 1929). English translation, Freshfield, E. H., *Roman Law in the Later Roman Empire* (Cambridge, 1932). Slavic translation, *Kormchaia*, chap. l in the editions of 1650 and 1653; chap. xlix in subsequent editions.

*Procheiron*, Zachariä von Lingenthal, ed. (Heidelberg, 1837). English translation, Freshfield, E. H., *A Manual of Eastern Roman Law* (Cambridge: Cambridge University Press, 1928). Slavic translation, *Kormchaia*, chap. xlix in the editions of 1650 and 1653; chap. xlviii in subsequent editions.

### B. Bulgarian Law

*Court Law for the People (Zakon Sudnyi Liudem)*, Saturník, T., ed., *Příspěvky k šíření Byzantského práva u Slovanů* (Prague, 1922), pp. 143–164.

### C. Canon Law

V. BĚNESHEVICH, "Singagoga v 50 titulov," *RAOKZ, 8* (1914).
—— *Kanonicheskii Sbornik XIV titulov* (St. Petersburg, 1905).
—— Ed., *Drevne-Slavianskaia Kormchaia*, I (St. Petersburg, 1906).
*Kormchaia (Nomocanon)* (1st ed. Moscow, 1650); revised by Patriarch Nikon, 1653; reprinted many times since.

### D. Russian Law

GREKOV, B. D., ed., *Pravda Russkaia*, I (Moscow and Leningrad, 1940).
IUSHKOV, S. V., ed., *Rus'ka Pravda* (Kiev, 1935). Of the versions of the text edited

by Grekov, the Short Version (Academy copy) and the Expanded Version (Trinity copy) translated into English by Vernadsky, G., *Medieval Russian Laws* (*Records of Civilization*, A. P. Evans, ed., No. 41 [New York, Columbia University Press, 1947]).

### 3. Statutes and Charters

The Church Statute of Vladimir the Saint, Beneshevich, V. N., ed., *Pamiatniki drevne-russkogo kanonicheskogo prava, RIB*, XXXVI (Petrograd, 1920). For the history and criticism of the text, see Iuskhov, S. V., *Ustav Kniazia Vladimira* (Novouzensk, 1926).

The Church Statute of Iaroslav the Wise, *Khristomatiia*, I, 199–204.

"The Metropolitan's Justice" ("Pravosudie Mitropolichie"), Iushkov, S. V., ed., *LZ, 35* (1929), 115–117.

Prince Vsevolod's Statute (1125–36), *Khristomatiia*, I, 206–211.

Charter of Princes Mstislav and Vsevolod to the Monastery of St. George (1130). *idem*, pp. 112–113.

Prince Vsevolod's charter to the Church of John the Baptist (around 1135), *idem*, pp. 212–216.

Prince Sviatoslav's statute (1137), *idem*, pp. 217–218.

Prince Rostislav's charter (1150), *idem*, pp. 219–224.

Bishop Manuil's charter (1150), *idem*, p. 224.

### 4. Deeds and Wills

Land deed of Antoni Rimlianin (prior to 1147), *Khristomatiia*, I, 114.

Varlaam's donation of land to the Monastery of Christ the Redeemer (around 1192), *idem*, p. 115.

Will of Kliment the Novgorodian (thirteenth century), *idem*, pp. 118–120.

## III. Chronicles, Historical and Geographical Treatises, and Sagas

### 1. Slavic

The Laurentian Chronicle (1377), *PSRL*, I, Fasc. 1 (2d ed. Leningrad, 1926); Fasc. 2 (2d ed. Leningrad, 1927). Fascicle 1: *Book of Annals*. English translation by Cross (see Abbreviations). Fascicle 2: The Suzdalian Chronicle.

The Hypatian Chronicle (early fifteenth century), *PSRL*, II, Fasc. 1 (3d ed. Petrograd, 1923); Fascicle 2 (1st ed. St. Petersburg, 1843). Fascicle 1: *Book of Annals*. Fascicle 2: The Kievan Chronicle and the Volynian and Galician chronicles.

The Radziwill Chronicle, also known as Königsberg Chronicle (fifteenth century). Illustrated. Photomechanical reproduction, *OLDP*, CXVIII (1902). Contents similar to Laurentian.

The Novgorodian Chronicles (thirteenth to fifteenth centuries). The First Nov-
gorodian Chronicle, *Novgorodskaia Letopis' po Sinodalnomu Kharateinomu
Spisku* (St. Petersburg, 1888). Also *PSRL*, III (1841). English translation,
Michell, R. and Forbes, N., with an introduction by Beazley, C. R., in *Camden
Third Series*, XXV (London, 1914).
The Second Novgorodian Chronicle, *PSRL*, III (1841); 2d ed., Bychkov, A. F.,
*Novgorodskie Letopisi* (St. Petersburg, 1879).
The Third Novgorodian Chronicle, *ibid.*
The Fourth Novgorodian Chronicle, *PSRL*, IV, (1848).
The Voskresensk Chronicle (sixteenth century), *PSRL*, VII (1856). Contains a
revised text of the *Book of Annals* and a digest of Novgorodian, Vladimirian
(Suzdalian), and other chronicles.
The Nikon Chronicle (sixteenth century), *PSRL*, IX (1862) and X (1885). Con-
tents similar to the Vokresensk Chronicle.

## 2. Greek

AKOMINATUS (ACOMINATUS), NIKETAS, *Chronographia*, Bekker, I., ed. (Bonn,
1835). Also *PG*, CXXXIX.
ANNA KOMNENA (COMNENA), *Alexias*, Schopen, J., and Reifferscheid, A., eds.
(Bonn, 1839–78). 2 vols. Also *PG*, CXXXI. English translation, Dawes, E. A. S.
(London, K. Paul, Trench, Trübner & Co., 1928).
ATTALIATES, MICHAEL, *Historia*, Brunet de Presle, W., ed. (Bonn, 1853).
CEDRENUS, see Kedrenus.
CINNAMUS, see Kinnamus.
CONSTANTINE PORPHYROGENITUS, *De Administrando Imperio, PG*, CXIII, cols.
157–422.
—— *De Cerimoniis Aulae Byzantinae*, Reiske, J., ed. (Leipzig, 1751–54), 2 vols.;
reprinted in the Bonn series (Bonn, 1829–30) and in *PG*, CXII. New edition,
with French translation, Vogt, A. (Paris, 1935–40), Vols. I–II (incomplete).
KEDRENUS (CEDRENUS), GEORGIUS, *Historiarum Compendium*, Bekker, J., ed.
(Bonn, 1838–39). 2 vols. Also *PG*, CXXXI–CXXXII. For the period 811–1057, the
text is actually an abridged edition of I. Skylitzes' work; the latter is still un-
published.
KINNAMUS, IOANNES, *Epitomae Historiarum*, Meineke, A., ed. (Bonn, 1836).
Also *PG*, CXXXIII.
LEO DIACONUS, *Historiae Libri decem*, Hase, B., ed. (Bonn, 1828). Also *PG*,
CXVII.
MANASSES, CONSTANTINE, *Chronicon*, Bekker, J., ed. (Bonn, 1837). Also *PG*,
CXXVII. Slavic translation, Bogdan, J., ed., *Cronica lui Constantin Manasses,
traducere mediobulgara* (Bucharest, 1922). See Weingart, M., *Byzantské
Kroniky v literature cirkevneslovanské*, I (Bratislava, 1922), 160–219.
PSELLUS, MICHAEL, *Chronographia*, Sathas, C., ed., *The History of Psellus* (Lon-
don, Methuen & Co., 1899); French translation, Renauld, E., ed., *Michel Psel-
los: Chronographie* (Paris, 1926–28). 2 vols.
SKYLITZES, IOANNES, see Kedrenus.
SYMEON MAGISTER AND LOGOTHETES (PSEUDO-SYMEON), *Chronicon*, Bekker, J.,
ed. (Bonn, 1838). Also *PG*, CIX. Slavic translation, Kunik, A. A., Vasilievsky,

V. G., and Sreznevsky, V. I., eds., *Simeona Metafrasta i Logofeta Spisanie Mira ot Bytiia i Letovnik* (St. Petersburg, 1905). See also Ostrogorsky, G., "Slavianskii perevod Khroniki Simeona," *SK, 5* (1932), 17–36.

ZONARAS, IOANNES, *Epitomae Historiarum*, Pinder, M. and Büttner-Wobst, T., eds. (Bonn, 1841–97), 3 vols.; Dindorf, L., ed. (Leipzig, 1868–75). 6 vols. Also *PG*, CXXXIV and CXXXV.

On Slavic translations, see Weingart, M., *Byzantské kroniky*, I, 84–159. *Paralipomen Zonarin*, Bodiansky, M., ed., *Chteniia*, XIV (1847).

## 3. Latin

ADAM OF BREMEN, *Gesta Hammaburgensis Ecclesiae Pontificum*, Schmeidler, B., ed. (Hannover and Leipzig, 1917).

COSMAS, see Kosmas.

DLUGOSZ, JAN, *Historiae Polonicae Libri XII* (Krakow, 1873–78). 5 vols.

HELMOLD, PRIEST OF BOSAU, *Cronica Slavorum*, Schmeidler, B., ed. (Hannover and Leipzig, 1909). English translation, Tschan, F. J., in *Records of Civilization, 21* (New York, Columbia University Press, 1935).

HENRICUS LETTUS, *Chronicon Lyvoniae*, Pertz, G. H., ed. (Hannover, 1874).

KADLUBEK, VINCENTIUS, *Chronica Polonorum*, Przezdziecki, A., ed. (Krakow, 1862).

KOSMAS (COSMAS) PRAGENSIS, *Chronica Boemorum*, Bretholz, B., ed. (Berlin, 1923).

LAMBERTUS MONACHUS HERSFELDENSIS, *Opera*, Holder-Egger, O., ed. (Hannover and Leipzig, 1894), pp. 1–304.

SAXO GRAMMATICUS, *Gesta Danorum*, Holder, A., ed. (Strassburg, 1886). Olrik, J., and Raeder, H., eds. (Copenhagen, 1931). 2 vols.

THIETMAR OF MERSEBURG, *Chronicon*, Kurze, F., ed. (Hannover, 1889).

VINCENTIUS, see Kadlubek.

## 4. Norse

Saga of Odd
    *Örvar-Odds Saga*, Boer, R. C., ed. (Halle, 1892). Partial Russian translation, Liashchenko, A. I., "Letopisnye skazaniia o smerti Olega Veshchego," *ANORI, 29* (1924), 254–288.

Saga of Olaf Trygvasson
    "Ólafs saga Tryggvasonar," Rafn, C. C., Rask, R. K., and Gudmunson, T., eds., *Fornmanna Sögur*, I–III (Copenhagen, 1825–27). English translation, Sephton, J., *The Saga of King Olaf Tryggwason* (London, D. Nutt, 1895).

The Eymund Saga
    "Saga Ólafs Konungs hins Helga," *Fornmanna Sögur*, V (1830), 267–298. Russian translation, Senkovsky, O. I., *Sobranie Sochinenii*, V (St. Petersburg, 1858), 511–573.

SNORRI STURLUSON, *Heimskringla*, Monsen, E., ed., translated with the assistance of Smith, A. H. (New York, 1932).

## 5. Oriental

## A. Arabic and Persian*

ATHIR, IBN AL, *Chronicon*, Tornberg, C. J., ed., IX (Leyden, 1863).

AUFI, "Jami al-Hikayat," Barthold, V., ed., *VOZ, 9* (1896), 262–267.

BAKRI, *Kitab al-Masalik wa'l Mamalik*, Kunik, A. and Rosen, Baron V., eds. *ANZ, 32*, Suppl. No. 2 (1878), with Russian translation (including Ibrahim ben Yakub's report).

BIBI, IBN AL, "History of the Seljuq Dynasty," Houtsma, M. T., ed., *Recueil de textes relatifs à l'histoire des Seldjoucides, 4* (1902). Excerpt in Russian translation by Iakubovsky, A. Iu., *Vizantiiskii Vremennik, 25* (1927), 54–58.

FIRDAUSI, *Shah-nama*, translated into English by Warner, A. G. and Warner, E. (London, K. Paul, Trench, Trübner & Co., 1905–25). 9 vols.

HAUQAL, IBN, *Viae et Regna, BGA*, II (1873). Excerpts in Russian translation, (1) Harkavy, A., *Skazaniia musulmanskikh pisatelei* (St. Petersburg, 1870), pp. 218–222; (2) Karaulov, N. A., *Sbornik materialov dlia opisaniia mestnostei i plemen Kavkaza*, XXXVIII (1908), 81–118.

HUDUD AL ALAM, Barthold, V., ed. (Leningrad, 1930). Phototypical reproduction of the manuscript.

—— Translation and explanation, Minorsky, V. (London, 1937).

IBN AL-ATHIR, see Athir.

IBN-AL-BIBI, see Bibi.

IBN HAUQAL, see Hauqal.

IBN-MISKAWAIHI, see Miskawaih.

KHAQANI, see Minorsky, V., "Khaqani and Andronicus Comnenus," *BSOAS*, 1945, 11, Pt. 3.

MARVAZI, SHARAF AL-ZAMAN TAHIR, *Marvazi on China, the Turks and India*, Minorsky. V., ed., with an English translation and commentary (London, The Royal Asiatic Society, 1942).

MISKAWAIH, IBN, AHMAD IBN MUHAMMED, *The Eclipse of the Abbasid Caliphate*, edited, translated, and elucidated by Amedroz, H. F. and Margoliouth, D. S. (Oxford, B. Blackwell, 1920–21). 7 vols. Excerpt on the Russians, translated into Russian by Florovsky, A. V., *SK, 1* (1925), 178–182; by Iakubovsky, A. Iu., *VV, 24* (1926), 64–69.

YAHYA OF ANTIOCH, *Histoire de Yahya-ibn-Said d'Antioche*. Edited and translated into French by Kratchkovsky, J., [Krachkovsky, I.] and Vasiliev, A., in *Patrologia Orientalis*, Graffin, R. and Nau, F., eds., *18* (1924).

## B. Armenian and Georgian

ASOGHIG, STEPHEN, of Daron, *Histoire universelle par Étienne Asolik de Taron*, Pt. 2, translated and annotated by Macler, F. (Paris, 1917). Russian translation, Emin, N., *Vseobshchaia Istoriia Stepanosa Taronskogo Asokhika* (Moscow, 1862).

BROSSET, M., *Histoire de la Géorgie*, I (St. Petersburg, 1849).

* Diacritical marks in the transliteration of the Arabic and Persian names and titles are omitted.

## C. Chinese

BICHURIN, IAKINF, *Sobranie svedenii o narodakh obitavshikh v srednei Azii* (St. Petersburg, 1851).
BRETSCHNEIDER, E., *Mediaeval Researches from Eastern Asiatic Sources* (London, K. Paul, Trench, Trübner & Co., 1910). 2 vols.
WITTFOGEL, K. A. and FENG CHIA-SHENG, *History of Chinese Society: Liao* (forthcoming).

## D. Hebrew

KOKOVTSOV, P. K., *Evreisko-Khazarskaia perepiska v X veke* (Leningrad, 1932).

## E. Syriac

AB-UL-FARAJ, GREGORY (Bar Hebraeus), *Chronographia*, Burns, P. J., and Kirsch, G. G., eds., with Latin translation (Leipzig, 1788). Budge, E. A. W., ed, with English translation (London, 1932).

# IV. Travels, Memoirs, and Letters

## 1. Travels

BENJAMIN OF TUDELA, *The Itinerary of Rabbi Benjamin of Tudela*, Asher, A., tr. and ed. (London and Berlin, A. Asher & Co., 1841). 2 vols.
BRUNO, see St. Bruno.
FADHLAN, IBN, *Kitab* (report of his mission to the Volga Bulgars), Krachkovsky, I. Iu., ed., *Puteshestvie Ibn-Fadlana* (Moscow and Leningrad, 1939). Phototypical reproduction of the text, Russian translation, and commentary. Togan, A. Zeki Validi, ed., "Ibn Fadlan's Reisebericht," *Abhandlungen für die Kunde des Morgenlandes* (Leipzig, 1939), with German translation and commentary.
IBRAHIM BEN YAKUB [Report of Travels in Slavic Countries], Kunik, A. A. and Rosen, Baron V., eds., see Bakri, sec. III, 5, above. Kowalski, T., ed., *MPH*, New Series, I. (1946).
PETHAHIAH OF REGENSBURG (PETACHIA), B. Jacob Ha-Laban, *Travels*, French translation, Carmoly, E., ed. (Paris, 1831). Benish, A., ed. and tr. (London, 1856).
ST. BRUNO OF QUERFURT, Letter [travel report] to Emperor Henry II of Germany (1008), Bielowski, A., ed., *MPH*, I (1864), 224–228. Giesebrecht, W. von, ed. *Geschichte der deutschen Kaiserzeit*, II (5th ed. Leipzig, 1885), 102–105.

## 2. Memoirs and Letters

EMPEROR MICHAEL VII DUCAS, Two Letters [to Prince Vsevolod of Kiev], Sathas, C., ed., *Bibliotheca Graeca Medii Aevi*, V (1876), 385–392. Russian translation, Vasilievsky, V. G., *Trudy,* II (St. Petersburg, 1909), 8–14. There is no name of addressee in the original; that the letters were addressed to Prince Vsevolod is Vasilievsky's conjecture.

VLADIMIR MONOMACH, PRINCE, Autobiography ("Testament"), Laur., cols. 240–252. English translation, Cross, pp. 301–309.

—— Letter to Prince Oleg, Laur., cols. 252–255. English translation, Cross, pp. 310–312.

## V. Biographies and Lives of Saints

AVRAAMI OF SMOLENSK, MONK
Rozanov, S. P., ed., *Zhitiia prepodobnogo Avraamia Smolenskogo* (St. Petersburg, 1912).

BORIS AND GLEB, PRINCES
Iakov, Monk (attributed to), "Skazanie strastei i pokhvala sviatuiu mucheniku Borisa i Gleba." Nestor, Monk, "Chtenie o zhitii i o pogublenii blazhennuiu strastoterptsu Borisa i Gleba." Both edited by Abramovich, D. I., "Zhitiia sviatykh Borisa i Gleba," *Pamiatniki drevnerusskoi literatury,* II (Petrograd, 1916). Bugoslavsky, S. A., ed., *Pam'iatki pro kniaziv Borisa i Gleba* (Kiev, 1928). Inaccessible to me.

FEODOSI, ABBOT
Nestor, Monk, "Zhitie prepodobnogo Feodosiia," *Chteniia,* 1858, Pt. 3; 1879, Pt. 1; 1899, Pt. 2.

OLGA, PRINCESS
Life of St. Olga, Makarii, I, 268–270.

VLADIMIR, THE SAINT, PRINCE
Iakov, Monk, "Pamiat' i pokhvala kniaziu Vladimiru," Makari, I, 249–257.

—— "Life of Prince Vladimir," *idem,* I, 257–261.

Ilarion, Metropolitan, "Pokhvala Kaganu Vladimiru," Ponomarev, I, 69–76.

Hagiographical Collections
*Paterik* (Patericon) of the Kievan Monastery of the Caves, Iakovlev, V., ed., *Pamiatniki russkoi literatury XII i XIII vekov,* I (St. Petersburg, 1872). Abramovich, D. I., ed., *Paterik Kievo-Pecherskogo Monastyria* (St. Petersburg, 1911).

*Prolog* (Menology)
Collection containing abridged lives of saints and other readings arranged according to the yearly cycle of church services. Known in several versions. The first printed edition of a version of *Prolog,* Moscow, 1641 (reprinted and revised several times).

Selection of lives of Russian saints from *Prolog,* Ponomarev, II and IV (for the months September to April).

A version of *Prolog* (according to a Bulgarian manuscript of the fourteenth century), *OLDP,* CXXXV (1916).

## VI. Epistles and Sermons

FEODOSI, ABBOT, "Poucheniia," Ponomarev, I, 33–43.
IAKOV, MONK, "Poslanie k Dimitriu" [i.e., to Prince Iziaslav I], Makarii, II, 324–327.
ILARION, METROPOLITAN, "On Law and Grace," Ponomarev, I, 59–69.
KIRILL OF TUROV, BISHOP, "Slova i poucheniia," Ponomarev, I, 126–177.
KLIMENT OF SMOLENSK, METROPOLITAN, "Poslanie k presviteru Fome" (revised by Afanasi), Loparev, Kh., ed., *OLDP*, XC (1892). See also Nikolsky, N. K., *O literaturnykh trudakh* Klimenta Smoliaticha (St. Petersburg, 1892).
LUKA ZHIDIATA, BISHOP, "Pouchenie," Ponomarev, I, 14–16.

*For belles-lettres and folklore, see* BIBLIOGRAPHY, XI.

# SUPPLEMENT TO SOURCES, 1973

### Chronicles: Slavic

LIKHACHEV, D. S., ed. and commentator, *Povest' vremennykh let* (*Book of* ANNALS). (Moscow and Leningrad, 1950). 2 vols.

### Legal Sources: Russian Law

SZEFTEL, M., *Documents de droit public relatifs à la Russie médiévale* (Bruxelles, 1963).
VERNADSKY, George, trans. and commentator, *Medieval Russian Laws* (New York, Columbia University Press, 1947). Reprinted by Octagon Books, Inc., New York, 1965.

# BIBLIOGRAPHY

## I. Historiography and Source Study

BAGALII (BAHALII), D. *Narys Ukrains'koi istoriografii* (Kiev, 1923–25). 2 parts.

DOROSHENKO, D., *Ogliad Ukrains'koi istoriografii* (Prague, 1923).

GAPANOVITCH, J. J., *Historiographie russe (hors de la Russie)*, Nikitine, B. P., ed. and tr. (Paris, 1946). Preface by Taube, Baron M.

IKONNIKOV, V. S., *Opyt Russkoi istoriografii* (Kiev, 1891–1908). 2 vols., each in 2 parts.

MAZOUR, A. G., *An Outline of Modern Russian Historiography* (Berkeley, University of California Press, 1939).

MILIUKOV, P. N., *Glavnye techeniia russkoi istoricheskoi mysli* (2d ed. Moscow, 1898).

RUBINSHTEIN (RUBINSTEIN), N. L., *Russkaia istoriografiia* (Moscow, 1941).

TIKHOMIROV, M. N., *Istochnikovedenie istorii SSSR s drevneishikh vremen do kontsa XVIII veka* (Moscow, 1940).

VOLGIN, V. P., TARLE, E. V., and PANKRATOVA, A. M., eds., *Dvadtsat' piat' let istoricheskoi nauki v SSSR* (Moscow and Leningrad, 1942).

## II. Historical Geography and Ethnography

BARSOV, N. P., *Ocherki Russkoi istoricheskoi geografii* (2d ed. Warsaw, 1885).

KUDRIASHOV, K. V., *Russkii istoricheskii atlas* (Moscow and Leningrad, 1928).

KUZNETSOV, S. K., *Russkaia istoricheskaia geografiia* (Moscow, 1910).

LIUBAVSKY, M., *Russkaia istoricheskaia geografiia v sviazi s istoriei kolonizatsii* (Moscow, 1909).

PYPIN, A. N., *Istoriia Russkoi etnografii* (St. Petersburg, 1890–92). 4 vols.

SAVITSKY (SAVICKIJ), P. N., *Šestina světa* (Prague, 1932).

SEREDONIN, S. M., *Istoricheskaia geografiia* (Petrograd, 1916).

SPITZYN, A. A., *Russkaia istoricheskaia geografiia* (Petrograd, 1917).

ZAMYSLOVSKY, E., *Uchebnyi atlas po Russkoi istorii* (2d ed. St. Petersburg, 1887).

—— *Ob'iasneniia k uchebnomu atlasu* (St. Petersburg, 1887).

ZELENIN, D., *Russische (ostslavische) Volkskunde* (Berlin and Leipzig, 1927).

## III. General Histories of Russia, Ukraine, and White Russia

ALLEN, W. E. D., *The Ukraine* (Cambridge, Cambridge University Press, 1940).

BESTUZHEV-RIUMIN, K. N., *Russkaia istoriia*, I (St. Petersburg, 1872).

DOROSHENKO, D., *Narys istorii Ukrainy*, I (Warsaw, 1932).

DOVNAR-ZAPOLSKY, M. V., ed., *Russkaia istoriia v ocherkakh i stat'iakh*, I–II (Moscow, 1904–11).

GITERMAN, V., *Geschichte Russlands*, I (Zürich, 1944).

HRUSHEVSKY (GRUSHEVSKY), M., *A History of Ukraine* (New Haven, Yale University Press, 1941).

—— *Istoriia Ukrainy-Rusi*, I–III (2d ed. Lvov, 1904–05).

ILOVAISKY, D. I., *Istoriia Rossii*, I (Moscow, 1876).

KARAMZIN, N. M., *Istoriia Gosudarstva Rossiiskogo*, I–III (6th ed. St. Petersburg, 1851).

—— *Primechaniia k Istorii Gosudarstva Rossiiskogo*, I–III (St. Petersburg, 1852).

KLIUCHEVSKY, V. O., *A History of Russia*, Hogarth, C. J., tr. (New York, E. P. Dutton & Co., 1911–12), I–II.

—— *Kurs Russkoi istorii*, I–II (Petrograd, 1918).

KOVALEVSKY, P. E., *Istoricheskii put' Rossii* (Paris, 1946–47). 2 parts.

—— *Manuel d'histoire russe* (Paris, 1947).

LEBEDEV, V. I., GREKOV, B. D., and BAKHRUSHIN, S. V., eds., *Istoriia SSSR*, I (Moscow, 1939).

MILIUKOV, P. N., SEIGNOBOS, and EISENMANN, L., *Histoire de Russie* (Paris, 1932), I.

MOUSSET, A., *Histoire de Russie* (Paris, 1945).

PARES, B., *A History of Russia* (revised ed. New York, A. Knopf, 1947).

PICHETA, V., *Gistoryia Belarusi*, I (Moscow, 1924).

PLATONOV, S. F., *Histoire de la Russie des origines à 1918* (Paris, 1929).

—— *History of Russia*, Aronsberg, E., tr., Golder, F. A., ed. (New York, The Macmillan Co., 1925).

POKROVSKY, M. N., *History of Russia*. Clarkson, J. D. and Griffiths, M. R. M., trs. and eds. (New York, International Publishers, 1931).

PRESNIAKOV, A. E., *Lektsii po russkoi istorii*, I (Moscow, 1938).

RIASANOVSKY (RIAZANOVSKY), V. A., *Obzor Russkoi kultury*, I (New York, published by the author, 1947).

ROZHKOV, N. A., *Obzor Russkoi istorii s sotsiologicheskoi tochki zreniia*, I (St. Petersburg, 1903).

—— *Russkaia istoriia v sravnitelno-istoricheskom osveshchenii*, I (Petrograd and Moscow, 1919).

SHMURLO, E., *Kurs Russkoi istorii*, I (Prague, 1931). Mimeographed.

SOLOVIEV, S. M., *Istoriia Rossii s drevneishikh vremen*, I–III (Moscow, 1851–53).

STÄHLIN, K., *Geschichte Russlands*, I (Berlin and Leipzig, 1923).

SUMNER, B. H., *A Short History of Russia* (New York, Reynal & Hitchcock, 1943).

TATISHCHEV, V. N., *Istoriia Rossiiskaia*, I–III (Moscow, 1768–74).

VERNADSKY, G., *Political and Diplomatic History of Russia* (Boston, Little, Brown, and Co., 1936).

WELTER, G., *Histoire de Russie* (Paris, 1946).

## IV. General Outlines of the Kievan Period

GREKOV, B. D., *Kievskaia Rus'* (4th ed. Moscow and Leningrad, 1944).

—— *The Culture of Kiev Rus* (Moscow, 1947).

MAVRODIN, V. V., *Drevniaia Rus'* (Moscow, 1946).

—— *Obrazovanie drevnerusskogo gosudarstva* (Leningrad, 1945).

SIMÕES DE PAULA, E., *O comercio varegue e o Grão-Principado de Kiev* (São Paulo, Brasil, 1942).

## V. Political and Diplomatic History

GREKOV, B. D., *Bor'ba Rusi za sozdanie svoego gosudarstva* (Moscow and Leningrad, 1945).

LIKHACHEV, D. S., "Russkii posolskii obychai XI–XIII vekov," *Istoricheskie Zapiski, 18* (1946), 42–55.

LINNICHENKO, I. A., *Rus' i Polsha do kontsa XII veka* (Kiev, 1884).

POTEMKIN, V. P., ed., *Istoriia diplomatii,* I (Moscow, 1941).

PRESNIAKOV, A. E., *Kniazhoe pravo v drevnei Rusi* (St. Petersburg, 1909).

SOLOVIEV, S. M., *Istoriia otnoshenii mezhdu Russkimi kniaziami Riurikova doma* (Moscow, 1847).

—— *Ob otnosheniakh Novgoroda k velikim kniaziam* (Moscow, 1845).

TAUBE, BARON M., "Études sur le développement historique du droit international dans l'Europe Orientale," Académie de Droit International, *Recueil des Cours,* 1926, Pt. 1, pp. 345–533.

## VI. Economic and Social History

ARISTOV, N. IA., *Promyshlennost' drevnei Rusi* (St. Petersburg, 1866).

BEREZHKOV, M., *O torgovle Rusi s Ganzoiu do kontsa XV veka* (St. Petersburg, 1879).

DIAKONOV, M. A., *Ocherki obshchestvennogo i gosudarstvennogo stroia drevnei Rusi* (4th ed. St. Petersburg, 1912).

DOVNAR-ZAPOLSKY, M. V., *Istoriia Russkogo narodnogo khoziaistva,* I (Kiev, 1911).

ECK, A., *Le Moyen Âge russe* (Paris, 1933).

GOETZ, L. K., *Deutsch-russische Handelsgeschichte des Mittelalters* (Lübeck, 1922).

—— *Deutsch-russische Handelsverträge des Mittelalters* (Hamburg, 1916).

GREKOV, B. D., Krestiane na Rusi s drevneishikh vremen do XVII veka (Moscow, 1946).

IUSHKOV, S. V., *Narysy z istorii vynyknennia i pochatkovogo rozvytku feodalizmu v Kyivs'kii Rusi* (Kiev, 1939).

KAVELIN, K. D., "Vzgliad na iuridicheskii byt drevnei Rossii," *Sobranie Sochinenii* (St. Petersburg, 1904), I, cols. 5–66.

KULISHER, I. M. (KULISCHER, J.), *Istoriia Russkogo narodnogo khoziaistva,* I (Moscow, 1925).

—— *Russische Wirtschaftsgeschichte,* I (Jena, 1925).

LEONTOVICH, F., "Zadruzhno-obshchinnyi kharakter politicheskogo byta drevnei Rossii," *ZMNP, 173* (1874), 201–244; *174* (1874), 120–151, 194–233.

MAVOR, J., *An Economic History of Russia* (2d ed. London and Toronto, J. M. Dent & Sons, Ltd., 1925), I.

NEVOLIN, K. A., "Obshchii spisok Russkikh gorodov," *Polnoe Sobranie Sochinenii,* VII (St. Petersburg, 1859), 27–95.

ROZHKOV, N. A., Gorod i derevnia v Russkoi istorii (St. Petersburg, 1902).

SVIATLOVSKY, V. V., *Primitivno-torgovoe gosudarstvo kak forma byta* (St. Petersburg, 1914).

TIKHOMIROV, M. N., "Drevnerusskie goroda," *MU, 99* (1946), 3–254.

## VII. Government and Administration

GAGEMEISTER (HAGEMEISTER), IU. A., *Razyskaniia o finansakh drevnei Rossi* (St. Petersburg, 1833).

GRADOVSKY, A. D., "Gosudarstvennyi stroi drevnei Rossii," *Sobranie Sochinenii* (St. Petersburg, 1899), I, 339–381.

KLIUCHEVSKY, V., *Boiarskaia Duma drevnei Rusi* (4th ed., Moscow, 1909).

NEVOLIN, K. A., "O preemstve veliko-kniazheskogo Kievskogo prestola," *Polnoe Sobranie Sochinenii*, VI (St. Petersburg, 1859), 587–634.

SERGEEVICH, V. I., *Drevnosti Russkogo prava* (St. Petersburg, 1908–11). 3 vols. (Vols. I–II: 3d ed.; Vol. III: 2d ed.).

TOLSTOY, COUNT D. A., *Istoriia finansovykh uchrezhdenii Rossii* (St. Petersburg, 1848).

## VIII. Law and Institutions

DIUVERNUA (DUVERNOIS), N. L., *Istochniki prava i sud v drevnei Rossii* (Moscow, 1866).

GOETZ, L. K., *Das russische Recht* (Stuttgart, 1910–13). 4 vols.

LASHCHENKO, R., *Lektsii po istorii Ukrains'kogo prava*, I (Prague, 1923).

NEVOLIN, K. A., "Istoriia Rossiiskikh grazhdanskikh zakonov," *Polnoe Sobranie Sochinenii*, III–V (St. Petersburg, 1857–58).

SATURNÍK, T., *Přispěvky k šíření Byzantského práva u Slovanů* (Prague, 1922).

SERGEEVICH, V. I., *Lektsii i issledovaniia* (4th ed. St. Petersburg, 1910).

TIKHOMIROV, M. N., *Issledovanie o Russkoi Pravde* (Moscow and Leningrad, 1941).

VERNADSKY, G., *Zvenia Russkoi kultury*, I (Bruxelles, 1938), 178–225.

VLADIMIRSKY-BUDANOV, M. F., *Khristomatiia po istorii Russkogo prava*, I (6th ed. St. Petersburg and Kiev, 1908).

—— *Obzor istorii Russkogo prava* (7th ed. Petrograd and Kiev, 1915).

## IX. Church and Religion

FEDOTOV, G. P., *The Russian Religious Mind: Kievan Christianity* (Cambridge, Mass., Harvard University Press, 1946).

GOETZ, L. K., *Das Kiever Höhlenkloster als Kulturzentrum des vormongolischen Russlands* (Passau, 1904).

—— *Kirchengeschichtliche und Kulturgeschichtliche Denkmäler Altrusslands* (Stuttgart, 1905).

GOLUBINSKY, E., *Istoriia kanonizatsii sviatykh v Russkoi tserkvi* (2d ed. Moscow, 1903).

—— *Istoriia Russkoi tserkvi*, I, Pts. 1 and 2 (2d ed. Moscow, 1901–04).

LEIB, B., *Rome, Kiev et Byzance à la fin du XI-e siècle* (Paris, 1924).

MAKARII, METROPOLITAN, *Istoriia Russkoi Tserkvi*, I–III (3d ed. St. Petersburg, 1888–89).

NEVOLIN, K. A., "O prostranstve tserkovnogo suda v Rossii do Petra Velikogo," *Polnoe Sobranie Sochinenii*, VI (St. Petersburg, 1859), 251–389.

NIKITSKY, A. I., *Ocherk vnutrennei istorii tserkvi v Velikom Novgorode* (St. Petersburg, 1879).

NIKOLSKY, N. K., "O drevne-russkom khristianstve," *Russkaia Mysl*, 1913, No. 6.

NIKOLSKY, N. M., *Istoriia Russkoi Tserkvi* (2d ed. Moscow and Leningrad, 1931).

POLONSKAIA, N. D., "K voprosu o khristianstve na Rusi do Vladimira," *ZMNP, 71* (1917), 33–80.

PRISELKOV, M. D., *Ocherki po tserkovno-politicheskoi istorii Kievskoi Rusi* (St. Petersburg, 1913).

TELBERG, G. G., *Zaria khristianstva na Rusi* (Shanghai, 1939).

*Vladimirskii Sbornik* (Belgrade, 1938).

## X. Language and Paleography

DURNOVO, N., *Ocherk istorii Russkogo iazyka* (Moscow and Leningrad, 1924).

JAKOBSON, R., "Remarques sur l'évolution phonologique du russe," *Travaux du Cercle Linguistique de Prague*, 2 (1929).

KARSKY, E. F., *Slavianskaia Kirillovskaia paleografiia* (Leningrad, 1928).

NIKULIN, A. S., *Istoricheskaia grammatika russkogo iazyka* (Leningrad, 1945).

OBNORSKY, S. P., *Ocherki po istorii Russkogo literaturnogo iazyka starshego perioda* (Moscow and Leningrad, 1946).

SHAKHMATOV, A. A., "Ocherk drevneishego perioda istorii Russkogo iazyka," *Entsiklopediia Slavianskoi filologii*, XI, Pt. 1 (Petrograd, 1915).

SHCHEPKIN, V. N., *Uchebnik russkoi paleografii* (Moscow, 1918).

SOBOLEVSKY, A. I., *Slaviano-Russkaia paleografiia* (St. Petersburg, 1908).

SREZNEVSKY, I. I., *Materialy dlia slovaria drevnerusskogo iazyka* (St. Petersburg, 1893–1912). 3 vols.

VINOGRADOV, V., *Velikii Russkii iazyk* (Moscow, 1945).

VINOKUR, G., *Russkii iazyk* (Moscow, 1945).

## XI. Literature and Folklore

ANICHKOV, E. V., BOROZDIN, A. K., and OVSIANIKO-KULIKOVSKY, D. N., *Istoriia Russkoi literatury*, I–II (Moscow, 1908).

CHADWICK, N. K., *Russian Heroic Poetry* (Cambridge, Cambridge University Press, 1932).

GRÉGOIRE, H., JAKOBSON, R., *et al.*, "La Geste d'Igor," *Annuaire, 8* (forthcoming).

GUDZII, N. K., *Istoriia drevnei Russkoi literatury* (3d ed. Moscow, 1945).

HAPGOOD, J. F., *The Epic Songs of Russia* (New York, Charles Scribner's Sons, 1886).

HRUSHEVSKY (GRUSHEVSKY), M., *Istoriia Ukrains'koi literatury*, I–IV (Kiev, 1923–25).

ISTRIN, V. M., *Ocherk istorii drevnerusskoi literatury* (Petrograd, 1922).

KELTUIALA, V. A., *Kratkii kurs istorii Russkoi literatury*, I (St. Petersburg, 1912).

KHALANSKY, M. E., *Velikorusskie byliny Kievskogo tsikla* (Warsaw, 1885).

MAGNUS, L. A., *The Heroic Ballads of Russia* (London, K. Paul, Trench, Trubner & Co.; New York, E. P. Dutton & Co., 1921).

 BIBLIOGRAPHY 383

MILLER, V. F., *Ekskursy v oblasti Russkogo narodnogo eposa* (Moscow, 1892).
—— *Ocherki Russkoi narodnoi slovesnosti* (Moscow, 1897–1910). 2 vols.
MIRSKY, PRINCE D. S., *A History of Russian Literature* (New York, A. Knopf, 1927).
NIKOLSKY, N. K., *Materialy dlia povremennogo spiska Russkikh pisatelei i ikh sochinenii* (St. Petersburg, 1906).
ORLOV, A. S., *Drevniaia Russkaia literatura* (Moscow and Leningrad, 1945).
—— *Slovo o Polku Igoreve* (Moscow and Leningrad, 1938).
—— Adrianova-Peretts, V. P. and Gudzii, N. K., eds., *Istoriia Russkoi literatury*, I (Moscow and Leningrad, 1941).
PETRUNKEVITCH, A., "The Lay of the War-Ride of Igor," *Poet-Lore, 30* (1919), 289–303.
PETUKHOV, E. V., *Russkaia Literatura: drevnii period* (2d ed., Iuriev, 1912).
PYPIN, A. N., *Istoriia Russkoi literatury*, I (St. Petersburg, 1898).
RALSTON, W. R. S., *The Songs of the Russian People as Illustrative of Slavonic Mythology and Russian Social Life* (2d ed., London, Ellis, 1872).
*Russian Fairy Tales*, Guterman, N., tr., folkloristic commentary by Jakobson, R., illustrations by Alexeieff, A. (New York, Pantheon, 1945).
SAKULIN, P. N., *Russkaia literatura*, I (Moscow, 1928).
SKAFTYMOV, A. P., *Poetika i genezis bylin* (Moscow and Saratov, 1924).
SOKOLOV, IU. M., *Russkii folklor* (Moscow, 1938).
SPERANSKY, M. N., *Istoriia drevnei Russkoi literatury*, I (Moscow, 1921).
—— *Russkaia ustnaia slovesnost'* (3d ed. Moscow, 1917).
STASOV, V. V., "Proiskhozhdenie Russkikh bylin," *Sobranie Sochinenii,* III (St. Petersburg, 1894), 948–1259.
TRAUTMANN, R., *Die Volksdichtung der Grossrussen,* I (Heidelberg, 1935).
VESELOVSKY, A. N., "Iuzhno-russkie byliny," *ANZ, 39,* Suppl. No. 5 (1881); *ANORS, 22,* No. 2 (1881); *36,* No. 3 (1884).
VLADIMIROV, P. V., *Drevniaia Russkaia literatura Kievskogo perioda* (Kiev, 1900).
ZHDANOV, I. N., *Russkii bylevoi epos* (St. Petersburg, 1895).

## XII. Art and Archeology

AINALOV, D. V., *Geschichte der russischen Monumentalkunst* (Berlin and Leipzig, 1932–33). 2 vols.
—— and REDIN, E., *Kievo-Sofiiskii Sobor* (St. Petersburg, 1889).
ALPATOV, N. and BRUNOV, N., *Geschichte der altrussischen Kunst* (Augsburg, 1932). 1 vol. of text and 1 vol. of plates.
ANISIMOV, A. I., "Domongolskii period drevnerusskoi zhivopisi," *Voprosy Restavratsii,* II (1928).
—— *Vladimirskaia ikona Bozhiei Materi* (Prague, 1928).
ARTSIKHOVSKY, A. V., *Drevnerusskie miniatiury kak istoricheskii istochnik* (Moscow, 1944).
BOBRINSKOY, COUNT A. A., *Reznoi kamen' v Rossii,* I (Moscow, 1918).
BUXTON, D. R., *Russian Mediaeval Architecture* (Cambridge, Cambridge University Press, 1934).
GOTIE (GOT'E), IU. V., *Zheleznyi vek v Vostochnoi Evrope* (Moscow and Leningrad, 1930).

GRABAR, I., *Istoriia Russkogo iskusstva*, I, V, VI (Moscow, n.d. [around 1912]).
—— *Die Freskomalerei der Dimitrikathedrale in Wladimir* (Berlin, 1925).
HALLE, F., *Die Bauplastik von Wladimir Ssusdal* (Berlin, 1929).
KONDAKOV, N. P., *The Russian Icon* (Oxford, Clarendon Press, 1927).
—— *Russkaia ikona* (Prague, 1933). 2 vols. of text and 2 vols. of plates.
—— *Russkie klady*, I (St. Petersburg, 1896).
LAZAREV, V. N., "Dva novykh pamiatnika Russkoi stankovoi zhivopisi XII–XIII vekov," *IIM, 13* (1936), 67–76.
—— "Novgorodskaia zhivopis' XII–XIV vekov," *SIF, 2* (1944), 60–74.
MIASOEDOV, V., *Freski Spasa Nereditsy* (Leningrad, 1925).
MURATOV, P. P., *Les icones russes* (Paris, 1927).
NEKRASOV, A. I., *Drevnerusskoe izobrazitelnoe iskusstvo* (Moscow, 1937).
—— *Ocherki po istorii drevnerusskogo zodchestva XI–XVII vekov* (Moscow, 1936).
NIEDERLE, L., *Rukovet' Slovanské archeologii* (Prague, 1931).
NIKOLSKY, V., *Istoriia Russkogo iskusstva* (Berlin, 1923). Preface by P. P. Muratov.
POLONSKAIA, N. D., *Istoriko-kulturnyi atlas po Russkoi istorii*, I (Kiev, 1913).
SOLNTSEV, F. G., illustrator, *Drevnosti Rossiiskogo Gosudarstva* (Moscow, 1849–53). 6 vols.
TOLSTOY, COUNT I. I. AND KONDAKOV, N. P., *Russkie drevnosti* (St. Petersburg, 1889–99). 6 vols.
VORONIN, N., *Ocherki po istorii Russkogo zodchestva* (Moscow, 1934).

## XIII. Music

BUKETOFF, I., "Russian Chant," in Reese, G., *Music in the Middle Ages* (New York, W. W. Norton & Co., 1940), pp. 95–104.
FINDEIZEN (FINDEISEN), N., *Ocherki po istorii muzyki v Rossii*, I (Moscow and Leningrad, 1928).
METALLOV, V. M., *Bogosluzhebnoe penie Russkoi tserkvi: period domongolskii* (Moscow, 1908).
—— *Osmoglasie znamennogo raspeva* (Moscow, 1900).
—— *Russkaia semiografiia* (Moscow, 1912).
PEKELIS, M., ed., *Istoriia Russkoi muzyki*, I (Moscow and Leningrad, 1940).
RAZUMOVSKY, D. V., *Krug drevnego tserkovnogo peniia znamennogo raspeva* (St. Petersburg, 1884).
SWAN, A. J., "The Nature of the Russian Folk-Song," *Musical Quarterly, 29* (1943), 498–516.
—— "The Znamenny Chant of the Russian Church," *Musical Quarterly, 26* (1940), 232–243, 365–380, 529–545.

## XIV. Humanities

CHIZHEVSKY, D., "Platon v drevnei Rossii," *RIOP, 2* (1930), 71–82.
FLOROVSKY, G., *Puti Russkogo bogosloviia* (Paris, 1937).
ISTRIN, V. M., "Moravskaia Istoriia Slavian i Istoriia Poliano-Rusi," *BS, 3* (1931), 308–331; *4* (1932), 36–55.

LIKHACHEV, D. S., *Natsionalnoe samosoznanie drevnei Rusi* (Moscow and Leningrad, 1945).
—— *Russkie letopisi* (Moscow and Leningrad, 1947).
NIKOLSKY, N. K., "Povest' Vremennykh Let," *ANSR*, II, Pt. 1 (1930).
PHILIPP, W., "Ansätze zum geschichtlichen und politischen Denken im Kiewer Russland," *Jahrbücher für Geschichte Osteuropas*, Suppl. No. 3 (Breslau, 1940). Reviewed by A. Florovsky, *BS, 8,* 292–296; inaccessible to me.
PRISELKOV, M. D., *Istoriia Russkogo letopisaniia XI–XV vekov* (Leningrad, 1940).
SHAKHMATOV, A. A., *Povest' Vremennykh Let,* I (Petrograd, 1916).
—— "Povest' Vremennykh Let i ee istochniki," *ODRL, 4* (1940), 11–150.
—— *Razyskaniia o sostave drevneishikh letopisnykh svodov* (St. Petersburg, 1908).
SHAKHMATOV, M. V., "Platon v drevnei Rusi," *RIOP, 2* (1930), 49–70.
—— *Ucheniia Russkikh letopisei domongolskogo perioda o gosudarstvennoi vlasti* (Prague, 1927). 2 vols. Mimeographed.
VALDENBERG, V., *Drevnerusskie ucheniia o predelakh tsarskoi vlasti* (Petrograd, 1916).
WEINGART, M., *Byzantské kroniky v literature cirkevneslovanské* (Bratislava, 1922–23). 2 vols.

## XV. Sciences, Medicines, and Technology

BOBYNIN, V. V., "Sostoianie matematicheskikh znanii v Rossii do XVI veka," *ZMNP, 232* (1884), 183–209.
RAINOV, T., *Nauka v Rossii XI–XVII vekov* (Moscow and Leningrad, 1940).
SVIATSKY, D. O., "Astronomicheskie iavleniia v Russkikh letopisiakh s nauchno-kriticheskoi tochki zreniia," *ANORI, 20* (1915), Pt. 1, pp. 87–208; Pt. 2, pp. 197–288.

## XVI. Education

LAVROVSKY, N. A., *Rassuzhdenie o drvenikh russkikh narodnykh uchilishchakh* (Kharkov, 1854).
POGODIN, M. P., "Obrazovanie i gramotnost' v drevnem periode Russkoi istorii," *ZMNP, 153* (1871), 1–28.
WANCZURA, A., *Szkolnictwo w starej Rusi* (Lvov, 1923).

## XVII. Regional History

ANDRIASHEV, A., *Ocherk istorii Volynskoi zemli* (Kiev, 1887).
BAGALEI (BAHALII), D. I., *Istoriia Severskoi zemli* (Kiev, 1882).
DANILEVICH, V. E., *Ocherk istorii Polotskoi zemli* (Kiev, 1896).
DOVNAR-ZAPOLSKY, M. V., *Ocherk istorii Krivichskoi i Dregovichskoi zemel* (Kiev, 1891).
GOLUBOVSKY, P. V., *Istoriia Severskoi zemli* (Kiev, 1881).
—— *Istoriia Smolenskoi zemli* (Kiev, 1895).
HRUSHEVSKY (GRUSHEVSKY), A., *Ocherki istorii Turovskogo kniazhestva* (Kiev, 1902).
HRUSHEVSKY (GRUSHEVSKY), M., *Istoriia Kievskoi zemli* (Kiev, 1891).

ILOVAISKY, D. I., *Istoriia Riazanskogo kniazhestva* (Moscow, 1858).

IVANOV, P. A., *Istoricheskie sud'by Volynskoi zemli* (Odessa, 1895).

KOSTOMAROV, N. I., *Severno-russkie narodopravstva* (St. Petersburg, 1863). 2 vols.

LIASKORONSKY, V., *Istoriia Pereiaslavskoi zemli* (Kiev, 1903).

MOLCHANOVSKY, N., *Ocherk izvestii o Podolskoi zemle* (Kiev, 1885).

NIKITSKY, A. I., "Istoriia ekonomicheskogo byta Velikogo Novgoroda," *Chteniia,* 1893, Pts. 1–2.

ZUBRITSKY, D., *Istoriia drevnego Galichsko-Russkogo kniazhestva*, I (Lvov, 1852). Inaccessible to me.

# SUPPLEMENT TO BIBLIOGRAPHY, 1973

## Historiography and Source Study

NECHKINA, M. V., ed., *Istoriia istoricheskoi nauki v SSSR*. Dooktiabrskii period. Bibliografiia (Moscow, 1965).

## General Histories of Russia, Ukraine, and White Russia

RIASANOVSKY, NICHOLAS V., *A History of Russia* (New York, Oxford University Press, 1962).

SHASKOLSKY, I. P., *Normanskaia teoriia v sovremennoi burzhuaznoi nauke* (Moscow and Leningrad, 1965).

STÖKL, GÜNTHER, *Russische Geschichte von den Anfängen bis zur Gegenwart* (Stuttgart, 1962).

## General Outlines of the Kievan Period

GREKOV, B. D., "Kievskaia Rus'," in *Izbrannye trudy* II (Moscow, 1959), 13–410.

## Art and Archeology

ALPATOV, M. V., *Russian Impact on Art* (New York, Philosophical Library, 1950).

GRABAR, I., ed., *Istoriia russkogo Iskusstva*, vols. 1–4 (Moscow, 1953–59).

HAMILTON, GEORGE H., *The Art and Architecture of Russia* (Baltimore, Maryland, Penguin Books, 1954).

LAZAREV, V. N., *Feofan Grek i ego shkola* (Moscow, 1961).

—— *Istoriia vizantiiskoi zhivopisi* (Moscow, 1947). 2 vols.

—— *Old Russian Murals and Mosaics from the XI to the XVI Century* (London, Phaidon Press, 1966).

POWSTENKO, O., *The Cathedral of St. Sophia of Kiev* (New York, The Ukrainian Academy of Arts and Sciences in the United States, 1954).

## Literature and Folklore

GRÉGOIRE, H., JAKOBSON, R., et al., *La Geste du Prince Igor, epopée russe du douzième siècle* (Annuaire, 8) (New York, 1948).

TSCHIŽEWSKIJ, D., *Geschichte der altrussischen Literatur in 11., 12. und 13. Jahrhundert*. Kiever Epoche. (1948).

# GENERAL INDEX

Aa River, 233
Abydos, 64
"Acceleration" of historical process, 213
Adalbert, bishop, 41
Adam, 156, 269, 281
Adelheid. *See* Evpraxia
Adyge. *See* Kosogians
Administration, 187–189; financial, 39, 40
Adriatic Sea, 318
Afghanistan, 361
Africa, 2
Agnes. *See* Anna, Queen of France, 343
Agricultural cycle, 248; laborers, 126, 142; religion, 49; tools, 109
Agriculture, 99–101, 107–109, 127, 128, 157, 169, 170
Akun. *See* Haakon the Blind
Alani-As, 37
Alano-Slavic tribes, 355
Alans, people, 55, 122, 133, 145, 354, 355
Albania, 319
Albert von Buxhoewden, bishop, 232
Albigenses, 269
Alësha Popovich, *byliny* character, 250
Alexander the Great, 272
Alexander Nevsky, prince, 17
Alexandria, 348, 364
Aliens, 215
Alimpi, icon painter, 262
Alp-Arslan, sultan, 356, 361
Alta River, 75
Americas, the, 2
Anastasius of Korsun, priest, 65
Anatolia, 34, 62, 63, 78, 235, 257, 261, 273, 362
Anatolian art, 258; commerce, 235
Andrei Bogoliubsky, prince, 181, 210, 211, 220–222, 259–262, 278, 358
Andrei, son of Vladimir II, 97
Andrew I, king, 329
Andrew II, king, 226–228, 329
Andrew, son of King Andrew II, 228
Andronicus Komnenus, emperor, 352, 353
Andronicus Komnenus, nobleman, 352
Angeli, house of, 351, 352
Anglo-Saxon guild, 134; language, 244; law, 293

Anglo-Saxons, 136, 187
Ani, kingdom of, 356
Animal style, 263
Anna, princess, wife of Vladimir I, 63, 65, 75, 83, 357
Anna, Queen of France, 278, 342, 343
Anna, daughter of Mstislav the Daring, 228
Anna, daughter of Vsevolod I. *See* Ianka
Antes, people, 7, 20, 55, 101, 112, 135, 138, 145, 176, 355
Antian princes, 178; tribes, 158, 333
Antioch, 348, 363
Antoni, monk. *See* St. Antoni
Apiculture, 106
Apocrypha, 267–269, 272, 281, 328
Apollo, 54
Appanages, 177, 314
Apsheron Peninsula, 33
Aquarius, 43
Arabia, 4
Arabic scientists, 295
Arabs, 5, 7, 20, 338, 345, 355, 356
Architecture, 256–261; pre-Christian, 257
Archives, office of, 269
Arctic Ocean, 12, 107, 200, 223
Aristocracy, 16, 17, 135, 139, 177
Aristocratic element of government, 182–185, 289
Arkona, 119, 318, 323
Armenia, 356, 359
Armenian architects, 259; art, 259, 359; churches, 260; doctors, 297; merchants, 119, 359; missionaries, 355; painters, 262, 359
Armenians, 355, 356, 359
Armor, 193, 398
Army, 192, 193
Arpad, Magyar *voevoda*, 24
Arrow-throwers, 300
*Artel*, 135
Artisans, 125, 143
Asia, 1, 10, 13, 239
Asia Minor, 34, 112, 235
Asians (As), 354. *See also* Iasians
Askold, ruler of Kiev, 23, 24
Astronomy, 43, 44, 296

# INDEX OF AUTHORS CITED

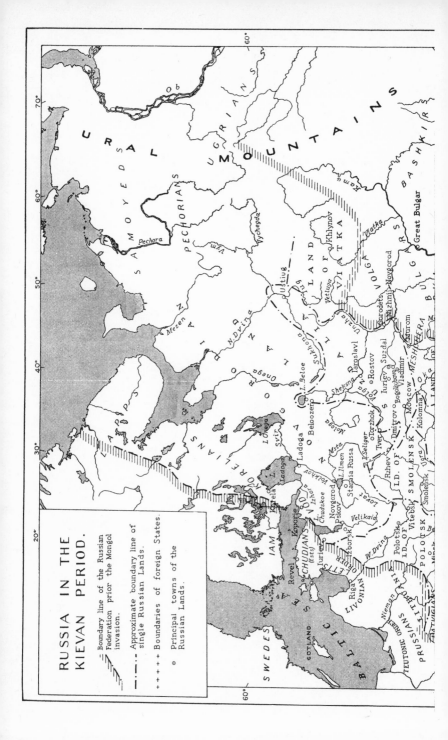

RUSSIA IN THE
KIEVAN PERIOD.

|||||| Boundary line of the Russian
Federation prior the Mongol
invasion.

—·—·— Approximate boundary line of
single Russian Lands.

+ + + + + Boundaries of foreign States.

⊙ Principal towns of the
Russian Lands.

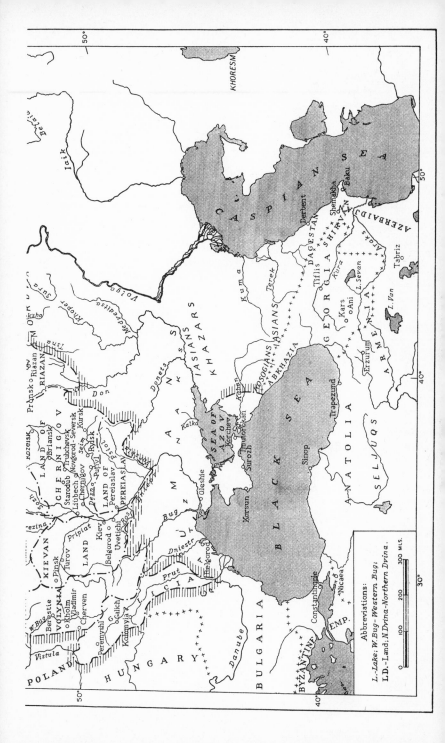